Lecture Notes in Economics and Mathematical Systems

For information about Vols. 1–100, please contact your bookseller or Springer-Verlag

Vol. 101: W. M. Wonham, Linear Multivariable Control. A Geometric Approach. X, 344 pages. 1974.

Vol. 102: Analyse Convexe et Ses Applications. Comptes Rendus, Janvier 1974. Edited by J.-P. Aubin. IV, 244 pages. 1974.

Vol. 103: D.E. Boyce, A. Farhi, R. Weischedel, Optimal Subset Selection. Multiple Regression, Interdependence and Optimal Network Algorithms. XIII, 187 pages. 1974.

Vol. 104: S. Fujino, A Neo-Keynesian Theory of Inflation and Economic Growth. V, 96 pages. 1974.

Vol. 105: Optimal Control Theory and its Applications. Part I. Proceedings 1973. Edited by B. J. Kirby. VI, 425 pages. 1974.

Vol. 106: Optimal Control Theory and its Applications. Part II. Proceedings 1973. Edited by B. J. Kirby. VI. 403 pages. 1974.

Vol. 107: Control Theory, Numerical Methods and Computer Systems Modeling. International Symposium, Rocquencourt, June 17–21, 1974. Edited by A. Bensoussan and J. L. Lions. VIII, 757 pages. 1975.

Vol. 108: F. Bauer et al. Supercritical Wing Sections II. A Handbook. V, 296 pages. 1975.

Vol. 109: R. von Randow, Introduction to the Theory of Matroids. IX, 102 pages. 1975.

Vol. 110: C. Striebel, Optimal Control of Discrete Time Stochastic Systems. III, 208 pages. 1975.

Vol. 111: Variable Structure Systems with Application to Economics and Biology. Proceedings 1974. Edited by A. Ruberti and R. R. Mohler. VI, 321 pages. 1975.

Vol. 112: J. Wilhelm, Objectives and Multi-Objective Decision Making Under Uncertantly. IV, 111 pages. 1975.

Vol. 113: G. A. Aschinger, Stabilitätsaussagen über Klassen von Matrizen mit verschwindenden Zeilensummen. V, 102 Seiten 1975.

Vol. 114: G. Uebe, Produktionstheorie. XVII, 301 Seiten. 1976.

Vol. 115: Anderson et al., Foundations of System Theory: Finitary and Infinitary Conditions. VII, 93 pages. 1976

Vol. 116: K. Miyazawa, Input-Output Analysis and the Structure of Income Distribution. IX, 135 pages. 1976.

Vol. 117: Optimization and Operations Research. Proceedings 1975. Edited by W. Oettli and K. Ritter. IV, 316 pages. 1976.

Vol. 118: Traffic Equilibrium Methods, Proceedings 1974. Edited by M. A. Florian. XXIII, 432 pages. 1976.

Vol. 119: Inflation in Small Countries. Proceedings 1974. Edited by H. Frisch. VI, 356 pages. 1976.

Vol. 120: G. Hasenkamp, Specification and Estimation of Multiple-Output Production Functions. VII, 151 pages. 1976.

Vol. 121: J. W. Cohen, On Regenerative Processes in Queueing Theory. IX, 93 pages. 1976.

Vol. 122: M. S. Bazaraa, and C. M. Shetty, Foundations of Optimization VI. 193 pages. 1976

Vol. 123: Multiple Criteria Decision Making. Kyoto 1975. Edited by M. Zeleny. XXVII, 345 pages. 1976.

Vol. 124: M. J. Todd. The Computation of Fixed Points and Applications. VII, 129 pages. 1976.

Vol. 125: Karl C. Mosler. Optimale Transportnetze. Zur Bestimmung ihres kostengünstigsten Standorts bei gegebener Nachfrage. VI, 142 Seiten. 1976.

Vol. 126: Energy, Regional Science and Public Policy. Energy and Environment I. Proceedings 1975. Edited by M. Chatterji and P. Van Rompuy. VIII, 316 pages. 1976.

Vol. 127: Environment, Regional Science and Interregional Modeling. Energy and Environment II. Proceedings 1975. Edited by M. Chatterji and P. Van Rompuy. IX, 211 pages. 1976.

Vol. 128: Integer Programming and Related Areas. A Classified Bibliography. Edited by C. Kastning. XII, 495 pages. 1976.

Vol. 129: H.-J. Lüthi, Komplementaritäts- und Fixpunktalgorithmen in der mathematischen Programmierung. Spieltheorie und Ökonomie. VII, 145 Seiten. 1976.

Vol. 130: Multiple Criteria Decision Making, Jouy-en-Josas, France. Proceedings 1975. Edited by H. Thiriez and S. Zionts. VI, 409 pages. 1976.

Vol. 131: Mathematical Systems Theory. Proceedings 1975. Edited by G. Marchesini and S. K. Mitter. X, 408 pages. 1976.

Vol. 132: U. H. Funke, Mathematical Models in Marketing. A Collection of Abstracts. XX, 514 pages. 1976.

Vol. 133: Warsaw Fall Seminars in Mathematical Economics 1975. Edited by M. W. Loś, J. Loś, and A. Wieczorek. V. 159 pages. 1976.

Vol. 134: Computing Methods in Applied Sciences and Engineering. Proceedings 1975. VIII, 390 pages. 1976.

Vol. 135: H. Haga, A Disequilibrium – Equilibrium Model with Money and Bonds. A Keynesian – Walrasian Synthesis. VI, 119 pages. 1976.

Vol. 136: E. Kofler und G. Menges, Entscheidungen bei unvollständiger Information. XII, 357 Seiten. 1976.

Vol. 137: R. Wets, Grundlagen Konvexer Optimierung. VI, 146 Seiten. 1976.

Vol. 138: K. Okuguchi, Expectations and Stability in Oligopoly Models. VI, 103 pages. 1976.

Vol. 139: Production Theory and Its Applications. Proceedings. Edited by H. Albach and G. Bergendahl. VIII, 193 pages. 1977.

Vol. 140: W. Eichhorn and J. Voeller, Theory of the Price Index. Fisher's Test Approach and Generalizations. VII, 95 pages. 1976.

Vol. 141: Mathematical Economics and Game Theory. Essays in Honor of Oskar Morgenstern. Edited by R. Henn and O. Moeschlin. XIV, 703 pages. 1977.

Vol. 142: J. S. Lane, On Optimal Population Paths. V, 123 pages. 1977.

Vol. 143: B. Näslund, An Analysis of Economic Size Distributions. XV, 100 pages. 1977.

Vol. 144: Convex Analysis and Its Applications. Proceedings 1976. Edited by A. Auslender. VI, 219 pages. 1977.

Vol. 145: J. Rosenmüller, Extreme Games and Their Solutions. IV, 126 pages. 1977.

Vol. 146: In Search of Economic Indicators. Edited by W. H. Strigel. XVI, 198 pages. 1977.

Vol. 147: Resource Allocation and Division of Space. Proceedings. Edited by T. Fujii and R. Sato. VIII, 184 pages. 1977.

Vol. 148: C. E. Mandl, Simulationstechnik und Simulationsmodelle in den Sozial- und Wirtschaftswissenschaften. IX, 173 Seiten. 1977.

Vol. 149: Stationäre und schrumpfende Bevölkerungen: Demographisches Null- und Negativwachstum in Österreich. Herausgegeben von G. Feichtinger. VI, 262 Seiten. 1977.

Vol. 150: Bauer et al., Supercritical Wing Sections III. VI, 179 pages. 1977.

Vol. 151: C. A. Schneeweiß, Inventory-Production Theory. VI, 116 pages. 1977.

Vol. 152: Kirsch et al., Notwendige Optimalitätsbedingungen und ihre Anwendung. VI, 157 Seiten. 1978.

Vol. 153: Kombinatorische Entscheidungsprobleme: Methoden und Anwendungen. Herausgegeben von T. M. Liebling und M. Rössler. VIII, 206 Seiten. 1978.

Vol. 154: Problems and Instruments of Business Cycle Analysis. Proceedings 1977. Edited by W. H. Strigel. VI, 442 pages. 1978.

Vol. 155: Multiple Criteria Problem Solving. Proceedings 1977. Edited by S. Zionts. VIII, 567 pages. 1978.

Vol. 156: B. Näslund and B. Sellstedt, Neo-Ricardian Theory. With Applications to Some Current Economic Problems. VI, 165 pages. 1978.

continuation on page 377

Lecture Notes
in Economics and
Mathematical Systems

Managing Editors: M. Beckmann and W. Krelle

247

Optimization and Discrete Choice in Urban Systems

Proceedings of the International Symposium
on New Directions in Urban Systems Modelling
Held at the University of Waterloo, Canada
July 1983

Edited by
Bruce G. Hutchinson, Peter Nijkamp and Michael Batty

Springer-Verlag
Berlin Heidelberg New York Tokyo

Editors

Prof. Dr. Bruce G. Hutchinson
Department of Civil Engineering, University of Waterloo
Waterloo, Ontario, Canada

Prof. Dr. Peter Nijkamp
Department of Economics, Free University
Amsterdam, The Netherlands

Prof. Dr. Michael Batty
Department of Town Planning
University of Wales, Institute of Science and Technology
Cardiff, Wales, United Kingdom

ISBN 978-3-540-15660-4 ISBN 978-3-642-51020-5 (eBook)
DOI 10.1007/978-3-642-51020-5

Library of Congress Cataloging in Publication Data. International Symposium on New Directions in Urban Systems Modelling (1983: University of Waterloo) Optimization and discrete choice in urban systems. (Lecture notes in economics and mathematical systems; 247) 1. City planning–Mathematical models–Congresses. 2. Urban economics–Congresses. I. Hutchinson, Bruce. II. Nijkamp, Peter. III. Batty, Michael. IV. Title. V. Series. HT166.I625 1983 307.1'2'0724 85-14812
ISBN 978-3-540-15660-4

2142/3140-543210

PREFACE

The papers contained in this volume were originally presented at the International Symposium on New Directions in Urban Systems Modelling held at the University of Waterloo in July, 1983. The papers have been reviewed and rewritten since that time. The exception is the introductory paper written specially by Manfred Fischer and Peter Nijkamp as an introduction to this volume.

The manuscript was prepared in the word processing unit in the Department of Civil Engineering, University of Waterloo. The sustained work of Mrs. I. Steffler in preparing this manuscript is gratefully acknowledged. Mr. R. K. Kumar provided excellent assistance with the editorial process.

The Symposium and the preparation of this manuscript were supported financially by the Natural Sciences and Engineering Research Council of Canada, The Academic Development Fund and the Department of Civil Engineering, University of Waterloo.

TABLE OF CONTENTS

CATEGORICAL DATA AND CHOICE ANALYSIS IN A SPATIAL CONTEXT

Manfred M. Fischer
Department of Geography
University of Vienna
Vienna
Austria
and
Peter Nijkamp
Department of Economics
Free University
Amsterdam
The Netherlands

Abstract. This paper provides a comprehensive review of the techniques available for categorical data and discrete choice analysis in a spatial context. The first half of the paper reviews the class of models known as generalized linear models including log-linear models, linear logit regression models and latent class models. The second half of the paper focusses on techniques that may be used for categorical spatial choice analysis including utility-based models, multiattribute preference models and heuristic choice techniques.

INTRODUCTION

In recent years, social science research has been marked by profound changes. First of all, our complex and highly dynamic world exhibiting sometimes stuctural changes has demanded effective research strategies in order to provide adequate insight into the key factors governing the evolution of modern societies. In addition, there has been an increase in public intervention (via regulations and planning strategies) in almost all countries. These factors have led to a need for quantitative analyses of complex patterns and processes (such as urban growth, demographic developments, and residential location patterns).

The increased use of quantitative analyses in social science research (including geography and regional science) has been stimulated by advances in such disciplines as mathematics, statistics and econometrics which have provided the tools for a formal, systematic and quantitative research methodology. Progress in these fields was also favoured by the explosive growth of computer hardware and software for scientic research. Illustrations and surveys of statistical and econometric modelling techniques in the area of regional economics and geography can be found in Bahrenberg, et al (1984), Issaev, et al (1982) and Nijkamp, et al (1984).

In the present paper some recent developments in categorical (or discrete) spatial data analysis are discussed. Categorical variables have a low degree of measurement precision as they are normally using values on an ordinal, or nominal measurement scale (see Roberts, 1979). Such data are often the outcomes of panel studies, interviews or questionnaires, but they may also be due to measurement problems, especially in case of latent and multi-dimensional variables.

Two classes of approaches to handling categorical data may be identified and these are exploratory and explanatory data analysis. Now the present paper focusses on the latter class.

Exploratory data analysis refers to attempts at identifying structures in complex phenomena without the explicit aim of testing hypotheses. Often, such exploratory analyses take the form of statistical data analysis (for instance, contingency table analysis, partitioning of chi-square, and cross-classifications). In a spatial context, there is a wide variety of exploratory discrete data methods, such as log-linear models, correspondence analysis, multidimensional and homogeneous scaling analysis, iterative proportional fitting procedures and the like.

Explanatory data analysis aims at analyzing cause-effect relationships such as in the context of micro- or macro-spatial choice behaviour. Models for causal inference are usually based on a stimulus-response structure so that behavioural hypotheses can be tested by means of appropriate statistical and econometric techniques. It should be added that causality concepts, from a methodological viewpoint, do not refer to real cause-effect patterns, but only to the structure of the underlying model (Blommestein and Nijkamp, 1983).

In the area of spatial data analysis a remarkable shift in attention from conventional metric data analysis (eg., in the field of spatial interaction modelling) towards categorical data analysis can be observed. This development started mainly in transportation research, but is now covering many more fields such as residential choice research, migration analysis and location analysis. Another remarkable trend is that much more attention, compared to past decades, is being focussed on disaggregate (or micro) spatial data analysis such as by means of panel studies.

Explanatory discrete spatial data analysis has received a great deal of attention in modern spatial research; witness the increased popularity of dummy variable regression models (dichtomous and polytomous), linear logit models, ordinal regression models, generalized linear models, various classes of discrete spatial choice models, and so forth. In recent years dynamic spatial discrete models have also come to the fore so that the field of discrete spatial data analysis is nowadays exhibiting a highly dynamic trajectory. The present paper attempts to identify some major lines of recent development in the field of explanatory categorical spatial research methods.

CATEGORICAL SPATIAL DATA ANALYSIS

Explanatory data analysis has grown rapidly during the last two decades. Research on explanatory methods and models with categorical variables has primarily two sources and these are (i) categorical explanatory data analysis which aims to analyze cause-effect relationships between a set of independent (stimulus) variables and one or more dependent (response) variables, where at least the dependent variable(s) is (are) discrete; and (ii) categorical choice analysis which aims to study the behaviour of populations of individuals in a given choice context.

Although the relationship between categorical explanatory data analysis and categorical choice analysis is rather close, it seems to be reasonable to separate these two subfields from a pedagogical point of view. This section is devoted to categorical explanatory data analysis while the following section discusses categorical choice analysis.

Table 1 shows a classification of statistical problems based on the types of dependent and independent variables involved. The last row in Table 1 corresponds to problems which can be tackled by means of standard multivariate analysis including conventional regression analysis, dummy variable regression models, and (co) variance models. Explanatory categorical data analysis is related to problems of types (i) to (iii) and there is a variety of models for dealing with such problems. Those which have become most widely used, especially in cases (i) - (iii), are linear logistic regression and linear logit models. Cell (i) of Table 1 corresponds to cross-classified discrete data problems. Such problems can also be dealt with by means of a subclass of the general (symmetric) log-linear models which are known as asymmetric log-linear models because they recognize a distinction between independent and dependent variables.

TABLE 1

CLASSES OF STATISTICAL PROBLEMS

Dependent Variables	Independent Variables		
	Categorical	Metric	Mixed
Categorical	(i)	(ii)	(iii)
Metric	(iv)	(v)	(vi)

Source: Fienberg (1981)

Recently progress has been made in integrating different models for categorical data analysis into a generalized linear models approach provided by Nelder and Wedderburn (1972) and implemented in the GLIM (Generalized Linear Interactive Modelling) computer package. The class of generalized linear models (GLMs) is obtained by extending classical regression models to allow a distribution from an exponential family and a link function which relates mean and linear predictor. The unifying methodology enables all members of the class of GLMs to be fitted by means of a common unified estimation procedure, the iterative weighted least squares procedure. GLMs for categorical data include linear logit models, probit models and log-linear models as special cases. Enlarging the generalized linear model methodology by adding an additional composite link function defined by Thomson and Baker (1981) permits the expected value of an observation to depend on more than one linear predictor. Then models for ordinal data such as the proportional odds and the proportional hazards models as suggested by McCullagh (1980) as well as latent class models can also be subsumed under the GLM framework (see Arminger, 1984).

Log-Linear Models

Log-Linear models closely resemble the regression and analysis of variance models for metric data. They are linear in the logarithms of the expected cell frequencies of a p-dimensional contingency table. Extensive discussions of the theory of log-linear models can be found in Bishop et al (1976), Haberman (1978, 1979) and Fienberg (1981) where procedures for handling structural zeros in incomplete contingency tables and for dealing with the contingency tables with ordered categories are discussed (also Aufhauser and Fischer, 1984). When all variables in a dependence relation are discrete (see cell (i) in Table 1), the sample data can be displayed in the form of an asymmetric contingency table where one dimension is treated as the dependent variable.

Let us consider now the general (symmetric) log-linear model for a 3-dimensional I x J x K table. Suppose that the total of the counts is n and let n_{ijk} be the observation for the (i,j,k) entry in the contingency table and let m_{ijk} denote the corresponding expected value for the (i,j,k) cell under some parametric model. Then the most general log-linear model takes the form

$$\ell n m_{ijk} = \ell n E(n_{ijk}) = u + u_{1(i)} + u_{2(j)} + u_{3(k)} + i_{12(ij)} + u_{13(ik)} + u_{23(jk)} + u_{123(ijk)} \quad (1)$$

subject to the usual ANOVA-like constraints

$$\sum_{i=1}^{I} u_{1(i)} = \sum_{j=1}^{J} u_{2(j)} = \sum_{k=1}^{K} u_{3(k)} = 0 \quad (2)$$

and

$$\left.\begin{aligned} &\sum_{i=1}^{I} u_{12(ij)} = \sum_{j=1}^{J} u_{12(ij)} = \sum_{i=1}^{I} u_{13(ik)} = 0 \\ &\sum_{k=1}^{K} u_{13(ik)} = \sum_{j=1}^{J} u_{23(jk)} = \sum_{k=1}^{K} u_{23(jk)} = 0 \\ &\sum_{i=1}^{I} u_{123(ijk)} = \sum_{j=1}^{J} u_{123(ijk)} = \sum_{k=i}^{K} u_{123(ijk)} = 0 \end{aligned}\right\} \quad (3)$$

where u represents the overall mean effect; $u_{1(i)}$, $u_{2(j)}$ and $u_{3(k)}$ mean effects (ie., deviations from the overall mean effect); $u_{12(ij)}$, $u_{13(ik)}$ and $u_{23(jk)}$ first-order interaction effects and $u_{123(ijk)}$ a second-order interaction effect. Extensions of eqns. (1) - (3) to higher dimensional contingency tables is straightforward.

The general model (1) - (3) imposing no restrictions on the $\{m_{ijk}\}$ is termed saturated and has as many independent parameters as there are entries in the table. By imposing restrictions on the parameters (ie., by equating different u-terms zero or some a priori specified values), a wide range of unsaturated and hybrid log-linear models describing the relationship between the dependent and independent variables can be specified. If the number of dimensions of a contingency table increases the number of possible log-linear models will also increase. The question as to which model may be considered to be reasonable and adequate should be solved on the basis of the principle of parsimony and its goodness-of-fit to the data at hand. For this crucial task there are different approaches which are based inter alia on F-statistics, partitions of the likelihood-ratio chi-square, standardized values of the parameter estimates and residual analysis.

The parameters and the expected cell frequencies can be estimated by means of (non-) iterative weighted least squares procedures, or alternatively by means of the iterative proportional fitting approach combined with linear contrasts of the design matrix method.

No further analytical problems arise when log-linear models are used for explanatory purposes. Only the marginals of the contingency table corresponding to the independent variables have to be treated as fixed and, consequently, the product multinominal sampling scheme with independent multinomial samples for each independent by independent variable combination has to be taken. Then log-linear models can be utilized to assess the effects of the independent variables on the dependent ones. Furthermore the interrelationships between the dependent variables can be determined.

Symmetric log-linear models and to some degree, asymmetric log-linear models, have received increasing attention by geographers and regional scientists. This increasing attention is reflected in publications of Wrigley (1979, 1981, 1984a,b), Willekens (1984), Willekens and Guvenc (1984), Aufhauser and Fischer (1984) and Fingleton (1981, 1983). In Bahrenberg et al (1984) the use of symmetrical and asymmetric log-linear models in a spatial context is illustrated. Willekens (1984) showed that log-linear modelling has also a great potential for analyzing spatial dyad structrues (see also Aufhauser 1984). In particular, conventional spatial interaction models can be reformulated as log-linear models. When log-linear models are applied to spatially dependent problems, standard model selection procedures (such as Brown's (1976) screening procedure and Aitkin's (1979) simultaneous test procedure) may erroneously detect interaction effects between variables which are spurious as a consequence of the spatial dependence of the measurements. An important step in the direction of including spatial dependence in the inferential process of choosing an adequate log-linear model has been undertaken by Fingleton (1983). Hutchinson (this volume) and Monkman and Shortreed (this volume) describe some applications of log-linear models.

Linear Logistic Regression and Linear Logit Regression Models

Let $y_1, \ldots y_I$ be statistically independent measurements of a binary random variable which takes values 0 and 1 with

$$\mathrm{Prob}(y_i = 1) = p(1/i) = p_{i1} \qquad i = 1,\ldots,I \tag{4}$$

$$\mathrm{Prob}(y_i = 0) = p(0/i) = p_{i0} \qquad i = 1,\ldots,I \tag{5}$$

Furthermore let x_{ik} $(i=1,\ldots,I;\ k=1,\ldots,K)$ denote the values of K independent variables for y_i. Then the general linear logistic regression model for a binary dependent variable has the form

$$p(1/i) = \frac{\exp(\beta_0 + \sum_{k=1}^{K} \beta_k x_{ik})}{1 + \exp(\beta_0 + \sum_{k=1}^{K} \beta_k x_{ik})} \qquad i = 1,\ldots,I \tag{6}$$

and

$$p(0/i) = \frac{1}{1 + \exp(\beta_0 + \sum_{k=1}^{K} \beta_k x_{ik})} = 1 - p(1/i) \tag{7}$$

where $\beta_k (k=0,1,\ldots,K)$ are unknown parameters. Note that the independent variables may be categorical and/or metric. Categorical independent variables are included in eqns. (6) and (7), for example, by adopting the principle of dummy coding.

The maximum likelihood estimates $\hat{p}(1/i)$ coincide with the sufficient statistics of (6) and (7) and thus

$$\sum_{i=1}^{I} y_i = \sum_{i=1}^{I} \hat{p}(1/i) \tag{8}$$

and

$$\sum_{i=1}^{I} x_{ik} y_i = \sum_{i=1}^{I} x_{ik}\, \hat{p}(1/i) \tag{9}$$

The solution for the (K+1) βs in eqns. (8) and (9) can be obtained by means of an iterative weighted least squares approach (see the algorithms proposed by Nelder and Wedderburn, 1972; Nerlove and Press, 1973; Fienberg, 1981). In the cases of (ii) and (iii) of Table 1 (when some or all independent variables are metric) it is not possible to carry out an overall goodness-of-fit, or to use an easily interpretable criterion such as an R-square for assessing the predictive power of the fitted model. Categorizing the metric variables may allow the construction of a corresponding logit regression model whose goodness-of-fit can be evaluated.

The logistic regression model in eqns. (6) and (7) can easily be reformulated and be shown to be equivalent to a linear model in the logits

$$\ln \frac{p(1/i)}{1 - p(1/i)} = \beta_0 + \sum_{k=1}^{K} \beta_k x_{ik} \tag{10}$$

where the left-hand side of eqn. (12) shows a transformation of the probabilities, which is known as the logit transformation and eqn. (10) is termed a linear logit model. This logit model is a categorical data analysis approach which closely resembles the regression and analysis of variance models for metric variables and can be regarded as a categorical counterpart.

In contrast to the classical regression models which can be efficiently estimated by ordinary least squares, logit models require other estimation procedures, such as the non-iterative weighted least squares procedure described by Grizzle et al (1969), or the iterative weighted least squares procedure suggested by Nelder and Wedderburn (1972). The non-iterative weighted least squares approach, also known as the GSK-approach, is however only appropriate when the sample under study includes a sufficiently large number of repeated observations (Wrigley, 1976).

Although linear logit and log-linear models look quite different it is possible to show that every logit model with categorical independent variables can be represented by an equivalent asymmetric log-linear model (Fienberg, 1981). Consequently all results achieved for log-linear models also apply to linear logit models. Often when logit models are formulated in terms of the log odds or logit scale they are easier to interpret than log-linear ones.

Logit models are also members of a more general class of models which are known as quantal response models (Finney, 1971). A quantal response model is defined by its distribution function F with an associated inverse function. Assuming the logistic function the following logit model is obtained

$$F(-\beta_0 - \sum_{k=1}^{K} \beta_k x_{ik}) = \exp(-\beta_0 - \sum_{k=1}^{K} \beta_k x_{ik}) / \{1 + \exp(-\beta_0 - \sum_{k=1}^{K} \beta_k x_{ik})\} \tag{11}$$

The main advantage of this distribution function is its closed-form expression in contrast to, for example, the normal one which leads to the following probit model

$$F(-\beta_0-\sum_{k=1}^{K}\beta_k x_{ik}) = \int_{-\infty}^{-\beta_0-\sum_{k=1}^{K}\beta_k x_{ik}} (2\Pi)^{-1/2} \exp(-1/2t^2)dt \qquad (12)$$

Note that when F corresponds to a continuous distribution the result obtained for logit analysis can be readily applied to general quantal response models.

Due to computational tractability and mathematical simplicity, logit analysis has been used more often than probit analysis, for instance, in the field of travel demand analysis. The models discussed so far can easily be extended to handle polytomous dependent variables (Fischer and Nijkamp, 1984). In case of an ordinal dependent variable it is useful to define a set of logits based on continuation ratios (Fienberg, 1981).

$$\ln \frac{p_{il}}{\sum_{\ell>1} p_{i\ell}} \qquad i = 1,\ldots,I \quad l = 1,\ldots,L \qquad (13)$$

It is worthwhile to note that this continuation ratio logit approach shows the asymptotic independence property. This means that if the ML-procedure is used, estimation can be carried out separately for each member of the set. The individual chi-square statistics can be added up to the overall goodness-of-fit statistic for the whole set of models. Furthermore, the L models can be assessed independently.

Dichotomous and polytomous single equation linear logit models have been applied in a variety of contexts, particularly in transportation studies to handle problems such as mode choice in work and shopping trips (Bahrenberg, et al, 1984). Special formulations of the linear logit model which are of particular interest for geography and regional science can be obtained by specifying categorical variable analogues to space-time forecasting models and to the traditional trend surface model which became known under the name probability surface model (Wrigley, 1977).

Moreover, it should be noted that a natural extension of discrete single-equation models described above are discrete recursive simultaneous system models with categorical dependent variables which allow a simultaneous assessment of all interrelationships between a set of variables (Goodman, 1973; Heckman, 1978).

It is worthwhile to note that when data are collected which correspond to a number of discrete time points, some variables may sometimes simultaneously be both dependent and independent variables within the system at hand. They may be considered as dependent from the temporally preceding variables, and as independent concerning the variables which temporally succeed them (Goodman, 1973). Some recent developments in discrete non-recursive simultaneous system modelling can be found in Manski and McFadden (1981a), where, for example, in Schmidt (1981) special attention is given to mixed discrete-linear systems which do not have a linear reduced form and thus yield specific difficulties in parameter estimation. Further progress in dynamic discrete simultaneous system modelling which would bring a significant advance over the static modelling of present discrete multivariate data analysis, would need strong research efforts in geography and regional science.

Latent Class Models

In latent class modelling the cause-effect relationships between a set of categorical manifest and latent variables are analyzed. Roughly speaking latent class models can be considered as a categorical analogue to structural equation models with latent variables. An extensive discussion of this field can be found in Goodman (1978), Haberman (1979) and Bartholomew (1983).

There are numerous latent class models. In most models the assumption is made that the manifest variables are conditionally independent given the latent variable(s). Principally two broad families of latent class models can be distinguished and there are (i) unrestricted and (ii) restricted models.

For the sake of simplicity the following general restricted latent class model with three categorical manifest variables and a categorical latent variable may be taken as an illustration.

Let $A=\{A_i\}$ with $i=1,\ldots,I$; $B=\{B_j\}$ with $j=1,\ldots,J$ and $C=\{C_k\}$ with $k=1,\ldots,K$ denote three (dichotomous or polytomous) categorical manifest variables. These three variables constitute a 3-dimensional contingency table cross-classifying a sample of n individuals with respect to A, B and C. Suppose that there is a (polytomous) categorical latent variable X with T categories (termed latent classes) which is able to explain the relationships among the variables in the 3-dimensional contingency table. Assume also that each individual in the population under consideration is in one and only one of the T latent classes, then

$$p^{ABC}_{ijk} = \sum_{t=1}^{T} p^{ABCX}_{ijkt} \qquad \begin{array}{l} i=1,\ldots,I \\ j=1,\ldots,J \\ k-1,\ldots,K \end{array} \qquad (14)$$

where $p^{ABC}_{ijk} = p(A=i,\ B=j,\ C=k)$ is the probability of being in cell (i,j,k) and p^{ABC}_{ijkt} the (unknown) probability of an observation belonging to cell (i,j,k,t) of the 4-dimensional table.

The assumption that the manifest variables are conditionally independent given the latent variable X (local independency assumption) leads to the following latent class model

$$p_{ijkt}^{ABCX} = p_{it}^{A|X} \, p_{jt}^{B|X} \, p_{kt}^{C|X} \, p_t^X \tag{15}$$

$$\text{where } p_t^X = p(X=t) = \sum_{i=1}^{I} \sum_{j=1}^{J} \sum_{k=1}^{K} p_{ijkt}^{ABCX} \tag{16}$$

is the probability of being in latent class t and $p_{it}^{A|X}$ the conditional probability of category i of A, given the value t of X. $p_{jt}^{B|X}$ and $p_{kt}^{C|X}$ are defined in an analogous way. The usual restrictions such as the following are of course also fulfilled in this case

$$\sum_{t=1}^{T} p_t^X = 1 \; ; \; \sum_{i=1} p_{it}^{A|X} = 1 \; ; \; \sum_{j=1}^{J} p_{jt}^{B|X} = 1 \; ; \; \sum_{k=1}^{K} p_{kt}^{C|X} = 1 \tag{17}$$

$(p_t^X, p_{it}^{A|X}, p_{jt}^{B|X}, p_{kt}^{C|X})$ denotes the vector of parameters in the general latent class model. When the number T of latent classes is unknown, T has to be determined within the analysis by considering various possible values for T.

In the simple latent class model of eqns. (15) to (17), the manifest variables A, B and C are affected by the latent variable X, but these manifest variables do not have any direct effects upon each other. Thus, it can be said that the latent variable X explains the relationships among the manifest variables. Evidently eqn. (15) defines a log-linear model for the unknown probabilities p_{ijkt}^{ABCX}. Since the x_ts are unknown, the frequencies n_{ijkt} are not known either, so that p_{ijkt}^{ABCX} cannot be estimated by cell frequencies as in the case of the ordinary log-linear model. In this case, one may employ a maximum-likelihood (ML) procedure for estimating conditional probabilities on the basis of observed marginal totals, by using an iterative proportional fitting method. Fisher's scoring procedure, a variant of the Newton-Raphson procedure, can be applied to any latent class model based on a log-linear model. Thus, latent class modelling can be considered as a special case of GLMs with a composite link function defined by Thomson and Baker (1981), (see also Arminger, 1984). For details on estimation see Goodman (1978, p. 542). Despite a general resemblance of the ML-equations of this general latent class model to those for ordinary log-linear models there are many difficulties arising which are not present in ordinary log-linear modelling. ML-estimates are not uniquely determined, because multiple solutions exist and also solutions exist which are not ML-estimates. Thus, special attention must be paid to a proof that the solution obtained is really an ML-estimate (Haberman, 1979).

As in confirmatory factor analysis restricted latent class models are defined by specific patterns of a priori fixed values of the conditional probabilities or by equality restrictions of conditional probabilities in the same latent class (such as eg., $p_{11}^{A|X} = p_{21}^{B|X}$ or by equality restrictions of conditional probabilities in different latent classes (such as $p_{11}^{A|X} = p_{12}^{A|X} = p_{23}^{B|X}$). The estimation procedure mentioned above can be modified in a straightforward manner for such restricted latent class models.

More general (restricted and unrestricted) latent class models include several latent variables where the latent variables are related to each other (structural relationships) and to a set of manifest variables (measurement relationships). In this case specific care must be taken that the parameters are identifiable. Such latent class models are discussed in Goodman (1978). Muthén (1979) presents a simultaneous equation system with dichotomous manifest variables of metric latent variables which makes use of the probit transformation. Furthermore, it is noteworthy that the LISREL model approach originally designed for metric variables has been extended by means of tetrachoric, ordered polytomous and metric manifest variables of latent variables.

The Generalized Linear Models Methodology as Unifying Framework

The generalized linear models (GLM) of Nelder and Wedderburn (1972) provides a framework for integrating the categorical data models discussed in the previous sections and also relates them to conventional linear metric data models. A detailed discussion of this GLM-approach can be found in Nelder and Wedderburn (1972), Nelder (1974), Arminger (1982), McCullagh and Nelder (1983), and O'Brien and Wrigley (1984) among others.

Let $y=(y_1,\ldots,y_I)$ be a dependent variable whose distribution is one of the exponential family of probability distributions with the density function

$$f(y;\ \theta,\Phi) = \exp(|y\theta - b(\theta)|/a(\Phi) + c(y,\Phi)) \qquad (18)$$

where $a(\Phi)$, $b(\theta)$ and $c(y,\Phi)$ are suitable monotonic functions. θ is the canonical parameter of the exponential family and Φ is the fixed, non-negative scale parameter. Table 2 lists some examples of specific members of the exponential family of probability disributions.

TABLE 2

CHARACTERISTICS OF SOME SPECIFIC PROBABILITY DISTRIBUTIONS OF THE EXPONENTIAL FAMILY (Arminger, 1982, pp. 20)

Characteristics	Normal	Poisson	Binomial
range of y	$(-\infty,\ \infty)$	0,1,2,...	(0, 1)
$a(\Phi)$	Φ	1	1/I
$b(\theta)$	$1/2\ \theta^2$	e^θ	$\ln\ (1+e^\theta)$
$c(y,\Phi)$	$-\ 1/2(\frac{y^2}{\Phi} + \ln\ 2\pi\Phi)$	$-\ \ln\ y\ !$	$\ln\ \binom{I}{Iy}$
$\mu=E(y)=b'(\theta)$	Φ	e^θ	$\frac{e^\theta}{1+e^\theta}$
Variance function $b''(\theta)$	1	μ	$\mu(1-\mu)$

Then a generalized linear model may be expressed as

$$y_i = g^{-1}(\eta_i) + \varepsilon_i \qquad i = 1,\ldots,I \tag{19}$$

where ε_i denotes a randomly distributed error and where

$$\eta_i = \sum_{k=1}^{K} \beta_k x_{ik} \tag{20}$$

is the linear predictor (linear-additive hypothesis) with parameter vector $\beta=(\beta_k)$, $k=1,\ldots,K$, and measurements x_{ik} of the K (metric and/or categorical) independent variables. $g^{-1}(\eta_i)$ is the inverse of the (monotonic twice differentiable) link function

$$\eta_i = g(\mu_i) \tag{21}$$

which relates the linear predictor to the theoretical mean

$$\mu = \frac{\partial b}{\partial \theta} = b(\theta) \tag{22}$$

The specification of a certain GLM refers to three components and these are the linear predictor, the link function and the error distribution. The specification of the linear predictor depends highly on the process of data generation and on the experimental design of the analysis. Table 3 outlines some standard members of the GLM family characterized by its specific link function and error distribution. There are a wide variety of link functions available.

TABLE 3

SOME IMPORTANT GENERALIZED LINEAR MODELS

Model	Link Function	Error Distribution
Classical linear regression	identify : $\eta = \mu$	normal
Symmetric log-linear	logarithmic: $\eta = \ln\mu$	Poisson
Asymmetric log-linear	logit : $\eta = \ln\frac{\mu}{1-\mu}$	binomial or multinomial
Logit regression	logit : $\eta = \ln\frac{\mu}{1-\mu}$	binomial or multinomial
Probit regression	probit : $\eta = F^{-1}(\mu)$ where F is the cumulative normal distribution function	binomial or multinomial

For categorical data models appropriate link functions are provided by the logit transformation (such as in the case of the asymmetric log-linear model and the linear logit regression model), by the probit transformation (such as in the case of the probit regression model) or the logarithmic transformation (such as in the case of the symmetric log-linear model). Evidently other variants of link functions such as the identity funtion in the case of linear metric data regression models, or the complementary log-log transformation can be specified within the GLM-framework.

The exponential family of possible density functions includes several continuous and discrete probability functions where the Poisson distribution plays a similar central role in categorical data analysis as the normal distribution in metric data anaysis. Generalizations of the Poisson distribution lead to the binomial and to the multinomial distribution which can be considered as constrained Poisson distributions. Binomial and multinomial distributions underlie the asymmetric log-linear, the logit regression and the probit regression models as shown in Table 3. The error components of the asymmetric log-linear, the logit regression and the probit regression models are either defined by the binomial or the multinomial distribution as indicated by Table 3.

Nelder and Wedderburn (1972) show that ML-estimates can be obtained for all sub-classes of GLMs by using the iterative weighted least-squares procedure in order to maximize the log-likelihood function L which can be expressed in canonical form as

$$L(\theta,\Phi|y) = \sum_{i=1}^{I} L_i(\theta_i,\Phi|y) = \sum_{i=1}^{I} \frac{(y_i\theta_i - b(\theta_i))}{a_i(\Phi)} + c(y_i,\Phi) \tag{23}$$

Obviously using eqn. (23) the ML equations for β can be derived. The solution of the ML equations can be shown to be equivalent to the results of an iterative weighted least squares approach. For more details on estimating GLMs, see Nelder and Wedderburn (1972), Arminger (1982) and Fischer and Nijkamp (1984).

Recently progress has also been made in extending the GLM-approach by integrating composite link function models, quasi-likelihood models and mixture models. In contrast to the simple form of the link function defined by a (1,1)-relationship between μ_i and η_i (see eqn. (21)), composite link functions allow each μ_i to be linear combination of some intermediate quantities which are themselves functions of η_i. Composite link functions are inter alia used in latent class modelling and in proportional odds and proportional hazards models suggested by McCullagh (1980) for ordinal data (see also Arminger, 1984; Flowerdew and Aitkin, 1982; and Nelder, 1984).

Some Concluding Remarks on Categorical Data Analysis

So far only a few attempts have been made to combine the categorical data analysis methodology with the spatial or spatio-temporal auto-correlation methodology. In this area, spatial data analysis is still facing many challenges.

Wrigley (1984b) shows that some first steps in this direction have already been undertaken. For example, Odland and Barff (1982) have recently attempted to link the logic of existing space-time interaction tests to categorical data models in order to model the space-time patterns of housing deterioration in an American city. Furthermore, Fingleton (1983) has tried to explore some of the fundamental features of complex categorical data sample survey designs in order to accommodate spatial dependence effects in the context of log-linear modelling. He also showed that considerable care is necessary when log-linear models are applied to spatially dependent data because standard model selection procedures such as Brown's (1976) screening procedure or Aitkin's (1979) simultaneous test procedure may erroneously detect interaction effects between variables which are spurious as a consequence of the spatial dependence of the measurements. Fingleton's solution to this problem is based on modifying the standard calculation of Pearson's chi-square statistic (this statistic will take on an inflated value in the presence of positive spatial dependence). Naturally, there is a continuing need to combine categorical data models with methods and models for analysing spatially dependent data. Still many research efforts will have to be made to tackle this important issue in spatial data analysis.

CATEGORICAL SPATIAL CHOICE ANALYSIS

Spatial choice and interaction analysis already has a long history. This issue was essentially the heart of economic geography and regional economics, in so far as these disciplines focussed attention on the location of firms or the settlement patterns of families or groups in a country.

The first formal contributions to spatio-temporal aspects of choice behaviour can be found in traditional space-time geography (Hägerstrand 1970). In a modelling framework, location-allocation models based on programming theory have played an important role in aggregate spatial choice and interaction analysis. In the 1970s, categorical spatial choice models focussing on distinct alternative choices have come to the fore (Bahrenberg et al, 1984; Clark, 1983; van Lierop and Nijkamp, 1984a; Nijkamp et al, 1984). Categorical spatial choice models aim at describing, explaining and forecasting disaggregate choice behaviour in a spatial context, for instance, in the housing market, transportation and labour market analysis (Fischer and Maier, 1984).

Later panel studies and longitudinal data analysis also have drawn a great deal of attention in spatial choice research (Coleman, 1981; Halperin,1984), while simultaneously the spatial activity-based approach came into existence (Damm, 1983). Very recently event-history analysis has demonstrated its potential in discrete spatial choice analysis (Hannan and Tuma, 1984).

Spatial choice models may be classified on the basis of criteria such as (van Lierop and Nijkamp, 1984b) (i) the level of aggregation; (ii) the nature of the choice process; and (iii) the element of time.

On the basis of these criteria, the following main classes of spatial choice models may be distinguished (i) micro simulation models; (ii) deterministic utility-based models; (iii) conventional random utility models; (iv) generalized random utility models; (v) psychometric behavioural models; (vi) activity-based choice models; and (vii) search models.

Micro simulation models serve to analyze spatial behaviour of individuals and groups when micro survey information is not available. This is a potentially powerful approach but not firmly rooted in theoretical and empirical choice analysis. Hence this approach will not be treated here any further.

The three classes of utility-based models from the above list are extremely relevant in the framework of discrete spatial choice analysis and are treated later. The psychometric behavioural, activity-based and search models may be regarded as complementary to the utility models and will be discussed after the utility-based models.

Utility-based Spatial Choice Models

Deterministic Utility-based Models. Utility maximizing models stem from conventional consumer theory in economics which takes for granted the existence of an individual utility function as the basis for rational individual choice behaviour. This traditional paradigm implies that each individual actor making a choice out of a finite set of (spatial) categorical alternatives (eg., transportation modes, residential locations, shopping facilities, recreational areas, etc.) has consistent preferences providing a ranking of the discrete alternatives which can be represented by utility function. Utility is defined on the set of attributes characterizing the choice-alternatives. Furthermore, it is assumed that each choice-maker chooses on the basis of the principle of utility maximization (Richards and Ben-Akiva, 1975). Sometimes also 'satisficer' approaches have been used in this context (Clark and Cadwallader, 1973).

Specific examples of such utility approaches can be found among others in Zahavi (1979) and Leonardi (1983). Zahavi has developed a utility-based model that aims at maximizing the total distances covered by specific transport modes on an average day by an average individual trip-maker by selecting an optimal mix of transport modes within constraints emerging from travel and time budgets. Leonardi has designed a dynamic model in which the successive stages of spatial choice behaviour of multiple actors are analyzed in the framework of an optimal control model.

Deterministic utility-based models have been criticized on several grounds. In particular their deterministic nature has been considered as a major drawback.

Conventional Random Utility Models. The analysis of spatial choice behaviour has progressed enormously due to the increased use of random utility models. In contrast to deterministic models random utility models consider the choice of an alternative as a random process.

Thus, a probabilistic approach to spatial choice analysis has various advantages as it takes into account that a choice-maker chooses an alternative in the presence of bounded rationality and that certain choice relevant attributes are unobserved or omitted by the analyst. Given the fact that individual preferences and perceptions are in general different, a variation in spatial choice behaviour across individuals may emerge. Such aspects as well as classical measurement errors are represented in the stochastic component of the utility function. Though individuals may be confronted with the same set of alternatives that are characterized by the same set of attributes, individual choices may thus be different. Random utility models aim to provide an operational framework for spatial choice problems by regarding choices as events with a certain probability distribution, so that the probability of a certain event is co-determined by the observable attributes of the choice alternatives. Compared with deterministic utility models, random approaches evidently enable a more adequate treatment of behavioural aspects of the choice process as well as a more precise description of actual spatial interaction patterns (van Lierop and Nijkamp, 1984b).

In a random framework the utility of a certain choice alternative for an actor is composed of two parts and these are (i) a deterministic component reflecting systematic impacts of alternative and individual specific attributes; (ii) a random component representing effects of unobserved or omitted (sometimes psychological) aspects.

Then the standard utility function of actor i (i=1,...I) with regard to choice alternative a (a=1,...A) can be written as

$$u_{ai} = V(z_{ai}) + E(z_{ai}) \qquad \begin{array}{l} a=1,\dots,A \\ i=1,\dots,I \end{array} \qquad (24)$$

where u_{ai} = utility of choice alternative a for individual actor i; z_{ai} = set of attributes characterizing the choice item a with regard to individual i; $V(z_{ai})$ = deterministic component of the individual utility function; and $E(z_{ai})$ = random component of the individual utility function (including individual tastes, classical measurement errors, etc.).

Then the probability p_{ai} that an individual i chooses alternative a is given by

$$p_{ai} = \text{Prob}\{[V(z_{ai}) + E(z_{ai})] \geq [V(z_{a'i}) + E(z_{a'i})] \quad a,a' = 1,\ldots,A\} \tag{25}$$

Conventional random utility models make use of a logit specification. The multinomial logit model approach assumes that the error terms in eqn. (25) are independently and identically distributed (IID) by means of a Weibull distribution. This IID assumption implies that individuals with identical observed attributes have identical tastes and that the correlation between omitted attributes across individuals and choice attributes is zero. When alternatives in the choice set are close substitutes for each other, the independence from irrelevant alternatives (IIA) property of the logit approach, which is caused by restrictive assumptions on cross-substitution in the variance-covariance structure, may lead to inconsistent choice probabilities and to counter-intuitive behavioural predictions (Fischer and Nijkamp, 1984; Horowitz, 1984; van Lierop and Nijkamp, 1982; Longley, 1984; Manski, 1981; Wrigley, 1984a). Nevertheless, the multinomial logit model approach has become a common tool in discrete spatial choice research, in particular due to its computational tractability. Lerman (this volume), Koppelman and Rose (this volume), Ortuzar and Donoso (this volume), Sinha et al (this volume) and van Lierop (this volume) discuss applications of random utility models.

Generalized Random Utility Models. The class of generalized random utility models aim to overcome the restrictions implied by the multinomial logit approach especially the independence from irrelevant alternatives axiom and the empty covariance structure. Various classes of generalized random utility models aiming to relax the IIA assumptions may be identified.

The general extreme value family of random utility models may easily be derived from the assumption of a broader class of multivariate extreme-value distributions of the random terms. Such models allow a general pattern of positive correlations among the error terms. It can be shown that the multinomial logit model approach is a special case of this family (McFadden, 1978). Another important special case leads to the subclass of multinomial nested logit models. In this approach a nested form of the choice pattern is assumed (Amemiya, 1976; Ben-Akiva and Lerman, 1979; Sobel, 1980). The nested logit model has become a major operational tool, as it is able to handle correlated error terms in the utility function (thus allowing cross-substitution) without leading to cumbersome computational problems.

The dogit class of models characterized itself by allowing the possibility that some pairs of alternatives exhibit the IIA-property, while other pairs may be free from this property. Under specific conditions this model approach turns into a multinomial logit model, but in general this model does not necessarily suffer from the IIA axiom (Gaudry and Dagenais, 1979; Hensher and Johnson, 1981).

The prominence theory of choice models is based on the idea that choice alternatives should especially be examined in regard to their degree of similarity (Yu, 1979). Then the relative prominence of a choice alternative becomes a relevant choice criterion. Under certain conditions this model is not suffering from the restrictive IIA axiom and may be regarded as a generalization of a multinominal logit model.

With negative exponential distribution models the error terms are assumed to be mutally independent, exponentially distributed with a zero mean but different standard deviation. Thus the error terms are not necessarily identically exponentially distributed (Daganzo, 1979).

Multinomial probit models allow a more flexible specification of the utility structure of choice alternatives, while it is also very suitable for panel data and categorical information. This model approach is characterized by error terms with a joint multivariate normal distribution with a zero mean and an arbitrary variance-covariance matrix. Thus the variances of the error terms are allowed to be different while the error terms themselves are allowed to be mutually correlated. Consequently, these models may be considered as generalizations of general extreme value models and of negative exponential distribution models (Daganzo, 1979). The computational problems of multinomial probit models are not easy to solve, though by means of the Clark approximation the calibration problem may be reduced to one of sequential univariate integration (Sheffi et al, 1982). This method enables one to calculate the choice probabilities for a reasonable number of alternatives very quickly (Hausman and Wise, 1978). The Hausman-Wise variant is even able to include individual taste variations and inter-actor interdependencies in panel studies (Daganzo and Schoenfeld, 1978).

It is clear that the choice in favour of one of the above-mentioned spatial choice models is not unambiguous as this depends on the nature of the data and the specific research aims. In general, however, the multinomial probit model has many advantages compared to other candidates, such as greater flexibility, statistical robustness, avoidance of the IIA assumption and so on (van Lierop and Nijkamp, 1984b).

Alternative Categorical Choice Models

The category of alternative utility-based discrete choice models consists of behavioural models that implicitly or explicitly are based on rational choice behaviour by means of individual preference mechanisms, though they are not necessarily based on a random utility approach. Three classes of alternative approaches are treated in the following paragraphs.

Psychometric behavioural models have mainly been developed in the area of quantitative psychology, but may be used also in the field of discrete spatial choice modelling. These models deal mainly with individual psychological responses and attitudes regarding stimuli emerging from various choice items. Examples of such models are the elimination by aspects model based on sequential judgement processes of attributes (Tversky, 1972; Young, this volume); the elimination by tree method and the hierarchical elimination method (Tversky and Sattath, 1979). Both direct (prior) preference and perception methods had revealed (posterior) preference and perception methods have been designed in this field (Hartgen, 1974). An alternative example of a psychometric choice model is the experimental conjoint measurement model (Dix, 1981). This model is essentially emerging as a linear-in-parameters additive multiattribute specification of the systematic part in a random utility function (Timmermans, 1984). A major problem of all such models however is how to reach a consistency between a priori expressed attitudinal responses and a posteriori measured actual behaviour (Burnett and Hauser, 1979; Louviere and Meyer, 1981). Though these models do not explicitly have their basis in utility theory, they have a strong individual behavioural component and may be regarded as a useful complement to utility-based choice models.

Activity-based choice models aim at analyzing in a comprehensive way the individual trip pattern of an actor over a longer period (eg., a day). Instead of focussing attention on separate trips, these models study the chain of trip making through a daily activity pattern. Consequently, much emphasis is placed on time allocations, scheduling of activities, constraints on activity choices, multiple purpose trips and the like. Those models stem essentially from space-time geography (Hägerstrand, 1970). Most activity-based models are based on household survey and panel data. The estimation of the various individual reaction and preference parameters may be based on logit or probit models, although this is not necessary (Carpenter and Jones, 1983; Damm, 1982; Hensher and Stopher, 1979; Lerman, 1979). Some limitations of activity-based models are (Dix, 1981): the limited sample size caused by expensive panel and longitudinal studies and the neglect of long-run spatial responses to policy controls. Despite these limitations significant progress has been made recently in this area (Golob, 1984; Koppelman and Pas, 1984).

Search models place much emphasis on the process nature of discrete choices, especially in a dynamic context. Such models require great attention for the definition and specification of choice alternatives, the definition of explanatory variables for choice processes, the evaluation process of all relevant alternatives, the level of transition costs, and the individual willingness to make a spatial trio (Clark and Smith, 1982; Rogerson, 1983; Smith and Lundberg, 1984; Weibull, 1982).

Search models stress the importance of the way in which an individual organizes, retrieves and updates a representation of the real world as a determinant of choice behaviour. Decision making is considered as an iterative heuristically guided and non-algorithmic search. Search occurs in the physical world as well as in the individual's representation of the real world where the accessed heuristic knowledge guides the search for an acceptable choice alternative from a space of alternatives. Several examples of domain-specific heuristics and their application to decision making are provided in Smith and Lundberg (1984). Search models seem to be extremely valuable, particularly in gaining more insight into the nature of bounded rationality.

At the end of this section, it should be noted that the set of classes of discrete spatial choice models discussed above is by no means exhaustive. For instance, individual deterministic welfare optimizing models have not been dealt with. Furthermore, some models may not unambiguously be assigned to one category (van Lierop and Rima, 1984). In the next subsection some other specific models and approaches for discrete spatial choice analysis will be discussed.

Recent Advances in Models for Categorical Spatial Choice Analysis

In this subsection a small set of recent advances in the area of categorical choice modelling will be discussed. The contributions described here are not meant to be exhaustive, but represent some interesting new directions.

Decompositional Multiattribute Preference Models

Decompositional multiattribute preference models are usually the result of controlled choice experiments involving hypothetical alternatives so that the limited range of attribute levels in normal survey data can be relaxed. Such models may allow extrapolation of choice predictions to the unobserved attribute mixes which are likely to define any new alternatives that might enter the choice set (Timmermans, 1983). The same author has also designed a methodology for testing the strict assumption inherent in logit models with additive linear utility components and other specifications of the utility component in the systematic part of a utility function.

Furthermore, Timmermans (1984) develops a conceptual model for individual decision processes by making a distinction between a cognitive phase, a preference phase and a decision phase. The preference phase may be guided by either compensatory rules (implying trade-offs among relevant attributes) or non-compensatory rules without explicit trade-offs.

Choice Models with Inter-Actor Dependencies

The probabilistic choice models discussed so far assume that an individual chooses among various alternatives with their level of utilities independent of the number of individuals who chooses each alternative. In a spatial context (eg., housing market) it is plausible to assume that the utility of a given spatial choice will depend on the number of others who choose neighbouring locations. Consequently, congestion or agglomerative economies may emerge.

In such situations one may assume that the utility associated with a specific alternative is an increasing or decreasing function of the number of individuals who choose that alternative (Miyao and Shapiro, 1981). This problem is essentially an equilibrium problem in which the probability that an alternative on the average will be selected is equal to the share of the total population which has selected that alternative. The proof that such an equilibrium does exist can be based on a multi-actor allocation model characterized by micro-economic utility functions with crowding effects as arguments.

Panel and Longitudinal Data Approaches

In recent years there has been a surge of interest in developing more reliable discrete panel models for spatial choice behaviour, sometimes on a longitudinal basis (Coleman, 1981; Halperin, 1984; Hensher and Johnson, 1982). Conventional panel data models are essentially of a cross-sectional nature leaving aside dynamic aspects of choices, but more recently dynamic models have also been designed in order to take into account the intertemporal aspects of spatial choices.

Major advances in the field of dynamic panel data models have been by Heckman (1981) who has used conditional probability models for predicting the occurrence of a certain event given its occurrence in previous periods. Such intertemporal influences may be caused by either spurious state dependence (serial correlation in the unobservables) or structural state dependence (impacts of past experiences upon the choice spectrum in subsequent periods). Furthermore, especially panel data based on longitudinal research may provide a genuinely behavioural or explanatory approach to analyzing spatial choice behaviour. Finally, new directions in this field can also be found in stochastic discrete panel data models based inter alia on negative binomial distributions (Wrigley, 1980) or on multivariate beta distributions (Chatfield and Goodhart, 1982).

Event History Analysis

Event history analysis is a recent development in social science research. Conventional multi-period research in many fields is based on stationary processes described by stable Markov models. Event history analysis aims at recording relevant information on all changes in a state variable within some observation period, with a particular emphasis on discrete changes (events) in the evolution of a phenomenon (Hannan and Tuma, 1984). Next the probability of occurrence of each of these events may be assessed by means of past data on the basis of statistical techniques, such as survivor functions, waiting-time distribution functions, and hazard functions. Applications of event-history analysis can be found in labour market analysis, marital status analysis and migration analysis. Some further contributions to event-history analysis are contained in Johansson and Nijkamp (1984). Such event-history models may provide a useful framework for individual choice analysis.

Heuristic Choice Analysis

Heuristic choice theory takes for granted that decision making is essentially based on heuristic choice procedures (Smith and Lundberg, 1984). Such procedures are necessary in case of complex choice problems in which exhaustive research is infeasible. Then heuristic approaches are useful in a decision context in which time and effort are major criteria for identifying an efficient search procedure. Consequently, the decision-maker's memory and his perception of the choice context are major determinants for individual heuristic choice analysis.

Models for such choice analyses models may be constructed in such a way that (i) they incorporate the view that choice behaviour presupposes a joint, heuristically-guided search of a physical space and its mental representation; (ii) they are able to incorporate individual variability in both mental representation and choice behaviour; (iii) they provide potential predictions of individual choices; and (iv) they are able to generate macro choice models from individual choice models. Various models of such individual choice processes are discussed in Smith and Lundberg (1984). Furthermore, various heuristic rules (such as conjunctive decision rules and lexicographic decision rules) are dealt with by the same authors. Such heuristic approaches to disaggregate choice analysis support the contention that human decision making should focus attention on the way individual actors structure their knowledge bases and on the processes by which these knowledge bases are assessed and modified.

PROSPECTS OF EXPLANATORY CATEGORICAL SPATIAL DATA AND CHOICE ANALYSIS

In the past decades, geography and regional economics have made a vigorous attempt at providing an explanation for real-world spatial configurations and development patterns. In recent years, significant progress has been made in the treatment of categorical variables. In the field of both parametric and non-parametric statistics and econometrics a wide variety of methods and models have been designed that treat categorical variables in an appropriate manner and have resulted in such terms as soft econometrics, soft modelling, qualitative statistics, non-metric data analysis and so on. Many of these techniques are also increasingly being applied in geography and regional economics such as in the field of consumer choice behaviour, locational perception and preference analysis, contingency table analysis, qualitative impact analysis and non-metric conflict analysis.

Whilst disciplines such as psychology and sociology have been extensive users of categorical data and have well developed experimental designs and statistical methods for dealing with such data, the spatial science disciplines in general have been late entrants to this new area and are still in an experimental phase.

In many cases, there is still a long way to go in fields such as polyhedral dynamics, differential topology, discrete-to-continuous transformations, qualitative spatial filter and aggregation analysis, but remarkable advances have been made in fields such as generalized linear models, latent variable approaches, correspondence analysis, fuzzy set analysis and discrete choice analysis.

A major bottleneck in designing methodologies for categorical data analysis useful in empirical research practice is the lack of attention to behavioural theories supporting or underlying the mathematical/statistical methodologies and models. As a consequence often the results of applications cannot be meaningfully interpreted.

In particular several distinct advances in the area of explanatory categorical choice analysis have to be mentioned (Nijkamp et al, 1984) and examples are

1. Recent extensions with generalized linear models including composite link models, mixture models, models with compound dispersion parameters, and quasi-likelihood procedures.

2. Extensions of spatial choice models with non-compensatory attributes and context dependent parameters.

3. Developments in the field of decompositional multiattribute preference models, in the case of large variations in underlying preferences or strategies due to structural changes in the set of alternatives.

4. Recent achievements in estimating choice models in the context of more complicated types of sampling processes involving exogenous and endogenous stratification simultaneously.

5. Advances in longitudinal, panel and event-history analysis allowing a more adequate treatment of time-space activity data.

The conclusion may be drawn from this brief survey that the field of categorical spatial data analysis is apparently becoming an extremely rich research area in urban and regional research and that this field is likely to continue its development at a rapid pace in the near future.

REFERENCES

Aitkin, M., 1979, A Simultaneous Test Procedure for Contingency Table Models, Applied Statistics 28, 233-242.

Amemiya, T., 1976, Specification and Estimation of a Multinominal Logit Model, Technical Report 211, Institute of Mathematical Studies in the Social Sciences, Stanford University, Stanford, CA.

Arminger, G., 1982, Klassische Anwendungen Verallgemeinenter Linearer Modelle in der Empirischen Sozialforchung, FB 6, Universität-Gesamthochschule Wuppertal (mimeographed).

Arminger, G., 1983, Regressionsmodelle in der Exponentielle Familie, Arbeitspapiers des Fachbereichs Wirtschaftswissenschaft der Universität-Gesamthochschule Wuppertal, 18.

Arminger, G., 1984, Analysis of Qualitative Individual Data of Latent Class Models with Generalised Linear Models, in Measuring the Unmeasurable, Nijkamp, P., Heitner, H. and Wrigley, N. (Eds.), Martinus Nijhoff, The Hague.

Aufhauser, E., 1984, Log-lineare Modelle und Ihre Anwendung zur Analyse Räumlicher Interaktionsmatrizen, MA Thesis, Department of Geography, University of Vienna.

Aufhauser, E. and Fischer, M.M., 1984, Log-linear Modelling and Spatial Analysis, paper presented at the 24th European Regional Science Conference, Milan.

Bahrenberg, G., Fischer, M.M. and Nijkamp, P. (Eds.), 1984, Recent Developments In Spatial Data Analysis: Methodology, Measurement, Models, Gower, Aldershot.

Bartholomew, P.J., 1983, Latent Variable Models for Ordered Categorical Data, Journal of Econometrics 22, 229-243.

Ben-Akiva, M.E., 1974, Structure of Passenger Travel Demand Models, Transportation Research Record 526, 26-42.

Ben-Akiva, M.E. and Lerman, S.R., 1979, Disaggregate Travel and Mobility Choice Models and Measures of Accessibility, in Behavioural Travel Modelling, Hensher, D.A. and Stopher, P.R. (Eds.), Croom Helm, London, 654-679.

Bishop, Y.M.M., Fienberg, S.E. and Holland, P.W., 1976, Discrete Multivariate Analysis: Theory and Practice, 2nd Edition, MIT Press, Cambridge, MA.

Brown, M.B., 1976, Screening Effects in Multidimensional Contingency Tables, Applied Statistics 25, 37-46.

Burnett, P. and Hanson, S., 1979, A Rationale for an Alternative Mathematical Paradigm for Movement as Complex Human Behaviour, Transportation Research Record 723, 11-24.

Carpenter, S. and Jones, P. (Eds.), 1983, Recent Advances in Travel Demand Analysis, Gower, Aldershot.

Chatfield, C. and Goodhart, G., 1975, Results Concerning Brand Choice, Journal of Marketing Research 12, 110-113.

Clark, W.A.V., 1983, Structures for Research on the Dynamics of Residential Search, in Evolving Geographical Structures, Griffith, D.A. and Lea, A.C. (Eds.), Martinus Nijhoff, The Hague, 372-397.

Clark, W.A.V. and Cadwaller, M.T., 1973, Residential Preferences: An Alternative View of Intra-urban Space, Environment and Planning A, 5, 693-703.

Clark, W.A.V. and Smith, T.R., 1982, Housing Market Search Behaviour and Expected Utility Theory, Environment and Planning A, 14, 717-737.

Coleman, J.S., 1981, Longitudinal Data Analysis, Basic Books, New York.

Daganzo, C.F. and Schoenfeld, L., 1978, CHOMP User's Manual, Research Report UCB-ITS-RR-78-7, Institute of Transportation Studies, University of California at Berkeley, CA.

Daganzo, C.F., 1979, Multinomial Probit. The Theory and Its Application to Demand Forecasting, Academic Press, New York.

Damm, D., 1982, Parameters of Activity Behaviour for Use in Travel Analysis, Transportation Research A, 16, 135-138.

Dix, M.C., 1981, Structuring our Understanding of Travel Choices, in New Horizons in Travel Behaviour Research, Stopher, P.R., Meyburg, A.H. and Brög, W. (Eds.), Lexington Books, Lexington, MA, 89-109.

Domencich, T.A. and McFadden, D., 1975, Urban Travel Demand: A Behavioural Analysis, North-Holland, Amsterdam.

Fienberg, S.E., 1981, The Analysis of Cross-Classified Categorical Data, 2nd Edition, MIT Press, Cambridge, MA.

Fienberg, S.E. and Meyer, M.M., 1983, Loglinear Models and Categorical Data Analysis with Psychometric and Econometric Applications, Journal of Econometrics, 22, 191-214.

Fingleton, B., 1981, Loglinear Modelling of Geographical Contingency Tables, Environment and Planning A, 13, 1539-1551.

Fingleton, B., 1983, Log-Linear Models with Dependent Spatial Data, Environment and Planning A, 15, 801-813.

Finney, D.J., 1971, Probit Analysis, 3rd Edition, Cambridge University Press, London.

Flowerdew, R. and Aitkin, M., 1982, A Method for Fitting the Gravity Model Based on the Poisson Distribution, Journal of Regional Science, 22, 191-202.

Fischer, M.M. and Maier, G., 1984, Discrete Choice and Labour Supply Modelling, paper presented at the Besancon Symposium of the IGU Working Group on Systems Analysis and Mathematical Models, August 21-23, 1984

Fischer, M.M. and Nijkamp, P., 1984, Explanatory Discrete Spatial Data and Choice Analysis: A State-of-the-art Review, Research Memorandum, Department of Economics, Free University, Amsterdam.

Gaudry, M.J.I. and Dagenais, M.G., 1979, The Dogit Model, Transportation Research B, 13, pp. 105-111.

Golob, Th. F., 1984, Analysing Activity Pattern Data Using Qualitative Multivariate Statistical Methods, in Measuring the Unmeasurable, Nijkamp, P., Heitner, H. and Wrigley, N. (Eds.), Martinus Nijhoff, The Hague.

Goodman, L.A., 1973, The Analysis of Multidimensional Contingency Tables when some Variables are Posterior to Others: A Modified Path Analysis Approach, Biometrika 60, 179-192.

Goodman, L.A., 1978, Analysing Qualitative/Categorical Data. Log-Linear Models and Latent Structure Analysis, Addison-Wesley, London.

Grizzle, J.E., Starmer, C.F. and Koch, G.G., 1969, Analysis of Categorical Data by Linear Models, Biometrics, 25, 489-504.

Haberman, S.J., 1978, Analysis of Qualitative Data. Vol. 1: Introductory Topics, Academic Press, New York.

Haberman, S.J., 1979, Analysis of Qualitative Data, Vol. 2: New Developments, Academic Press, New York.

Hägerstrand, T., 1970, What About People in Regional Science, Papers of the Regional Science Association, 24, 7-21.

Halperin, W.C., 1984, The Analysis of Panel Data for Discreter Choices, in Measuring the Unmeasurable, Nijkamp, P., Leitner, H. and Wrigley, N. (Eds.), Martinus Nijhoff, The Hague.

Hannan, M.T. and Tuma, N.B., 1984, Dynamic Analysis of Qualitative Variables: Applications to Organizational Demography, in Measuring the Unmeasurable, Nijkamp, P., Leitner, H. and Wrigley, N. (Eds.), Martinus Nijhoff, The Hague.

Hartgen, D.T., 1974, Attitudinal and Situational Variables Influencing Urban Mode Choice, Transportation, 3, 377-392.

Hausman, J.A. and Wise, D.A., 1978, A Conditional Probit Model for Qualitative Choice, Econometrica, 46, 403-426.

Heckman, J.J., 1978, Dummy Endogenous Variables in a Simultaneous Equation System, Econometrica, 46, 931-959.

Heckman, J.J., 1978, Statistical Models for Discrete Panel Data, in Structural Analysis of Discrete Data with Econometric Applications, Manski, C.F. and McFadden, D. (Eds.), MIT Press, Cambridge, MA, 114-178.

Hensher, D.A. and Johnson, L.W., 1981, Applied Discrete Choice Modelling, Croom Helm, London.

Hensher, D.A. and Stopher, P.R. (Eds.), 1979, in Behavioural Travel Modelling, Croom Helm, London.

Horowitz, J.L., 1984, Random Utility Models as Practical Tools of Travel Demand Analysis, in Transportation and Mobility in an Era of Transition, Jansen, G.R.M., Nijkamp, P. and Ruijgrok, C. (Eds.).

Hutchinson, B.G., Contingency Table Analysis and Urban Travel Accounts, this volume

Issaev, B., Nijkamp, P., Rietveld, P. and Snickars, F. (Eds.), 1982, in Multiregional Economic Modelling: Practice and Prospect, North-Holland, Amsterdam.

Johansson, B. and Nijkamp, P., 1984, Analysis of Episodes in Urban Event Histories, Working Paper, International Institute for Applied Systems Analysis, Laxenburg, Austria.

Johnson, L. and Hensher, D., 1982, Application of Multinomial Probit to a Two-period Panel Data Set, Transportation Research A, 16, 457-464.

Koppelman, F.S. and Pas, E.I., 1984, Travel-activity Behaviour in Time and Space: Methods for Representation and Analysis, in Measuring the Unmeasurable, Nijkamp, P., Leitner, H. and Wrigley, N. (Eds.), Martinus Nijhoff, The Hague.

Koppelman, F.S. and Rose, G., Geographic Transfer of Travel Choice Models: Evaluation and Procedures, this volume.

Leonardi, G., 1983, An Optimal Control Representation of a Stochastic Multi-stage-multiactor Choice process, in Evolving Geographical Structures, Griffith, D.A. and Lea, A.C. (Eds.), Martinus Nijhoff, The Hague, 62-72.

Lerman, S., 1979, The Use of Disaggregate Choice Models in Semi-Markov Process Models of Trip Chaining Behaviour, Transportation Science, 13, 273-291.

Lerman, S., Random Utility Models of Spatial Choice, this volume

Lierop, W.J.F. van and Nijkamp, P., 1982, Disaggregate Models of Choice in a Spatial Context, Sistemi Urbani, 3, 331-368.

Lierop, W.J.F. van and Rima, A., 1984, Trends and Prospects of Qualitative Disaggregate Spatial Choice Models, in Measuring the Unmeasurable, Nijkamp, P., Leitner, H. and Wrigley, N. (Eds.), Martinus Nijhoff, The Hague.

Lierop, W.J.F. van and Nijkamp, P., 1984a, Perspectives of Dissagregate Choice Models on the Housing Market, in Discrete Spatial Choice Models, Pitfield, D.A. (Ed.), Pion, London, 141-162.

Lierop, W.J.F. van and Nijkamp, P., 1984b, Disaggregate Residential Choice Models: Review and Case Study, Research Memorandum, Department of Economics, Free University, Amsterdam, (mimeographed).

Lierop, W.J.F. van, Residential Mobility With a Probit Model, this volume.

Longley, P.A., 1984, Discrete Choice Modelling and Complex Spatial Choice: An Overview, in Recent Developments in Spatial Data Analysis: Methodology, Measurement, Models, Bahrenberg, G., Fischer, M.M. and Nijkamp, P. (Eds.), Gower, Aldershot, 375-392.

Louviere, J.J. and Meyer, R.J., 1981, A Composite Attitude-Behaviour Model of Traveler Decision Making, Transportation Research B, 15, 411-420.

Manheim, M.L., 1979, Fundmentals of Transportation Systems Analysis, MIT Press, Cambridge, MA.

Manski, C.F., 1981, Structural Models for Discrete Data: The Analysis of Discrete Choice, in Sociological Methodology 1981, Leinhardt, S. (Ed.), Jossey-Bass, San Francisco, 58-109.

Manski, C.F. and McFadden, D. (Eds.), 1981a, in Structural Analysis of Discrete Data with Econometric Applications, MIT Press, Cambridge, MA.

Manski, C.F. and McFadden, D., 1981b, Alternative Estimators and Sample Designs for Discrete Choice Analysis, in Structural Analysis of Discrete Data with Econometric Applications, Manski, C.F. and McFadden, D. (Eds.), MIT Press, Cambridge, MA, 2-50.

McCullagh, P., 1980, Regression Models for Ordinal Data, Journal of the Royal Statistical Society B, 42.

McCullagh, P. and Nelder, J.A., 1983, Generalized Linear Models, Chapman and Hall, London.

McFadden, D., 1978, Modelling the Choice of Residential Location, in Spatial Interaction Theory and Planning Models, Karlqvist, A., Lundqvist, L., Snickars, F. and Weinbull, J.W. (Eds.), North-Holland, Amsterdam, 75-96.

Miyao, T. and Shapiro, P., 1981, Discrete Choice and Variable Returns to Scale, International Economic Review, 22, 257-273.

Monkman, N. and Shortreed, J., Transport Impacts of Changing Household Structure, this volume

Muthén, B., 1979, A Structural Probit Model with Latent Variables, Journal of the American Statistical Association 74, 807-811.

Muthén, B., 1983, Latent Variable Structural Equation Modelling with Categorical Data, Journal of Econometrics, 22, 43-65.

Nelder, J.A., 1974, Log-Linear Models for Contingency Tables: A Generalization of Classical Least Squares, Applied Statistics 23, 323-329.

Nelder, J.A., 1984, Statistical Models for Qualitative Data, in Measuring the Unmeasurable, Nijkamp, P., Leitner, H. and Wrigley, N. (Eds.), Martinus Nijhoff, The Hague.

Nelder, J.A. and Wedderburn, R.W.M., 1972, General Linear Models, Journal of the Royal Statistical Society A, 135, 370-384.

Nerlove, A. and Press, S.J., 1973, Univariate and Multivariate Log-linear and Logistic Models, Technical Report R-1306-EDA/NIH, Rand Corporation, Santa Monica, CA.

Nijkamp, P., Leitner, H. and Wrigley, N. (Eds.), 1984, in Measuring the Unmeasurable, Martinus Nijhoff, The Hague.

O'Brien, L.G. and Wrigley, N., 1984, A Generalized Linear Models Approach to Categorical Data Analysis, in Recent Developments in Spatial Data Analysis: Methodology, Measurement, Models, Bahrenberg, G., Fischer, M.M. and Nijkamp, P. (Eds.), Gower, Aldershot, 231-252.

Odland, J. and Barff, R., 1982, A Statistical Model for the Development of Spatial Patterns: Applications to the Spread of Housing Deterioration, Geographical Analysis, 14, 327-339.

Ortuzar, J.D. and Donoso, P.C.F., Modal Choice Modelling for Several Alternatives: Application of Disaggregate Choice Models in Santiago, Chile, this volume.

Richards, M.G. and Ben-Akiva, M., 1975, A Disaggregate Travel Demand Model, Saxon House, Farnborough.

Roberts, F.S., 1979, Measurement Theory with Applications to Decisionmaking, Addison-Wesley, Reading, MA.

Rogerson, P., 1983, The Effects of Job Search and Competition on Unemployment and Vacancies in Regional Labor Markets, in Evolving Geographical Structures, Griffin, D.A. and Lea, A.C. (Eds.), Martinus Nijhoff, The Hague, 349-371.

Schmidt, P., 1981, Constraints on the Parameters in Simultaneous Tobit and Probit Models, in Structural Analysis of Discrete Data with Econometric Applications, Manski, C.F. and McFadden, D. (Eds.), MIT Press, Cambridge, MA. and London.

Sheffi, Y., Hall, R. and Daganzo, C.F., 1982, On the Estimation of the Multinomial Probit Model, Transportation Research A, 16, 447-456.

Sinha, H.K., Khanna, S.K. and Arora, M.G., Choice of Urban Transport Modes for Work Trips, this volume.

Smith, T.R. and Lundberg, C.G., 1984, Psychological Foundations of Individual Choice Behaviour and a New Class of Decision Making Units, in Recent Developments in Spatial Data Analysis: Methodology, Measurement, Models, Bahrenberg, G., Fischer, M.M. and Nijkamp, P. (Eds.), Gower, Aldershot, 335-373.

Sobel, K., 1980, Travel Demand Forecasting with the Nested Multinomial Logit Model, Transportation Research Record, 775, 48-55.

Stopher, P.R. and Meyburg, A.H. (Eds.), 1976, in Behavioural Travel-Demand Models, Lexington Books, Lexington, MA.

Thomson, R. and Baker, R.J., 1981, Composite Link Functions in Generalized Linear Models, Applied Statistics, 30, 125-131.

Timmermans, H.J.P., 1983, Decompositional Multiattribute Preference Models in Spatial Choice Analysis: A Review of Some Recent Developments, Progress in Human Geography.

Timmermans, H.J.P., 1984, Decision Models for Predicting Preferences Among Multiattribute Choice Alternatives, in Recent Development in Spatial Analysis: Methodology, Measurement, Models, Bahrenberg, G., Fischer, M.M. and Nijkamp, P. (Eds.), Gower, Aldershot, 337-354.

Tversky, A., 1972, Choice-by-Elimination, Journal of Mathematical Psychology, 9, 341-367.

Tversky, A. and Sattath, S., 1979, Preference Trees, Psychological Review, 86, 542-573.

Wedderburn, R.W.M., 1974, Quasi-Likelihood Functions, Generalized Linear Models and the Gauss-Newton Method, Biometrika, 61, 439-447.

Weibull, J.W., 1982, A Dynamic Model Framework for Analysis and Simulation of Housing Markets, paper IIASA Workshop on Spatial Choice Models in Housing, Transportation and Land Use Analysis, Laxenburg.

Willekens, 1984, Log-linear Modelling of Spatial Interaction, Papers of the Regional Science Association, 52, 187-206.

Willenkens, F. and Guvenc, 1984, Hybrid Log-linear Models, in Measuring the Unmeasureable, Nijkamp, P., Leitner, H. and Wrigley, N. (Eds.) Martinus Nijhoff, The Hague.

Wrigley, N., 1976, An Introduction to the Use of Logit Models in Geography, Concepts and Techniques in Modern Geography 10, Geo Abstracts, Norwich.

Wrigley, N., 1977, Probability Surface Mapping. An Introduction with Examples and Fortran Programmes, Concepts and Techniques in Modern Geography 16, Geo Abstracts, Norwich.

Wrigley, N., 1979, Developments in the Statistical Analysis of Categorical Data, Progress in Human Geography, 3, 315-355.

Wrigley N., 1980, An Approach to the Modelling of Shop-Choice Patterns, in Geography and the Urban Environment, Herbert, D.T. and Johnston, R.J. (Eds.), John Wiley, Chichester, 45-85.

Wrigley, N., 1981, Categorical Data Analysis, in Quantitative Geography: A British View, Wrigley, N. and Bennett, R.J. (Eds.), Routledge and Kegan Paul, 111-122.

Wrigley, N., 1984a, Statistical Models for Discrete Choice Analysis, Proceedings of the 3rd European Conference on Theoretical and Quantitative Geography, Bahrenberg, G. and Fischer, M.M. (Eds.), Bremer Beiträge zur Geographie und Ramplanung 5, University of Bremen, Bremen.

Wrigley, N., 1984b, Categorical Data Methods and Discrete Choice Modelling in Spatial Analysis: Some Directions for the 1980s, in Measuring the Unmeasurable, Nijkamp, P., Leitner, H. and Wrigley, N. (Eds.), Martinus Nijhoff, The Hague.

Young, W., The Application of an Elimination-by-aspects Model in Urban Location Decisions, this volume

Yu, W., 1979, A Prominence Theory of Choice, Working Paper 10, Regional Science Department, University of Pennsylvania, Philadelphia, PA.

Zahavi, Y., The UMOT Project, Report DOT-RSPA-DPB-20-79-3, U.S. Department of Transportation, Office of Systems Engineering, Washington, D.C.

Optimization Models

A COMBINED LINEAR/NON-LINEAR PROGRAMMING MODEL OF EMPLOYMENT, TRANSPORTATION, AND HOUSING IN AN URBAN ECONOMY

Hans-Jürg Büttler
Swiss National Bank
8022 Zurich
Switzerland

Abstract. The purpose of this paper is to describe a model which is normative, allocates resources efficiently, incorporates all economic features which are prerequisite to the existence of cities, and serves as a tool for town planning. The model is organized as a linear program when population distributions are known and as a non-linear program when these distributions are to be predicted. Relationships to existing macro-economic models such as Mills' (1972) model are sketched, and suggestions are made for further development of this model framework.

INTRODUCTION

If a well organized spatial structure is the outcome of town planning alone, then one can say that town planning is as old as cities themselves. For instance, spatially well organized cities can be found in Mesopotamia, in the Roman Empire, and existed throughout the Middle Ages. Many would argue that modern cities have lost this clear-cut spatial structure. If this is the case, the question of why this happened has to be answered. There appear to be two reasons for this view. Firstly, the town planning of modern cities is subject to more uncertainties than in ancient cities. In particular, the considerable growth of population and transportation since World War II, rapid changes in technology, and structural changes in demand for housing are very difficult to forecast. Predicting these variables, however, is essential, if town planning is to provide a plan which is viable in the long run where the cost of structural change is kept to a minimum. Secondly, in democratically organized countries, town planning in the final outcome is a political process. This follows readily from the fact that any town-planning policy has an immediate impact on both the allocation and the distribution of resources. For instance, Hochman (1979) has shown that there are at least two environmental policies against air pollution: either a Pigouvian tax or land-use zoning. While both rules, if correctly applied, are efficient, they exhibit an entirely different distribution of resources. In the former case, revenues from the Pigouvian tax can, in principle, be distributed equally to all residents of the city, while in the latter case, these revenues go to landlords who benefit from higher land rents. As far as town planning deals with the distribution of resources, it is mainly predicted as the outcome of a political process (Henderson, 1977). Therefore, it is not surprising that theoretical approaches to town planning deal mostly with the question of efficient resource allocation, leaving the problem of distribution aside.

Recent analytical approaches to town planning have three bases. Firstly, models which are descendants of the spatial interaction tradition such as the Lowry model. In these models, the spatial allocation of employment within an urban area is explained by means of fixed labour ratios, with economic variables such as prices and incomes usually absent (Batty, 1976; Anas, 1983; Echenique, 1983). Secondly, models which primarily focus on the housing market. Both empirical models and simulation models are used. However, some of these models lack economic variables and some are not suited to application. Thirdly, models which tackle the land use and trip distribution of an urban area by minimizing net economic costs (Sharpe, this volume). All three attempts are directed towards the question of how resources can be efficiently allocated within an urban area given some social consensus about the distribution of resources among residents.

Other attempts to approach the normative task of town planning have been made in urban economics literature, but without widespread application to real cities. Perhaps the first attempt in this field was that by Herbert and Stevens (1960). They considered the equilibrium in the land and housing market of a two-dimensional city by means of a linear programming model. Due to the enormous amount of data required, computer simulations to date have not been performed. Mills (1972a, 1972b) considered both the normative aspect and the computer application of a two-dimensional city model, while Kim (1979) primarily addressed the question of how different transportation modes should be efficiently used within an urban area. Both Mills and Kim minimize total resource costs of a city, while household's preferences are ignored. Following Kanemoto's approach (1981) to a symmetrical and featureless city, the welfare of city residents will be maximized here, while being subject to resource constraints. The purpose of this paper is to describe a model which is normative, allocates resources efficiently, incorporates all economic features which are prerequisite to the existence of cities, and serves as a tool for town planning. To make the model operational, a combined linear/non-linear programming model is chosen.

The outline of the paper is as follows. The following section describes the basic model. The model is that of the closed city with city population, capital stock, and export demand given. A specific town is divided into rectangular zones which serve as plane coordinates. The objective function to be maximized is the Benthamite welfare function of the urban economy. Consequently, the individual utility functions are stepwise linear. For each zone, relationships between housing, employment, production, and transportation are described. Two important features which are prerequisite to the existence of cities are introduced: increasing returns to scale in the production of commodities and comparative advantages of certain locations. In order to consider increasing returns to scale, activities are distinguished by both input-output technology and land use intensity. On the other hand, export nodes exhibit comparative advantages. Moreover, the model considers several transport modes: private vehicles, buses, tramways, subways, etc. It is shown that an efficient resource allocation requires maximization of the non-linear welfare function with regard to the populations to be allocated to each zone. This maximization is subject to two conditions: firstly, the sum of all populations residing in each zone must be equal to the exogenously given city population; secondly, the value of the welfare function must be evaluated by a linear programming model. This combined linear/non-linear approach has the advantage that all endogenous variables except the populations residing in each zone can be determined by a linear programming model and therefore makes a computer application possible. At the optimum, there exists a dual program to the linear subprogram which determines shadow prices of resources and shadow incomes of households. The model serves as a tool for town planning when varying exogenous variables. For instance, the forecast of the city population may be varied since it is a random variable, ie., a point estimate with confidence interval. Further, it may be desirable to study the sensitivity of land use zoning when new export nodes are developed in the city.

In the final section, several extensions are briefly discussed: the method of finite elements, traffic congestion, imports, local public goods, different resource endowments of the city residents, and application to the small, open city.

THE MODEL

Discrete Plane Coordinates

Based on urban economics literature, a city is defined as its metropolitan area. A city may therefore consist of several political communities. In this context, the jurisdictional fragmentation of the city must not influence the efficient resource allocation within the urban area, but it naturally plays a crucial role in the allocation of local public goods. To make the model operational, discrete plane coordinations are introduced. Fig. 1 considers the map of a hypothetical city, for which rectangular or squared zones are defined. The rectangular coordinates allow a convenient presentation of the model but in the final section it is shown that a triangular map could reduce the number of variables considerably. In Fig. 1, there are $j=1,\ldots,J$ segments on the abscissa and $i=1,\ldots,I$ segments on the ordinate. The segments can be of different size and their number is arbitrary but should be chosen so as to allow for all activities within the urban area. Unless the city is symmetric, the origin of the map can arbitrarily be chosen. The topographical features of the city are considered by technical coefficients of the model which are defined for each rectangular zone. Shaded zones in Fig. 1 denote export nodes where specific commodities are exported to and imported from other cities. The location of these export nodes, which may exist or be planned, are exogenous to the model but should be chosen so as to exhibit locational comparative advantages in terms of transportation costs such as a harbour, railway station, airport, or highway junction.

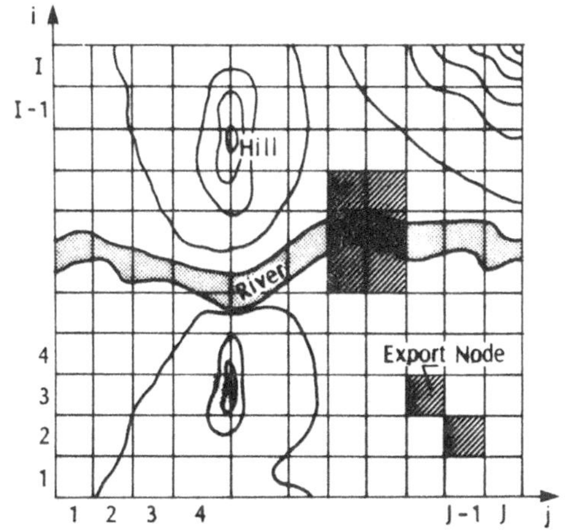

Figure 1 - Rectangular Network

Production and Transportation

There are $r=1,\ldots,R$ industries in the city which each produce a single commodity where the Rth good is floor space. Since all production activities are assumed to be linear, the definition of distinct industries should preferably be taken from an input-output table of the city in question, if it exists. Commodities are produced in buildings with a floor-to-land ratio of g_s, where the index runs from 1 to S. Hence, each industry can be described by a set of linear production activities, the single activities of which are distinguished by different building densities. In other words, increasing returns to scale are considered by introducing building densities. There are $m=1,\ldots,M$ transportation modes, eg., automobiles, buses, tramways, subways, etc. While people can use all transport modes, it is assumed that commodities can only be transported by automobiles (including trucks). If necessary, the latter assumption can easily be relaxed. The model will not only assign transport modes to residents and commodities efficiently but also compute commuting flows.

List of Variables

A list of all exogenous variables is given below. Many of them, however, may be varied due to uncertainty so as to evaluate the sensitivity of the optimal resource allocation.

E_r = export of commodity r (r=1,...,R) where the export of locally consumed goods is zero,

P = city population,

d(i,j) = mean distance to travel within zone (i,j),

A(i,j) = available land for construction and transportation activities in zone (i,j).

K = available physical capital stock of the city, except building capital,

g_s = building density (floor-to-land ratio), where s=1,...,S and $g_{s+1} > g_s$; for instance, g_1 denotes the density of a one-story, single-family house, while g_S denotes the density of the tallest building. (The maximum height of a building to be considered depends both on structure and soil),

$a_{r,q,s}$ = quantity of commodity r (r=1,...,R) required to produce one unit of commodity q (q=1,...,R-1) when production of commodity q takes place in a building with density g_s (input-output coefficients and factor ratios could depend on zone (i,j) in order to consider topographical differences),

$a_{r,R}$ = quantity of commodity r (r=1,...,R-1) required to produce one unit of floor space in commercial buildings or residences, respectively,

$a_{R+1,q}$ = number of person equivalences for one unit of good q (q=1,...,R-1),

$b_{q,r,s}$ = quantity of factor q (q=1,...,3) required to produce one unit of commodity r (r=1,...,R-1) when production of commodity r takes place in a building with density g_s; the factors are labour (q=1) capital (q=2) and land (q=3),

$b_{q,R+m}$ = quantity of factor q (q=1,...,3) required to produce one unit of transportation service with transport mode m (m=1,...,M),

α_r^u = marginal utility over interval u (u=1,...,3) of commodity r (r=1, ...,R-1),

$\alpha_{R,s}^u$ = marginal utility of floor space (r=R) in a building with density g_s (s=1,...,S) where u=1,...,3,

$\overline{Y}_r^u$ = lower boundary of interval u (u=1,...,3) for commodity r (r=1,...,R).

Endogenous variables are determined by the programming model, namely

$Y_r^u(i,j)$ = quantity of commodity r (r=1,...,R-1) over interval u=1,...,3, consumed by a household residing in zone (i,j),

$Y_{R,s}^u(i,j)$ = floor space (r=R), over interval u=1,...,3, in a building with density g_s, which is consumed by a household residing in zone (i,j),

$E_r(i^*,j^*)$ = export of commodity r (r=1,...,R-1) in an export node (i*,j*),

$Z_{r,s}(i,j)$ = production of commodity r (r=1,...,R-1) in a building with density g_s which is located in zone (i,j),

$Z_R(i,j)$ = production of floor space in commercial buildings and residences in zones (i,j),

$F_r^b(i,j)$ = quantity of commodity r (r=1,...,R-1) shipped across bth boundary (b=1,...,4) of zone (i,j),

$P(i,j)$ = population residing in zone (i,j) and this is an exogenous variable for the linear programming model,

$D_r(i,j)$ = final demand for commodity r (r=1,...,R-1) produced in zone (i,j).

$D_{R+m}(i,j)$ = number of persons moved by transport mode m (m=1,...,M) in zone (i,j),

$Z_{R+m}(i,j)$ = transportation services, as measured by persons times distance, of mode m (m=1,...,M) in zone (i,j), where m=1 is automobile,

$H^b(i,j)$ = number of persons moved across bth boundary (b=1,...,4) of zone (i,j), or the commuting flow.

Objective Function

The objective is to maximize the Benthamite welfare function of city residents which is defined as the sum of individual utilities. In a first stage, it is assumed that all individuals are identical in that they have the same utility function. In order to obtain a linear objective function, the monotonically increasing and strictly concave utility function is linearized. This situation is depicted in Fig. 2a for the first R-1 commodities. The domain of each commodity is divided into three intervals u=1(1,...,3) over which the marginal utility is constant. The lower boundary of the first interval $\bar{Y}_r^1$ is assumed to be nil. Accordingly, total demand for each commodity is divided into three variables Y_r^u(u=1,...,3). The situation is different in case of demand for floor space by residents. In Fig. 2b, it is assumed that the utility function depends not only on floor space but also on housing attributes (Büttler and Beckmann, 1980). Naturally, a resident prefers a flat in a low-density building to the same flat in a high-density building. Hence, marginal utilities as depicted in Fig. 2b tend to fall with increasing building density g_s. Although all individuals (or households in this context) are treated as if they were identical, it is well known that at the optimum they are treated unequally (Mirrlees, 1972; Kanemoto, 1980). The model, however, can be modified by using the Rawlsian welfare function so that equal individuals are treated equally at the optimum. Given the assumptions above, the objective function to be maximized is

$$W[P(i,j)] = \max \sum_{i=1}^{I} \sum_{j=1}^{J} \sum_{r=1}^{R-1} \sum_{u=1}^{3} \alpha_r^u \, Y_r^u(i,j) P(i,j)$$

$$+ \sum_{i=1}^{I} \sum_{j=1}^{J} \sum_{u=1}^{3} \sum_{s=1}^{S} \alpha_{R,s}^u \, Y_{R,s}^u(i,j) \; P(i,j) \qquad (1)$$

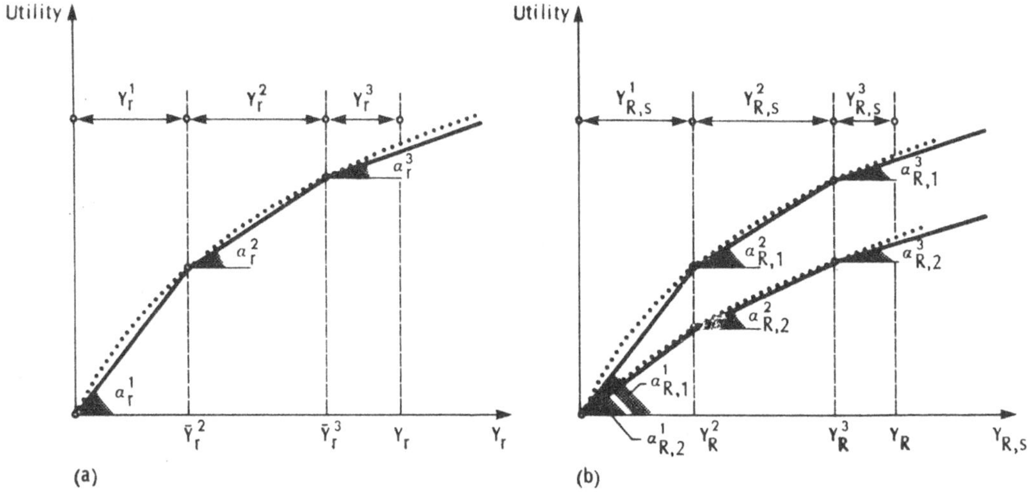

Figure 2 - Linearized Utility Functions

The first term on the right-hand side is the total utility of all city re-residents obtained from the first R-1 commodities, and the second term is the utility from floor space in buildings with different densities. For the linear programming model (LPM), the welfare is maximized with regard to all endogenous variables except the populations P(i,j) residing in zone (i,j). The latter are treated as constant parameters in the LPM. Hence, the welfare W evaluated at the optimum of the LPM is a function of populations P(i,j). The sum of all populations P(i,j) residing in zones (i,j) must be equal to the city population

$$P = \sum_{i=1}^{I} \sum_{j=1}^{J} P(i,j) \qquad (2)$$

There are constraints on the demand components $Y_r (r=1,\ldots,R-1)$ due to the linearized utility function in Fig. 2a

$$0 \leq Y_r^1(i,j) \leq \bar{Y}_r^2 \qquad (3a)$$

$$0 \leq Y_r^2(i,j) \leq \bar{Y}_r^3 - \bar{Y}_r^2 \tag{3b}$$

$$0 \leq Y_r^3(i,j) \tag{3c}$$

$$\alpha_r^u > \alpha_r^{u+1}, \; u=1,2 \tag{3d}$$

Inequality eqn. (3d) tells us that the marginal utility tends to fall with increasing consumption. Similar constraints are obtained for floor space demand

$$0 \leq Y_{R,s}^1(i,j) \leq \bar{Y}_R^2 \tag{4a}$$

$$0 \leq Y_{R,s}^2(i,j) \leq \bar{Y}_R^3 - \bar{Y}_R^2 \tag{4b}$$

$$0 \leq Y_{R,s}^3(i,j) \tag{4c}$$

$$\alpha_{R,s}^u > \alpha_{R,s}^{u+1}, \; u=1,2 \tag{4d}$$

$$\alpha_{R,s}^u > \alpha_{R,s+1}^u, \; s=1,\ldots, S-1; \; u=1,\ldots, 3 \tag{4e}$$

$$\sum_{s=1}^{S} Y_{R,s}^1(i,j) \leq \bar{Y}_R^2 \tag{4f}$$

$$\sum_{s=1}^{S} Y_{R,s}^2(i,j) \leq \bar{Y}_R^3 - \bar{Y}_R^2 \tag{4g}$$

Eqns. (4a)-(4d) are the same as (3a)-(3d). Eqn. (4e) tells us that the marginal utility tends to fall with increasing building density. Eqns. (4f) and (4g) are introduced to avoid the LPM choosing the first or second component of total floorspace demand from different building densities. Since $Y_{R,1}^1$ yields the greatest possible utility, the LPM will first exhaust, if feasible, the first interval in Fig. 2b. Condition (4f) impedes the LPM from choosing $Y_{R,2}^1$, if $\alpha_{R,2}^1 > \alpha_{R,1}^2$, because the same apartment cannot be located in a building with different densities. It is possible, however, that a solution still exists for which components of floorspace demand are chosen from different densities. In this case, the LPM could be rerun excluding some densities.

Export

The export of commodity r in prespecified export nodes (i*,j*) must be at least as great as the exogenous demand for exports

$$\sum_{i=i^*} \sum_{j=i^*} E_r(i,j) \geq E_r, \; r=1, \ldots, R-1 \tag{5}$$

For locally consumed commodities E_r is zero.

Production

To consider transportation cost in terms of resources, each zone (i,j) is distinguished by four boundaries as shown in Fig. 3. The numbering of the boundaries follows in a clockwise rotation manner starting with the southbound boundary. To economize on notation, all zones are equally treated but boundary conditions of the urban area are given separately. The sum of final demand for, outflow of, and use as an input in other productions of a good in zone (i,j) cannot exceed the sum of inflow and production of that good; this is production constraint (6) for commodity r

$$[F_r^1(i+1,j) + F_r^2(i,j+1) + F_r^3(i-1,j) + F_r^4(i,j-1)] + \sum_s Z_{r,s}(i,j)$$

$$- \sum_s \sum_{q=1}^{R-1} a_{r,q,s}\, Z_{q,s}(i,j) - a_{r,R}\, Z_R(i,j) - \sum_{b=1}^{4} F_r^b(i,j) - E_r(i,j)$$

$$- D_r(i,j) \geqq 0 \;, \quad r=1, \ldots, R-1; \; i=1, \ldots, I; \; j=1, \ldots, J \tag{6}$$

The first term in brackets denotes the inflow of commodity r and the second term is production. The next two terms denote the use of commodity r as an input in the production of all other commodities. It has been assumed that floorspace production is independent of the building density because the construction industry is mobile. This allows one to distinguish the production of floorspace by building densities on the demand side, ie., in connection with the demand for floor space by residents. The last terms are outflow, export, and final demand. Exports are neglected in eqn. (6) if zone (i,j) is not an export node (i*,j*). Most of the input-output coefficients are not sensitive to changes in the building density and can therefore be kept constant, ie., $a_{r,q,s} = a_{r,q}$. However, in the absence of public goods in this model, at least one industry should exhibit increasing returns to scale in the sense that either its input-output coefficients $a_{r,q,s}$ or its factor ratios $b_{r,q,s}$, or both, depend on the building density. For the boundaries of the urban area, it is assumed that

$$F_r^b(I+1,j) = F_r^b(0,j) = 0 \;, \quad j=0,\ldots, J+1; \; b=1,\ldots, 4 \tag{7a}$$

$$F_r^b(i,J+1) = F_r^b(i,0) = 0 \;, \quad i=1,\ldots, I; \; b=1,\ldots, 4 \tag{7b}$$

$$F_r^3(I,j) = F_r^1(1,j) = 0 \;, \quad j=1,\ldots, J \tag{7c}$$

$$F_r^2(i,1) = F_r^4(i,J) = 0 \;, \quad i=1,\ldots, I \tag{7d}$$

Eqns. (7) ensure that there is no inflow or outflow of goods at thé boundaries of the urban area.

Final Demand (other than housing)

The model determines commuting trip flows but not shopping trip flows. Therefore, it simply requires total final demand for commodity r to be at least as great as total consumption by households

$$\sum_{i=1}^{I} \sum_{j=1}^{J} D_r(i,j) \geqq \sum_{i=1}^{I} \sum_{j=1}^{J} \sum_{u=1}^{3} P(i,j)\, Y_r^u(i,j) \;, \quad r=1, \ldots, R-1 \tag{8}$$

At the expense of additional endogenous variables the model can be modified to include shopping trips in the same way as is shown for commuting flows below.

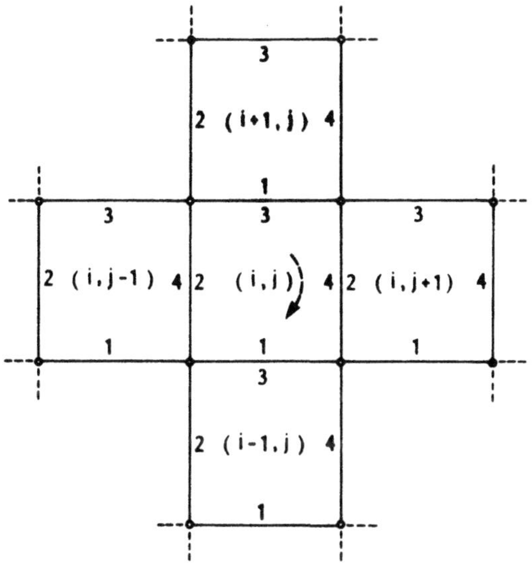

Figure 3 - Internal Numbering of Zones

Production of Floor Space

Total production of floor space in zone (i,j) must be at least as great as total demand for floor space by the R-1 industries and residents in that zone

$$Z_R(i,j) - \sum_{s=1}^{S} \sum_{q=1}^{R-1} a_{R,q,s}\, Z_{q,s}(i,j) - \sum_{u=1}^{3} \sum_{s=1}^{S} P(i,j) Y^u_{R,s}(i,j) \geqq 0 \,,$$

$$i=1, \ldots, I; \; j=1, \ldots, J \qquad (9)$$

To economize on variables, total floor space production could be substituted into eqn. (6).

Commuting and Employment

The model considers both commuting trip flows and commodity flows. It requires that the demand for labour by all industries which are located in zone (i,j) does not exceed the supply of labour in that zone. The latter is given by the sum of net inflow of labourers and residents in that zone

$$\sum_{r=1}^{R-1} \sum_{s=1}^{S} [b_{1,r,s} + b_{1,R,s}\, a_{R,r,s}]\, Z_{r,s}(i,j) + \sum_{u=1}^{3} \sum_{s=1}^{S} b_{1,R,s}\, P(i,j) Y^u_{R,s}(i,j)$$

$$\leqq [H^1(i+1,j) + H^2(i,j+1) + H^3(i-1,j) + H^4(i,j-1)] + P(i,j) - \sum_{b=1}^{4} H^b(i,j) \,,$$

$$i = 1, \ldots, I; \; j = 1, \ldots, J \qquad (10)$$

In order to account for the building density the production of floor space has been substituted from eqn. (9). The first term denotes the demand for labour by all industries including construction of commercial buildings. The demand for labour by housing construction is given in the second term. Population $P(i,j)$ residing in zone (i,j) plus inflow minus outflow of the labour force is defined as the supply of labour. Once again, increasing returns to scale can be considered by the labour ratio $b_{1,r,s}$ which should fall, at least in a certain range, with increasing building density. In high-rise buildings, however, the input of labour per unit of output could rise due to increasing communication within that building. For a closed urban economy it is required that

$$H^b(I+1,j) = H^b(0,j) = 0\ ,\ j=0,\dots,J+1;\ b=1,\dots,4 \tag{11a}$$

$$H^b(i,J+1) = H^b(i,0) = 0\ ,\ i=1,\dots,I;\ b=1,\dots,4 \tag{11b}$$

$$H^3(I,j) = H^1(1,j) = 0\ ,\ j=1,\dots,J \tag{11c}$$

$$H^4(i,J) = H^2(i,1) = 0\ ,\ i=1,\dots,I \tag{11d}$$

which ensures that there is no inflow or outflow of labour at the boundary of the city. Moreover, employment in transportation, which is not assigned to specific zones, is considered by eqn. (12).

$$\sum_{i=1}^{I}\sum_{j=1}^{J}\sum_{m=1}^{M} b_{1,R+m}\, Z_{R+m}(i,j)$$

$$+ \sum_{i=1}^{I}\sum_{j=1}^{J}\sum_{r=1}^{R-1}\sum_{s=1}^{S} [b_{1,r,s} + b_{1,R,s}\, a_{R,r,s}]\, Z_{r,s}(i,j)$$

$$+ \sum_{i=1}^{I}\sum_{j=1}^{J}\sum_{u=1}^{3}\sum_{s=1}^{S} b_{1,R,s}\, P(i,j)\, Y^u_{R,s}(i,J) \leqq P \tag{12}$$

The demand for labour by transportation and industries cannot exceed total city population.

Transportation

The LPM chooses those transport modes which are efficient in terms of resource costs, while tripmakers are indifferent to various modes, ie., individual utility functions are independent of commuting costs. It is assumed that commodities can be shipped by automobiles only. In constraint eqn. (13) the supply of transportation services of automobiles (ie., mode 1) must be at least as great as the demand for transportation services in zone (i,j)

$$Z_{R+1}(i,j) \geqq d(i,j)\ [\sum_{q=1}^{R-1} a_{R+1,q}\ [F^1_q(i+1,j) + F^2_q(i,j+1) + F^3_q(i-1,j) + F^4_q(i,j-1)]$$

$$+ \sum_{q=1}^{R-1}\sum_{b=1}^{4} a_{R+1,q}\ F^b_q(i,j) + D_{R+1}(i,j)]\ ,\ i=1,\dots,I;\ j=1,\dots,J \tag{13}$$

The same applies to the remaining modes in constraint eqn. (14). Total demand for transportation services in zone (i,j) is given by the sum of inflow and outflow of commuters. This is constraint eqn. (15).

$$Z_{R+m}(i,j) \geq d(i,j)\, D_{R+m}(i,j)\ ,\ m = 2,\ldots,M;\ i = 1,\ldots,I;\ j = 1,\ldots,J \tag{14}$$

$$\sum_{m=1}^{M} D_{R+m}(i,j) = H^{1}(i+1,j) + H^{2}(i,j+1) + H^{3}(i-1,j) + H^{4}(i,j-1)$$

$$+ \sum_{b=1}^{4} H^{b}(i,j)\ ,\ i = 1,\ldots,I;\ j = 1,\ldots,J \tag{15}$$

Capital Services

The city is given a fixed capital stock. The demand for capital services which depends on transportation services (first term), commodity production (second term), and housing construction (third term) must not exceed the fixed capital stock

$$\sum_{i=1}^{I} \sum_{j=1}^{J} \sum_{m=1}^{M} b_{2,R+m}\, Z_{R+m}(i,j)$$

$$+ \sum_{i=1}^{I} \sum_{j=1}^{J} \sum_{r=1}^{R-1} \sum_{s=1}^{S} [b_{2,r,s} + b_{2,R,s}\, a_{R,r,s}]\, Z_{r,s}(i,j)$$

$$+ \sum_{i=1}^{I} \sum_{j=1}^{J} \sum_{u=1}^{3} \sum_{s=1}^{S} b_{2,R,s}\, P(i,j)\, Y^{u}_{R,s}(i,j) \leq K \tag{16}$$

Land Constraints

In each zone, the use of land for transportation (first term), commercial buildings (second term), and housing (third term) cannot exceed the supply of land in that zone

$$\sum_{m=1}^{M} b_{3,R+m}\, Z_{R+m}(i,j) + \sum_{q=1}^{R-1} \sum_{s=1}^{S} \frac{a_{R,q,s}}{g_s}\, Z_{q,s}(i,j)$$

$$+ \sum_{u=1}^{3} \sum_{s=1}^{S} \frac{P(i,j)}{g_s}\, Y^{u}_{R,s}(i,j) \leq A(i,j)\ ,\ i=1,\ldots,I;\ j=1,\ldots,J \tag{17}$$

In contrast to earlier attempts (Mills, 1972a; Kim, 1979), this model distinguishes clearly between the demand for floor space and land by introducing the floor-to-land ratio. It is clear that at the optimum not all transport modes will necessarily be used. Both technology and topography of a specific city will decide whether a subway system, say, is efficient for a given endowment of resources.

Combined Linear/Non-Linear Programming

The objective function eqn. (1) and constraint eqns. (2)-(17) describe the LPM for fixed populations P(i,j) residing in zone (i,j). For each assignment of the city population to various zones, there exists an optimum welfare W which is given by the LPM. The final goal is to maximize this non-linear function

$$\max_{\{P(i,j)\}} W[P(i,j)] \tag{18a}$$

$$\text{s.t.} \quad \sum_{i=1}^{I} \sum_{j=1}^{J} P(i,j) = P \tag{18b}$$

$$W[P(i,j)] = LPM[\text{eqns.}(1)-(17)] \tag{18c}$$

where the welfare function W is defined by the LPM of eqns. (1)-(17). Naturally the model in eqns. (1)-(17) can be solved directly as a non-linear optimization problem assuming a computer is available to deal with this number of dependent variables. Given a CDC-6000 computer for example, the number of dependent variables is restricted to about one hundred in non-linear optimizations. This is far too low a capacity when compared to the number of dependent variables of this model, the latter being: $IJ[6+2M+8(R-1)+(R+2)S]+(R-1)I^*J^*$. For instance, with 50 zones, 4 modes, 4 industries (eg., retail, manufacturing, services, and construction), 5 densities, and 2 export nodes, the number of dependent variables is 3406. In the combined linear/non-linear programming model defined by eqn. (18), the number of endogenous variables of the non-linear optimization is equal to the number of zones (IJ), whereas the remaining dependent variables are determined by the LPM.

At the optimum, the efficient allocation of labour, capital, buildings, and land in each zone is given. In particular, the assignment of various activities to each zone is determined together with the efficient building density for each activity and zone. Moreover, the solution will decide which transport modes should be used by how much and if at all. The dual program to the primal LPM of eqns. (1)-(17) yields the economic evaluation of resources, ie., shadow incomes, capital rents, and land rents at the social optimum. Since populations $P(i,j)$ are exogenous to the LPM, it is clear that shadow incomes (hence utilities) are not constant between zones which is due to the Benthamite welfare function.

Land Use Policies

The present model could serve as a tool for town planning. Naturally, many exogenous variables are subject to forecast and measurement errors. Since land use zoning is quite expensive in terms of resources if binding, such regulations should be viable in the long run so that misallocations are avoided. Land use zoning should provide a framework within which residents and investors are free to choose from alternative activities, information is given to everybody at no or minimal cost, long run investments are not subject to unnecessary uncertainty, and future changes in land use regulations should be possible at minimal cost. With this in mind, the sensitivity of the model is evaluated when key variables are changed. For instance, changes in city population or production technology might have a big impact on the allocation of resources. In addition, it might be of interest to evaluate the effect of new export nodes to be developed in the city, ie., the model can be used as a basis for cost-benefit analysis. Similarly, restrictions on building densities or on building heights can be evaluated.

The practicality of implementing the model obviously depends on the specifications of the master plan in question. As implied earlier, the master plan of a particular city should be viable for a long time horizon, thus making exogenous variables subject to uncertainty. As a consequence, it is not desirable to collect extensive statistical data on input-output coefficients, factor ratios, floor-to-land ratios, and so forth. What is required are best guesses of possible, future technologies based on present knowledge and a few statistical samples, as well as imagination about the uncertainty involved in estimating future trends. Hence, it seems to me that the model can be implemented for real cities at low costs, considering the fact that modifications such as an irregular zoning system, zone-dependent coefficients to capture the topography of the city, etc., can easily be done by simply attaching locational coordinates to corresponding coefficients.

A Technical Digression

It is not intended to deal here with the problem of which numerical algorithm is best suited for the LPM described above (eg., a particular decomposition method as described in Sharpe, this volume). The structure of the linear/non-linear model, however, deserves some comments. Denote the number of endogenous variables (excluding P(i,j)) as ν and that of constraints as μ. Let $\underline{P}$ be the (ν x 1) row vector whose first I J elements are P(i,j) with the remaining elements equal to zero; $\underline{\alpha}$ the (ν x ν) matrix of marginal utilities; $\underline{x}$ the (ν x 1) column vector of endogenous variables; $\underline{A}$ a (μ x ν) matrix of constants, some elements of which contain P(i,j); $\underline{B}$ a (μ x ν) matrix of constants; and finally $\underline{b}$ a (μ x 1) vector of resource constraints. Then the LPM can be written in matrix notation:

$$W(\underline{P}) = \max_{\underline{x}} F = \underline{P}\,\underline{\alpha}\,\underline{x} \qquad (19a)$$

$$\text{s.t.} \quad \underline{A}\,\underline{x} - \underline{B}\,\underline{P}' \leq \underline{b} \qquad (19b)$$

A solution of the LPM exists if the opportunity set of $\underline{x}$, as described by eqn. (19b), is bounded and nonempty. By eqns. (2)-(17), consumption, production, and transportation ultimately use labour, capital, and land, total amounts of which are fixed. Hence, the opportunity set is bounded. Of course, the values of the exogenous variables must be set such that the opportunity set is nonempty. For instance, if there is a positive demand for exports, it must be possible to assign all production and residents to export nodes in order to satisfy at least that export demand while total transport costs and final demands are zero. The opportunity set is nonempty if there is no demand for exports because a solution with no activity ($\underline{x} = \underline{0}$) is feasible. If the number of endogenous variables is greater than the number of constraints, then the solution occurs at a vertex and is unique. In our case

$$\nu = IJ[5+2M+8(R-1) + (R+2)S] + (R-1)I^*J^* \tag{20a}$$

$$\mu = IJ[4+M+4(R-1)+3\,S] + 14 + 4R + 5S + 10(I+J) \tag{20b}$$

With the same values as in the last section, ν = 3,356 and μ = 1,955, given that I = 5, J = 10, and I J = 50. Therefore, it is very likely that in real applications the LPM solution is unique with regard to $\underline{x}$.

Let the constraints (19b) be partitioned and renumbered such that the first μ_1 constraints are satisfied as equalities at the optimum, while the remaining constraints are satisfied as strict inequalities. Then the welfare function can be written, when assuming a vertex solution, as

$$W(\underline{P}) = \underline{P}^1\underline{\alpha}^{11}(\underline{A}^{11})^{-1}(\underline{b}^1 + \underline{B}^{11}\underline{P}'^1) \tag{21}$$

where superscripts denote partitioning as described above. Since $\underline{A}^{11}$ may contain $\underline{P}^1$, the welfare function is at least quadratic, ie., non-linear. By the Weierstrass theorem, the global maximum of W exists (on its domain), if the opportunity set

$$\Pi = \{P(i,j)\,|\,\Sigma\Sigma P(i,j) = P\} \tag{22}$$

is nonempty and compact, and if the welfare function is continuous. In our case, both conditions are fulfilled. Moreover, the solution is unique, if the opportunity set is also convex, and if the welfare function is also strictly concave. While the former condition applies to eqn. (22), the latter is not easy to show. However, there are weaker conditions for a unique solution to hold.

EXTENSIONS

Finite Elements

In this section, several possible extensions are briefly discussed. The first extension of the model concerns the geometry of the zones. In order to reduce the number of variables, the topography of the city can possibly better be approximated by using triangular rather than rectangular zones. In Fig. 4, a hypothetical city map is divided into triangular zones where regions of no construction activity are not included in the network. The modification of the above equations to triangular zones is straightforward. Further, by analogy to the method of finite elements in mechanical engineering it is possible to change the method. The tentative outline of the finite element approach when applied to this situation is the following. Firstly, the city is divided into triangular zones. Secondly, the welfare maximization problem in its general, non-linear form is formulated for each zone independently and solved in closed form. If a closed form solution is not possible, find a best, parameterized approximation. The solution for each zone depends on both boundary conditions and dependent variables of the objective function. Thirdly, all zones are linked together by boundary conditions. The latter are known at the outskirts of the city. Hence, dependent variables not included in the objective function can be obtained by solving a linear equation system. Fourthly, optimal utilities are summed over all zones and maximized when subject to the linear equation system. It is left to future research, however, to answer the question whether this approach brings about numerical advantages.

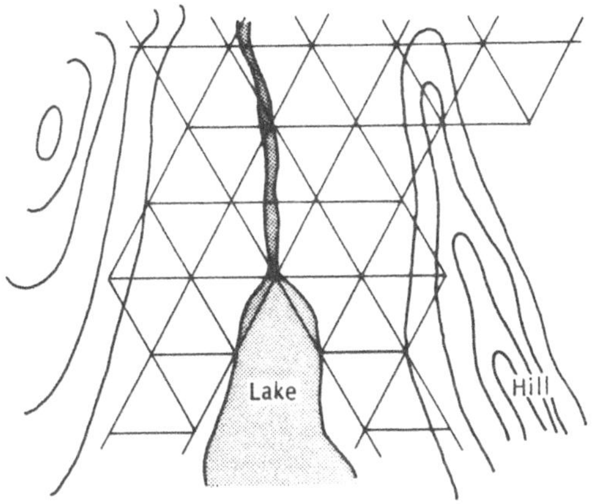

Figure 4 - Triangular Network

Traffic Congestion

It is a well known fact that traffic congestion in cities causes considerable social costs. Mills (1972a) has shown how traffic congestion can be introduced into a LPM by considering a stepwise linear marginal cost function. Of course, this requires the knowledge of the marginal cost function of a typical city (see also Hutchinson, 1974).

Imports

Imports can be considered in two ways in this model. Firstly, in the basic model exports were treated as variables net of imports. Secondly, imports can be dealt with as separate inputs whereas total imports are given exogenously. Moreover, import nodes need not be identical to export nodes.

Public Goods

Introducing public goods is not a straightforward matter. Initially, public goods should be distinguished by their degree of localness. While some of them provide services to all residents in the city, eg., a theatre, opera, etc. others are strictly local, ie., do not provide services to residents residing in adjacent zones. On the other hand, individual utilities now depend on public-goods consumption. Hence, the efficient allocation of households depends crucially on the spatial allocation of public goods if these are local in degree.

Different Resource Endowment

In the basic model, all households are equally endowed. To consider an unequal distribution of resources, different classes with regard to ability to work, capital, and land can be introduced. Define a joint density function

$$f(A_a, K_k, B_b) \tag{23a}$$

where a, k, and b denote indices for different classes of work ability (A), capital endowment (K), and land endowment (B). The sum of densities over all classes is equal to one

$$\sum_a \sum_k \sum_b f(A_a, K_k, B_b) = 1 \tag{23b}$$

The supply of labour, capital, and land in the city is given by:

$$\sum_a A_a \; P \sum_k \sum_b f(A_a, K_k, B_b) \tag{23c}$$

$$\sum_k K_k \; P \sum_a \sum_b f(A_a, K_k, B_b) \tag{23d}$$

$$\sum_b B_b \; P \sum_a \sum_k f(A_a, K_k, B_b) \tag{23e}$$

For each class, work places, living places, and commuting flows have to be determined in the same way a was shown in the basic model. The number of variables, however, will increase considerably even with a moderate number of classes.

The Small, Open City

In the basic model, the city was considered to be closed with both labour and capital supply fixed. This is one of two polar cases. In the other polar case the city is assumed to be open but small, ie., migration of labour and capital between the city and the rest of the economy does not affect the state of the rest of the economy. In other words, the utility of city residents is given by that obtained outside the city. In the case of a small open economy it is appropriate to maximize the city production net of resources costs when subject to the condition that all city residents attain the given utility level (Kanemoto, 1980). If neither of these polar cases is a good approximation to the city in question, a model should be formulated in which migration of labour depends on the welfare attainable in the city.

ACKNOWLEDGMENTS

Financial support from the University of Zurich and the Swiss Federal Institute of Technology (ETH) as well as comments by two anonymous referees are gratefully acknowledged.

REFERENCES

Anas, A., 1983, From Physical to Economic Urban Models: The Lowry Framework Revisited, a paper presented to the International Symposium on New Directions in Urban Modelling, University of Waterloo, Waterloo, Ontario.

Batty, M., 1976, Urban Modelling, Cambridge University Press, London.

Büttler, H.-J. and Beckmann, M.J., 1980, Design Parameters in Housing Construction and the Market for Urban Housing, Econometrica, 48, 201-225.

Echenique, M., 1983, The Practice of Modelling in Developing Countries, a paper presented to the International Symposium on New Directions in Urban Modelling, University of Waterloo, Waterloo, Ontario.

Henderson, J., 1977, Economic Theory and the Cities, Academic Press, New York.

Herbert, J.D. and Stevens, B.H., 1960, A Model for the Distribution of Residential Activity in Urban Areas, Journal of Regional Science, 2, 21-36.

Hochman, O. and Ofek, H., 1979, A Theory of the Behaviour of Municipal Governments: The Case of Internalizing Pollution Externalities, Journal of Urban Economics, 6, 416-431.

Hutchinson, B.G., 1974, Principles of Urban Transport Systems Planning, McGraw-Hill, New York.

Kanemoto, Y., 1980, Theories of Urban Externalities, North Holland, Amsterdam.

Kim, T.J., 1979, Alternative Transportation Modes in an Urban Land Use Model: A General Equilibrium Approach, Journal of Urban Economics, 6, 197-215.

Mills, E.S., 1972a, Markets and Efficient Resource Allocation in Urban Areas, Swedish Journal of Economics, 74, 100-113.

Mills, E.S., 1972b, Studies in the Structure of the Urban Economy, The Johns Hopkins University Press, Baltimore, MD.

Mirrlees, J.A., 1972, The Optimum Town, Swedish Journal of Economics, 74, 114-135.

Sharpe, Ron, 1984, An Optimum Economic/Energy Land-Use Transportation Model, this volume.

AN OPTIMUM ECONOMIC/ENERGY LAND-USE TRANSPORTATION MODEL

Ron Sharpe
CSIRO Division of Building Research
PO Box 56, Highett, VIC 3190
Australia

Abstract. The paper develops a combined land-use transportation planning model to minimize the total combined energy (or cost) of transport, land use development, and demolition of existing activity. The model takes the form of a large-scale linear programming problem with a sparse structure. The problem may be solved efficiently by decomposing it into sub-problems using Benders (1962) technique. The model is extended to include gravity type trip distributions, gaming solutions, multiple objectives, variable development densities, congestion and multiple planning periods.

INTRODUCTION

The increasing availability of efficient large-scale linear programming (LP) algorithms capable of solving problems involving tens of thousands of variables allows more powerful urban (and building) planning models to be developed. However, in the past there has been some resistance amongst urban modellers to using an LP approach because of its apparent restriction to strict cost minimization and its apparent treatment of land use transportation activities as simple homogeneous quantities, ie., without diversity. While LP has had a long association with strict cost minimization problems, it has also been adapted to solve a wide range of non-linear formulations, eg., the TOPAZ (Technique for the Optimum Placement of Activities in Zones) model (Brotchie, 1969; Sharpe and Brotchie, 1972; Brotchie, Dickey and Sharpe, 1980), mixed variable programming problems (Benders, 1962; Geoffrion, 1970; Geoffrion, 1972; Geoffrion and Graves, 1974), and non-linear or diversity problems of the gravity or entropy type (Brotchie, 1978, Harris, 1981).

A further unjustified criticism often levelled at linear programming is that it is restricted to solving problems with a single objective, whereas real-world problems usually involve multiple objectives held by competing groups. Again, LP has been extended to serve the latter, eg., in a competitive gaming format in the TOPAZ model (Sharpe and Karlqvist, 1980) and in a multi-objective framework (Van Delft and Nijkamp, 1976). Further development of TOPAZ as a multi-objective planning model will now be described.

OUTLINE OF METHOD

The approach to be used is similar to that developed for the TOPAZ model (Brotchie, 1969; Sharpe and Brotchie, 1972; Sharpe and Karlqvist, 1980; and in linear form by Roy and Brotchie, 1981). The objective is to determine a land-use and trip distribution pattern to (i) maximize the total benefits less costs of interaction plus, (ii) the total benefits less costs of establishing and operating the activities in the zones plus, and (iii) the total benefits less costs of demolishing or removing any development of an earlier period.

Benefits and costs may be in either economic or energy units. Activity and zone sizes and capacities are assumed to be expressed in consistent units. Activity increments and decrements in each zone are assumed to be additive.

The allocation is to be subject to the constraints that each activity is to be fully allocated and that each zone has a limited capacity. Additional planning and transport capacity constraints may also be included. For convenience, the model will be expressed in the equivalent form of minimizing costs less benefits.

The following notation is assumed

A_i = planned level of activity i including existing development,

b_{ij} = unit cost less benefit of incrementing the level of activity i in zone j,

$c_{ijk\ell}$ = cost less benefit per unit of interaction between activity i in zone j and activity k in zone ℓ,

d_{ij} = unit cost less benefit of decrementing the level of activity i in zone j,

e_{ij} = level of activity i existing in zone j at the start,

s_{ik} = level of interaction between a unit of activity i and a unit of activity k (assumed to be independent of zonal location of the activities),

r_{ik} = $s_{ik}A_i/A_k$,

$T_{ijk\ell}$ = level of interaction between activity i in zone j activity k in zone ℓ,

x_{ij} = amount of activity i to be allocated in zone j,

y_{ij} = amount of activity i to be removed from zone j, and

z_j = capacity of zone j including existing development.

Our earlier objective (at the start of this section) may now be expressed terms of the variables as follows

1. Minimize total costs less benefits of interaction. The simplest interpretation of this objective is to cost the flow between an activity pair (i,k) along a path (j,ℓ) as ($T_{ijk\ell}$ $c_{ijk\ell}$) and then minimize the sum of these over all activity pairs and paths. This is the objective of the

classical transportation (trip distribution) problem (eg., Bayer, 1965; Harris, 1981). The use of such an objective ignores any diversity that may occur in the trip distribution due to individuals pursuing their own separate objectives rather than complying with the objective to minimize total community cost (Wilson, 1970). However, this simple community objective provides a useful lower cost bound and a good starting point for objectives incorporation diversity, as will be shown later.

2. Minimize the total costs less benefits of establishing and operating the activities in the zones. The simplest form of this expression is to assume that these costs and benefits are constant per unit of activity in each zone and then sum over all activities and zones, ie., the sum of $b_{ij}x_{ij}$ for all i,j.

3. Minimize the total cost less benefits of demolishing or removing activity is similar to (ii), ie., minimize the sum of $d_{ij}y_{ij}$ for all i,j.

The planning objective is subject to the following constraints to ensure that the resulting solutions are practical

1. The transportation flows are linked to the net zonal activity levels (x_{ij}-y_{ij}+e_{ij}) via the trip origin and destination constraints of the classical transportation model. Firstly, the total trips from activity i in zone j to activity k in all zones ℓ are assumed equal to the net activity level of activity i in zone j times a unit trip generation rate s_{ik}. Secondly, the total trips arriving at activity k in zone ℓ from all zones j are assumed to be related in a similar manner to the net activity level times a trip destination rate r_{ik}.

2. Each activity target should be met. This is ensured by constraining the sum of all net activity levels over all the zones to be equal to the target level for each activity.

3. Each zone has a limited capacity which cannot be exceeded. In this case the total sum of all net activity levels in each zone is constrained to be less than or equal to that zone's capacity.

4. Individual activity levels in each zone and flows between zones may be constrained for both practical reasons and planning purposes. Firstly all variables can only have positive increments, since negative values have no physical meaning. Secondly planners may wish to impose minimum or maximum levels on new development, demolitions or flows. Thirdly it is necessary to ensure that the amount of a particular activity demolished in a zone does not exceed the existing level of that activity.

The overall problem may then be expressed mathematically as follows

$$Z = \mathrm{Min}_{T,x,y} \sum_{ijk\ell} T_{ijk\ell}\, c_{ijk\ell} + \sum_{ij} b_{ij}\, x_{ij} + \sum_{ij} d_{ij}\, y_{ij} \quad (1)$$

subject to

interaction origin-destination constraints,

$$\sum_{\ell} T_{ijk\ell} - s_{ik}(x_{ij} - y_{ij} + e_{ij}) = 0 \qquad \forall ijk \quad (2)$$

$$\sum_{j} T_{ijk\ell} - r_{ik}(x_{k\ell} - y_{k\ell} + e_{k\ell}) = 0 \qquad \forall ik\ell \quad (3)$$

each activity is fully allocated,

$$\sum_{j}(x_{ij} - y_{ij}) = A_i - \sum_{j} e_{ij} \qquad \forall i \quad (4)$$

each zone's capacity is not exceeded,

$$\sum_{i}(x_{ij} - y_{ij}) \leq Z_j - \sum_{i} e_{ij} \qquad \forall j \quad (5)$$

and constraint bounds,

$$0 \leq (x_{ij})_{min} \leq x_{ij} \leq (x_{ij})_{max} \quad (6)$$

$$0 \leq (y_{ij})_{min} \leq y_{ij} \leq (y_{ij})_{max} \leq e_{ij} \quad (7)$$

$$0 \leq (T_{ijk\ell})_{min} \leq T_{ijk\ell} \leq (T_{ijk\ell})_{max} \quad (8)$$

This formulation, with the exception of the demolition variables, is a special case of the TOPAZ formulation (Brotchie, 1969; Sharpe and Karlqvist, 1980). TOPAZ allows for a more general form of the transport cost component of the objective which includes entropy (or gravity) type costs (to be discussed later). In the earliest TOPAZ formulation, Brotchie (1969) presented another special case of the transport cost component of the objective using a quadratic form.

Solution Procedure by Decomposition

Most real-life applications of the problem are too large to be solved economically by existing general linear programming codes. For example, a typical urban planning problem involving say, 4 activities and 40 zones would generate an LP problem with 25,920 variables and 1324 constraints. However, the model has a special property that enables it to be decomposed or partitioned into smaller sub-problems. This involves, in our particular case, a separation of the problem defined by eqns. (1) to (8) into a master problem confined to the land use activity allocations and removals only, and a sub-problem involving the transportation distribution subject to fixed land uses.

In TOPAZ the decomposed formulation is solved as a competitive game involving two players, with one player sub-optimizing the land use (master) problem while the other sub-optimizes the transportation distribution (sub) problem. This non-cooperative game, in which each player sequentially makes optimizing decisions according to the last move of the other player, leads to a Nash equilibrium solution (eg., Rao and Hati, 1980; Roy and Lesse, 1983). In this Nash approach there is no direct cooperation between players and hence the final solution achieved is not expected to be as good as one in which the players make simultaneous decisions (Sharpe and Karlqvist, 1980).

A real-life interpretation of the two players in this strictly non-cooperative game is not straight forward. The first player might be represented by a ruthless land use planning authority seeking only to minimize its infrastructure costs and being totally disinterested in the transport costs of those travelling between activities (ie., the second player) and vice versa. This is unlikely to occur in practice, but the outcome is still of interest since it provides one extreme bound to reality. If players cooperate to jointly optimize land use and trip distribution then the solution may be described as a Pareto optimum or Pareto equilibrium (eg., Rao and Hati, 1980). In the following solution procedure, this joint cooperation is achieved between the two players through the use of Bender's (1962) decomposition technique, which always leads to a unique solution. This technique allows the transportation sub-problem to signal to the master problem the effect of land use changes on total transportation cost, through the use of marginal cost (dual) variables. Additional constraints (called Benders cuts) are then generated for the master problem to constrain it to move towards the global (Pareto) optimum.

Benders Decomposition

The following procedure follows that used by Geoffrion (1970) and Geoffrion and Graves (1974). Matrix subscripts are occasionally suppressed for convenience.

<u>Step 0</u> - Select a convergence tolerance parameter $\varepsilon \geq 0$

Initialize the upper bound, $UB = \infty$, the lower bound, $LB = -\infty$, and the iteration count, $H = 0$.

<u>Step 1</u> - Solve the current master problem

$$Z_1 = \text{Min}_{x,y,Z_0} \sum_{ij} \left[b_{ij}\, x_{ij} + d_{ij}\, y_{ij} \right] + Z_0 \tag{9}$$

subject to eqns. (4) to (7) and, if $H > 0$,

$$Z_o - \sum_{ijk} [\pi^h_{ijk} s_{ik}(x_{ij} - y_{ij} + e_{ij}) + \mu^h_{ijk} r_{ki}(x_{ij} - y_{ij} + e_{ij})] = 0 \;\forall\; h=1,\ldots H \qquad (10)$$

where π, and μ are dual variables to be obtained from the transportation sub-problem constraints (2) and (3) respectively.

Let $(x^{H+1}, y^{H+1}, Z_o^{H+1})$ be the optimal solution and put LB equal to the optimal values of eqn. (9), $LB = Z_1^{H+1}$, which is a lower bound on the optimal value of eqn. (1)-(8).

Terminate if $UB \leq LB + \varepsilon$.

<u>Step 2</u> - (a) Solve the transportation sub-problem.

$$Z_2 = \mathrm{Min}_T \sum_{ijk\ell} T_{ijk\ell}\, c_{ijk\ell} \qquad (11)$$

subject to eqns. (2), (3) and (8) with $x = x^{H+1}$, $y = y^{H+1}$ using a capacitated transportation algorithm (eg., Bayer, 1965). Denote the optimal solution as T^{H+1} and the value of the objective in eqn. (11) as Z_2^{H+1}. The upper bound to the problem defined by eqns. (1) to (8) is then

$$UB^{H+1} = Z_1^{H+1} + Z_2^{H+1} - Z_o^{H+1}$$

Store the solution $(x,y,T)^{H+1}$ if $UB^{H+1} < UB$ and set $UB = UB^{H+1}$.

Terminate if $UB \leq LB + \varepsilon$.

(b) Determine an optimal dual for eqn. (11) subject to the constraints (2), (3) and (8), for the current solution, and denote it by

π^{H+1} corresponding to constraint (2), and
μ^{H+1} corresponding to constraint (3).

Set $H = H+1$ and return to Step 1.

Comments on the Solution Technique

Firstly, the dual solution to the transportation sub-problems is degenerate since the number of active constraints is one less than the number of dual variables. Hence, although the primal solution is uniquely defined, the dual solution is not unique. This often leads to weak Benders cuts and slows the solution convergence (Magnanti and Wong, 1981). Early experience with the above formulation also showed this. Magnanti and Wong have reported that some researchers have improved the convergence procedure by imposing more limits on each solution step and this was subsequently implemented in the above formulation with success. The move limits imposed take the following form for the x variables (y variables are also treated in a similar manner)

$$(x^H - \Delta x) \leq x^{H+1} \leq (x^H + \Delta x)$$

where $\Delta x = \phi\,(x_{max} - x_{min})$

These move limits are also subject to any bounds constraints imposed by eqns. (6) and (7). A value of $\phi = 0.15$ has proved satisfactory.

Secondly, the transportation problem in Step 2(a) is most easily solved as a set of independent transportation sub-problems for each activity pair, i and k

$$Z_{2(ik)} = \text{Min} \sum_{j\ell} T_{ijk\ell}\, c_{ijk\ell} \tag{12a}$$

subject to

$$\sum_{\ell} T_{ijk\ell} = s_{ik}(x_{ij} - y_{ij} + e_{ij}) \quad \forall\, j \tag{12b}$$

$$\sum_{j} T_{ijk\ell} = r_{ik}(x_{k\ell} - y_{k\ell} + e_{k\ell}) \quad \forall\, \ell \tag{12c}$$

and eqn. (8) as before.

The sizes of the linear programming tableaux are substantially reduced over that required for solution as one large problem. For example, the 4-activity, 40-zone case considered earlier would now generate an LP tableau involving 321 variables and (44+H) constraints for the master problem, and a 40 x 40 tableau for the transportation sub-problem, compared to 25,920 variables x 1324 constraints required in a combined problem formulation.

A further substantial core saving is achieved by decomposing the master problem into a capacitated transhipment problem composed of eqns. (4,5,6,7 and 9, without the Z_0 term), and a small LP consisting of the Z_0 term in eqns. (9) and (10). The decomposition used employs the Dantzig Wolfe technique (Geoffrion, 1970) involving a capacitated transhipment algorithm (Kallio, Por and Soismaa, 1979) and a revised simplex LP (Gass, 1964) for the sub-problem generated.

Entropy (Gravity) Trip Distribution Sub-Model

It is often desirable in urban planning studies to replace the transportation sub-model (eqns. 11,2,3 and 8) with a gravity-type model to reflect the diversity of the community in trip distribution patterns. In this case a model of the following form is appropriate (Wilson, 1970)

$$Z_2^B = \text{Max}_T \left[- \sum_{ijk\ell} T_{ijk\ell}(\log T_{ijk\ell} + \beta_{ik}\, c_{ijk\ell})/\beta_{ik}\right] \tag{13}$$

$$= \text{Min} \left[Z_2 + \sum_{ijk\ell} T_{ijk\ell}(\log T_{ijk\ell})/\beta_{ik}\right] \tag{14}$$

subject to constraints (2,3 and 8), and where β_{ij} is the gravity exponent for activity pairs, i and k.

Since the transportation sub-problem is now non-linear, it is necessary to use Generalized Benders Decomposition (Geoffrion, 1972) to determine an optimal solution. Again the solution is unique. The solution procedure is similar to that for the linear sub-problem with the duals of the linear sub-problem being replaced by the Lagrangian multipliers generated by the gravity model solution.

Once again the dual variables are not unique giving rise to the possibility of weak Benders cuts and slow convergence. Geoffrion (1972) and Magnanti and Wong (1981) have suggested ways in which an optimal set of duals may be selected to give strong cuts. However, the use of move limits (described earlier) has been found easier to implement and to produce rapid convergence.

The solution to the gravity model for a particular i, k trip sub-set is given by Wilson, (1970)

$T_{j\ell} = A_j B_\ell O_j D_\ell \exp(-\beta\ c_{j\ell})$

where O_j = number of trips originating in zone j = $s_{ik}\ (x_{ij}-y_{ij}+e_{ij})$; D_ℓ = number of trip destinations in zone ℓ; $A_j = 1/\sum_\ell B_\ell D_\ell \exp\ (-\beta c_{j\ell})$; and $B_\ell = 1/\sum_j A_j O_j \exp(-\beta c_{j\ell})$.

A_j and B_ℓ are solved by recursive iteration from an arbitrarily assumed set of values for one of them, eg. all $A_j = 1$. The dual variables are then given by

$$\pi_j = -\log\ (A_j O_j)/\beta$$
$$\mu_\ell = -\log\ (B_\ell D_\ell)/\beta$$

PLANNING GAMES

The Nash (non-cooperative) and Pareto (cooperative) games provide two bounds of reality, and it is expected that actual outcomes involve partial cooperation and thus lie somewhere in between. Nash solutions are not unique unlike Pareto solutions, and as the degree of cooperation moves between these extremes there will be a transition from unique to non-unique solutions. The land use authority will have interests in the transport costs of the community, and also the land consumed by the transport network, while the travelling community will have interests in saving public infrastructure costs as these are eventually paid from community taxes. Hence we expect the objectives of the two players to be mixed, and the level of cooperation to vary over space and time as perceived needs change. Thus it is of interest to examine how the outcomes vary as the level of cooperation and weighting given to various components of cost in eqns. (1) and (13) change.

Firstly, the objective of the planning authority may be expressed as a weighted sum of the components in eqn. (1) (subscripts suppressed)

$$P = \alpha_1 bx + \alpha_2 dy + \alpha_3 cT \qquad (15)$$

Secondly, the objective of the individuals in the community can be shown to have a group travel objective expressed by a gravity model (eqn. 13) to which an infrastructure cost component would be added

$$Q = \alpha_4 (T\log T + \beta\ cT)/\beta + \alpha_5 b\ x + a_6 dy \qquad (16)$$

A more general case is to treat cost c as being of a different form for the planning authority and individuals, rather than a linear transformation as shown here (Sharpe, Roy and Taylor, 1982).

Pareto Game

In a Pareto planning game these objectives may be combined so that the overall objective is given by

$$Z = (\alpha_1+\alpha_5)bx + (\alpha_2+\alpha_6)dy + (\alpha_3+\alpha_4)cT + \alpha_4(T\log T)/\beta$$

To reproduce eqn. (1), set $(\alpha_1+\alpha_5) = (\alpha_2+\alpha_6) = \alpha_3 = 1$; $\alpha_4 = 0$.

To reproduce eqn. (1) with a gravity model replacing the minimum transport cost model, set $(\alpha_1+\alpha_5) = (\alpha_2+\alpha_6) = \alpha_4 = 1$; $\alpha_3 = 0$.

Other examples of interest are as follows;

To minimize planning authority building costs only, set $\alpha_1 = \alpha_2 = 1$; $\alpha_3 = \alpha_4 = 0$.
To minimize transport costs only, set $\alpha_1 = \alpha_2 = \alpha_4 = 0$; $\alpha_3 = 1$.
To maximize the transport entropy objective, set $\alpha_1 = \alpha_2 = \alpha_3 = 0$; $\alpha_4 = 1$.

In the cases where the travelling individuals perceive their travel costs differently to travel costs perceived by the authority, α_3 and α_4 can be used to weight cT in an appropriate fashion. For example, the planners may wish to minimize energy consumption cost, $\alpha_3 cT$, whereas the travelling individuals may wish to minimize generalized travel costs (including time costs), $\alpha_4 cT$.

The signs of the α variables may be also changed ($\alpha = -1$) to produce maximum cost solution extremes, which may provide a useful upper bound for judging the performance of solutions in between the best and the worst.

Nash Game

The Nash (competitive) game generated by the original TOPAZ can be reproduced by a two-stage iterative process involving the above sub-models.

Step 1 - Solve the master sub-problem as per the Benders approach with H=0 in eqn. (10) to generate solution $(x,y)^o$, ie.,

$$P = \text{Min}_{x,y}\ (\alpha_1 bx + \alpha_2 dy)$$

Step 2 - Solve the appropriate transportation sub-problem to generate the trip distribution $T^o(x,y)$.

Step 3 - Calculate psuedo cost coefficients for the planning authority objective (eqn. 15) using

$$b'_{ij} = b_{ij} + a_{ij}$$

$$d'_{ij} = d_{ij} - a_{ij}$$

where $a_{ij} = 0.5\ \alpha_3\ (\Sigma\ c_{ijk\ell} T^o_{ijk\ell})/(x-y+e)^o_{ij}$

Repeat step 1 with b and d replaced by b' and d' and then steps 2 and 3. Continue to repeat the process until x and y converge.

Weighting factors. The problem of how appropriate weighting factors (α) should be selected has long been a point of criticism levelled at optimization modelling. To overcome the problem four alternatives are available and these are (i) ask the decision makers to select their weightings; (ii) calibrate the weighting factors against past performance; (iii) use the model to explore the range of acceptable solutions, with satisficing constraints; and (iv) use a rule based (or expert systems) approach.

The first may be useful as a learning process for decision makers to obtain an appreciation of the problem by manipulating the weightings to see what impact it has on the outcome. The second option is acceptable only if the political system is to continue with previous objectives without change of emphasis. The third alternative involves seeking minimum acceptable levels for each objective component and applying these as constraints, which will then reduce the range of feasible solutions. In the fourth alternative, decision makers may state their preferences in natural language terms (Dickey, 1983). For example, "highest priority must be given to reducing energy consumption and also to do this in an efficient and economic manner" might be interpreted as placing a weighting of $\alpha=1.0$ on energy cost and a lesser weighting on economic cost, eg., $\alpha=0.5$.

In the real world political process, the weighting of various objectives is often strongly contested and hence it should not be expected to be easy to select weightings for models. The main advantage of modelling should be seen as providing information on the impact of various weightings and solution sensitivity to changes in emphasis.

FURTHER EXTENSIONS

Multiobjective Economic and Energy Modelling

So far the model has been presented as one which treats costs in one set of units, namely economic or energy units. In Sharpe, Roy and Taylor (1982) it is shown how a multiobjective form involving both economic and energy terms may be developed. For example, assume that in the original notation, b, c, and d represent unit economic costs, and let $\bar{b}$, $\bar{c}$ and $\bar{d}$ represent corresponding unit energy costs. Further, as discussed earlier, assume that the unit transport costs are separately identified as c' and c" with c' representing planning authority costs (including system operation, pollution, construction and maintenance costs) and c" representing individual user costs (including fares, fuel, vehicle ownership and maintenance, etc.)

The planner's objective, eqn. (15), may now be extended to include energy costs as follows

$$P = \alpha_1 b'x + \alpha_2 d'y + \alpha_3 c'T + \delta_1 \bar{b}x + \delta_2 \bar{d}y + \delta_3 \bar{c}T \qquad (17)$$

while the objective representing all individuals can be expressed as

$$Q = \alpha_4 (T\log T + \beta c''T)/\beta + \alpha_5 bx + \alpha_6 dy \qquad (18)$$

Pareto and Nash solutions may now be generated as before to provide cooperative and non-cooperative multiobjective solutions.

Variable Density of Development

The initial model presented in this paper implies that the density of development for each activity is constant across all zones. If desired, this assumption may be relaxed by subdividing activities into sub-activities with different densities, eg., low, medium and high density.

Unit development and demolition costs are postulated as being of the form shown in Fig. 1. Energy for construction of both buildings and infrastructure is expected to be inversely related to density in a similar manner to economic construction costs. Social costs are expected to show an overall increase with density due to crowding effects, although at very low densities social costs may be high due to isolation effects. When the social and economic construction costs are combined, a U-shaped curve results.

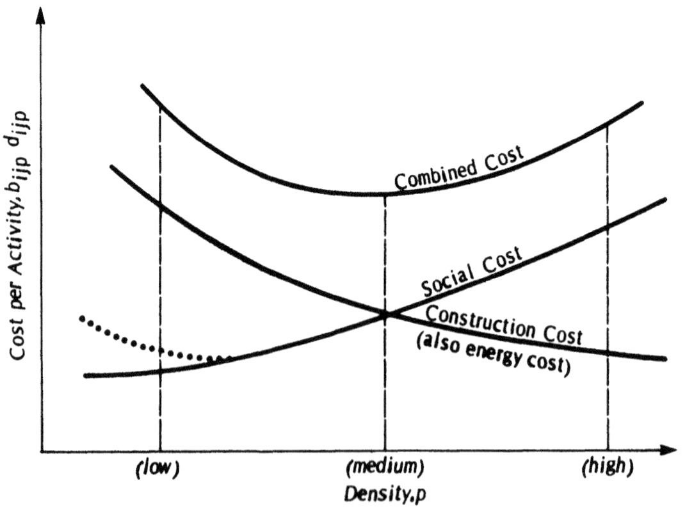

Figure 1 - Activity Costs vs Density

Fig. 1 purposely excludes one other very important cost, namely land cost or land rent. If such a curve was included, it would be expected to take a similar form to the construction cost curve, with its slope being dependent upon location within the urban area. It would generally have a high price (high slope) in highly accessible areas, eg. in the Central Business District, and a low-slope at the periphery.

However, as land price is generally inversely related to transport cost (ie. land price is proportional to accessibility), and as the model already included transport cost effects in determining location, only the non-transport cost component needs be included as an extra component. The operation of the model is expected to place high density development in high accessibility areas, and low density development in low accessibility areas.

The modifications necessary for the introduction of sub-activities of different densities, ρ, are as follows

Let $x_{ij\rho}(y_{ij\rho})$ = amount of activity i of density ρ allocated (demolished) in zone j; $e_{ij\rho}$ = amount of existing $x_{ij\rho}$; $b_{ij\rho}(d_{ij\rho})$ = development (demolition) cost for $x_{ij\rho}(y_{ij\rho})$; and $s_{ik\rho}(r_{ik\rho})$ = unit interaction level for $s_{ik}(r_{ik})$ for density level ρ.

Eqns. (1)-(5)) are modified in the original model by replacing

$\sum_{ij} b_{ij}x_{ij}$ by $\sum_{ij\rho} b_{ij\rho}x_{ij\rho}$

$s_{ik}x_{ij}$ by $\sum_{\rho} s_{ik\rho}x_{ij\rho}$

$r_{ik}x_{k\ell}$ by $\sum_{\rho} r_{ik\rho}x_{k\ell\rho}$

x_{ij} by $\sum_{\rho} x_{ij\rho}$

y_{ij} and e_{ij} are treated in a similar manner.

Eqns. (6)-(7) are changed by appending a subscript ρ to each element. This modification increases the number of land use variables by a factor equal to the number of density levels, but it is not expected to greatly increase computation since it only leads to an increase in the number of columns in the master problem LP tableau which only marginally increases computation difficulty. It is also interesting to note that the trip generation factors, $s_{ik\rho}$ and $r_{ik\rho}$ can now be related to density.

Different Socio-Economic Groups

A logical alternative to the above is to treat the sub-activities as being of different socio-economic groups, ρ, rather than different densities. If desired, such socio-economic groups could also be further split into density groupings.

Transport Network Congestion and Land Consumption

Another interesting trade-off that might be included in the model is to decide what levels of transport congestion are optimal given that the transport network competes against other activites for space in urban areas (Mills, 1972; Sharpe and Karlqvist, 1980).

At the same time, construction costs for the transport network might also be considered. Fig. 2 shows expected cost curves developed for different levels of congestion and parallels the development of the density curves in Fig. 1. Energy cost curves would be expected to also adopt a similar form.

Let c_{tn} = total cost per unit flow at congestion level n

x_{tJn} = land consumed by the transport network in zone J at congestion level n.

$$= p_n V_J L_J \tag{19}$$

where p_n = land required per unit of flow at congestion level n (including garages, buffer zones, etc.); L_J = average length of path passing through zone J; and V_J = flow volume passing through, starting or ending in zone J

$$= \sum_{ijk\ell} \delta_{j\ell J} T_{ijk\ell} \tag{20}$$

$\delta_{j\ell J}$ = 1 if $T_{ijk\ell}$ passes completely through J (ie. $j \neq J$)

= $(0.5 + \Delta)$ if trip starts or ends in J (ie. j or ℓ = J)

Δ = correction factor for additional space required for origin of destination parking and servicing.

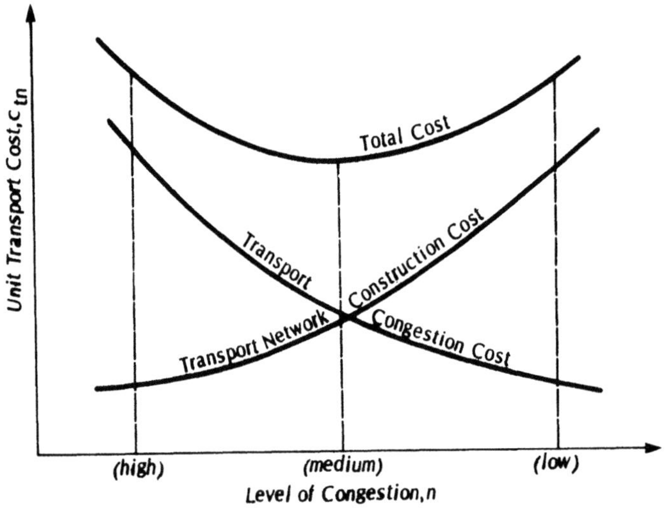

Figure 2 - Transport Costs vs Level of Congestion

The original model is modified as follows:

An additional cost term $\sum_{jn} c_{tn} x_{tjn}$ is added to eqn. (1) and eqn. (5) becomes

$$\sum_i (x_{ij} - y_{ij}) + \sum_n x_{tjn} \leq z_j - \sum_i e_{ij} \quad \forall j \tag{21}$$

and an additional equation is required

$$\sum_{ijk\ell} \delta_{j\ell J} T_{ij\ell} \leq (\sum x_{tJn}/p_n)/L_J \quad \forall J \tag{22}$$

Eqn. (22) becomes part of the transportation sub-problem, and requires that this sub-problem be decomposed in order to generate a solution.

Alternatively, an iterative procedure might be used

1. Assume x_{tjn} for each zone, eg. set x_{tjn} to existing or planned values where known.
2. Solve the transportation sub-problem to generate flows $T_{ijk\ell}$, and calculate V_J using eqn. (20).
3. Generate a land use constraint using eqn. (19), ie.,

$$\sum_n (x_{tJn}/p_n) = V_J L_J \tag{23}$$

4. Add this constraint into the master problem (eqns. (9) and (10)) and solve to generate a new solution which will include revised x_{tjn} values.

Multiple Transport Modes

If multiple transport modes are required, a modal split sub-model may be added, eg., a logit model. Modal split might be combined with transportation distribution to form a multi-mode trip distribution sub-model. Transport network congestion and land consumption as described above could also be extended for the multi-mode case.

Multiple Time Periods

These may be incorporated by subdividing the variables into their components for individual periods, m, ie., x_{ijm}, y_{ijm}, and $T_{ijk\ell m}$. Discounting the future benefits and costs may be used to reflect the higher opportunity benefits and costs of development in earlier periods, ie., eqn. (1) becomes

$$\text{Min} \sum_m \left[\gamma_{1m}(Tc)_m + \gamma_{2m}(bx)_m + \gamma_{3m}(dy)_m\right] \tag{24}$$

where γ_{1m}, γ_{2m} and γ_{3m} are present value factors. The constraints (2,3,4,5,6 and 8) take the same form as before with separate sets being written for each time period. Constraint (7) needs additional treatment to ensure that any demolition does not exceed the total development (or part thereof) up to the previous period, ie.,

$$x_{ijm-1} - y_{ijm} \geq e_{ij} \ \forall\ i,\ j;\ m > 1 \tag{25}$$

Constraint (25) is the only link between the variables of different time periods and generally will not be binding, so rather than generate a large master problem, it would be efficient to decompose it into sub-problems, one for each time period. Any violations of (25) could be remedied by iteration with y values being constrained by the x values from the previous period. This procedure gives a sequential planning approach in which each time period is planned without concern for subsequent future costs, ie. no feedback is incorporated. An alternative formulation which retains the feedback effect of (25) but is also decomposable could be generated by the construction of a higher level master problem using the Dantzig-Wolfe decomposition approach (Geoffrion, 1970). Both the sequential and the latter (simultaneous) alternatives provide interesting planning cases (Sharpe, Brotchie, Ahern and Dickey, 1974).

Additional Planning Constraints

Additional constraints may be readily incorporated into the master problem, such as zoning constraints restricting the level of development of certain activities in certain zones before, after, or during certain periods, as in the original TOPAZ formulation (Brotchie, Dickey and Sharpe, 1980).

Operational Version of Model

The model presented in Section 2 has been successfully programmed in FORTRAN for a Cyber 76 computer and is called TOPAZ82 (Sharpe, Wilson and Pallot, 1984). A test problem involving 3 activities and 41 zones involving over 15,000 variables and over 700 constraints has been solved for Pareto problems with a range of values including infinity. The expected efficiency in terms of working space and execution speed have been borne out (working space approximately 10,500 words and execution times in the range of 1 to 15 seconds). These results will be reported in a subsequent paper.

TOPAZ82 has been also successfully modified for an 8-bit micro-computer with 64 k storage, and is currently being adapted to a 16-bit micro-computer with 128 k minimum storage, with interactive colour graphics.

CONCLUSIONS

The paper presents a large scale programming formulation of a combined land use trip distribution planning problem in energy and economic terms and indicates how it may be solved efficiently using the Bender's decomposition technique. An extension to an entropy trip distribution sub-problem is developed indicating that the structured approach leads to a practical solution technique.

The use of the model in a gaming format would appear to be helpful to planners to explore a range of outcomes and the benefits that might be achieved through cooperation between different groups. The model also has the potential to explore problems involving multiple economic and energy objectives. A number of extensions to include variable development densities, various socio-economic groups, transport network congestion and land consumption, multiple time periods and additional planning constraints, are indicated.

REFERENCES

Baver, G., 1965, Algorithm 258, Communications of the Association for Computing Machinery, 8, 381-382.

Benders, J.F., 1962, Partitioning Procedures for Solving Mixed-Variables Programming Problems, Numerische Mathematik, 4, 238-252.

Brotchie, J.F., 1969, A General Planning Model, Management Science, 16, 265-266.

Brotchie, J.F., 1978, A Model Incorporating Diversity in Urban Allocation Problems, Applied Mathematical Modelling, 191-200.

Brotchie, J.F., Dickey, J.W. and Sharpe, R., 1980, TOPAZ - General Planning Technique and its Applications at the Regional, Urban and Facility Planning Levels, Springer-Verlag, Heidelberg.

Dickey, J.W., 1984, Computer Consultant Systems, a paper presented at the International Symposium on New Directions in Urban Modelling, University of Waterloo, Waterloo, Ontario.

Gass, S.I., 1964, Linear Programming, McGraw-Hill, New York.

Geoffrion, A.M, 1970, Elements of Large-Scale Mathematical Programming, Parts I and II, Management Science, 16, 652-691.

Geoffrion, A.M., 1972, Generalized Benders Decomposition, Journal of Optimization Theory and Applications, 10, 237-260.

Geoffrion, A.M. and Graves, G.W., 1974, Multicommodity Distribution System Design by Benders Decomposition, Management Science, 20, 822-844.

Harris, B., 1981, An Extended Programming Experience, Environment and Planning A, 13, 19-27.

Kallio, M., Por, A. and Soismaa, M., 1979, A FORTRAN Code for the Transhipment Problem, WP-79-26, International Institute for Applied Systems Analysis, Laxenburg, Austria.

Magnanti, T.L. and Wong, R.T., 1981, Accelerating Benders Decomposition: Algorithmic Enhancement and Model Selection Criteria, Operations Research, 29, 464-484.

Rao, S.S. and Hati, S.K., 1980, Optimum Design of Shock and Vibration Isolation Systems Using Game Theory, Engineering Optimization, 4, 215-226.

Roy, J.R. and Brotchie, J.F., 1981, Alternative Approaches to Land-Use Transportation Modelling, CSIRO, Australia Division of Building Research Report, Melbourne.

Roy, J.R. and Lesse, P.F., 1983, Planning Models for Non-Cooperative Situations: A Two-Player Game Approach, Regional Science and Urban Economics, 13, 195-211.

Sharpe, R. and Brotchie, J.F., 1972, An Urban Systems Study, Royal Australian Planning Institute Journal, 10, 105-118.

Sharpe, R., Brotchie, J.F., Ahern, P. and Dickey, J.W., 1974, Evaluation of Alternative Growth Patterns in Urban Systems, Computers and Operations Research, 1, 345-362.

Sharpe, R. and Karlqvist, A., 1980, Towards a Unifying Theory for Modelling Urban Systems, Regional Science and Urban Economics, 10, 241-257.

Sharpe, R., Roy, J.R. and Taylor, M.A.P., 1982, Optimizing Urban Futures, Environment and Planning B, 9, 209-220.

Sharpe, R., Wilson, B.G. and Pallot, R.G., 1984, Computer User Manual for TOPAZ82, CSIRO, Australia Division of Building Research Report, Melbourne.

Van Delft, A. and Nijkamp, P., 1976, A Multi-Objective Decision Model for Regional Development, Environmental Quality Control and Industrial Land Use, Papers of the Regional Science Association, 36, 35-57.

Wilson, A.G., 1970, Entropy in Urban and Regional Modelling, Pion, London.

INFORMATION FLOWS AND DECISION-MAKING IN URBAN MODELS

John R. Roy and Paul F. Lesse
CSIRO Division of Building Research
P.O. Box 56, Highett
Victoria 3190
Australia

Abstract. In urban systems, the behaviour of various interest groups is determined by perceptions of their own goals as well as by perceived reactions to their decisions by other interacting groups, particularly those with faster speeds of adjustment. When modelling the actions of such groups, information theory may be used, with constraints related to observed behaviour of each group, including measures of variability describing the behaviour of faster adjusting groups. These concepts are applied to an urban modelling framework where a rationale is provided for simplifying the complex interaction patterns by identification of certain recursive sequences. In addition, when interacting spatial decisions are made at different levels of aggregation, methods are described for nesting or embedding the finer-level behavioural decisions in more macro-level decision structures which often consist of multi-objective land use planning policy instruments and moreover attempts at a synthesis of optimizing and behavioural model frameworks. Special attention is given to leader-follower behaviour, model estimation procedures, appropriate model sequences, primal and dual solution approaches, stability properties of the various equilibria, as well as measures of intrinsic model value.

INTRODUCTION

Scope of Problem

An urban system can be treated as a set of sub-systems which interact spatially and temporally with each other via interchange of people, goods, money and information. The art of urban modelling would appear to be related to obtaining a mathematically tractable representation of this complex interaction pattern, which on one hand accounts for observed behavioural influences, whilst on the other provides guidance on application of policy instruments related to achieving certain performance levels of the physical system. Most existing land use transportation models can either be regarded as primarily behavioural or primarily normative. Behavioural models usually handle spatial policy instruments as exogenous constraints, grouped according to alternative scenarios or scenario combinations. The estimated model parameters describe the user response to prevailing conditions in the system, including influences of existing planning controls, implying forecasts tending to project effects of current planning policies into the future. On the other hand, normative models provide the values of land-use policy instruments which optimize certain policy criteria, but often at the expense of weak representation of behavioural decisions not amenable to explicit planning control. Whereas the institutional planning frameworks in some countries may strongly support one or the other of these two divergent approaches, cases will often arise when either a more endogeneously policy-related behavioural model or a more behaviourally-consistent normative model is desired. The current paper examines some structural and implementation issues involved in the development of such models, and makes specific suggestions on the form of certain of the submodels as well as a scheme for their interconnection.

Land Use Policy Instrument Determination under Behavioural Influences

This model framework treats the supply side of the transportation system as an exogenous input, which may be changed for different future scenarios. The normative level concentrates on providing values of macro land use supply policy instruments as a means of optimal compromise satisfaction of alternative planning goals related primarily to relative efficiency and equity in the performance of the system. If the behavioural response of the system is defined at a finer, more micro level of aggregation than that of the macro land use policy instruments, and if the land use policy goals are defined directly in terms such macro policy instruments (eg., such as minimizing land use infrastructure costs), a sequential solution approach can be adopted. The solution of the macro land use problem can then be directly attached as constraints to the spatial interaction (behavioural) problem, or alternatively, the system objective can be handled simultaneously with the spatial interaction surplus objective in a Pareto framework, following the Embedding Theorem (Wilson, Coelho, Macgill and Williams, 1981). However, more general planning objectives, such as those used in TOPAZ (Brotchie, Dickey and Sharpe, 1980), may contain components related to equity or efficiency at the behavioural level, such as transport energy consumption, which if combined with the spatial interaction objectives in a Pareto framework, would force the spatial interaction results to be out of equilibrium. Thus, in the following development, a non-cooperative Nash equilibrium is sought (Intriligator, 1971) between the objectives of the land use authority and groups of households and firms, corresponding to a Stackelberg leader-follower problem in oligopoly theory (Johansson, 1978). In this case, the land use authority, acting as the leader, is taken to allow for the reactions to application of its optimal land use policy instruments by households and firms (the followers), with the latter adapting to the land use constraints as given. This is achieved (Roy and Lesse, 1983a) by constraining the spatial interaction models (after their estimation) by unknown values of the corresponding macro land use supply policy instruments (eg., area of light-industrial land to be released for development at a certain time), thus enabling the solutions of these models to be expressed as either functions of the policy instruments, or of the duals on constraints which connect these (unknown) macro land use supply instruments with demand at the micro or spatial interaction level. Such functions are then directly embedded into the micro level components (eg., transport energy consumption) of the land use objective (or objectives), which in conjunction with physical land use capacity constraints and market clearing conditions can then be solved entirely in terms of the land use policy instruments of the authority or the corresponding duals. In this way, the sensitivity of the behavioural response of the system to macro land use policy instrument changes is accounted for in the optimizing of the policy objectives, which corresponds to the philosophy of the Stackelberg leader-follower problem (Johansson, 1978; Roy, Johansson and Leonardi, 1983). In this endeavour, the micro or behavioural part of the system is simulated by a modified Lowry-type model. By embedding such relations at the macro policy instrument level, we are implicitly assuming that such aggregate behaviour provides a reliable highly-peaked fit to observed actions, that is, it can be essentially treated as deterministic.

Formulation and Interconnection of Behavioural Sub-models

In considering interactions between groups in the behavioural or market part of the system, one of the main difficulties is to identify reasonable decision sequences within the possible network of simultaneously connected decisions. Current practice, for instance in Lowry-type models, is to locate the various groups in a fixed sequence, with merely common zonal supply or demand parameters connecting the decisions between the groups. In earlier versions, the location of new exogenous basic industry was taken to be the driving force of the model. In more unified input/output representations (Wilson, Coelho, Macgill and Williams, 1981), a simultaneous location sequence of all industrial sectors was implied. In the following, we suggest maintaining an essentially sequential model structure, but dividing industry (with the exception of the housing, retail and service sectors) into stagnating or declining sectors as well as growth sectors, as inspired by Wegener, Gnad and Vannahme (1983). Although not developed in this paper, vintage and accessibility data could be initially used to locate the most probable pattern of industry closures, with the property thus vacated, plus further land released by the planning authority, becoming available for location of the growth industries, which then form the driving force of the model. These latter are simultaneously located using available regional input/output information, where flows from industry to the household, retail and service sectors of the previous time period are included, but flows from and between the household, retail and service sectors are handled using separate sub-models. Note also, that in our model, the land use authority, as the coordinator of land use policy goals for all the sectors, can influence the relative spatial advantage of any sector, and thus affect its eventual viability.

After location of the growth industries, the location of the household and service (retail) sectors is handled. With the fast growth of the service (including quaternary) sectors, it may be preferable to locate the new service activity before the household activity, that is, to locate the service activity at time t about household activity at time period (t-1); the choice of either alternative is determined according to which approach better fits the observed state of the system, using an iterative sequential model estimating procedure as pioneered by Batty (1983). In the body of the paper, the more usual order of locating the household sector before the service sector is illustrated. However, as household location is partly influenced by accessibility to services, as well as to employment, a nested recursive entropy approach (Roy and Lesse, 1983b) is proposed, to nest the influence of service accessibility into the household location model. This implies maximizing a weighted sum of housing choice, conditional job choice and service choice entropies (Boyce, Leblanc, Chon and Lin, 1983; Roy and Lesse, 1983b) rather than the pure sum given earlier in Wilson, Coelho, Macgill and Williams (1981). It is also the entropy equivalent of the nested logit approach adopted by Anas (1983).

In addition, the use of nested recursive approaches within the sub-models may achieve further benefits (Roy and Lesse, 1983b), with models for the faster adjusting groups eg., customers in retail models, being estimated first. This implies that, in the shorter term, the more slowly-adjusting groups allow for marginal reactions to their decisions by faster-adjusting groups, but not vice-versa. Information-theoretic criteria can be used to determine the sequences which use the constraint information most efficiently. In cases where behaviour of several economic agents, such as retailers and property developers, is being modelled, a multi-level Stackelberg oligopoly structure is defined, for customers, retailers and developers (Roy, Johansson and Leonardi, 1983).

Most existing Lowry-type models, with the current exception of CATLAS (Anas) and MEP (Echenique) have an inadequate treatment of housing and service sector supply, and consider prices and rents as exogenous. In the current presentation, this weakness is overcome for the service model above, where the equilibria consider retail prices and floorspace rents as endogenous (Roy, Johansson and Leonardi, 1983). Further work needs to be done for the housing sector, but the improved random bidding formulations of Lerman and Kern (1983) may well supersede the Alonso bid-rent approach. A further challenge is to attempt to integrate these ideas within the comprehensive framework presented by Batty (1983), particularly the consideration of embedding functional relations of land use policy instruments obtained from the chosen sequence of behavioural sub-models into behavioural components of the land use planning goals.

Further Issues

Using the unifying framework of information theory, it is possible to regard the so-called estimating and forecasting stages of a land use/transport model as system states with different levels of prior knowledge (Roy and Lesse, 1983b), with Legendre transforms of the original Shannon entropy functions being used for forecasting (Lesse, 1982). In non-doubly constrained models, where the attractiveness of the supply side plays an important role, Kullback information gain criteria (Snickars and Weibull, 1977) can be applied to estimate at unconstrained nodes the size component of attractiveness which cannot be explained by constraints on quality, as well as to separate out cleanly the accessibility effects from zonal attractiveness effects (Roy, 1983).

Finally, within the macro land use policy level itself, the role of conflicting criteria is examined. This area has already received considerable attention, such as in the general work in Nijkamp (1978) and Rietveld (1979), as well as in the urban modelling applications discussed in Roy and Batten (1982) and Batten (1984). Within the multilevel model framework being discussed in the current paper, the general embedding or leader-follower approach described in Roy and Lesse (1983a) is introduced into the multiple objective scheme. This ensures that when any of the objectives possess micro-behavioural or interaction terms which are not directly controllable by the planning authority, the sensitivity of these terms to changes in the macro land use policy instruments is taken into account.

We will now describe the ways in which these ideas are to be developed here. The first section describes the behavioural models for location of industrial, household and service activity. It also indicates the way in which these models are interconnected, including provision for recursive feedback effects. In the second section, the method and philosophy for embedding the behavioural level at the macro policy instrument level are described, ensuring that expected behavioural responses to land use policy instrument changes are considered in determining endogeneous values of these instruments. Finally, we examine the multi-objective macro-spatial policy level, where compromises are sought between partially conflicting objectives, whilst also allowing for the above behavioural interactions.

BEHAVIOURAL SUB-MODELS AND THEIR INTERCONNECTION

Nakamura, Hayashi and Miyamoto, (1983) suggest that, independent of the model being used, certain large-scale industries, as well as key government, cultural, sporting and recreational activities, should be located a priori. Alternative locations of sets of these activities can be provided as inputs to the model proper, and handled using a scenario approach. In addition, we attempt to obtain the most probable spatial distribution of closures for declining or stagnating industries. In the model described, the remainder of the urban activity is divided into industrial growth, residential and business/service groups, which are handled sequentially, but with the improved feedback mechanisms and iterative estimation mentioned in the introduction, which may indicate a reversal of the treatment of the residential and service sectors. Descriptions of models for the location of these three groups now follow.

Location of Growth Industries

Previous Work. In earlier applications of Lowry-type models, the location of industry was treated as exogenous input to the system. More recently, input/output statistics have been used in industrial location models to pick up the interdependencies between economic sectors (Wilson, Coelho, Macgill and Williams, 1981; Batten and Roy, 1982; Batty, 1983). This approach is followed here, where flows from and between the retail and household sectors are omitted from the combined scheme. As firms in different sectors have different areal requirements and different transport costs per dollar of output, we segment industrial activity in each sector into average-sized firms, each with certain average spatial requirements, transport costs and output levels. These form the basis of transport cost and land rent constraints, reflecting the trade-offs between rent and accessibility (Roy and Batten, 1982). Note that, in the estimation phase, nested transport constraints related to commuting costs of the labour force could also be included. Also, the sectors may be reasonably subdivided into two groups, national or footloose sectors, and regional sectors (eg., building and construction) whose products are not transferable between zones (Batten and Roy, 1982).

Despite the sophistication implied in the input/output approach, it is difficult to quantify certain criteria influencing industrial location. However, in the incremental procedure applied in this model, where industrial growth sectors are located about themselves plus the labour force, the location of existing activity exerts a strong influence on future location patterns, as the reallocation of existing demand is usually permitted, but not existing infrastructure supply (except through demolitions and conversions, as mentioned earlier).

Data Availability and Aggregation Levels. In principle, technical input/output coefficients in industrial location models can be regarded as analogous to trip generation coefficients, representing normalized money flows. Often, they are only available at the national level as a_{ij}, the proportion of input from sector i in the output of sector j. In some cases, one may be fortunate enough to have coefficients obtained from survey data for the actual urban region being modelled. If one possessed only partial survey information at the level of the urban region, this raw information can be directly used as constraints in the industrial location model, rather than having to go through the intermediate step of estimating a regional table from this partial data. In general the most detailed information available would be the complete set of regional coefficients $\bar{a}_{ij}$ for the particular metropolitan region - these will rarely be available as $\bar{a}_{ij}^{rs}$ or even $\bar{a}_{ij}^{r}$ for particular zones r and s, or even for aggregations of these zones eg., inner ring, middle ring, outer ring. The models must be sufficiently flexible to adapt to this relative scarcity of data.

In order that the computational effort not be excessive in this phase of the model, an appropriate degree of aggregation must be sought at the sectoral level, such as 10 to 15 sectors. Such economies in the consideration of sectors will permit interzonal flows to be considered both by zones and by sectors, similarly as in interregional analysis. In addition, to separate the intraregional flows from those flowing outside the urban region and into the region from outside, it may be advisable to use a dog-leg input/output table (Batten, 1982), which also separates the external flows into interregional and trade components. A future research task is to use all the information in such a table (or the partial information directly, if a full table is not available) in the constraints of our industrial location model.

Modelling the Linked Decision Processes. Finally, in considering the decisions involved, it is seen that if the receivers of inputs are taken to pay the transport costs, the firms make location decisions which are strongly conditional on the expected locations of their suppliers. Rather than considering the location and supplier choices simultaneously, as implied in previous work, it will usually be more efficient to consider a nested recursive approach to this problem (Roy and Lesse, 1983b), where the average conditional entropy of choice of suppliers given location is firstly maximized under the transport cost and flow balance constraints. Then, the surplus representation of this conditional entropy is evaluated and attached as a constraint in the locational model, leading to definition of composite transport costs for the supply of inputs to firms of each sector in their potential location sites. For instance, if the system of events is defined as firms of sector i, class m (m=1 national, footloose, m=2 regional) and status n (n=1 newly locating, n=2 existing) located in region r receiving their inputs of sector j class v from zone s, the conditional entropy objective of choice of suppliers given location is expressed as

$$\overline{S} = \max_{p^{s/r}_{jv/imn}} - \sum_{imnr} q^{r}_{imn} \sum_{jvs} p^{s/r}_{jv/imn} \log p^{s/r}_{jv/imn} \quad (1)$$

where $p^{s/r}_{jv/imn}$ is the probability that a firm will obtain supplies of sector j, class v from zone s, given that it is a sector i firm of class m, status n, located in zone r. In the initial run through the estimation procedure, q^{r}_{imn} is the joint observed probability that a firm of sector i, class m and status n is located in zone r, which after the first run through the following location stage could be replaced by estimated model probabilities p^{r}_{imn} for further iterations, thus optionally replicating the results of a superior class of simultaneous model (Boyce, LeBlanc, Chon and Lin, 1983), and improving on nested logit (Roy and Lesse, 1983b).

Coordination with Planning Policy. As a final step, constraints should be applied to ensure that the more micro location patterns emerging in this industrial location model conform with the unknown macro industrial location policy instruments being evaluated at the planning authority level. Of course, such macro location policy instruments are endogenously determined in this class of model by appropriate embedding of the behavioural model at the upper policy level (Roy and Lesse, 1983a). This procedure is illustrated later for residential location policy.

Residential Location Model

The sectoral distribution of industry enables job requirements for each socio-economic group in each zone to be evaluated. Initial estimates of service jobs are also made (corrected in later iterations, as in the Lowry model), so that the total job demand by zone and socio-economic group is obtained. However, if the service sector is treated first, as suggested previously, the complete employment distribution would be available at this stage. The macro land supply constraints set by the authority are endogenous in the complete model structure. In the absence of explicit consideration of the land development process, we assume that released zonal supply and realized demand are in equilibrium.

A Nested Model for Conditional Job Choice. We shall briefly summarize the ideas behind a model which has been recently developed (Roy and Lesse, 1983b). Treating locational choice as preceding job (and service) choice, the conditional job choice model is estimated first. However, as described later, if the relative coefficient θ_e on the average job accessibility constraint on the locational model turns out to be greater than unity, the order should be reversed, and locational choice made conditional on job choice (already available as d_{ml}, the proportion of jobs for group 1 in zone m). Consider thus the choice of job in zone m given zone of residence i and socio-economic group 1, the latter being taken as the segmentation criterion for households as well as for jobs. Denote $p_{m/il}$ as the probability that a worker will find a job at m, given that he lives in zone i and belongs to socio-economic group 1, and let q_{il} be the observed (or estimated) probability that persons of socio-economic group 1 live in zone i. The conditional entropy of job choice given locational choice averaged over the locational choices is maximized as

$$\overline{S} = \max_{p_{m/il}} - \sum_{il} q_{il} \sum_{m} p_{m/il} (\log p_{m/il} - 1) + \sum_{il} \omega_{il} (1 - \sum_{m} p_{m/il})$$
$$+ \sum_{ml} \eta_{ml} (d_{ml} - \sum_{i} q_{il} p_{m/il})$$
$$+ \beta (c - \sum_{iml} c_{im} q_{il} p_{m/il}) \tag{2}$$

In the constraints, c is the mean journey to work cost and c_{im} the journey to work cost between zones i and m. Also, ω_{il}, η_{ml} and β are unknown Lagrange multipliers. The solution comes out as

$$p_{m/il} = \exp-(x_{iml}) / \sum_{m} \exp-(x_{iml}) \tag{3}$$

where $x_{iml} = \eta_{ml} + \beta c_{im}$. The Legendre transforms $\hat{S}$ of the Shannon entropy, defined by Lesse (1982), or its surplus representation, may then be evaluated numerically as

$$\hat{S} = \sum_{il} q_{il} \sum_{m} p_{m/il} (\log p_{m/il} + x_{iml}) \tag{4}$$

Upon substitution of eqn. (3) into eqn. (4), and following the definition of composite commuting costs $\hat{c}_{il}$ of (Williams, 1977) as

$$\hat{c}_{il} = -(1/\beta) \log [\sum_{m} \exp-(x_{iml})] \tag{5}$$

eqn. (4) transforms to the following constraint at the residential location stage (Roy and Lesse, 1983b)

$$- \beta \sum_{il} p_{il} \hat{c}_{il} = \hat{S} \tag{6}$$

where p_{il} are the unknown model residential location probabilities.

Recursive Linking of Sub-models. Now, before proceeding to the location phase, we clarify a means of meeting the desire to provide more recursive linking between certain stages of such models, thus attempting to counteract some disadvantages in the assumed sequence of handling the sub-models. For instance, it is clear that accessibility to shops and services influences residential location decisions, in addition to accessibility to jobs. In the current stage of the estimation, we have no model information on current flows to service activity. Thus, in the first iteration through the residential sub-model we may approximate service accessibility effects using flows from the previous time period. However, as soon as the initial estimation of the service sub-model is performed, and values $p_{j/il}$ obtained for the probability of shopping at centre j given that one is of socio-economic group l living in zone i and for the Lagrange multiplier β on the shopping travel time constraint, the Legendre transform or surplus form of this entropy may be computed as $\overset{\Delta}{S}$, and weighted composite travel time t_{il} defined as in eqn. (5) (that is, assuming that travel time has a key influence on shop choice), leading to a constraint

$$- \bar{\beta} \sum_{il} p_{il} \hat{t}_{ij} = \overset{\Delta}{S} \tag{7}$$

analogous to eqn. (6). Note that, as an iterative sequence is used anyhow in Lowry-type models to correct the housing demand from the distribution of service employees (as well as sometimes to correct for the results of traffic congestion), we can readily take advantage of this scheme to introduce linking constraints such as eqn. (7).

<u>Locational Phase.</u> For the location phase itself, the choice for each socio-economic group l encompasses not only zone of residence i, but also housing type k. Note that, index k was superfluous for the previous model of job and location choice given residential location. However, the p_{il} terms in eqns. (6) and (7) can be simply expressed as $(\sum_k p_{ikl})$ when evaluating the location probabilities p_{ikl} for choice by socio-economic group l of housing of type k in zone i. In specifying the constraints, r_{ik} is the average rent of housing of type k in zone i, r_k is the average rent paid for such housing over the urban area and λ_k the corresponding Lagrange multiplier. In addition, b_{il} is the average housing budget of people of socio-economic group l living in zone i and b_l its mean value over each socio-economic group, noting that $\sum_l b_l = \sum_k r_k$. Also θ_e and θ_s are the multipliers on the composite travel cost time constraints for employment and service activity respectively, obtained from eqns. (6) and (7). Finally, h_i (with associated multiplier ψ_i) represents the endogenous housing supply allocation to be determined at the planning level, that is, the proportion of total housing which is to be situated in zone i. This provides the key linkage between the behavioural level and the policy level, the mechanics of which is described in the policy section. Thus a formulation for the residential location choice stage is given as

$$\begin{aligned} \bar{S}_L = \max & - \sum_{ikl} p_{ikl}(\log p_{ikl} - 1) + \Omega(1 - \sum_{ikl} p_{ikl}) \\ & + \sum_k \lambda_k (r_k - \sum_{il} p_{ikl} r_{ik}) + \sum_i \alpha_i (b_l - \sum_{ik} p_{ikl} b_{il}) \\ & - \theta_e (\hat{S} + \beta \sum_{ikl} p_{ikl} \hat{c}_{il}) - \theta_s (\overset{\Delta}{S} + \bar{\beta} \sum_{ikl} p_{ikl} \hat{t}_{il}) \\ & + \sum_i \psi_i (h_i - \sum_{kl} p_{ikl}) \end{aligned} \tag{8}$$

which yields

$$p_{ikl} = h_i \exp-(\bar{z}_{ikl}) / \sum_{ikl} \exp-(\bar{z}_{ikl}) \tag{9}$$

where $\bar{z}_{ikl} = (\lambda_k r_{ik} + \alpha_l b_{il} + \theta_e \beta\ \hat{c}_{il} + \theta_s \vec{\beta}\ \hat{t}_{il})$. If the value of $p_{il} = (\sum_k p_{ikl})$ computed via eqn. (9) is close to the observed value q_{il} used in the estimation of eqn. (2), the process is complete, and we may simply obtain the work trip probabilities p_{iml} as $[(\sum_k p_{ikl}) p_{m/il}]$. Otherwise, we can substitute p_{il} from eqn. (9) for q_{il} in eqn. (2), reevaluate $p_{m/il}$ and then p_{ikl} etc., until convergence.

Limitations. An obvious weakness of the above class of model is that, whereas it uses observed rents r_{ik} in the estimation problem, their values must be assumed exogenously for forecasting applications. Rather than trying to develop an operational Alonso-type model to eliminate this weakness, one approach may be to try to combine the above procedure with the method of Nakamura, Hayashi and Miyamoto (1983) where land price functions are estimated at the macro-level and competition allowed for at a more micro-level. A further development would be the use of a random bidding approach, with direct evaluation of willingness-to-pay (Lerman and Kern, 1983). Finally, one may be able to use the shadow-price transformation of the housing supply constraint multipliers ψ_i to correct the base rents r_{ik}, as suggested by Los.

Service Location Model

Previous Work. In most applications of Lowry-type models (except Anas, 1983), the location of service activity has been treated in a demand framework, with no feedback between floorspace supply and projected demand. In certain applications, such as in Mackett (1982), floorspace supply from the preceding time period was used as a component of demand attractiveness values in the current time period. It was not until the work of Harris and Wilson (1978) that a supply/demand equilibrium form of such models was presented, formalizing the more intuitive approach suggested by Lakshmanan and Hansen (1965). This work was expanded by Wilson, Coelho, Macgill and Williams (1981). A profit-maximizing framework was introduced by Roy and Johansson (1981). Finally, in Roy, Johansson and Leonardi (1983), rents and prices were treated as endogenous and the investment side was included via the property developers. Some aspects of this most recent work are summarized in the following.

Customer Choice Model. A key element in any service location model is to determine customer demand for a given distribution of service floorspace. Usually a simultaneous model form has been developed to determine the probability p_{ijl} that persons of socio-economic group l emanating from zones i shop (or obtain service) at centres j. However, in Roy (1983), a nested recursive approach was suggested for this problem, which conveniently decouples the macro-accessibility influences from the more micro quantity and quality components of attractiveness at the facilities themselves. In brief, the first step is to estimate conditional probabilities $p_{il/j}$ that a customer comes from zone i and belongs to socio-economic group l given that he shops at centre j. In this context, the only relevant constraints are related to shopping travel time and flow of purchasing power from zone i, in addition to the usual origin constraint. If q_j is the observed probability of shopping in centre j, the following conditional entropy averaged over centres j

$$\overline{S} = -\sum_j q_j \sum_{il} p_{il/j} \log p_{il/j} \tag{10}$$

is maximized in terms of $p_{il/j}$ under the above constraints, yielding

$$p_{il/j} = \exp(x_{ijl})/\sum_{il} \exp-(x_{ijl}) \tag{11}$$

where x_{ijl} is a weighted sum of the constraint parameters. From eqn. (11), the Legendre transform or surplus form of the conditional entropy $\hat{S}$ can be computed as

$$\hat{S} = -\sum_j q_j \sum_{il} p_{il/j}(\log p_{il/j} + x_{ijl}) \tag{12}$$

If weighted composite travel times $\hat{t}_j$ are defined as

$$\hat{t}_j = -(1/\overline{\beta})\log[\sum_{il} \exp-(x_{ijl})] \tag{13}$$

where $\overline{\beta}$ is the Lagrange multiplier on the travel time constraint attached to eqn. (10), the value of S is maintained in the nested destination choice model if the following constraint is applied

$$-\overline{\beta}\sum_j p_j \hat{t}_j = \hat{S} \tag{14}$$

where p_j is the sought value of the probability of choosing centre j. For the destination choice decision, the following Kullback information gain function

$$\overline{T} = \sum_j p_j \log(p_j/p_j^s) \tag{15}$$

is minimized in terms of p_j under chosen destination quality constraints plus eqn. (14), p_j^s is the residual destination probability just related to the size component of attractiveness, usually given as $(W_j^\alpha / \sum_j W_j^\alpha)$, where α is a positive index and W_j the occupied floorspace in centre j. This index α can be obtained via another Kullback minimization, this time between the observed destination probabilities q_j and the model values p_j. The solution comes out as

$$p_j = p_j^s \exp-(y_j+\theta\overline{\beta}\hat{t}_j)/[\sum_j p_j^s \exp-(y_j+\theta \overline{\beta}\hat{t}_j)] \tag{16}$$

where y_j contains the destination constraint contributions and θ is the Lagrange multiplier on eqn. (14). The joint customer probability p_{ijl} may be directly obtained by multiplication of eqns. (11) and (16). Note that, as p_{ij1} also equals $p_{i1}p_{j/i1}$, where p_{i1} is the known housing location probability, it is possible to evaluate $p_{j/i1}$ and thus the Legendre transform of the average conditional entropy of the $p_{j/i1}$ distribution, from which composite average travel times t_{i1} may be extracted for the shopping accessibility constraint of eqn. (7) in the housing location phase. Finally, the above nested recursive approach needs to be compared in practice with the alternative simultaneous procedure, both from the standpoint of solution efficiency (Roy, 1983), as well as from increasing the redundancy of the estimated model (Lesse, Batty and Batten, 1983), in which the redundancy is defined as $(S_{max} - S_{model})/S_{max}$, where S_{model} is the entropy of the p_{ij1} distribution and S_{max} its unconstrained maximum value.

Equilibrium States for Economic Agents. After describing the behaviour of the customers for a given distribution of occupied floorspace, it is now necessary to address the treatment of the retailers, property developers and planning authority. In the context of a strategic land use model, it is advisable to project the determination of land use policy from long run equilibrium behaviour of the retailers and developers rather than from a transient state, as the former at least represents a stable position toward which the system is moving.

Retailers. The retailers in each centre are treated as independent agents, who maximize profits via floorspace decisions W_j and price decisions y_j, according to perceptions of the expected response of customers. The prices y_j occur in the constraints on the customer demand problem of eqn. (10), thus implying that customer decisions p_{ij1} are a function of both the retailer location decisions W_j and the price decisions y_j. The non-linearity in these functional relationships implies that questions of existence and uniqueness of the equilibria need to be examined carefully, particularly in relation to the customer scale coefficient α.

Property Developers. The property developers, acting as independent agents at each centre, make decisions about the amount of infrastructure supply, and set rent levels r_j for the retailers. They act on perceptions of the expected response of the retailers to such decisions, and aim to maximize their rate of return on investment. Thus, the retailers anticipate expected customer response in making their decisions, and developers anticipate corresponding retailer response, thus indicating a two-level Stackelberg oligopoly solution (Johansson, 1978).

Role of Planning Authority. Finally, the planning authority would usually be expected to have the power to determine which sites in the urban area are suitable for new retail development or extensions of existing development. It may choose these from a larger number of available sites in order to achieve certain partial goals, such as reduction of expenditure on shopping travel and/or greater spatial equity in accessibility to sevices throughout the city. This would involve solution of an assignment problem at the upper planning policy level.

Work Required. There is clearly much further work to be done in estimating this series of linked models and applying them to real planning problems. Also, additional work needs to be done on examining the stability properties of the models, particularly to determine if the bifurcation phenomena identified in the simpler model structures of Harris and Wilson (1978) persist when lags or rigidities are introduced with respect to the different agents in the system. In addition, we should at least recognize the difference between the short-term adjustments away from an observed state caused by parameter changes, and the gradual adjustment of the system towards a long-run Nash equilibrium. Further details of our current progress may be obtained from Roy, Johansson and Leonardi (1983).

EMBEDDING THE BEHAVIOURAL LEVEL AT THE PLANNING POLICY LEVEL

Principles of Approach

A procedure for embedding behavioural relations at the macro land use policy instrument level in cases where the policy objectives contain micro behavioural level contributions has been presented by Roy and Lesse (1983a), and is briefly summarized here. As mentioned earlier, such cases fall outside the validity of application of the embedding theorem of Coelho and Wilson discussed in Wilson, Coelho, Macgill and Williams, (1981). Secondly, by embedding behavioural relations obtained from probabilistic theory in deterministic planning objectives, we are implicitly assuming that the estimated aggregate distribution is overwhelmingly the most probable, given the constraint information. Wilson (1967) has proved this result using analogies with maximum likelihood statistics. However, (i) we may not have included all relevant constraint information and (ii) some of the available constraint information may be in error. Thus, it is advisable to use sensitivity analysis on the behavioural side. We would primarily be interested in how sub-optimal the optimal planning policy instruments determined by the model may become under the influence of certain small parameter changes. A further reason for such sensitivity analysis would be to check the consequences of changes to the Lagrange multipliers on the behavioural constraints, which are assumed to retain their estimated values when the behavioural functions are embedded at the macro policy instrument level.

Application to Residential Location

As an illustration of the use of the embedding procedure, the residential location phase is discussed. Consider that the planning authority would like to direct its residential location policy towards minimizing commuting travel costs plus the cost of the provision of services, such as supply of electricity and water and waste disposal etc. If c_{iml} are average transport resource costs of people of socio-economic group 1 commuting between zones i and m (allowing for different modal split among different socio-economic groups) and c_{ik} the unit cost of providing public infrastructure services in zone i for houses of type k (eg., k=1 detached houses, k=2 town houses, k=3 apartments, etc.), then the residential objective C_H may be written as

$$C_H = \min_{h_i} \sum_{iml} p_{iml} c_{iml} + q \sum_{ikl} p_{ikl} c_{ik} \qquad (17)$$

where h_i is the proportion of housing to be allocated to zone i, which is the land supply policy parameter constrained to equal the demand in eqn. (8), and g a normalization ratio. Upon setting $\partial C_H/\partial h_i = 0$, the sensitivites of the locational and job choice probabilities within p_{ikl} and p_{iml} to the changes in macro land-use policy instruments h_i are taken into account via embedding eqns. (3) and (9) into eqn. (17). Thus, defining R_{iml} as $\exp-(x_{iml})$ and S_{ikl} as $\exp-(z_{ikl})$, eqn. (17) is given directly in terms of the policy variables as

$$C_H = \sum_{iml} h_i c_{iml} \{ R_{iml} (\sum_k S_{ikl}) / [(\sum_m R_{iml}) (\sum_{kl} S_{ikl})] \} + q \sum_{ikl} h_i c_{ik} \{ S_{ikl} / (\sum_{kl} S_{ikl}) \} \qquad (18)$$

The constraints for eqn. (18) include market clearing constraints, physical land capacity constraints and any exogenous land-use policy constraints. If the land capacity constraints relate to the sum of residential plus industrial activity, rather than each separately, the residential and industrial location stages will be coupled at the macro spatial policy instrument level. Further coupling constraints ensure consistency between the job requirements output from the industrial and service location models and the job demands d_{ml} input into the conditional job choice model in eqn. (2).

Estimation and Implementaton

In the estimation phase, the amount of housing taken up in the estimation time period is used for h_i, and the multipliers λ_k, θ_e and θ_h are obtained in eqn. (8). In the planning time period it is assumed that these multipliers remain unchanged as new values of h_i are endogenously determined to satisfy the planning goals, such as in eqn. (17). These assumptions may be unreasonable if these goals represent a strong departure from the criteria which led to the housing allocations h_i in the estimation time period, and sensitivity analyses should be carried out.

Now, p_{ikl} and p_{iml} in eqn. (17) are given as functions of the unknown policy instruments h_i. This is a situation which occurred in embedding micro travel behaviour in macro land use policy objectives in TOPAZ (Brotchie, Dickey and Sharpe, 1980). However, in the current model structure, we embed functions representing micro location behaviour, as well as micro travel behaviour, in the macro land use policy objective in terms of h_i, as well as implicitly allowing for a recursive sequence of connecting the behavioural sub-models. In addition, such functions in terms of the primal land use variables h_i are sometimes implicit in nature, and create numerical difficulties when embedded in the planning policy objectives. Thus, in Roy and Lesse (1983a), we presented a general embedding procedure which expresses the function p_{ikl} in terms of the corresponding duals ψ_i, and is thus embedded as an explicit function of ψ_i in eqn. (17). As the duals ψ_i and the primal values h_i are related to each other monotonically, the minimization of eqn.(17) can be alternatively carried out in terms of ψ_i. As the multipliers η_{ml} on the job constraints of eqn. (2) are also not explicitly known at the micro level due to the dependence of the job allocations d_{ml} on the macro industrial policy constraints to be determined at the planning level, terms such as p_{ijl} in eqn. (17) and its constraints become bilinear functions of (ψ_i, η_{ml}), and the solutions can be handled via geometric programming.

Future Developments

One current weakness of this general residential location framework is that it is being implicitly assumed that the macro land release allocations by the planning authority, made according to non-market criteria, are perfectly taken up by the market. This would only be realistic if the authority could apply subsidies, which is often not an available option in many cities. However, if a general supply/demand framework could be developed, for instance by coupling a housing supply model with a random bidding model and allowing for unsatisfied demand, a general consistent result could be obtained.

The industrial and service sub-models can be embedded in a similar way as above in the behavioural terms of the land use policy goals relating to industrial and service activity allocation respectively, and the outcomes of all the behavioural sub-models be coordinated in terms of the relevant policy instruments or corresponding duals to meet the complete set of partially conflicting land use policy goals.

COORDINATION OF LAND USE POLICY GOALS

General Approach

Usually planning policy is implemented in an environment of conflicting objectives which can often be identified with certain lobby groups. A method is sought for handling this problem which explicitly reveals the trade-offs involved in satisfying each objective to varying degrees. This general area has already been investigated in a planning context by Nijkamp (1978) and Rietveld (1979), among others. An approach is developed by Batten, (this volume) who uses information theory to ensure minimum divergence of each trial solution from a base solution. In a more positive model context, ie., when we are seeking the system response which diverges as little as possible from the current state whilst satisfying the new goal constraints, the base or prior distribution is given as the current state of the system. In a more normative planning situation, such as being investigated in this paper, the base distributions represent the ideal point distributions for each goal in turn, where the ideal point distribution is the optimal solution for each goal acting alone. In this latter context, the approach of Batten (this volume) is a sequential interactive method based on a measure of divergence rather similar to the Minkowski metric discussed in Nijkamp (1978), in which a weighted sum of differences of the compromise solution from each ideal point is minimized.

In order to ensure that the most important criteria have been introduced before the solution possibly goes infeasible, Batten suggests introducing the criteria sequentially in order of importance. This is an excellent procedure in an interactive design framework, as the participants gain a clear appreciation of trade-offs involved in loosening or tightening various goal constraints. In the usual operation of a land-use/transport model, the length of the computation may however often preclude the use of a direct interactive approach, and the modeller must often judge how to best run the model and present its results. A possible scheme is to check all possible combinations of pairs of criteria, and using the ideal point solutions, check their degree of conflict with each other. Then, if a set of desirable levels of each criterion has been supplied to the modeller by the planning agency, he will be in a good position to perceive any irreconcilable areas which may cause infeasibility, and suggest appropriate modifications to the goal constraints. Thus, rather than being confined by the automatic black-box nature of the Minkowski metric, one would gain considerable insight into the compromises required.

In conclusion, it should be noted that many important performance criteria are not directly expressible as goals or goal constraints. For instance, a constraint on peak pollution levels cannot be applied explicitly, but one must await the results of an extensive a posteriori analysis at the more micro level before seeing how well one has done. In such cases, intuition and experience are required, and a scenario approach is usually necessary.

Conflicting Criteria with Embedded Micro Behaviour

In the model structure described in this paper, the goals will hardly ever be simple functions of the policy variables, but because of the embedding of behavioural relations in any micro level parts of the planning policy goals, they will be, at the best, bilinear. Such problems can of course be solved by geometric programming, or sometimes using eigenvalue techniques (Roy and Lesse,

1983a). Once the values of the macro policy instruments eg., h_i (or the corresponding duals, eg., ψ_i) have been obtained by such techniques, the behavioural distributions such as p_{iml} can be evaluated immediately. One difficulty is the presence of local optima (Brotchie, Dickey and Sharpe, 1980) and bifurcations (Harris and Wilson, 1978). However, linear iterative approaches with random starting solutions have been successfully adopted in the former case, and considerable numerical experience has been gathered on likely difficult parameter values for the latter. Of course, if the difficulties of implementing such a comprehensive multilevel model appear too daunting, one may replace any or all parts of the upper level planning policy framework by exogenous constraints, which can be manipulated in various forms in relation to certain recognized goals.

One is finally left with the experimental art of urban modelling and that is how to include all perceived important factors, but at the same time keep the analysis computationally tractable. Still (luckily for all of us), neither a static nor a context-free process, and thus not possessing a unique solution!

ACKNOWLEDGEMENTS

The authors are particularly grateful to Börje Johansson, Regional and Urban Development Group, IIASA, Austria, whose insights into the modelling of economic behaviour are strongly influencing the conceptual development.

REFERENCES

Anas, A., 1983, From Physical to Economic Urban Models: The Lowry Framework Revisited, a paper presented at the International Symposium on Directions in Urban Modelling, University of Waterloo, Waterloo, Ontario.

Batten, D.F. and Roy, J.R., 1982, Entropy and Economic Modelling, Environment and Planning A, 14, 1047-1061.

Batten, D.F., 1982, On Interregional Cross-Hauling and the Dog-Leg Input-Output Table, Proceedings of 29th Annual Meeting of North American Section of the Regional Science Association, Pittsburgh, PA.

Batten, D.F., 1984, Conflict, Inertia and Adaptive Learning in Urban Systems Modelling, this volume.

Batty, M., 1983, Technical Issues in Urban Model Development: A Review of Linear and Nonlinear Model Structures, a paper presented at the International Symposium on New Directions in Urban Modelling, University of Waterloo, Waterloo, Ontario.

Boyce, D.E., LeBlanc, L.J., Chon, D.S. and Lin, K.T., 1983, Implementation and Computational Issues for Combined Models of Location, Destination, Mode and Route Choice, Environment and Planning A, 15, in press.

Brotchie, J.F., Dickey, J.W. and Sharpe, R., 1980, TOPAZ - General Planning Technique and its Applications at the Regional, Urban and Facility Level, Springer-Verlag, Berlin.

Harris, B. and Wilson, A.G., 1979, Equilibrium Values and Dynamics of Attractiveness Terms in Production-Constrained Spatial Interaction Models, Environment and Planning A, 10, 371-388.

Intriligator, M.D., 1971, Mathematical Optimization and Economic Theory, Prentice-Hall, New Jersey.

Johansson, B., 1978, Contributions to Sequential Analysis of Oligopolistic Competition, Memorandum No. 73, Nationalekonomiska Institutionen, University of Gothenburg, Gothenburg, Sweden.

Lakshmanan, T.R. and Hansen, W.G., 1965, A Retail Market Potential Model, Journal of the American Institute of Planners, 31, 134-143.

Lerman, S.R. and Kern, C.R., 1983, Hedonic Theory, Bid Rents and Willingness to Pay: Some Extensions of Ellickson's Results, Journal of Urban Economics, forthcoming.

Lesse, P.F., 1982, A Phenomenological Theory of Socio-Economic Systems with Spatial Interactions, Environment and Planning A, 14, 869-888.

Lesse, P.F., Batty, M. and Batten, D.F., 1983, A Theory of Model Evaluations: 1. Spatial Invariance, Transformations and Aggregations, submitted to Environment and Planning A.

Mackett, R., Lodwick, A.J. and King, J., 1982, The Leeds Integrated Land-Use/ Transport (LILT) Model, User Guide - Version 1, Report of Institute of Transport Studies, University of Leeds, Leeds, U.K.

Nakamura, H., Hayashi, Y., and Miyamoto, K., 1983, Land-Use Transportation Analysis System for a Metropolitan Area, Transportation Research Record, forthcoming.

Nijkamp, P., 1978, Compromise Choice in Spatial Interaction and Regional Planning Models, in Karlqvist, A., Lundqvist, L., Snickars, F. and Weibull, J.W., (Eds.). Spatial Interaction Theory and Planning Models, North Holland, Amsterdam, 289-306.

Rietveld, P., 1979, Multi-Objective Decision-Making and Regional Planning, Martinus Nijhoff, Boston.

Roy, J.R. and Johansson, B., 1981, On Planning and Forecasting the Location of Retail and Service Activity, a paper presented at the conference on Structural Economic Planning in Time and Space, University of Umea, Sweden.

Roy, J.R. and Batten, D.F., 1982, An Approach to Modelling Multilevel Decisions in Urban Systems, Sistemi Urbani, forthcoming.

Roy, J.R., 1983, Estimation of Singly-Constrained Nested Spatial Interaction Models, Planning and Design: Environment and Planning B, 10, 269-274.

Roy, J.R. and Lesse, P.F., 1983a, Planning Models for Non-Cooperative Situations: A Two Player Game Approach, Regional Science and Urban Economics, 13, 205-221.

Roy, J.R. and Lesse, P.F., 1983b, On Nested Recursive Entropy Models for Multistage Processes, submitted to Environment and Planning A.

Roy, J.R., Johansson, B. and Leonardi, G., 1983, Some Location and Price Equilibria in Facility Investment with Uncertain Demand, a paper presented at the 8th Conference of Pacific Region of the Regional Science Association, Tokyo, Japan (forthcoming in Papers of Regional Science Assocation).

Snickars, F. and Weibull, J.W., 1977, A Minimum Information Principle: Theory and Practice, Regional Science and Urban Economics, 7, 137-168.

Wegener, M., Gnad, F. and Vannahme, M., 1983, The Time Scale of Urban Change, a paper presented at the International Symposium on New Directions in Urban Modelling, University of Waterloo, Waterloo, Ontario.

Williams, H.C.W.L., 1977, On the Formation of Travel Demand Models and Economic Evaluation Measures of User Benefit, Environment and Planning A, 9, 285-344.

Wilson, A.G., 1967, A Statistical Theory of Spatial Distribution Models, Transportation Research, 1, 253-269.

Wilson, A.G., Coelho, J.D., Macgill, S.M. and Williams, H.C.W.L., 1981, Optimization in Locational and Transport Analysis, John Wiley, Chichester, UK.

CONFLICT, INERTIA, AND ADAPTIVE LEARNING IN URBAN SYSTEMS MODELLING

David Batten*
CSIRO Division of Building Research
P.O. Box 56
Highett, VIC 3190
Australia

Abstract. A composite multidimensional method, encompassing the complete typology of multi-objective programming models and multi-criteria evaluation methods, is developed for the interactive resolution of conflicting multilevel and multistage decisions in urban systems. The resulting compromise approach corresponds to a Harmonious Adaptive Learning Procedure (HALP). Compromise trajectories are generated using a development planning model in which resource allocation is determined by a stepwise interactive planning scheme of multistage decision processes at the macro and meso levels of the city system.

INTRODUCTION

It is often argued that urban planning or policymaking strategies must be designed to benefit the majority of a city's population. For political survival (so the argument goes), the average citizen must be satisfied with city hall's management of the urban system. In reality, however, urban planning policies have quite a different impact on each citizen because of the geographical, industrial and financial diversity which exists within each city. Some individuals, suburbs and industries benefit more than the average, while others are at a disadvantage. In such a complex system as an urban economy, the average citizen is clearly a misnomer.

More fruitful is the suggestion that an urban system exhibits considerable hierarchical structure, in so much as it contains a multiplicity of decisions by actors and groups of actors who influence different levels of the total planning process (Roy and Batten, 1983). In such a system, the metropolitan planning authority's major role is one of coordination, since it has only fragmentary knowledge about the micro-structure of the city and can boast only limited authority and ability to control the actions of various agents. To this end, multilevel programming models can provide a framework for the coordination of decisions made by the various actors who represent different components of such an economic system (Nijkamp and Rietveld, 1981).

---

*This paper was written during the author's stay as a visiting scientist at the International Institute for Applied Systems Analysis, A-2361 Laxenburg, Austria

One such multilevel system is depicted in Fig. 1 (typical goals for each subsystem are included). At the macro level, decisions taken concerning spatial policies may be based upon general efficiency or equity criteria for the city as a whole. These metropolitan policies impose certain constraints on feasible development options at the meso level, where subsystems of industries, trade unions, environmental agencies, and local authorities pursue their own conflicting objectives. Similarly, decisions taken at both the macro and meso levels impose further constraints on the individual decision-makers in smaller units at the micro level. Note that each component may have more than one goal, which introduces an additional dimension of complexity. Nevertheless, it should be stressed that the policies implemented at higher levels can coordinate but not completely control the goal-seeking activities at lower levels (Mesarovic, Macko and Takahara, 1970).

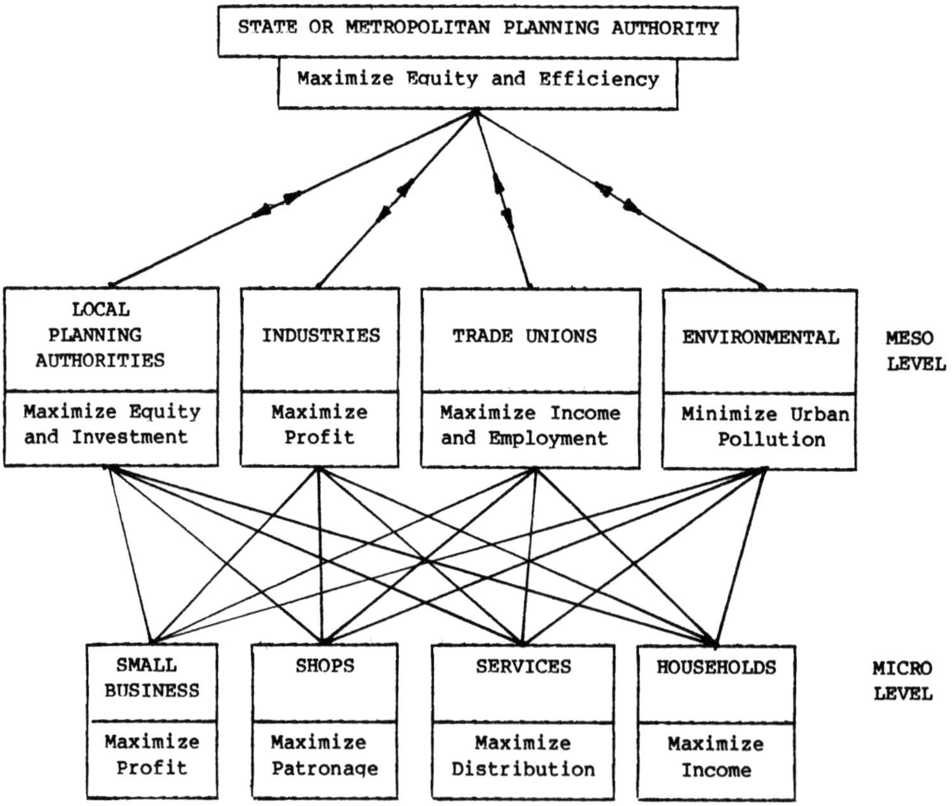

Figure 1 - Typical Decision-Makers in a Multilevel Urban System

Harmonious planning strategies for an urban system containing a variety of subsystems at both the meso and micro levels require methods for the resolution of conflicting interests and objectives arising from the interdependencies between the various components or subsystems. Planners and policy-makers at both the metropolitan and local levels must consider a range of policy objectives (implying a multidimensional welfare function) and a multiplicity of criteria (for example, efficiency, equity, environmental quality, etc.) to reflect the diverse goals and aspirations which exist amongst the community. Their collective decision-making must ultimately lead to an allocation of resources which reflects a meaningful compromise between the various policy options.

During the last decade, various methods for multidimensional decision-making have been proposed (see, for example, Cochrane and Zeleny, 1973; Zeleny, 1974, 1982; Wallenius, 1975; Keeney and Raiffa, 1976; Nijkamp and Rietveld, 1976; van Delft and Nijkamp, 1977; Nijkamp, 1977, 1979a; Blair, 1978; Cohon, 1978; Rietveld, 1980; Spronk, 1981; Hafkamp and Nijkamp, 1981; Voogd, 1982). A survey of these methods indicates that most have been classified into two definite groups, namely multiobjective programming (MOP) models and multicriteria evaluation (MCE) models. A second major subdivision into models which contain quantitative (hard) information and those which can handle qualitative (soft) information has also become apparent more recently. The result is a useful typology of multidimensional models (Nijkamp, 1979b).

There are, however, two important methodological aspects which have been largely overlooked in the majority of multidimensional models developed in the 1970s. Firstly, the typology just described is by no means unambiguous. Goals and objectives can easily be expressed as quantitative achievement levels (carrying discrete values), and then ranked in order of priority instead of being weighted in a multidimensional welfare function. A ranking of achievement levels is equivalent to the prioritization of decision criteria for an MCE model. Thus, clear distinctions between goals in an MOP model and criteria in an MCE model may sometimes be difficult. Furthermore, distinctions between cardinal (hard), ordinal (soft), and even more qualitative information can also be misleading. Much of the cardinal information currently used for planning purposes is based on guesstimates which are no more statistically reliable than qualitative statements. Once again, this area cannot be easily demarcated in an unambiguous manner.

The foregoing remarks suggest that it might be useful to develop a composite multidimensional methodology which is flexible enough to encompass the complete typology namely (i) conflicting objectives; (ii) conflicting decision criteria; (iii) quantitative information; and (iv) qualitative information. Following a discussion of multidimensional decision-making, a new methodology known as the Harmonious Adaptive Learning Procedure (HALP) is outlined.

A second deficiency inherent in the current suite of multidimensional models is the scant consideration given to the time dimension. Planning is clearly a dynamic process in which investment decisions made at one point in time have a dominant, but usually a delayed, impact on the trajectory of urban development. In other words, decision-making is a multistage process in which goal conflicts can be resolved either simultaneously or sequentially over time. The majority of multidimensional models developed so far have underplayed the role of time as a fundamental dimension for the achievement of compromise policies. Even the interactive decision models which are based on a series of iterative compromise solutions have neglected to explore the advantages (or otherwise) of multistage compromises compared with simultaneous tradeoffs. Adaptive learning procedures are an appropriate tool for the evaluation of multistage compromise solutions. Possibilities for the extension of the HALP procedure into this dynamic setting are discussed in the fourth part of the paper.

Finally, a dynamic planning model, first developed as a tool for analysing the feasibility, consistency, and tradeoffs between different national and regional objectives (using traditional optimzation techniques), is restructured as an adaptive learning procedure for urban systems planning. The result is a development planning model in which satisfactory resource allocation is based upon a stepwise interactive planning scheme at the metropolitan and local levels using multistage decision processes which allow for various compromises through time.

MULTIDIMENSIONAL DECISION-MAKING

The complex interactions between the three policy or decision levels (macro, meso, and micro) of our urban system depicted in Fig. 1, and inside the various components at each level, can only be analysed in an appropriate way if the guiding aspirations and interests of each actor are understood. The multidimensional nature of this problem implies at least three conflict categories, namely

1. Conflicts between various priorities, goals or targets within one component of the system (for example, frictions between efficiency and equity criteria at the metropolitan level).

2. Conflicts between various priorities, goals or targets set by different components at one level of the system (for example, frictions between business firms who strive to maximize profit and households who strive to maximize their income).

3. Conflicts between various priorities, goals or targets set by different components at different levels of the system (for example, frictions between business firms who strive to maximize profit and protection agencies who strive to minimize damage to the environment).

This picture reflects the duality of conflicting choices, viz., between goals and between system components. Goal conflicts have been studied extensively in the fields of multi-objective programming (MOP) and multi-criteria evaluation (MCE). The presence of several competing policy units (subsystems) leads to additional complications, however, since it introduces multiple choice conflicts. Consequently, an appropriate compromise framework has to be devised which leads to a satisfactory result for both the components and the objectives at various levels of our urban system.

Before discussing the complex problem of coordination of the multi-component level and simultaneous compromise at the multi-objective level, it is important to understand the nature of the main methods developed for multidimensional decision-making. The typology given in Table 1 is largely taken from Nikjamp (1979), where the characteristics of each method are summarized. It is not our intention to compare or contrast individual methods here, but rather to concentrate on the typology itself.

TABLE 1

METHODS FOR MULTIDIMENSIONAL DECISION-MAKING

	Hard (Quantitative) Information	Soft (Qualitative) Information
Multi-Objective Programming Models	Utility Models Penalty Models Goal Programming Models Constraint Models Hierarchical Models Min-Max Models Ideal Point Models	Fuzzy set models Stochastic Models Soft Econometric Models
Multi-Criteria Evaluation Methods	Trade-Off Analysis Expected Value Method Correspondence Analysis Discrepancy Analysis Concordance Analysis Goals-Achievement Method	Expected Value Method Lexicographic Method Multidimensional Scaling Regime Method Ordinal Concordance Analysis Eigenvalue Method Frequency Method

(after Nijkamp, 1979)

Multi-objective programming (MOP) models are based on a multidimensional view of welfare in the form of continuous objective functions, subject to various constraints. In general, an MOP model takes the form

$$\text{maximize } \omega(x),\ x \in K \qquad (1)$$

where $\omega(x)$ is an M-dimensional vector of objective functions, x is an N-dimensional vector of decision variables, and K is a feasible, M-dimensional

Euclidean space. A central role in these models is played by the Pareto frontier (efficiency frontier, set of non-dominated or non-inferior points). A Pareto solution reflects the fact that when a number of objectives conflict, the only way we can increase the value of one objective function subject to the constraints is to decrease the value of at least one of the remaining objective functions. Any feasible point that is not dominated by other points is a Pareto solution. For continuous MOP models, the entire set of Pareto solutions cannot normally be identified. It is usually sufficient to ascertain the extreme points.

A simple illustration of a Pareto frontier (or set of efficient solutions) for the case of two objective functions is given in Fig. 2. Only the points on the efficiency locus AB are relevant Pareto solutions, because all other points in the feasible set are dominated by a point on this locus. No point on the arc AB dominates any other point on the same arc.

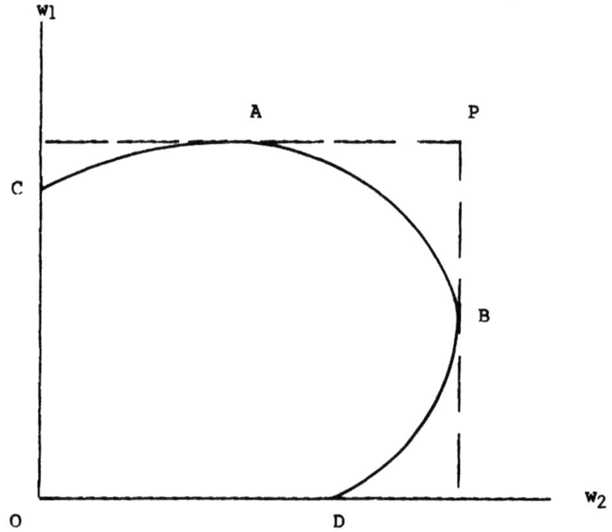

Figure 2 - Pareto Frontier for Two Conflicting Objectives

The point P in Fig. 2 dominates all feasible solutions. It corresponds to the point at which both objectives attain their maximum values and is known as the ideal solution. Ideal solutions like P may be used as reference points for evaluating various compromise solutions on the Pareto frontier. One might assume that the ultimate compromise solution is that point which has a minimum discrepancy with respect to the ideal point P. This approach, known as the ideal point method, requires normalization of the objective functions and an appropriate choice of a distance metric. The Minkovsky metric is frequently used.

Multi-criteria evaluation (MCE) methods are based on a comprehensive comparison of discrete alternatives (plans, projects or strategies). Given the multidimensionality of the decision criteria for a plan or project, a first step in all these methods is the construction of an impact matrix which reflects the outcomes of all alternatives with respect to all decision criteria (variables). Each element of this matrix reflects the relative value of each criterion with respect to each plan or outcome. Instead of using artificial prices for intangible goods, multi-criteria models assign priorities to certain decision criteria. These weights reflect the relative importance attached by decision-makers to the outcomes with respect to each criterion.

Goals and objectives can usually be expressed in the form of quantitative targets or achievement levels carrying discrete values. They can also be ranked in order of priority instead of being specified as a continuous multi-dimensional welfare function. Such a prioritization of achievement levels which ranks different (combinations of) decision variables corresponds closely to an MCE method. Yet it is also a permissible MOP model. This suggests that the distinction between these two classes of multidimensional model may not be unambiguous.

Moreover, the recent distinction between multidimensional choice models on the basis of information accuracy can also be misleading. Quantitative models are assumed to contain cardinal, deterministic or hard information. Qualitative models suffer by comparison since they are limited to ordinal, fuzzy or soft data. Yet realistic choice models must surely expect and be prepared for a mixture of quantitative and qualitative information. Moreover, some of the so-called cardinal information currently used for planning purposes is based on guesstimates which may be no more statistically reliable than qualitative statements.

Thus it seems worthwhile to explore various composite multidimensional methodologies which may be flexible enough to encompass the complete typology implied in Table 1, namely (i) conflicting objectives, (ii) priorities among decision criteria, (iii) quantitative information, and (iv) qualitative information. However, it is usually not sufficient to reduce such a composite methodology exclusively to a single mathematical optimization problem. In many planning and decision models, the first compromise solution obtained using one of the abovementioned methods may not be entirely satisfactory. Situations arise in which the decision-maker(s) is unable or unwilling to provide all the required goal or preference information a priori, since this implies complete knowledge about all possible actions (choices) and the trade-offs between these actions. Situations also arise in which the conflicting nature of certain goals may preclude the existence of any feasible solution. In such cases, interactive decision methods are needed.

Interactive decision procedures allow the decision-maker(s) to become more actively involved with the process of compromise, whereby they obtain greater insight into the trade-offs between different goals. The feedback process leads to closer cooperation and understanding between decision-makers and analysts. To this extent, the interactive approach can be interpreted as an operational example of learning theory (see, for example, Atkinson, Bower and Clothers, 1965 or Hilgard and Bower, 1969). One of the major learning effects induced by the interactive approach is that the decision-makers's perceptions of the decision problem or preferences may change during the interactive process.

HARMONIOUS ADAPTIVE LEARNING PROCEDURES FOR MULTIDIMENSIONAL CONFLICT MANAGEMENT

The composite multidimensional methodology which we shall now describe is of the interactive type, and will be referred to as the Harmonious Adaptive Learning Procedure (HALP). It represents a synthesis of some of the author's earlier work on hierarchical systems using information theory (Batten, 1983; Batten and Andersson, 1983) with interactive goal programming procedures (Spronk, 1981; Hafkamp and Nijkamp, 1981).

Consider a multilevel system (such as the one depicted in Fig. 1) in which there are R components or subsystems ($r=1,\ldots,R$). Each subsystem has a set of J objectives $\omega_r = (\omega_{1r},\ldots,\omega_{Jr})$ which are to be maximized and which depend on I decision variables $x_r = (x_{1r},\ldots,x_{Ir})$. If we assume that each subsystem can solve its internal goal conflicts, we can take for granted the existence of a component welfare function $\omega_r = \sum_j \lambda_{jr}\,\omega_{jr}$, where λ_{jr} is the weight attached to the objective j by subsystem r.

In such a system, a set of side-conditions which we shall call relational constraints delimit the action space of each decision-maker (for example, technical, economic, environmental and institutional constraints). These relational constraints are of two types

internal constraints: $A_r x_r \leqq a_r$,

joint constraints: $\sum_r B_r x_r \leqq b$.

No coordination by the planning authority is needed when only internal constraints prevail. The need for coordination arises from the occurrence of joint constraints.

In some multi-level studies, it is assumed that the metropolitan authority's objectives are simply the sum of the subsystem objectives ($\sum_r \omega_r$). We shall relax that assumption completely. Futhermore, we shall allow each subsystems's set of objectives to differ from the next. However, we shall assume that both the metropolitan authority (hereafter termed the authority) and each subsystem contain decision-makers who can perform the following functions (or steps)

1. Rank their set of objectives in order of importance on an ordinal scale, such as most important, next most important, and so on. This prioritization of goals corresponds to a lexicographic ordering of each set, which closely resembles the decision-making technique adopted by many policy-makers.
2. Relate each objective to a (minimally) acceptable achievement level so that each goal can be expressed in the form of an achievement constraint, namely

$$C_r x_r \geqq \omega_r\,(\min)$$

where C_r is a *JxI matrix of impact coefficients which are specified a priori in such a fashion that all x_r are nonnegative.

By asking each subsystem (including the authority) to rank each of its objectives, and to specify achievement levels for each, we can construct a priorities and targets matrix as shown in Table 2. A horizontal maximization across any row of this matrix would lead to a maximum value of the corresponding objective function, whereas a vertical maximization would favour a maximum value of all objective functions within one subsystem. In any event, Table 2 enables a lower threshold value to be computed for the objective functions and subsystems.

The analyst in each subsystem r must be prepared to calculate various ideal solutions by successively maximizing each of his J objectives $\omega_r = (\omega_{1r}, \ldots, \omega_{Jr})$ separately subject to various sets of (normalized) restrictions, denoting the maxima by $\omega^*_r = (\omega^*_{1r}, \ldots, \omega^*_{Jr})$ and the corresponding (normalized) combinations of the decision variables by $x^*_{jr} = (x^*_{1jr}, \ldots, x^*_{Ijr})$. At any stage, it is not necessary to accept a value of ω_{jr} (min) which is lower than the following

$$\omega_{jr}\,(\min) = \min_{k=1,J} \{\omega_{jr}\,(x^*_{kr})\}$$

and this pessimistic value may be compared with the corresponding target value in Table 2. The initial set of R ideal solutions will be termed independent because they are computed in the absence of any coordination by the authority through the distribution of common resources $(b_1, \ldots, b_R)$.

The following distance metric can be used to evaluate the minimum discrepancy between any compromise solution and the ideal solution

$$\text{Minimize } I_r = \sum_{j=1}^{J} \sum_{i=1}^{I} x_{ijr} \log (x_{ijr}/x^*_{ijr}) \qquad (2)$$

It should be understood that this discrepancy or penalty function is not a welfare or utility function, but is actually a measure of information gain

(Kullback, 1959). It is equivalent (at its first approximation) to the minimization of the Chi-square statistic

$$\sum_{j=1}^{J}\sum_{i=1}^{I}(x_{ijr}-x^{*}_{ijr})^{2}/x_{ijr} \tag{3}$$

and is therefore a suitable measure of deviation or goodness of fit. The arbitrary choice of this function for generating trial compromise solutions is no drawback in an interactive procedure where the decision-makers have the opportunity to adapt to each solution and reformulate their desires in a stepwise manner. Moreover, operational and efficient algorithms for the solution of this discrepancy function subject to linear constraint systems are readily available (Eriksson, 1980, 1981).

TABLE 2

PRIORITIES AND TARGETS MATRIX FOR A MULTILEVEL SYSTEM

		SUBSYSTEMS		
		Component 1	Component 2	....
Objective Functions	w_1	Rank j_{11} w_{11}(min)	Rank j_{12} w_{12}(min)	
	w_2	Rank j_{21} w_{21}(min)	Rank j_{22} w_{22}(min)	
	....			

The above gives rise to the following independent compromise model for each subsystem r:

Minimize I_r subject to (4)

internal constraints: $A_r\, x_r \leqq a_r$

achievement constraints: $C_r\, x_r \geqq \omega_r$ (min)

(in order or priority) $x_r \geqq 0.$

We shall approach the solution to this problem in a series of interactive steps to illustrate the adaptive learning procedure which is involved. Each trial compromise may be judged by the decision-maker in terms of its feasibility and desirability, and modifications can then be made.

The first step in our adaptive procedure consists of adding the achievement constraint carrying the highest priority (j=1) to the set of internal restrictions to define the first feasible region. The ideal solution (P_1) correspond ing to this region is computed, and the first compromise point is then obtained by minimizing I_r subject to the above-mentioned constraints. At this early stage, the decision-maker would not normally be invited to modify his preferences unless it is impossible to obtain a feasible solution.

The second step in this sequential process consists of adding the achievement constraint of second highest priority to the first set of constraints. The second feasible region so defined will be smaller than the first if the two objectives partly conflict. The resulting model necessitates the calculation of a second ideal solution (P_2) since the addition of a new constraint results in a displacement of the original ideal point. Once this second reference point has been identified, a second compromise solution can be determined by minimizing I_e subject to the appended constraint set.

In successive steps, additional achievement constraints are introduced in order of priority, a new ideal solution is computed for each new feasible region, and a new compromise solution is determined. The advantage of this sequential procedure arises from our ability to detect the precise constraint which may render the system infeasible. It is quite possible that the simultaneous presence of various achievement constraints precludes any feasible region. The sequential addition of each constraint permits us to detect any transition to infeasibility. Iterative revision of the offending achievement constraint, or some modification of earlier achievement levels, is then possible. The interactive learning character of this procedure is quite apparent.

Once a feasible region has been defined in which all J objectives (achievement constraints) are represented, the resulting trial compromise solution is presented to the decision-maker for his overall assessment. As a result of the learning procedure, his preferences may have altered. Further modifications to the achievement constraints can be taken into account, resulting in the calculation of new ideal solutions and compromise points. The interactive process continues until the decision-maker is finally satisfied, whereupon the final compromise solution is obtained.

The various steps in this adaptive learning procedure are summarized in Fig. 3. Although functions like information gain or directed divergence are minimally biased, it is really the interactive character of this procedure which prevents the policymaker from taking biased decisions on the basis of a single-step choice algorithm (Hafkamp and Nijkamp, 1981). The convergence properties of similar interactive procedures have already been discussed (for mathematical aspects, see Rietveld, 1980).

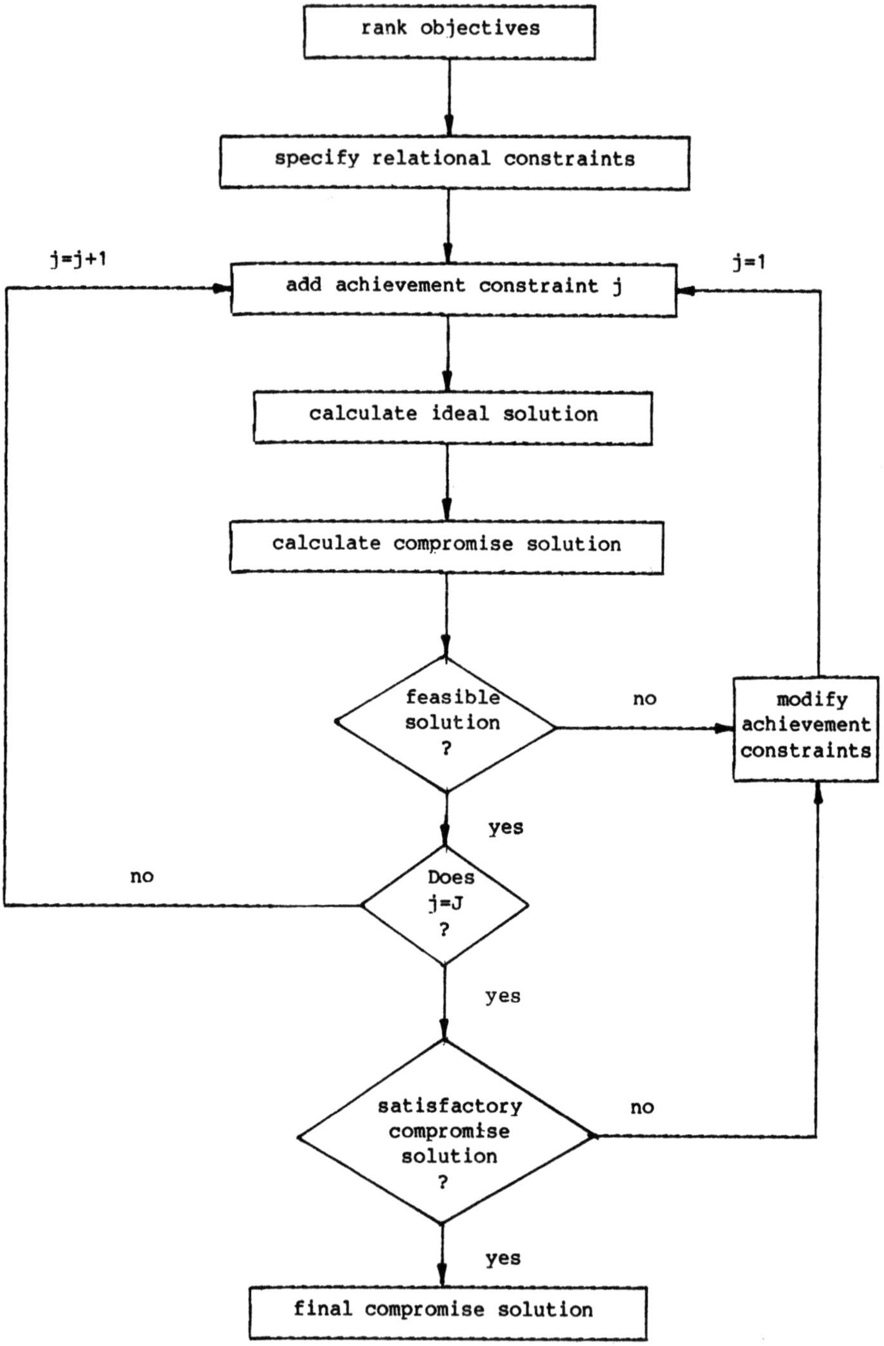

Figure 3 - An Adaptive Learning Procedure

The proposed adaptive learning procedure embodies the complete typology (Table 1) of multidimensional methodologies. The ranking of objectives in order of importance corresponds to the lexicographic method (soft MCE) of evaluation; and is also used in hierarchical optimization models (hard MOP). Specifying these objectives in the form of achievement constraints is the basis of the goals-achievement method (hard MCE), and largely corresponds to the approach adopted in many constraint models (hard MOP). Since these constraints can rarely be sharply defined, and may be modified during the learning procedure, they are synonymous with fuzzy set models (soft MOP). Finally, the use of the information gain measure as a distance metric for measuring the deviation between ideal solutions on the one hand, and a set of compromise solutions on the other hand, is consistent with the approach adopted in discrepancy analysis (hard MCE), penalty models (hard MOP) and ideal point models (hard MOP). The latter trio correspond closely to the method of displaced ideals (Zeleny, 1976).

This composite methodology is depicted in Fig. 4. The adaptive learning procedure implies the notion of satisficing rather than optimizing, in so much as the ultimate compromise solution complies with certain achievement levels specified by the decision-makers in each subsystem. However, this approach has so far been limited to the resolution of internal goal conflicts within each subsystem in the absence of any interdependencies between different components of our multilevel system. It is now time to consider the role of the authority as the coordinator of decision-making throughout the system.

Since each subsystem r has resolved its internal goal conflicts by means of the adaptive learning procedures outlined above, it now possesses a yardstick by which to measure further compromises. The internal constraints embodied in each subsystem's independent compromise model are now relayed to the authority, together with the resulting values of x_r so determined. The authority's planning problem may now be formulated as follows:

Minimize I subject to (5)

$$\begin{array}{llcl} \text{subsystem constraints:} & A_1 x_1 \quad \ddots & & \leqq a_1 \\ & & \ddots \; A_R\, x_R & \leqq a_r \\ \text{coordinating constraints:} & B_1 x_1 + \ldots + & B_R\, x_R & \leqq b \\ \text{achievement constraints:} & C_1 x_1 + \ldots + C_R x_R & & \geqq \omega \text{ (min)} \end{array}$$

where I is a similar distance metric to the one used for each subsystem, namely I_r as given in eqn. (2), but is summed over all R subsystems.

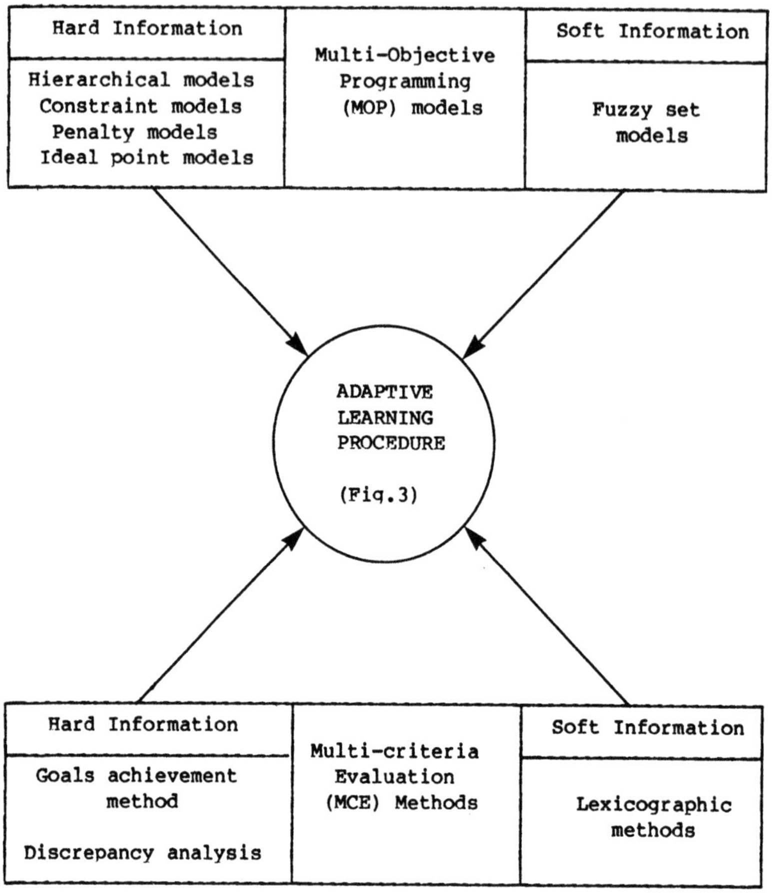

Figure 4 - Adaptive Learning as a Composite System of Miltidimensional Methods

The initial values of x_r provided by the subsystems allow the authority to calculate a set of resource distribution coefficients (B_1, ..., B_R) which satisfy $\sum_r B_r x_r = b$. Given this information, the authority then searches for an efficient compromise solution for the distribution of common resources by means of a similar adaptive learning procedure to that utilized by the subsystems. In this case, the relational constraints include the (internal) subsystem constraints and the (joint) coordinating constraints. The set of achievement constraints are based on the objectives of the authority itself, although some relaxation of these targets may be needed to find a feasible compromise solution.

Once this solution has been determined, the authority generates a provisional distribution of resources (b_1,..., b_R) to each subsystem. This gives rise to the following coordinated compromise model for each subsystem r

Minimize I_r subject to (6)

$$\begin{aligned} &\text{internal constraints:} && A_r x_r \leqq a_r \\ &\text{joint constraints:} && B_r x_r \leqq b_r \\ &\text{achievement constraints:} && C_r x_r \geqq \omega_r \text{ (min)} \end{aligned}$$

Once again, the subsystems solve their revised problems by means of an adaptive learning procedure, and then report the results back to the authority. In the direct method of multilevel programming (see Kornai, 1975 or Johansen, 1978), each subsystem reports the shadow prices Π_r of the common resources back to the authority. Given this information, the authority revises the distribution of resources and may also suggest that certain achievement levels set by the subsystems be relaxed. Once an efficient distribution of common resources $(b_1,...,b_R)$ which enables the authority and each sub-system to reach a satisfactory compromise solution is found, the coordination process is complete.

The resulting series of iterations between the authority and each subsystem necessitates further learning procedures in which each subsystem must also consider the conflicting interests of other subsystems. Harmonious planning strategies for a macroeconomic system result from the resolution of goal conflicts arising from the interdependence between all the components involved. This interactive process, which we have formulated as a series of adaptive learning procedures, will be known as the Harmonious Adaptive Learning Procedure (HALP).

In what follows, we shall attempt to extend the scope of this approach into a dynamic setting. The above-mentioned procedure has been formulated in a timeless space. Interactive processes and the relaxation of various aspirations have been treated as if they all occur simultaneously.

CONFLICT MANAGEMENT AS A MULTISTAGE PROCESS

The introduction of the time element into multidimensional decision-making may complicate our earlier formulations, but it nevertheless allows more realistic trajectories of learning and compromise to be developed. We begin by restating our compromise models [in eqns. (5) and (6)] in dynamic form. For the authority, we have

$$\text{Minimize } I = \sum_{r=1}^{R} \sum_{j=1}^{J} \sum_{i=1}^{I} x_{ijr}(t) \log[x_{ijr}(t)/x^*_{ijr}(t)] \tag{7}$$

subject to the following constraints for each stage or time period t:

$$\begin{array}{llll} A_1(t)\, x_1(t) & \ddots & & \leqq a_1(t) \\ & & A_R(t)x_R(t) & \leqq a_R(t) \\ B_1(t)\, x_1(t) & + \ldots + & B_R(t)x_R(t) & \leqq b(t) \\ C_1(t)\, x_1(t) & + \ldots + & C_R(t)x_R(t) & \geqq \omega(t). \end{array}$$

As before, we shall assume that the initial values of our state and decision variables, namely $x_r(0)$, are provided by the r subsystems, who first calculate compromise solutions which resolve their internal goal conflicts by adaptive learning in the absence of any coordination from the authority. Stage 1 begins with the calculation of a set of resource distribution coefficients $\{B_1(1),\ldots, B_R(1)\}$ which satisfy the following resource constraint for the first period, namely

$$\sum_r B_r(1)\, x_r(0) \leqq b(1).$$

Given this information, the authority must now search for an efficient compromise solution for the distribution of these common resources during the first period (t=1). The relational constraints include the internal (A) constraints and the coordinating (B) constraints. The set of achievement (C) constraints are largely based on the authority's own objectives.

Once this solution has been found, the authority generates a distribution of resources $\{b_1(1), \ldots, b_R(1)\}$ for each subsystem to consider at stage 1. This gives rise to the following coordinated compromise model for each subsystem r (in which t=1 at this stage)

$$\text{Minimize } I_r = \sum_{j=1}^{J} \sum_{i=1}^{I} x_{ijr}(t) \log[x_{ijr}(t)/x^*_{ijr}(t)] \tag{8}$$

subject to the following constraints:

$$A_r(t)x_r(t) \leqq a_r(t)$$

$$B_r(t)x_r(t) \leqq b_r(t)$$

$$C_r(t)x_r(t) \geqq \omega_r(t)$$

Once again, the subsystems can solve this revised problem by means of an adaptive learning procedure, report back to the authority, and then receive a new distribution of resources for the second stage (t=2). The resulting series of iterations between the authority and each subsystem is repeated until all T stages (time periods) have been completed.

In contrast to the single stage formulations discussed in the previous section, the multistage models in eqns. (7) and (8) facilitate a rich range of possible trajectories which can be followed according to various learning combinations and compromise decisions. The time element offers us much greater scope for achieving satisfactory conflict resolution. We shall now explore these additional options.

Firstly, in the single stage approach we limited the discrepancy functions I or I_r to the calculation of distance between any compromise solution $\{x_{ijr}\}$ and the ideal solution $\{x^*_{ijr}\}$. Once we adopt the multistage approach, however, $\{x^*_{ijr}(t)\}$ can be interpreted in a number of different ways

1. In a normative planning environment, use of the ideal solution as a reference point would still be appropriate.

2. In a more positive planning situation, the ultimate aim might be to obtain compromise solutions which deviate as little as possible from the most recent state of the system. Such a minimum disturbance principle would result in one of the following (normalized) reference points

$$x^*_{ijr}(t) = x_{ijr}(t-1)$$

or

$$x^*_{ijr}(t) = x_{ijr}(t-T) \tag{9}$$

In this case, a new reference point is no longer calculated as we introduce additional achievement constraints in the learning procedure, since the emphasis is on minimum disturbance instead of displaced ideals.

3. As an extension of the previous approach, we might prefer to assume that a priori states of the system are not just governed by the most recent historical pattern, but also by agreements and contracts established in earlier periods. If $z_{ijr}(t-\tau)$ denotes the normalized state of the system τ periods earlier, then we have

$$x^*_{ijr}(t) = F_{ijr}\left\{z_{ijr}(t-1),\ z_{ijr}(t-2),\ \ldots\right\} \tag{10}$$

where F_{ijr} denotes a positively differentiable function of the normalized states of the system in preceding periods. To discount certain periods and emphasize others, eqn. (10) could take the following form

$$x^*_{ijr}(t) = \sum_{\tau}\omega_j(\tau)x_{ijr}(t-\tau) \tag{11}$$

where $\sum_{\tau}\omega_j(\tau)=1$ and all $\omega_j(\tau) \geqq 0$.

4. In a more prescriptive planning situation the desired aim may be to obtain compromise solutions which deviate as little as possible from a preferred trajectory of future urban development. The preferred growth path may be determined by the authority, which still needs to consider a number of conflicting objectives. It is likely that control theory can assist in this situation with the use of a penalty function to stabilize deviations from the desired trajectory (Lesse and Sharpe, 1981).

Secondly, with multistage decision-making, it is possible for the authority to modify the availability of resources at various stages to meet the needs of certain subsystems more effectively, yet still not exceed the total pool of resources available for the complete period. In other words, an additional constraint of the form

$$\sum_{t=1}^{T} b(t) \leqq b \tag{12}$$

is added to the authority's budgeting system in eqn. (8), indicating that the authority must also determine an efficient allocation of their total resources b over the whole period prior to, or in conjunction with, the distribution of resources to each subsystem at each stage. We shall return to the authority's multistage control problem shortly.

Thirdly, in a multistage problem the lexicographic ordering of objectives becomes particularly important. It is quite possible to waive some of the lower-order objectives in the early stages in an attempt to achieve satisfactory harmony between the authority and its subsystems as quickly as possible. The authority itself may be prepared to postpone consideration of some of its own objectives of lower priority in order to allow each subsystem the freedom to resolve its own internal goal conflicts more effectively. The prioritization of objectives is therefore dependent on deadlines as well as goal preferences, and may be used to reduce the set of achievement constraints which warrant consideration at each particular stage.

The above mentioned features of the multistage compromise process accentuate the richer range of decision-making and learning procedures inherent in this dynamic form of conflict management. An additional consideration is the need to discount the later stages in order to place a greater emphasis on early compromises if the prioritization of objectives is not used for this purpose. Depreciation may also be included in the investment process as defined by the relational constraints.

But perhaps the most important additional feature which must be addressed in order to solve the multistage problem satisfactorily is the question of overall coordination and control by the metropolitan planning authority over the entire period of interest. As well as playing a major role in the harmonious process of adaptive learning through successive interactions with each subsystem at each stage, the authority must ensure that the compromise process has fulfilled certain conditions at the end of the final stage. This overall control problem can be formulated in a similar fashion to the single-stage models, although other approaches (such as a closed loop optimum control problem) are also possible. For the authority's overall control, we might have to minimize

$$I = \sum_{t=1}^{T} \sum_{r=1}^{R} \sum_{j=1}^{J} \sum_{i=1}^{I} x_{ijr}(t) \log[x_{ijr}(t) - x^*_{ijr}(t)] \qquad (13)$$

subject to the following time-coordination constraints

$$\sum_{t=1}^{T} A_r x_r(t) \leq a_r \qquad (r=1, \ldots, R)$$

$$\sum_{t=1}^{T} B_r x_r(t) \leq b$$

where $x^*_{ijr}(t)$ should be interpreted in a manner consistent with the authority's overall objectives (for example, as points on a trajectory of preferred development if minimum deviation from such a trajectory is desired, ie., compromise trajectories).

In reality, it is difficult to solve eqn. (13) in advance of the interactive solutions reached at each stage of the adaptive learning process. This is because the set of resource distribution coefficients $\{B_r\}$ are actually functions of the stage reached in the compromise process, and cannot usually be determined accurately in advance. However, it is possible to devise a monitoring scheme which allows the authority's overall progress to be assessed at each stage so that revisions can be made when deemed appropriate.

The schematic representation of a multistage process which allows for compromise solutions by adaptive learning at each stage, together with further compromises between stages and overall control by the authority, is depicted in Fig. 5. The key to this dynamic process is that it allows for harmonious adaptive learning procedures which cater for the interdependencies between all the components involved, as well as dynamic learning procedures which can resolve further conflicts via multistage compromises. The resource allocation monitor ensures that the total resources allocated over the entire period are within the means of the metropolitan planning authority.

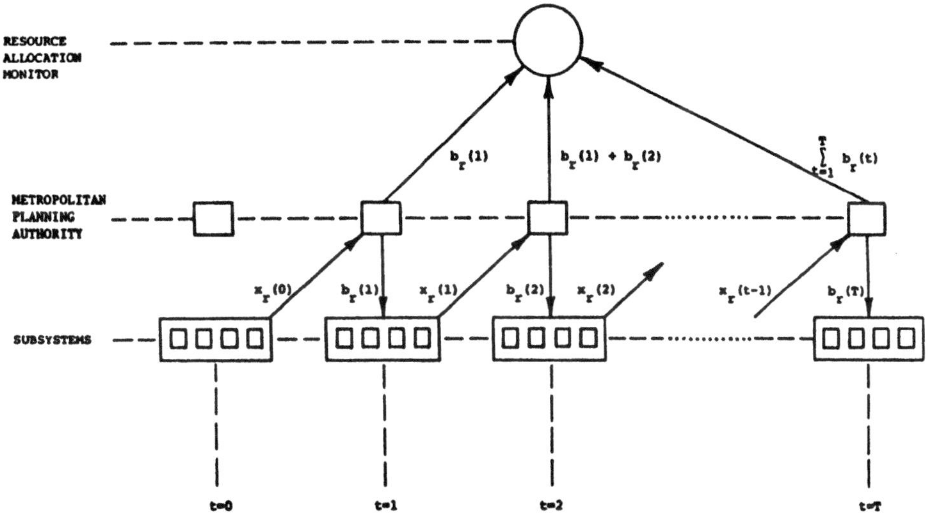

Figure 5 - Conflict Management by Multistage Compromise

ADAPTIVE LEARNING IN A DYNAMIC PLANNING MODEL

In this section, a dynamic multi-activity planning model which was previously developed to analyse the feasibility, consistency and tradeoffs between different national and regional objectives (Sharpe and Batten, 1976; Karlqvist et al., 1978; Sharpe, Batten and Anderson, 1981) is reorganized as a multistage adaptive learning procedure for urban systems. Known as DREAM (Dynamic Regional Economic Allocation Model), the original form of the model caters for multiple objectives by including each goal in the objective function and then assigning arbitrary weights to each goal in order to simulate potential tradeoffs. However, the specification of such a welfare function a priori presupposes complete information about all possible actions and tradeoffs between these actions. Since this information is rarely available, interactive decision methods are more appropriate. For this reason, the DREAM model will be reorganized as a multistage version of the Harmonious Adaptive Learning Procedure (HALP), to allow various urban decision-makers to become more actively involved with the multilevel process of compromise.

The basic structure of the DREAM model is defined through a set of relationships which can be classified under the following general headings: technical-economic relations, demographic relations, spatial relations, temporal relations and institutional-political relations. The temporal structure of the model is represented by a simple dynamic multiplier principle which relates the (gross) investment in fixed capital in a certain time period to activity in different sectors during the same time period by linear capital coefficients. The net change of capital (ie., gross investment less provision for depreciation) then serves as a constraint on the level of productive activity for the next time period.

The spatial flows of people, goods and services are fundamental features of an urban system. A distinction can be made between products from footloose sectors which are transferable between zones, and products which are not normally transferable, namely local products. Since the products of local sectors must be used within the zone where they are produced, the flow-stock relations in that case take a closed form similar to the usual dynamic Leontief (1966) model. For footloose sectors, flows of people and goods between zones and between the metropolis and the rest of the world must be taken into account.

The broad structure of the urban version of model is depicted in Fig. 6. It is essentially a set of relationship between (i) the urban population in different zones; (ii) the productive activities in different sectors and zones; and (iii) the flows of people, goods and services on a transport network with certain distance-cost characteristics.

These relationships are expressed in mathematical form using a set of linear constraint equations. We shall begin with the (internal and joint) relational constraints. Notation for the following is given in the Appendix.

Population-workforce relationship (internal constraints)

In this relationship, the labour required to produce output in each zone is equated to the total workforce employed in the zone, the latter being expressed as a function of the metropolitan population times the zonal employment activity rate, ie.,

Labour required for production in zone r = Workforce employed in zone r

$$\sum_{i}^{N} \lambda_{it}^{r} X_{it}^{r} = \alpha_{t}^{r} P_{t} \tag{14}$$

for all time periods t; $r=1, N_{ZON}$.

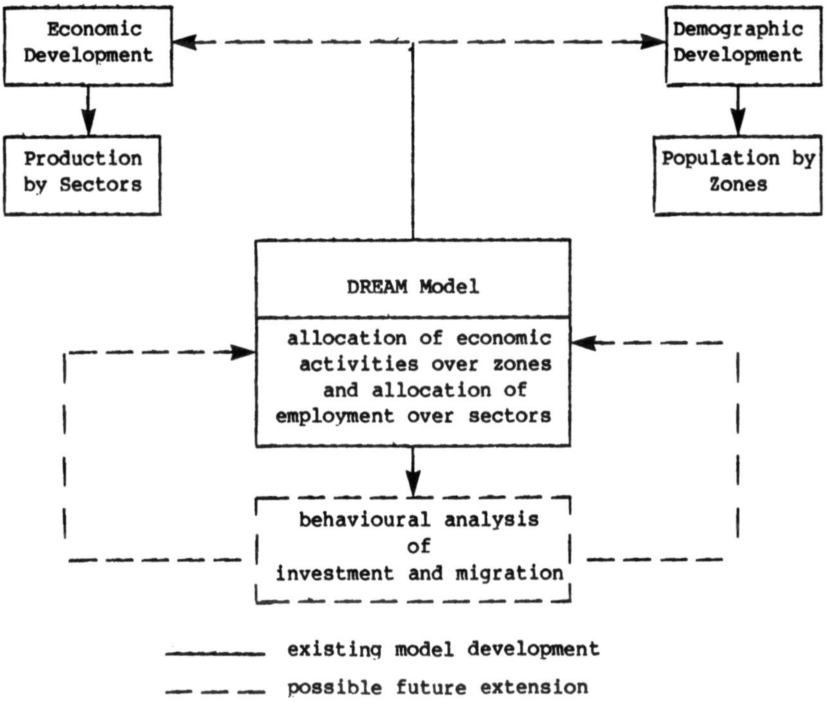

Figure 6 - Basic Structure of the Model

Zonal production relationship (internal constraints)

The dynamic input-output relationship of Leontief (1966) is adopted for flows between local sectors. In this relationship, the output from local sector i is consumed in part by other sectors j, and the remainder is required for stocks or investment by sectors j for production in a later time period

Zonal output of sector i - Input demand of sectors j (including consumption) - Capital demand of sector i by sectors j = 0

$$X_{it}^{r} - \sum_{j}^{N+1} a_{ij} X_{jt}^{r} - \sum_{j}^{N} b_{ij}^{r} I_{jt}^{r} = 0 \tag{15}$$

for $i \in I_{LOC}$; all t; $r=1, N_{ZON}$.

Production-investment-capacity relationship (internal constraints)

The zonal output of any sector i cannot exceed the available zonal capacity at time t

$$X^{r}_{it} \leq C^{r}_{it} \tag{16}$$

where the total capacity is equal to the depreciated capacity at time (t-1) to t

$$C^{r}_{ij} = \gamma_t C^{r}_{i(t-1)} + q_t I^{r}_{it} + h_t I^{r}_{i(t-1)} \tag{17}$$

Eqns. (16) and (17) may be combined into a more convenient form as follows

Output for sector i	-	Depreciated investments over previous periods	$\leq$	Depreciated initial capacity

$$X^{r}_{it} - \sum_{p=1,t} \frac{\rho_{it}}{\rho_{ip}} (q_p I^{r}_{ip} + h_p I^{r}_{i(p-1)}) \leq \rho_{it} C^{r}_{i0} \tag{18}$$

for i = 1, N; all t: r=1, N_{ZON}.

Economic activity for footloose sectors (joint constraints)

It is assumed that the total levels of economic activities for footloose sectors are to be constrained to projected target values at certain points in time

Total output over all zones = Target output

$$\Sigma X^{r}_{it} = \overline{X}_{it} \tag{19}$$

for $i \in I_{MOB}$: r=1, N_{ZON}; $t \in T_A$.

An alternative to having a strict equality is to relax the constraint to allow total economic activity to be greater than or equal to a minimum target value. In the latter situation, this constraint would be reclassified as an achievement constraint.

Flow Relationships (joint constraints)

Modified gravity models can be derived by entropy maximizing methods to calculate (i) the commodity flows from footloose sectors to all other sectors within and between zones, and (ii) the flows of employees to and from their workplaces within and between zones. The form of the gravity model is consistent with the Leontief relationship (eqn. 15) applied to footloose sectors (the formulation of an urban input-output model based on the microstates approach to entropy modelling can be found in Batten and Roy, 1982). The commodity flows f^{rs}_{ij} are constrained by the following origin and destination relations (time subscripts suppressed)

$$\sum_j \sum_s f_{ij}^{rs} = X_i^r \tag{20}$$

for r=1, N_{ZON}; for all j,s;

$$\sum_r f_{ij}^{rs} = a_{ij} X_j^s + b_{ij}^s I_j \tag{21}$$

for s=1, N_{ZON}; for all i,j,r

Similar constraints apply to the employees' trips to work. Note that flows from sectors outside the system and flows to sectors outside the system are not constrained. The outside supply and demand are assumed to absorb any flows into and out of the zonal system.

The total cost for different kinds of shipments from i to j is expressed by

$$\sum_r \sum_s c_{ij}^{rs} f_{ij}^{rs} = \bar{c}_{ij} \tag{22}$$

for all i,j, and the most probable distribution of flows can be found by maximizing the following entropy function (Shannon, 1948)

$$U = - \sum_{ijrs} f_{ij}^{rs} \log(f_{ij}^{rs}) \tag{23}$$

subject to eqns. (20) through (22). If a priori flow data exist, the maximum likelihood distribution may be improved by incorporating these flows into the objective function (in a similar form to eqn. 3).

In the above model, the production (X_{it}^r), investment (I_{jt}^r) and population (P_t^r) levels in each zone are the decision variables. The original formulation was completed by maximizing a single objective (eg., net exports less transporation costs) or a weighted sum of various objectives (e.g. employment, consumption and pollution expressed in terms of the above decision variables), expressed in linear or quasi-quadratic form. Such model formulations can be solved using iterative linear programming (Karlqvist et al, 1978) or entropy-maximizing techniques (Eriksson, 1981).

The specification of multi-objective welfare functions a priori (as weighted sums of various objectives) presupposes complete information about all the possible actions and the specific tradeoffs between these actions. In reality, this information is rarely available. Rather than weight the objectives beforehand, it is preferable to express them as target levels in the form of achievement constraints. The following constraints are typical examples which correspond to the pursuit of satisfactory employment and consumption levels in each zone.

Employment Constraints (achievement constraints)

The level of employment activity in any zone has an upper limit which is dependent on available labour. It is also desirable to control the level of unemployment by setting a lower limit on activity rate

$$\alpha^r_{t_{min}} \leq \alpha^r_t \leq \alpha^r_{t_{max}} \tag{24}$$

for all t; r=1, N_{REG}.

Eqns. (14) and (24) may be combined as follows

$$\alpha^r_{t_{min}} P_t \leq \sum_i^N \lambda^r_{it} X^r_{it} \leq \alpha^r_{t_{max}} P_t \tag{25}$$

for all t; r=1, N_{REG}.

Structural unemployment constraints (achievement constraints)

From political, social and technical considerations it may be desirable to limit the maximum increase or decrease in workforce in a sector in a zone over a period of time

Lower limit	$\leq$	Workforce change per year over period (t-1) to t	$\leq$	Upper limit	
$e^r_{it_{min}}$	$\leq$	e^r_{it}	$\leq$	$e^r_{it_{max}}$	(26)

The workforce at time t is related to the workforce at (t-1) as follows

$$\lambda^r_{it} X^r_{it} = (1+e^r_{it})^{(m_t - m_{t-1})} \lambda^r_{i(t-1)} X^r_{i(t-1)} \tag{27}$$

Minimum consumption constraints (achievement constraints)

A minimum per capita level of consumption (or minimum per capita wage rate) may be desirable to ensure a basic living standard in each zone

$$X^r_{it} \geq w^r P^r_t \tag{28}$$

for all t; i=N+1; r=1, N_{REG}.

Also, as an optional additional constraint, it may be desirable to equalize per capita consumption over all zones

$$X^1_{it}/P^1_t = Z^2_{it}/P^2_t = \ldots = X^r_{it}/P^r_t \tag{29}$$

for all t; i=N+1; r=1, N_{ZON} A number of other achievement constraints can be formulated in a similar manner.

CONCLUSIONS

Adaptive learning procedures are an appropriate tool for the interactive evaluation of multilevel and multistage compromise solutions. By developing a composite multidimensional methodology which is flexible enough to encompass the complete typology of multiobjective programming models and multicriteria evaluation models, the full set of interdependencies within conflicting subsystems and between conflicting goals can be assessed. The resulting compromise approach corresponds to a Harmonious Adaptive Learning Procedure (HALP).

When the dimension of time is included a much richer variety of decision-making options and learning procedures arises. Urban planning is clearly a dynamic process in which investment decisions taken at one point in time have a dominant but delayed impact on the feasible trajectory of urban development. Conflict management is therefore a multistage process in which goal conflicts can either be resolved simultaneously or sequentially over time. The notion of compromise trajectories has been demonstrated using a development planning model in which resource allocation in an urban system is determined by a step-wise interactive planning scheme of multistage decision processes at the metropolitan and local levels.

REFERENCES

Atkinson, R.C., Bower, G.H. and Clothers, E.J., 1965, An Introduction to Mathematical Learning Theory, John Wiley, New York.

Batten, D.F., 1983, Spatial Analysis of Interacting Economies, Kluwer-Nijhoff, Boston, MA.

Batten, D.F. and Andersson, S.E., 1983, Towards a Hierarchical System of Models to Coordinate National and Regional Economic Developments, Papers, Regional Science Association, 51, 21-41.

Batten, D.F. and Roy, J.R., 1982, Entropy and Economic Modelling, Environment and Planning A, 14, 1047-1061.

Blair, P., 1978, Multi-objective Regional Energy Planning, Martinus Nijhoff, Boston, MA.

Cochrane, J.L. and Zeleny, M., 1973, Multiple Criteria Decision-Making, University of South Carolina Press, Columbia, SC.

Cohon, J.L., 1978, Multiobjective Programming and Planning, Academic Press, New York.

van Delft, A. and Nijkamp, P., 1977, Multi-Criteria Analysis and Regional Decision-Making, Martinus Nijhoff, Boston, MA.

Eriksson, J., 1980, A Note on the Solution of Large Sparse Maximum Entropy Problems with Linear Equality Constraints, Mathematical Programming, 18, 146-154.

Eriksson, J., 1981, Algorithms for Entropy and Mathematical Programming, Doctoral Dissertation, Department of Mathematics, University of Linkoping, Linkoping, Sweden.

Granholm, A. and Ohlsson, O., 1975, A Note on Distribution Analysis in a Linear Programming Model, Regional Science and Urban Economics, 5, 483-491.

Hafkamp, W. and Nijkamp, P., 1981, Multiobjective Modelling for Economic-Environmental Policies, Environment and Planning A, 13, 7-18.

Hilgard, E.R. and Bower, G.H., 1966, Theories of Learning, Appleton-Century-Crofts, New York.

Johansen, L., 1978, Lectures on Macroeconomic Planning, North Holland, Amsterdam.

Karlqvist, A., Sharpe, R., Batten, D.F. and Brotchie, J.F., 1978, A Regional Planning Model and its Application to South-Eastern Australia, Regional Science and Urban Economics, 8, 57-86.

Keeney, R.L. and Raiffa, H., 1976, Decision Analysis with Multiple Conflicting Objectives, John Wiley, New York.

Kornai, J., 1975, Mathematical Planning of Structural Decision, North Holland, Amsterdam.

Kullback, S., 1959, Information Theory and Statistics, John Wiley, New York.

Leontief, W.W., 1966, Input-Output Economics, Oxford University Press, London.

Lesse, P. and Sharpe, R., 1980, A Control Theory Approach to Regional Stagnation, in Buhr, W. and Friedrich, P. (Eds.), Regional Development under Stagnation, Nomos Verlag, Baden-Baden, West Germany.

Mesarovic, M.D., Macko, D. and Takahara, Y., 1970, Theory of Hierarchical, Multilevel Systems, Academic Press, New York.

Nijkamp, P., 1977, Theory and Application of Environmental Economics, North-Holland, Amsterdam.

Nijkamp, P., 1979, Multidimensional Approaches to Environmental Analyses: A Non-Technical Survey, Man, Environment, Space and Time, 1, 64-95.

Nijkamp, P. and Rietveld, P., 1976, Multi-Objective Programming Models: New Ways in Regional Decision-Making, Regional Science and Urban Economics, 6, 253-274.

Nijkamp, P. and Rietveld, P., 1981, Multiobjective Multi-Level Policy Models: An Application to Regional and Environmental Planning, European Economic Review, 15, 63-89.

Rietveld, P., 1980, Multiple Objective Decision Methods and Regional Planning, North Holland, Amsterdam.

Roy, J.R. and Batten, D.F., 1983, An Approach to Modelling Multilevel Decisions in Urban Systems, submitted to Sistemi Urbani.

Shannon, C.E., 1948, A Mathematical Theory of Communication, Bell System Technical Journal, 27, 379-423 and 623-656.

Sharpe, R. and Batten, D.F., 1976, A DREAM Model for Regional Economic Planning, Papers, Regional Science Association, Australian-New Zealand Section, 1, 3-18.

Sharpe, R., Batten, D.F. and Anderson, M., 1981, Dynamic Modelling of an Urban Economy, Proceedings, 8th European Symposium on Urban Data Management MG2/6, 1-10.

Spronk, J., 1981, Interactive Multiple Goal Programming: Applications to Financial Planning, Martinus Nijhoff, Boston, MA.

Voogd, H., 1982, Multicriteria Evaluation for Urban and Regional Planning, Pion, London.

Wallenius, J., 1975, Interactive Multiple Criteria Decision Methods, Helsinki School of Economics, Helsinki, Finland.

Zeleny, M., 1974, Linear Multiobjective Programming, Springer, Berlin.

Zeleny, M., 1982, Multicriteria Decision-Making, McGraw Hill, New York.

APPENDIX

NOTATION FOR SECTION 5

a_{ij} = production or technical input-output coefficient.
= quantity of sector i absorbed per unit of total output of sector j.

b^r_{ij} = capital coefficient (urbanized)
= capital or stock of goods produced by sector i which sector j must hold per unit of its full capacity output for use in a later time period.

$\bar{c}_{ij}$ = transport cost per unit distance per unit flow from sector i to sector j.

c^{rs}_{ij} = transport cost per unit flow from sector i to sector j over path r-s.
= $D^{rs}\ \bar{c}_{ij}$.

C^r_{it} = zonal capacity to produce output i at time t.

C^r_{i0} = initial zonal capacity for output i.

d_i = depreciation rate for sector i.

D^{rs} = trip distance between zone r and zone s.

d^r_{it} = change in workforce per year in sector i of zone r over period (t-1) to t.

f^{rs}_{ijt} = average flow from sector i in zone r to sector j i n zone s over time

γ_t, g_t, h_t = constants implicitv defined in eqn. (17).

I_{MOB} = subset of footloose sectors.

I_{LOC} = subset of local sectors.

I^r_{jt} = level of capital investment per year in sector j in zone r at time t.

m_t = number of years from base year to the end of period t.

n_{ij} = gravity exponent for flows between sectors i and j.

N_{ZON} = number of zones (excluding rest of world).

N = total number of footloose plus local sectors.

N=1 = consumption sector.

P^r_t = projected population level in zone r in time t.

R = rest of world zone.

T = number of time periods.

T_A = subset of time periods for constraint eqn. (20).

W^r = minimum level of consumption or wage rate per capita in zone r.

X^r_{it} = level of output for sector i in zone r at time t.

$\overline{X}_{it}$ = total projected or target level of output for footloose sector i over all zones at time t.

α_t^r = activity employment rate (no. of workers per unit population) in zone r at time t.

λ_{it}^r = zonal labour-output coefficient at time t for sector i, zone r.

ρ_{it} = depreciation factor for sector i at time t.

$= (1-d_i)^{m_t}$.

Spatial Interaction

ON HOUSEHOLD TRAVEL CIRCUIT BENEFITS AND THEIR LOCATIONAL IMPLICATIONS

Frank Southworth
Transportation Group
Energy Division
Oak Ridge National Laboratory
P.O. Box X
Oak Ridge, TN 37831
United States of America

Abstract. A circuit-based measure of a household's locational accessibility to a variety of urban land uses is presented, using the workplaces of household members to derive an extended measure of locational benefit. The approach is then used to look at the other side of the problem: the implications for the accessibility of public and private facilities to the population of households they serve. Removing destinations from the system may affect the frequency of visits to other destinations both positively or negatively, in the latter case through the loss of circuitous travel options.

INTRODUCTION

Multi-destination daily travel circuits have been shown by a number of authors to be very popular with urban dwellers (see, for example, Hemmens, 1970; Vidakovich, 1974; Horowitz, 1978; Hanson, 1980; O'Kelly, 1981; Kitamura, 1982). Of particular interest to the urban planner are multi-purpose travel circuits since they link together a mixture of land uses and therefore have a significant bearing upon the efficiency of urban land use configuration. This paper is concerned with the tracing of a household's typical (say weekly) travel activity pattern. The emphasis is placed upon development of a model that will allow us to reproduce the sort of spatial interactions such household members typically have with their surrounding urban environment. In particular, the research focuses upon the development of circuit-based measures of locational accessibility. In the second part of the paper a new approach to the definition of a household's locational advantage with respect to multi-purpose travel opportunities is presented. This approach recognizes the importance of fixed workplace locations in the formation of multi-destination travel chaining. In the following section this approach is applied in the reverse context: that of recognizing a public or private facility's accessibility to its customer households. A numerical example is presented for a 15 shop, 7 recreation, 8 residental and 2 workplace location system. Finally, a brief summary is offered, and some remarks directed towards further research in this area.

To date very little progress has been made towards the explicit inclusion of travel circuits into our transportation planning models (or, for that matter into our policies). Since Marble's (1964) paper, a number of authors have tried to apply simple Markov chaining models to the problem (see Hanson, 1979, for a review). More recently, and supported by the empirical and statistical evidence provided by such authors as Kitamura and Kermanshah (1982), more elaborate trip linking models have been considered. While some recent beginnings in this area may be noted (such as Richardson and Young's (1982) two destination, single circuit logit model, O'Kelly's multi-shop trip model making use of Howard's (1976) methods, Lerman's (1979) semi-Markov trip chaining, mode and travel frequency model, and Kobayashi's (1979) travel corridor study), none of our more generally applicable urban travel models recognize either the presence or even the impact of multi-destination, multi-purpose travel circuits. The model presented below is a first operational version of a computer program called CIRCUS. The objective in developing CIRCUS (CIRCUit Selection model) is to generalize travel allocation models to incorporate all forms and levels of spatial interaction between any number of spatially separated locations. For the present paper it will be assumed that the automobile is universally available for multi-purpose travel circuits. The most popular approach to measuring the locational accessibility and of an household H to a set of spatially dispersed opportunities is to use a potential measure such as the Hansen (1959) index, for each trip purpose separately

$$a_H = \sum_{j \in J(H)} W_j^{\alpha} \exp(-\beta c_{Hj}) \qquad (1)$$

where W_j = attractiveness of destination j (usually a volume based index); c_{Hj} = cost of an H to j trip; α = activity size parameter; β = travel cost sensitivity parameter; and J(H) = relevant destination set. A combined, multi-purpose index then requires as appropriate cross-purpose weighting scheme, as discussed below.

Such a measure covers only direct diadic spatial interactions, and as such considerably oversimplifies the functional organizations of the activity space involved (Rouget, 1972; White, 1979; Southworth, 1982a,b; for discussion on this point, and for alternative graph-theoretic, point-pattern, and utility-based approaches respectively). As White (1979) concludes: "Moreover, it must now be recognized that individual facility accessibility may diverge considerably from, and may be sub-optimal when compared with, facility 'system' accessibility, ie., accessibility to a linked set of services required by users." The important word here is linked.

If, as Hensher (1976) claims, we can miss up to 30 percent of all tripmaking by ignoring multi-destination circuits, then to avoid modelling them can only give us a rather vague, and almost certainly misleading conception of how households will view, and will respond to, the siting of new urban facilities. Since the connectivity between households and service facilities is likely to be circuit-based, then the facility siting(s) plan should take this behaviour into account.

THE NEW APPROACH TO MEASURING LOCATIONAL ACCESSIBILITY

The Importance of Work Location to Household Accessibility

A largely neglected feature of the household's travel activity pattern is the important role played by the workplace(s) and, where appropriate, the school(s) as fixed extensions of the base of regular activities. Restricting subsequent discussion to the work location, such a location frequently acts as either an important transfer point or as a satellite terminal in the daily travel schedule of household members. In the former case, late afternoon and evening travel may begin from the workplace, prior to return home. In the latter case lunch-time work-based circuits may be made. The daily presence of a household member at such a work site ensures its importance to the household's overall locational accessibility.

Fig. 1 shows graphically this notion of an extended activity area. If we take boundaries A1 and A2 to represent the outer limits of home (H) and workplace (W) based circuits respectively, then the separation of H from W shown serves to extend the areal coverage of the household's travel activity pattern. (Of course the regularity of the areas shown is for illustrative purposes only here). Also shown in Fig. 1 are the sorts of circuits we might expect to find under such a home-workplace separation. Specifically, the following types of circuit are hypothesised (and substantiated by a number of empirical studies, as discussed in section 4 below)

1. simple single destination round-trip circuits, based on H (eg., circuit H-4-H in Fig. 1);
2. multi-destination H based circuits (eg., H-1-2-3-H; H-9-10-11-H);
3. simple work based circuits (eg., W-8-W); and
4. home-work-other travel circuits (eg., H-W-5-6-H; H-W-7-H).

No destinations out of the home and prior to arrival at the workplace are shown. Nor is the situation in which a second workplace is sufficiently close to the first that it encourages a carpooling to work circuit. What is shown in Fig. 1 are two different types of H-based multi-destination circuit: the clustered destination set (9-10-11) and the dispersed destination set (1-2-3). Also shown is the potential for a significantly large spatial separation of home and workplace to act as a factor in bringing within the household's travel hinterland such locations as destination 7, through the potential for a circuit of the type H-W-7-H. If, for example, we hypothesize a distance-decay function based on points H and W (see top right of Fig. 1), then we might expect a much less steep decay in the demand to visit locations such as 5, 6 and 7 where a significant amount of travel occurs between leaving work and returning home.

It is with the types of circuits shown in Fig. 1 that the rest of this paper will be concerned. This includes the restriction that all type 3 circuits listed above (ie., H-W-Other-W-H) may contain only a single work-based sub-circuit, typically as a result of time restrictions over the lunch hour. We will also restrict the maximum number of destinations per circuit, not counting the return home, to 3 in the example presented below. This restriction may easily be relaxed; although recent empirical studies suggest that daily travel circuits in urban areas rarely exceed 4 or 5 driving stages (see Richardson and Young, 1982; Kitamura, 1982).

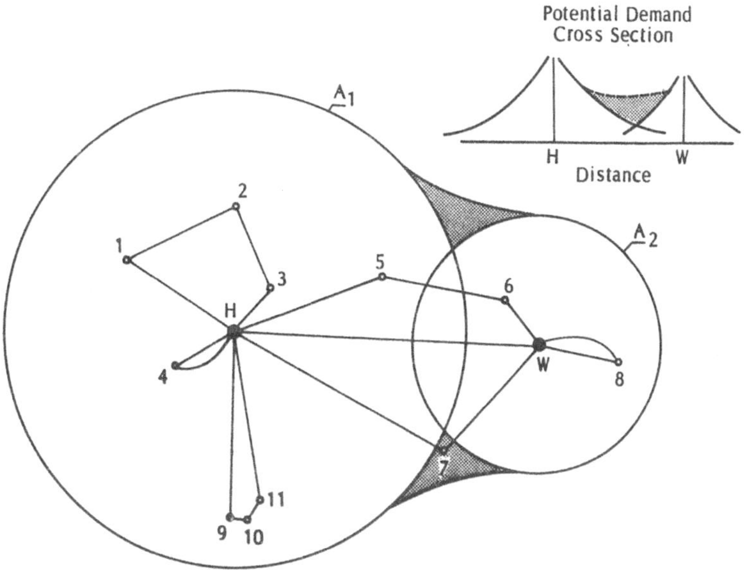

Figure 1 - An Extended Travel Activity Area with Circuit Types

Measuring Circuit-Based Accessibility

To obtain a suitable circuit-based locational benefit statistic, we need the following five pieces of information which we will treat below as five inter-related modelling steps (i) a suitable destination set; (ii) a suitable set of direct travel (ie., trip) connections between relevant diads; (iii) a suitable set of circuits (ie., trip sequences); (iv) a suitable measure of travel cost; and (v) a suitable measure of travel benefit.

Each of these steps poses problems for the urban modeller. We do not have a well defined procedure for specifying destination sets in any form of spatial analysis to date; and this problem is exacerbated by the inclusion of circuits, since any destination may owe its inclusion to one or more other destinations also being present in that same set. At the same time such destinations may also be competing for travellers who are limited in their activity levels by travel time and other cost constraints (the usual assumption of spatial interaction modelling). However, by tracing all likely circuits, subject to one or more empirically validated circuit duration and/or length rules, the possibility now exists to more realistically define the potential destination set of any household. Within large urban areas, where most households will have daily travel activity patterns covering only a small portion of the full urban system, the recognition of circuit-size constraints offers a more readily believable basis for destination set selection than any simple point (=house) based distance or cost decay rule. Subsequent destination elimination conditions might then be imposed to suit the socio-economic characteristics of the household members, as in a non-circuit based model. This notion, then, suggests that an information updating procedure may be feasible, through which better information on the structure of a household's trip circuits pattern leads to a better representation of the appropriate destination set such members choose to visit.

Such a procedure is represented by an iterative feedback loop in the computational model presented in Fig. 2. This figure shows in flow-chart form the structure of the computational model used to operationalize the above five step procedure. As noted earlier, this program has been called CIRCUS.

As a starting point we may invoke a simple distance based or areal coverage rule to obtain such a destination set. Given such a set, the next step is to determine which pairs of destinations ought to be linked directly, by what are termed trips below. Such trips form the basic links in the circuit-based travel chaining activity we are seeking to model. By eliminating from further consideration all highly unlikely direct diadic interactions at an early stage, we can considerably reduce the computational burden to be placed upon the subsequent circuit building algorithm. One option is to use a simple travel distance or, more generally, travel cost cut-off rule. A second option is to use a logistic spatial interaction model to obtain the likelihood $p(i,p|j)$ of a significant level of tripmaking to fulfill purpose p at location i, given current location j, and then apply the following rule (see Southworth, 1982a, 1983 for tests using such a rule to build urban truck circuits).

$$\lambda_{ji} = 1 \text{ if } P(i,p|j) \geq e \qquad (2)$$
$$= 0 \text{ otherwise}$$

where, for example

$$P(i,p|j) = \frac{\exp(\alpha_i^p \ln W_i^p - \beta c_{ji}p)}{\sum_{i \in J(H)} \exp(\alpha^p \ln W_i^p - \beta c_{ji}p)} \tag{3}$$

and where e is a suitably chosen cut-off probability.

The result is to produce a binary direct interaction matrix $\{\lambda_{ij}\}$. If a j to i diad has a 0 assigned to it, it is no longer considered in the subsequent circuit-building step. Other trip linkage inclusion rules besides eqns. (2)-(3) may be developed and considered, with perhaps a mixture of such rules being necessary to a multi-purpose travel chaining model.

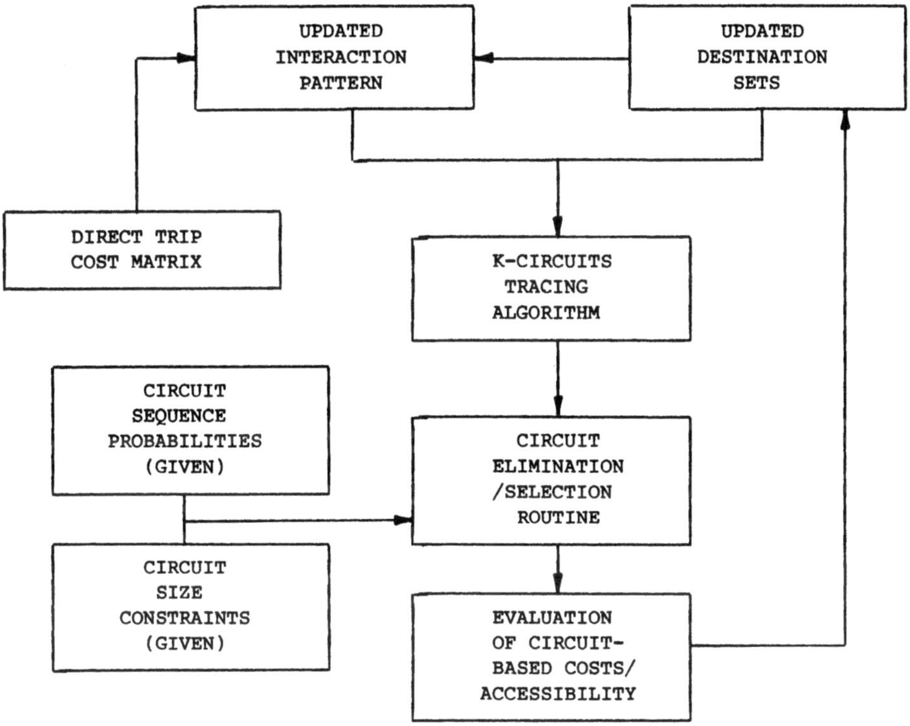

Figure 2. Flow Diagrams of Major Modelling Steps

The third step in this process is to define an appropriate set of circuits, through an appropriate set of trip chaining rules. The current model accomplishes this with the aid of Shier's (1974) Bureau of Standards program for tracing the k shortest paths between any two locations on a graph. Using the double-sweep method of path enumeration and information storage, the algorithm can at present generate twenty paths between any origin-destination pair. From such paths many more circuits can be extracted (300 circuits per origin were generated from the numerical example reported below). Referring again to Fig. 2, we now remove from this circuit set any unacceptable circuits. Any circuit which does not fit into the above defined four member typology is rejected. This includes all circuits in which any destination is visited more than once: notably the many redundant (ie., self-looping) circuits generated by the algorithm. It also included any circuits considered to be too costly, or to have too many trips. Given this reduced circuit set, a weighting procedure is then made available, by which the modeller can reduce the impact of less likely multi-purpose trip sequences upon the subsequent circuit cost and benefits averaging procedure, using prior information on the purpose sequence probabilities for different circuit sizes (ie., different numbers of trips per circuit).

To obtain the net spatial benefits associated with any site, this k-shortest path building algorithm can be used in one of two ways. We can either replace the idea of shortest by cheapest, build circuitous paths, and then derive the benefits associated with the resulting destination set; or we can deal with both travel costs and benefits simultaneously within the circuit-building process, as described by Southworth (1982a, 1982b). As an alternative to the use of this circuit constructing routine, we could also use a weighted matrix multiplication procedure on our binary interation matrix, to obtain the 1,2,3... powers of accessibility of H to its previously defined destination set (Rouget, 1972; Southworth, 1983). Whichever computational approach we choose, the most difficult problem at the conceptual level remains that of specifying an appropriate spatial benefits measure, against which to trade off the more easily averaged travel costs.

For N=4 (trips), we have the following total circuits cost measure, C(H)

$$C(H) = 2\left(\sum_{j=1}^{N} c_{Hj}\lambda_{Hj}\right) + \left(\sum_{\substack{j=1 \\ j\neq i}}^{N} \sum_{i=1}^{N} c_{HjiH}\lambda_{HjiH}\right) + \left[2\left(\sum_{\substack{j=1 \\ j\neq i}}^{J} \sum_{i=j}^{N} c_{ji}\lambda_{ji}\right) + \sum_{\substack{j=1 \\ j\neq i\neq \ell}}^{N} \sum_{i=1}^{N} \sum_{\ell=1}^{N} c_{Hji\ell H}\lambda_{HjiH}\right)\right] \quad (4)$$

where, for example

$$\lambda_{Hji\ell H} = \lambda_{Hj}\lambda_{ji}\lambda_{i\ell}\lambda_{\ell H} \quad (5)$$

and where j=1....J refers to the set of fixed workplace (and school) destinations used by members of H, and j=J+1,....N refers to other purpose specific destinations (such as the shop and recreation nodes used in the simplified system used below). The first term on the RHS of eqn. (4) refers to single destination circuits, the second to three trip circuits, and the third term to four trip circuits, including work-based secondary circuits as well as the H-W-other-H type.

If we let B(H) represent the total benefits associated with such a circuits set, and let b refer to the benefit of visiting any given location, we might also consider summing benefits in a similar manner, giving

$$B(H) = (\sum_{j=1}^{N} \lambda_{Hj} b_j) + [\sum_{\substack{j=1 \\ j \neq i}}^{N} \sum_{i=1}^{N} \lambda_{HjiH}(b_j + b_i)] + (\sum_{\substack{j=1 \\ j \neq i \neq \ell}}^{J} \sum_{i=j+1}^{N} \lambda_{ji} b_i)$$

$$+ [\sum_{\substack{j=1 \\ j \neq i \neq \ell}}^{N} \sum_{i=1}^{N} \sum_{\ell=1}^{N} \lambda_{HjiH}(b_j + b_i + b_\ell)] \quad (6)$$

However, such a summation poses a number of conceptual as well as practical problems. First, we have to consider whether we should really be including any purpose specific destination more than once, rather than once per circuit as above. Second, we need to consider the across-purpose weighting schemes most appropriate to a set of potentially widely different travel activity frequencies. Are destination purposes with higher frequencies of visitation to be assigned more importance in our definition of accessibility? Since the frequency of visits to some destinations may rest on the availability of a multi-purpose circuit or circuits, this latter problem is rendered more difficult to deal with than it would be under a conventional interaction modelling approach. Such issues have not to date been confronted by urban modellers. The specification of circuit-based locational benefits remains an interesting, yet rather difficult area for future research. Following Muraco's (1972) multi-index investigation of direct connectivity potential, we might simply count destinations visited in eqn. (6) above (ie., all b's=1.0), and calculate average cost per trip. We could then look for other measures of the benefit or attractiveness of this destination set, such as the activity size indices typically used in eqn. (1), and try to integrate these two bits of information in some way (a sort of multi-dimensional approach to the definition of locational accessibility). The sort of destination benefit measurement most useful is left open in this paper. The numerical example given below places most of its emphasis upon the problem of selecting an appropriate circuits set, and simply counts each time a destination is visited as one extra benefit. This gives the average cost C_H per circuit-based trip as

$$\bar{C}'_H = C(H)/B(H) \quad (7)$$

Implications for Facility Location

If we take the above representation of a household's locational accessibility as a realistic one, then it poses an interesting question for the location of both public facilities such as hospitals, and for private facilities such as shopping malls and recreational centres. Consider one such facility, located at j. The accessibility of H to j may be obtained by extracting all j-inclusive circuits from eqn. (7) above. Turning the problem around, j's accessibility to different H locations may be assessed relative to the accessibility of other activity centres in the area. If we now let r refer to a particular circuit, and define R(j) to be the set of all j-inclusive circuits sets of relevance, summing over all H residences given

$$\bar{c}'_j = [\sum_{r \in R(j)} (c(r)/n(r))]/n(j) \tag{8}$$

where n(r) refers to the number of destinations visited on circuit r (not counting the return to base H) and n(j) refers to the number of circuits involving destination j.

Now if we let θ refer to the probability of taking the particular multi-purpose trip sequence implied by circuit r, we get the following weighted average cost per circuit-based trip measure

$$\tilde{c}'_j = [\sum_{r \in R(j)} (c(r)/n(r))\theta(r)]/n(j) \tag{9}$$

The heart of the allocation of households to service facilities problem now becomes one of specifying the appropriate contribution of each circuit r to j's ability to remain accessible to (or to attract custom from) H. It is worth noting also that in order to derive a suitable measure of a facility's circuit-based accessibility to its customers, we need to first of all build such circuits from the point of view of the customers themselves (ie., the households). We cannot simply assume the sort of mirror accessibility indices produced by direct spatial interaction models to be applicable. That is, simply substituting an origin attraction weight for a destination attraction weight in an index such as eqn. (1) above will no longer suffice. Circuits must be built from the household (plus work) location. The public or private facility's locational benefit measure is then a derivative of this.

Alternatively, we can use this notion of average trip cost within a probabilistic weighting procedure. For example, if we assume that the choice of a circuit r is a logistic function of its average trip cost, then we have the following log-sum averaged (circuit-based) travel cost

$$\approx{c}'_j = \ln \sum_{r \in R(j)} \exp(-\beta(c(r)/n(r))\theta_r) \tag{10}$$

where β is a cost per trip sensitivity parameter.

If we also have prior information concerning preferences across the destination set, both within and between purposes, then we can use a second log-sum averaging procedure to include this circuit-averaged cost weighting within a subsequent destination allocation phase. If we let q(j) represent this prior probability of selecting location j, then we get the following measure of the circuit-based average cost per trip out of location H, where J(H) refers here to the relevant H-based destination set, and $\tilde{c}'_{JH}$ refers to the log-sum averaged H to j circuit travel cost (ie., H's contribution to R(j))

$$\tilde{c}'_H = \ln \sum_{j \in J(H)} \exp(-\lambda \tilde{c}'_{jH}\, q(j)) \tag{11}$$

The relevant j-based accessibility might use a similar prior q(H), if such data could be justified as useful and reliable information.

A NUMERICAL EXAMPLE

As an example of the program's performance, consider the multi-location system shown in Fig. 3. The point locations in this system are based on the position of each of 15 major shopping centres, and 7 recreational centres (cinemas, arenas, restaurants) in the town of Champaign-Urbana, in east-central Illinois. The two work sites are located on the University of Illinois campus, which dominates the town's employment. The 8 home locations used are randomly selected residental areas within the town. Typical in-vehicle plus parking time between each pair of locations is used as the measure of spatial separation in the tests reported below. There is relatively little traffic congestion in the town, but parking times do serve to reduce slightly the apparent relative advantage of the closer locational pairs shown. No attempt was made to reproduce existing travel patterns: the town's spatial structure was used only to help the author recognize any unlikely travel circuits generated by the model, given his close familiarity with the town's makeup.

The following system-wide circuit size and sequence probabilities were used in the testing reported below (based on the figures given by Kitamura, 1982) (i) single destination (ie., two trip) home-based circuits: 0.60; (ii) multi-destination (ie., 3 or 4 trip) non-work circuits: 0.20; (iii) home-work-other-work-home circuits: 0.15; and (iv) home-work-other-home circuits: 0.05. The results of some initial tests are shown in Fig. 3, which is used to compare four different measures of system average cost per trip, from each of the 17 shop and/or recreational activity (R) locations. Five of these activity locations contained both of these activities, and are circled in Fig. 3. No further trip purpose breakdown is considered (eg., durable versus non-durable goods shopping). The example is illustrative only. The four average trip cost measures computed are the following (i) a simple average cost of travel from location j to all 8 residential (H) locations in the system ($\bar{c}_j$); (ii) the circuit-based average cost from j to all locations, using eqn. (8) above, ($\bar{c}'_j$); (iii) the circuit-based average cost per trip from j to all locations, using the above circuit-type weightings, using eqn. (9) above, $(\tilde{c}'_j)$; and (iv) the log-sum averaged circuit-based cost per trip, using eqn. (10) above, weighted by the same circuit sequence probability as in 3, $(\tilde{\tilde{c}}'_j)$. For demonstration purposes a value of $\beta = 2.0$ was used, and the natural log of average within-circuit trip cost, $[c(r)/n(r)]$, was taken, (ie., we adopted the Newtonian gravity model for the initial testing).

To obtain the three circuit-based indices, (ii)-(iv) above, 300 circuits were generated out of each of the 8 household locations shown, from which were removed any circuits not falling into one of the four types of circuit described above. In addition H-W1-W2-H and H-W1-W2-Other-H carpooling circuits were allowed to occur out of each household location (as well as H-W2-W1-(other)-H circuits). All pairs of locations were allowed a direct trip connection in the initial tests. All results reported in this paper refer to a spatial system in which all destinations are equally weighted with respect to their attractiveness. The results may therefore be taken to reflect different notions of system connectivity, which imply an unweighted version of spatial accessibility.

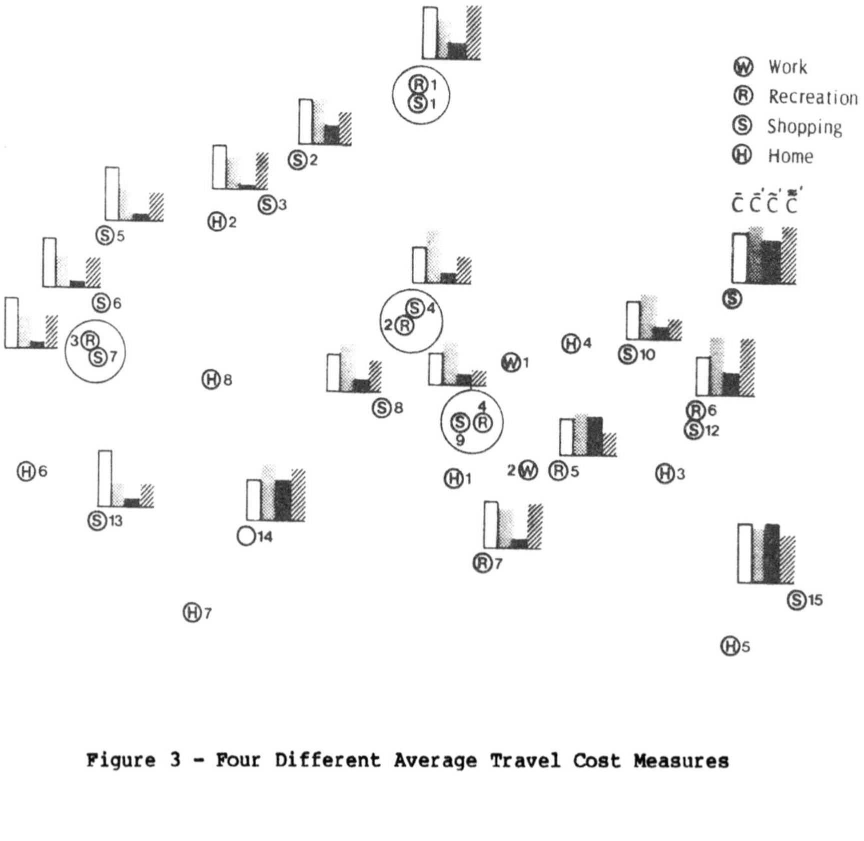

Figure 3 - Four Different Average Travel Cost Measures

The simple average cost per trip index $\bar{c}$ shows the expected result: central facility locations are more accessible on average than are peripheral ones. This index serves as our base for comparison. The cost per circuit-based trip index $\bar{c}'$ ranks the 17 activity locations quite differently, with some central facility locations having higher access costs per circuit based trip than a number of the western (ie., left hand side) peripheral locations. Introducing the circuit type probabilities into the picture causes further re-ranking of the activity centre, with the western locations having a particularly low set of average cost per trip statistics. Finally, the log-sum averaged index produces yet another across location ranking scheme, with something of a return to the original, simple $\bar{c}$ ranking scheme.

The sort of circuit-based travel activity patterns generated by the model are shown in Fig. 4, for household locations H1 (centrally located) and H6 (peripherally located). The circled locations in this figure refer to the only (3) activity centres common to both origin locations' destination sets. The key indicates at what stage in the process of circuit building a new trip linkage was introduced into this travel activity pattern. The bench-marks shown are at 60, 100, 200, and 300 circuits. The majority of these circuits, however, contain the redundancies referred to above. For example, of the 300 circuits traced for origin H1, only 47 circuits contained no unacceptable repeat destinations. Of these 47, a further subset might also be removed if we were to introduce additional restrictions on circuit trip purpose sequences. Certainly, if we were to build more circuits, including all 4 and 5 destination chains, many trip purpose sequences (such as H-S-R-S-R-H) might be considered unacceptable behaviour. Such restrictions would mean that the algorithm would need to generate an even larger percentage of unusable circuits as part of the activity pattern building process. The majority of unacceptable circuits formed are of the self-looping type. To date, no simple way of counting such redundant paths has been found for circuits with 4 or more trip linkages (see Luce and Perry, 1949, for a mathematical statement of this problem). Until we can come up with a way of removing redundant paths from such a tracing process, or, alternatively, integrate the circuit tracing and trip purpose selection sequence process in a consistent manner, we must accept this overproduction of circuits as part of the price we pay for an operational model. Application of the model to large-scale (ie., many location) systems, despite the rapid fall in computer costs, may require such a breakthrough if the procedure is to be applicable to much larger problems than the example given here.

SOME FINAL REMARKS

For a suitably validated direct interactions inclusion rule based on eqns. (2)-(3) above, we can now look at the questions of how the addition or removal of one or more destinations affects the selection of any other destination, by adding or removing the appropriate circuit subset. This approach presupposes that such changes in the travel environment will not significantly affect the behaviour of households, except to encourage compensations internal to the new destination set. In theory it allows us to consider the effects of, say, a shopping mall closure upon the patronage of a (not too distant) recreational centre. It also implies that where we have two or more locations providing the same service, that we can recognize both competitive and supportive aspects of the system's spatial organization within a single framework. As such the approach described here offers an alternative to the recent work on destination agglomeration effects in spatial interaction models proposed by Fotheringham (1982).

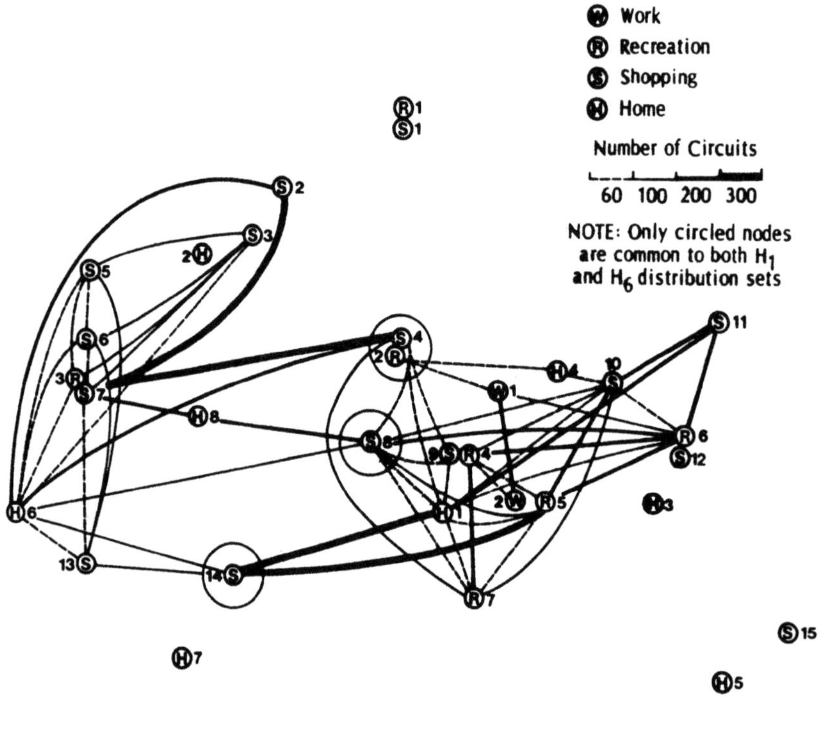

Figure 4 - Two Household Based Circuitous Travel Sets (Simulation)

Finally, it is worth taking a little time to consider just how the data required for the proposed approach might be collected. For an appropriately sampled population, the usual idea of collecting a set of household travel diaries covering a particular week's travel activity pattern may not be sufficient to the needs of a model based on all regularly used circuits. At the risk of commiting sampling heresy, it seems necessary for the analyst to collect data from households on both their frequently used circuits and on those circuits which they consider important to their current life-style. Infrequent, but potentially imperative health-care trips fall into this latter category; and the access to such services from workplace and school as well as from home is likely to be of concern to most families. There is a need, then, to formulate an appropriately worded questionnaire; one less interested in ascertaining trip volume counts than in identifying the physical nature of the household's spatial connectivity pattern and its implications for service (or market) area coverage.

The time-frame covered by such a questionnaire needs further discussion and research. The need to sample a particular set of travel dates should not, however, be of primary concern. It would be particularly useful to learn whether household members actually view their travel activity patterns as made up of circuits, and how they view potential circuit-based savings in trip miles and time availability. It would also be useful to know which locations would not be visited regularly by one or more members of a household if such locations did not contribute to an efficient travel circuit. Once again we come up against the problem of defining a suitably general, operational version of (the household's) locational accessibility. (The discussion and reference cited in Pirie (1979) bear directly upon this issue.) The notion of potential spatial access developed in the second section of the paper could certainly be refined in a number of ways: to include mode of travel restrictions, and to reduce the subset of trips used to form circuits even further, by imposing time-of-day or week-specific, or total household travel time and cost specific budgets upon the likely circuit set. There will inevitably be a trade-off in the use of such restrictions, between the need to add further assumptions to the modelling approach, and the use of additional constraints to reduce the computational burden involved in evaluating such spatial benefits. What we cannot afford to do is to ignore the need to come to grips with circuit-inclusive models of spatial interaction.

REFERENCES

Adler, T. and Ben-Akiva, M., 1979, A Theoretical and Empirical Model of Trip Chaining Behavior, Transportation Research B, 13, 243-257.

Fotheringham, S., 1982, Some Theoretical Aspects of Destination Choice and Their Relevance to Production-Constrained Gravity Models, a paper presented at the 29th North American Regional Science Association Meetings, Pittsburgh, PA.

Hansen, W.G., 1959, How Accessibility Shapes Land use, Journal of the American Institute of Planners, 25, 31-35.

Hanson, S., 1979, Urban Travel Linkages: A Review, in Hensher, D.A. and Stopher, P.R. (Eds.), Behavioral Travel Modelling, Croom Helm, London, 81-100.

Hanson, S., 1980, Spatial Diversification and Multipurpose Travel: Implications for Choice Theory, Geographical Analysis, 12, 245-257.

Hemmens, G.C., 1970, Analysis and Simulation of Urban Activity Patterns, Socio-Economic Planning Sciences, 4, 53-66.

Hensher, D.A., 1976, The Structure of Journeys and Nature of Travel Patterns, Environment and Planning A, 8, 655-672.

Horowitz, J., 1978, Disaggregate Demand Models of Nonwork Travel, Transportation Research Record, 673, 65-71.

Horowitz, J., 1980, Random Utility Models of Urban Nonwork Travel Demand: A Review, Papers of the Regional Science Association, 45, 125-137.

Howard, R.A., 1971, Dynamic Probabilistic Systems, 1, John Wiley, New York.

Kitamura, R., 1982, A Sequential History Dependent Approach to Trip Chaining Behavior, a paper presented at the 62nd Annual Meeting of the Transportation Research Board, Washington, DC.

Kitamura, R. and Kermanshah, M., 1982, Identifying Time and History Dependencies of Activity Choice, a paper presented at the 62nd Annual Meeting of the Transportation Research Board, Washington, DC.

Kobayashi, K., 1979, An Activity Model and its Validation, in Hensher, D.A. and Stopher, P.R. (Eds.), Behavioral Travel Modelling, Croom Helm, London, 101-115.

Lerman, S.R., 1979, The Use of Disaggregate Choice Models in Semi-Markov Process Models of Trip Chaining Behavior, Transportation Science, 13, 273-291.

Luce, R.D. and Perry, D., 1949, A Method of Matrix Analysis of Group Structures, Psychometrika, 14, 95-116.

Marble, D.F., 1964, A Simple Markovian Model of Trip Structure in a Metropolitan Region, Papers of the Regional Science Association, Western Section, 4, 150-156.

Muraco, W.A., 1972, Intraurban Accessibility, Economic Geography, 48, 388-405.

O'Kelly, M.E., 1981, A Model of the Demand for Retail Facilities, Incorporating Multistop, Multipurpose Trips, Geographical Analysis, 13, 134-148.

Pirie, G.H. 1979, Measuring Accessibility: A Review and Proposal, Environment and Planning A, 11, 299-312.

Richardson, A.J. and Young W., 1982, A Measure of Linked-Trip Accessibility, Transportation Planning and Technology, 7, 73-82.

Rouget, B., 1972, Graph Theory and Hierarchisation Models, Regional Science and Urban Economics, 2, 263-296.

Shier, D.R., 1974, Computational Experience With an Algorithm for Finding the K Shortest Paths in a Network, Journal of Research of the National Bureau of Standards, Mathematical Sciences, 78B, 3, 139-165.

Southworth, F., 1982a, An Urban Goods Movement Model: Framework and Some Results, Papers, Regional Science Association, 50, (forthcoming).

Southworth, F., 1982b, The Spatial Accessibility of Truck Terminals in the Presence of Multi-Destination Truck Circuits, Modeling and Simulation Proceedings, 13, 1073-1080.

Southworth, F., 1983, Circuit Based Locational Accessibility Indices, Environment and Planning B, 10, 249-260.

Vidakovich, V., 1974, A Study of Individual Journey Series: An Integrated Interpretation of the Transportation Process, in Newell, G.F. (Ed.), Traffic Flows and Transportation, Elsevier, New York, 57-70.

White, A.N., 1979, Accessibility and Public Facility Location, Economic Geography, 55, 18-55.

A STOCHASTIC MULTI-STAGE MOBILITY CHOICE MODEL

Giorgio Leonardi
International Institute for Applied Systems Analysis (IIASA)
Regional and Urban Development Group
A-2361 Laxenburg
Austria

Abstract. The paper proposes a dynamic framework for spatial mobility, where a random-utility approach is used to relate transition probabilities to other state variables for the system. Although the framework is quite general, housing mobility is a useful applied reference. First-order non-linear differential equations are derived for the expected population sizes and for the expected utilities in the individual evaluation process. The qualitative features of the dynamic behaviour are analyzed for a small-scale example, and it is shown how simple exogenous shocks, like changes in the housing stock and in the transport network, may lead easily to periodic behaviour and instabilities.

INTRODUCTION

This paper explores a non-linear dynamic formulation of a spatial population redistribution process. The point of view adopted is that individuals change state (eg., they move to a new location and dwelling) according to an explicit evaluation and choice process. The main sources of nonlinearity in this process are (i) the limited capacity (eg., limited housing stock) in each state (eg., location), which induces interactions among potential movers; and (ii) the market-type shortage signals (prices), reflecting the competition among potential movers in bidding for new states to be occupied (eg., vacant dwellings).

A distinctive feature of the proposed model is the use of a random-utility maximizing approach for the evaluation process of each individual. Moreover, the building up of individual expected utilities is itself a dynamic process, accounting for changing conditions in each state (mainly changing idle capacity and prices) and for expectations on benefits due to future moves.

The dynamic properties of the resulting dynamic system are explored for a simple two-states example. Even in this simplified case, the analysis reveals how changes in the physical structure of the environment (like changing the available capacity or the distance between zones) may lead to non-smooth changes in the dynamic behaviour, causing waves, bifurcations and instability.

POPULATION MOBILITY AND EVALUATION PROCESS

Consider a total population of size T, made up of individuals which can occupy different states labelled $1,\dots,m$. Each individual is assumed to have a residential behaviour and a moving behaviour, in the sense that a typical history of his life will be a sequence of stays in some states alternated to moves from one state to the other. Moreover, each state j is supposed to have a finite capacity Q_j, $j=1,\dots,m$, such that not more than Q_j individuals can be in state j at the same time. In order for such a system to exist, it is of course required that

$$T \leq \sum_{j=1}^{m} Q_j$$

If one wants to model the dynamic behaviour of such a system in deterministic terms, he is led to a very simple set of differential equations. Define: $p_j(t)$ = the population size in state j at time t; $\dot{p}_j(t)$ = the time derivative of $P_j(t)$; r_{ij} = the rate of flow from i to j (that is, r_{ij} is defined in such a way that the number of moves from i to j in a small time interval, given that a population $P_i(t)$ occupies state i at the beginning of that interval, is $P_i(t)r_{ij}\Delta$); and assume that both T and Q_j, $j=1,\dots,m$ are constant. Then the balance of inflows and outflows for each state is ensured by the following accounting equations

$$\dot{P}_j(t) = \sum_{i=1}^{m} P_i(t)r_{ij} - P_j(t)\sum_{i=1}^{m} r_{ji}, \quad j=1,\dots,m \tag{1}$$

A conservation property holds for eqn. (1), since

$$\sum_{j=1}^{m} \dot{p}_j(t) = \sum_{i=1}^{m} P_i(t)\sum_{j=1}^{m} r_{ij} - \sum_{j=1}^{m} P_j(T)\sum_{i=1}^{m} r_{ij} = 0$$

So far, nothing has been assumed on the rates r_{ij}, so that eqn. (1) is fairly general.

In order to provide the structure of the moving decisions with some economic underpinnings, resort to a random-utility approach will be made. While the main results on static random-utility based choice models can be considered as known (reference can be made to Manski, 1973; Domencich and McFadden, 1975; Williams, 1977; Ben-Akiva and Lerman, 1979 for its standard disaggregate treatment; and to Leonardi, 1982a and 1982b; for its more general asymptotic extreme value treatment; further results on the mathematical structure of random-utility models are found in Leondardi, 1981; and Smith, 1982), its use in a dynamic context needs some new theoretical effort. Although the idea of using random-utility choice models to derive flow rates in a set of equations like (1) is not quite new (see De Palma and Ben-Akiva, 1981, for instance), with almost no exception the dynamic nature of the evaluation process has been ignored.

The main aim of this section is to introduce a new way of looking at the dynamics of the evaluation process, relating them to an explicit micro-economic phenomenon, the formation of expectations over future. This approach, called here time-nested random-utility theory, has been proposed in Leonardi and Campisi (1981); and further developed in Leonardi (1983a).

The idea behind the approach is very simple and is clarified by the following example. Suppose an individual is subject to a mobility process of the type described by eqn. (1). Assume he behaves in such a way as to maximize the utility of his choices, and define: $h_i(t)$ = the gain per unit time due to staying in state i, $i=1,\dots,m$; v_{ij} = the utility associated with the action of moving from state i to state j, $i,j=1,\dots,m$; in most applications, v_{ij} will typically have a negative sign and be interpreted as the cost of moving between states i and j; $V_i(t)$ = the expected utility an individual gets from an unbounded-horizon process starting in state i at time t, $i=1,\dots,m$; α = the time-discount parameter in estimating future benefits; since continuous time is considered here, this means each individual is assumed to discount the future according to an exponential decay function with parameter α; $F(x)$ = the probability distribution for the random-utility term each individual will add to its evaluations.

One needs a further assumption on the state of the knowledge each individual has at any given time. It will be assumed that, in a small time interval Δ starting at time t, the amount of available alternatives considered for evaluation is

$$\lambda[Q_j - P_j(t)]\Delta$$

where λ is a non-negative constant. Using the terms defined above, a set of recurrence equations for the $V_i(t-\Delta)$ and $V_i(t)$ is obtained (see Leonardi, 1983a)

$$V_i(t-\Delta) = h_i(t)\Delta + (1-\alpha\Delta)\ E \max\left\{V_i(t) + \tilde{\theta}_i,\ \max_{(j)}[v_{ij} + V_j(t) + \tilde{\theta}_j]\right\} \qquad (2)$$

where the symbol $\max_{(j)}$ denotes maximization over all available alternatives in state j and over all states $j=1,\dots m$; the symbol $\tilde{\theta}_j$ denotes a random variable with distribution function $F(x)$; and the symbol E denotes taking expectation with respect to the sequence of random variables $\{\tilde{\theta}_j\}$.

In order to derive differential equations from eqn. (2), additional assumptions on the distribution $F(x)$ are needed. A frequently used one is (Manski, 1973; Domencich and McFadden, 1975)

$$F(x) = \exp(-e^{-\beta x}),\ \beta < 0 \qquad (3)$$

Recent work by Leonardi (1982a, 1982b) has shown that, under mild conditions, the same results derived by using the tight assumption (3) can be obtained as well from a much broader family of distributions for which the following requirement is met

$$\lim_{x\to\infty} \frac{F'(x)}{1-F(x)} = \beta \text{ , } \beta > 0 \tag{4}$$

No matter whether assumption (3) or (4) is preferred, both yield when applied to (2) (Leonardi, 1983b)

$$\alpha V_i(t) - \dot{V}_i(t) = h_i(t) + \frac{\lambda}{\beta} \sum_{j=1}^{m} [Q_j-P_j(t)] e^{\beta v_{ij}} e^{\beta[V_j(t)-V_i(t)]} \tag{5}$$

where $\dot{V}_i(t)$ denotes the time derivative of $V_i(t)$ (eqn. (5) is of course obtained by letting $\Delta \to 0$ in eqn. (2)).

Eqn. (5) thus provides a dynamic model for the value formation process, explicitly stated in terms of the parameters and state-variables of the stock-flow process. In order to derive the flow rates consistent with eqn. (5), one can observe that both assumptions (3) and (4) imply a multinomial logit model with dispersion parameter β and alternatives

1. staying in the place currently occupied in state i; there is just one such alternative* and its utility (besides the random term) is $V_i(t)$, and
2. moving to a new place in some state $j=1,\dots,m$; for each j there are $\lambda[Q_j-P_j(t)]\Delta$ alternatives available and each of them has utility (besides the random term) $v_{ij} + V_j(t)$.

Therefore, if one defines $P_{ij}(t,\Delta)$ = the probability that an individual in state i at time t makes a move towards state j within a small time interval Δ; the standard multinomial logit formula yields

$$P_{ij}(t,\Delta) = \frac{\Delta\lambda[Q_j-P_j(t)]e^{\beta[v_{ij}+V_j(t)]}}{\Delta\lambda \sum_{j=1}^{m} [Q_j-P_j(t)]e^{\beta[v_{ij}+V_j(t)]} + e^{\beta V_i(t)}}$$

and one gets for $r_{ij}(t)$

$$r_{ij}(t) = \lim_{\Delta\to 0} \frac{P_{ij}(t,\Delta)}{\Delta} = \lambda[Q_j-P_j(t)]e^{\beta[v_{ij}+V_j(t)-V_i(t)]} \tag{6}$$

---

*Staying in the currently occupied place in i is different in this model from moving to another place available in state i.

Substitution of result (6) into eqn. (5) yields for the value information process the more concise expression

$$\alpha V_i(t) - \dot{V}_i(t) = h_i(t) + \frac{1}{\beta} \sum_j r_{ij}(t) \tag{7}$$

showing that the rate of change in expected utilities can be split into two terms

1. a local contribution $h_i(t)$, unspecified as yet, and
2. an interaction contribution $\frac{1}{\beta} \sum_j r_{ij}(t)$, proportional to the total rate of outflow from a place in state i.

While the interaction term is well specified in terms of the physical parameters and state variables of the system, the local term is still a black box. In the next section new assumptions will be introduced which will clarify the nature of this term.

A RANDOM-UTILITY PRICE-FORMATION MECHANISM

So far just one type of actor has been considered in the general mobility process, namely the individuals consuming the capacity offered in the system and making moves among different states. Let a new type of actor now be introduced, and assume a standard market mechanism is at work: suppliers charge prices for the use of the offered capacity, and they set them so as to maximize their revenues. However, the total capacities Q_j, $j=1,\ldots,m$ are held constant, so that no investments in capacity expansion are made by suppliers.

Since suppliers are maximizing revenues, the price for each unit of capacity, in each state, in each small time interval Δ, will be adjusted so as to reach the maximum level which does not discourage the highest bidding consumer from paying for it. Due to the random nature of consumer's behaviour, the highest bids will also be random variables, for which the distribution and expected value will now be determined. In order to simplify notation, time dependency will not be indicated explicitly any more from now on, but it is understood that it is still there.

If there were no prices, an individual currently in state i would move to state j if a place were available there, which is better than any other alternative (including the currently used one). In other words, he would move if

$$v_{ij} + V_J + \tilde{\theta}_j - \max[V_i + \tilde{\theta}_i, \max_{(k)}(v_{ik} + V_k + \tilde{\theta}_k)] \geq 0 \tag{8}$$

If a price were charged in j, higher than the left-hand side of (8), then the individual from i would not find the place in j attractive any more, and he would consider other choices or stay in the current state. The maximum price level beyond which no individual in the system would consider a place in j as a convenient choice is therefore

$$\max_{(i)}\left\{v_{ij}+V_j+\tilde{\theta}_j - \max[V_i+\tilde{\theta}_i,\ \max_{(k)}(v_{ik}+V_k+\tilde{\theta}_k)]\right\} \tag{9}$$

where $\max_{(i)}$ indicates maximization both over every P_i on state i and over every $i=1,\ldots,m$. From the usual assumptions on the distribution of the random terms it is easily derived that the random variables

$$v_{ij} + V_j + \tilde{\theta}_j$$

have distribution

$$R_{ij}(x) = \exp(-A_{ij}e^{-\beta x}) \tag{10}$$

where

$$A_{ij} = \lambda\Delta e^{\beta(v_{ij}+V_j)} \tag{11}$$

while the random variables

$$\max[V_i+\tilde{\theta}_i,\ \max(v_{ik}+V_k+\tilde{\theta}_k)]$$

have distribution

$$S_i(x) = \exp(-B_i e^{-\beta x}) \tag{12}$$

where

$$B_i = e^{\beta V_i} + \lambda\Delta \sum_{k=1}^{m} e^{\beta(v_{ik}+V_k)} \tag{13}$$

Both eqns. (10) and (12) are therefore of the Gumbel type. The distribution of the difference between the two variables (that is, of the term within curly brackets in eqn. (9)) is given by

$$D_{ij}(x) = \int_{-\infty}^{\infty} R_{ij}(x+y)dS_i(y) = \int_{-\infty}^{\infty} \beta B_i \exp[-A_{ij}e^{-\beta(x+y)}]\exp(-B_i e^{-\beta y})e^{-\beta y}dy$$

$$= \frac{B_i}{B_i + A_{ij}e^{-\beta x}} = \frac{1}{1 + \frac{A_{ij}}{B_j} e^{-\beta x}} \tag{14}$$

a logistic distribution. Using definitions (11) and (13) and neglecting higher order terms in Δ, eqn. (14) becomes approximately

$$D_{ij}(x) = \frac{1}{1 + \lambda\Delta f_{ij}e^{\beta(V_j-V_i)}e^{-\beta x}} \exp[-\lambda\Delta f_{ij}e^{(V_j-V_i)}e^{-\beta x}] \tag{15}$$

where $f_{ij} = e^{\beta v_{ij}}$, again a Gumbel-type distribution. Finally, the distribution for the random quantity defined in eqn. (19) is

$$H_j(x) = \prod_{i=1}^{m} D_{ij}^{P_i}(x) = \exp[-e^{-\beta x}\lambda\Delta \sum_{i=1}^{m} P_i f_{ij} e^{\beta(V_j-V_i)}][1 - \lambda\Delta\psi_j e^{-\beta x}] \tag{16}$$

having defined

$$\psi_j = \sum_{i=1}^{m} P_i f_{ij} e^{\beta(V_j - V_i)} \tag{17}$$

Now the price in state j will be set equal to the random variable with distribution $H_j(x)$, if it is greater than 0. If this condition is not met, it means that even the highest bidding consumer will never choose to move to state j, no bargaining with the supplier will take place, and no price adjustment will be made. Therefore the average price set in state j at time t, as adjusted during the time interval (t, t+Δ), is given by

$$\int_0^\infty x dH_j(x) = \lambda\beta\Delta\psi_j \int_0^\infty x e^{-\beta x} dx = \frac{\lambda}{\beta} \psi_j \Delta \tag{18}$$

If one compares eqn. (17) with eqn. (6), one can write

$$\lambda\psi_j = \frac{\sum_{i=1}^{m} p_i r_{ij}}{O_j - P_j}$$

therefore, from eqn. (18) the unit price in j is

$$\frac{1}{\beta} \frac{\sum_{i=1}^{m} p_i r_{ij}}{O_j - P_i} \tag{19}$$

The numerator in expression (19) is the total inflow of individuals to state j per unit time, while the denominator is the available capacity in j. The rather lengthy mathematics of this section have thus proved a very simple and intuitive result: average prices are proportional to the ratio between attracted consumers and available capacity, the proportionality factor being 1/β.

The local term in eqn. (7), h_i, can now be redefined as

$$h_i = a_i - \frac{\lambda}{\beta} \psi_i \tag{20}$$

where a_i is a residual local utility term, depending on specific features of state i other than prices. This term, which might or might not be time-dependent, can now be considered as exogenously given.

In analogy with definition (17), one can define the quantity

$$\phi_i = \sum_{j=1}^{m} f_{ij} (O_j - P_j) e^{\beta(V_j - V_i)} \tag{21}$$

Eqn. (7) can finally be rewritten in the form

$$\alpha V_i - \dot{V}_i = a_i + \frac{\lambda}{\beta} (\phi_i - \psi_i) \tag{22}$$

A further theoretical result, not discussed in this paper, is the existence of an optimal control problem which, by maximizing a suitably defined functional subject to eqn. (1) as constraints, embeds both the transition rates in eqn. (6) and eqn. (22) for the value-formation process. The details on this embedding property are found in Leondardi (1983a, 1983b). What makes the embedding optimal control problem approach appealing is the structure of the objective function, which is a dynamic version of the entropy-type functions used to embed static spatial interaction models (Wilson, 1970). However, a closer look at some of the behavioural assumptions used so far reveals some weaknesses, which suggest to proceed to a slight revision of the model, rather than to theoretical refinement. This is pointed out in the following section.

ANTICIPATION VERSUS PAST MEMORY

The approach used so far is anticipatory, in the sense that the future trajectory of the system determines the current evaluation. This appears clearly in the way the recurrence eqn. (2) is built. Except for the expectation operator, eqn. (2) has the same structure of a dynamic programming problem. In principle, they must be solved by backward induction, starting from the end of the process and going back to the current time. Even after randomness and uncertainty are introduced, this way of evaluating alternatives still remains a formidable task, and it is perhaps questionable as a behavioural assumption.

As an alternative to the anticipatory assumption, let now a very simple memory effect be introduced. It will be assumed that the actor does not try at all to conjecture on the future trajectory of the system, but rather updates his past experiences. Let the symbols be defined as previously and consider the relationship among the values of V_i, the expected utility in state i, at times t, t+Δ.

Assume an actor in state i updates V_i at time t+Δ by adding the following two components (i) the gain $h_i(t+\Delta)\ \Delta - h_i(t)\ \Delta$ in the interval $(t+\Delta,t+2\Delta)$; and (ii) the expected utility (taking possible moves into account) at time $t+2\Delta$.

However, he is assumed not to know $V_i(t+2\Delta)$; his most recent memory is on the value of V_i just before time t+Δ, that is, he remembers $V_i(t)$. He then tries to find the value of the best alternative, whose expected utility is given by

$$\max\{V_i(t) + \tilde{\theta}_i,\ \max_{(j)}[v_{ij}+V_j(t)+\tilde{\theta}_j]\} \tag{23}$$

an expression which is identical to the second term on the right-hand side of eqn. (2), except for the discount factor.

Discounting must be introduced to this case as well. But it will also be assumed that the actor is aware he has used knowledge dated Δ time units back, therefore he inflates the expected utility given by eqn. (23) in order to express it in values at time $t+2\Delta$. If α_1 is the inflation rate and α_2 is the discount rate, expression (23) will be multiplied by

$$(1+2\alpha_1\Delta)(1-\alpha_2\Delta) = 1 - (\alpha_2-2\alpha_1)\Delta = 1 - \alpha\Delta$$

having defined $\alpha = (\alpha_2-2\alpha_1)$.

Once this is done, an equation quite similar to eqn. (2) is obtained, but for $V_i(t+\Delta)$, rather than $V_i(t-\Delta)$

$$V_i(t+\Delta) = h_i(t)\ \Delta + (1-\alpha\Delta)\ E\ \max\{V_i(t)+\tilde{\theta}_i\ ,\ \max_{(j)}[v_{ij}+V_j(t)+\tilde{\theta}_j]\} \tag{24}$$

Arguing as for eqn. (2), taking the limit of eqn. (24) for $\Delta \to 0$ yields the following differential equation

$$\alpha V_i + \dot{V}_i = h_i + \frac{\lambda}{\beta} \sum_{j=1}^{m} (Q_j-P_j) f_{ij} e^{\beta(V_j-V_i)} \tag{25}$$

where $f_{ij} = e^{\beta v_{ij}}$.

In spite of the different behavioural assumptions used to derive them, eqn. (25) looks very much like eqn. (5). The only formal difference is a reversal of the time direction: $\dot{V}_i$ appears with a plus, rather than a minus sign. This might imply in general a completely different dynamic behaviour, although it is evident that eqns. (5) and (25) have the same equilibrium points. Another important difference is the way α is defined. Being the difference between two non-negative quantities (the discount and the inflation rate), α can now take any real values, including negative ones. This has also implications on the quality of the dynamic behaviour, as the next section will show.

STABILITY, WAVES AND BIFURCATIONS

Though a general analysis of the structure of equilibrium points to the dynamic systems considered so far is difficult to perform, some insights in the problem is given by considering a simple example. With reference to a pure residential mobility model, suppose a system of just two zones is given, with no local differentiation both in utility a_i and in housing stock Q_i.

Define: T = the total population; Q = the total housing stock; it is understood that the stock in each zone is $Q/2$; P = the population living in the first zones; $T-P$ is therefore the population living in the second zone; x = the difference between the expected utility in the first zone and that in the second zone; in the two-zones case this variable is enough to describe the evaluation and choice process.

By means of the appropriate substitutions and rearrangements on eqns. (1) and (22), one ends up with the following system

$$\alpha\, x - \dot{x} = F(x,P) \tag{26}$$

$$\dot{P} = G(x,P) \tag{27}$$

where

$$F(x,P) = \frac{\lambda}{\beta}\left\{ \left[\frac{Q}{2} + (T-2P)\right](1-fe^{\beta x}) - \left[\frac{Q}{2} - (T-2P)\right](1-fe^{-\beta x})\right\} \tag{28}$$

$$G(x,P) = \lambda(T-P)\left(\frac{Q}{2} - P\right)fe^{\beta x} - \lambda P\left(\frac{Q}{2} - T + P\right)fe^{-\beta x} \tag{29}$$

and $f = e^{-\beta C}$ is a decreasing function of the distance (or travel cost) C between the two zones.

In a similar way, for a memory-based system as discussed in the previous section, one obtains the equations

$$\alpha x + \dot{x} = F(x,P) \tag{30}$$

$$\dot{P} = G(x,P) \tag{31}$$

An important question to be asked is to what extent and in which way the structure of the equilibrium point of systems (26)-(27) and (30)-(31) depends on some parameters (like α), as well as on the distance C and the housing stock O. These are indeed the two main interlinks between the housing mobility system and the physical structure of the settlement.

First of all, it is clear from intuitive considerations that both systems above have the equilibrium solution

$$P = \frac{T}{2}\,,\ x = 0 \tag{32}$$

since the two zones have no intrinsic relative advantages. The Taylor-expansion approximation of F(x,P) and G(x,P around (0,T/2) yields

$$\bar{F}(x,P) = -\lambda fQ \cdot x + \frac{4\lambda}{\beta}(1-f)\cdot\left(P-\frac{T}{2}\right)$$

$$\bar{G}(x,P) = \lambda\beta f\frac{T}{2}(Q-T)\cdot x\ \lambda fQ \cdot \left(P-\frac{T}{2}\right)$$

Therefore, the behaviour of the equilibrium point (32) can be deduced (for small perturbations) by analyzing the linear system

$$\dot{x} = \alpha x - \bar{F}(x,P)$$

$$\dot{P} = \bar{G}(x,P)$$

for the anticipatory case, and the linear system

$$\dot{x} = \bar{F}(x,P) - \alpha x$$

$$\dot{P} = \bar{G}(u,P)$$

for the past memory case.

For the anticipatory case, the coefficient matrix is

$$\begin{bmatrix} \alpha + \lambda fQ & , -\frac{4\lambda}{\beta}(1-f) \\ \lambda\beta f\frac{T}{2}(Q-T) & , -\lambda fQ \end{bmatrix}$$

and its eigenvalues y_1, y_2 are the roots of the equation

$$y^2 - \alpha y - A = 0 \qquad (33)$$

where $A = \lambda f[Q(\alpha+\lambda f) + 4(1-f)\frac{T}{2}(Q-T)]$

Since by assumption $\alpha > 0$ and $Q > T$ ($f \leq 1$ by definition) it is true that $A > 0$.

The two roots of eqn. (33) are

$$y_1 = \frac{1}{2}(\alpha + \sqrt{\alpha^2+4A}) > 0$$

$$y_2 = \frac{1}{2}(\alpha - \sqrt{\alpha^2+4A}) < 0$$

Therefore, within the above assumptions for the parameters, this system is structurally very stable, but the equilibrium point is an unstable one: a saddle point (since the eigenvalues are both real and always opposite in sign). This means that no trajectory in the (x,P) plane, except two (the two opposite branches of one separatrix) will converge to the equilibrium. This unrealistic rigidity is one more reason to replace the anticipatory assumption with the past memory one.

For the past memory case, the coefficient matrix is

$$\begin{bmatrix} -(\lambda fQ+\alpha) & , -\frac{4\lambda}{\beta}(1-f) \\ \lambda\beta f\frac{T}{2}(Q-T) & , -\lambda fQ \end{bmatrix}$$

and its eigenvalues are the roots of the equation

$$y^2 + (\alpha+2\lambda fQ)y + \lambda f[\lambda fQ^2 + 2\lambda T(Q-T)(1-f) + \alpha Q] = 0 \qquad (34)$$

Some calculations yield

$$y_1 = \frac{1}{2}[-(\alpha+2\lambda fQ) + \sqrt{\alpha^2-8\lambda^2T(Q-T)f(1-f)}]$$

$$y_2 = \frac{1}{2}[-(\alpha+2\lambda fQ) - \sqrt{\alpha^2-8\lambda^2T(Q-T)f(1-f)}]$$

When the eigenvalues are real and $\alpha > 0$, one has

$$y_1 < -\lambda fQ < 0$$

$$y_2 < 0$$

and the equilibrium point is a stable node, ie., every trajectory ends in it.

When $\alpha > 0$ but the eigenvalues are complex, damped oscillations are produced and the equilibrium point becomes a stable focus, ie., the trajectories are spirals converging to it.

In order to analyze how the oscillatory behaviour depends on the stock level and the distance between the two zones, define: $Y = Q-T$ the total vacant stock.

Then the solution of the inequality

$$\alpha^2 \leq 8\lambda^2 TYe^{-\beta C}(1-e^{-\beta C})$$

(which is the condition for having complex eigenvalues) can be plotted on the (C,Y) plane as in Fig. 1.

It seems from Fig. 1 that increasing the excess capacity Y beyond a certain threshold produces oscillations. The threshold depends on the distance between the zones, and for $C < \frac{1}{\beta} \log 2$ it is decreasing while for $C > \frac{1}{\beta} \log 2$ it is increasing. It is important to notice that for $C = 0$ there can be no oscillation, and the eigenvalues become

$$y_1 = -\lambda Q < 0$$
$$y_2 = -(\alpha + \lambda) < 0$$

corresponding to a stable node.

This means that distance is mainly responsible for waves to appear. It is also interesting to see how the damping speed and the period depend on Y. The damping factor is

$$\alpha + 2\lambda f(T+Y)$$

therefore increasing Y will also fasten the damping process. However, if Y is small compared to T, the damping speed will not be affected significantly.

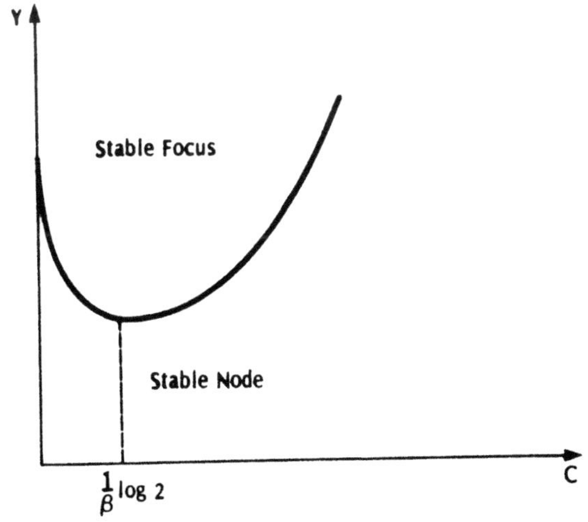

Figure 1 - Changes in Equilibrium as a Function of the Distance Between the Zones, C, and the Vacant Stock Y. First Case $\alpha > 0$.

The period is

$$\frac{2\Pi}{\sqrt{8\lambda^2 TYf(1-f) - \alpha^2}}$$

and it is decreasing with Y. Therefore, in general, low excess capacity levels produce long waves fading out slowly, while high excess capacity produces short waves fading out rapidly.

The situation becomes more complex when $\alpha < 0$. The changes in the type of equilibrium plotted on the (C,Y) plane, appear as in Fig. 2. The positive orthant of the (C,Y) plane is divided into five regions, corresponding to five different types of equilibrium points. The region of the saddle points is the region where the inequality

$$y_1 y_2 < 0$$

holds, ie., where the eigenvalues are opposite in sign. From elementary algebra it is known that the value of the product $y_1 y_2$ is equal to the constant term in eqn. (34), hence the inequality defining the saddle point region is

$$\lambda f(T+y)^2 + 2\lambda TY(1-f) + \alpha(T+Y) < 0 \tag{35}$$

where $f = e^{-\beta C}$.

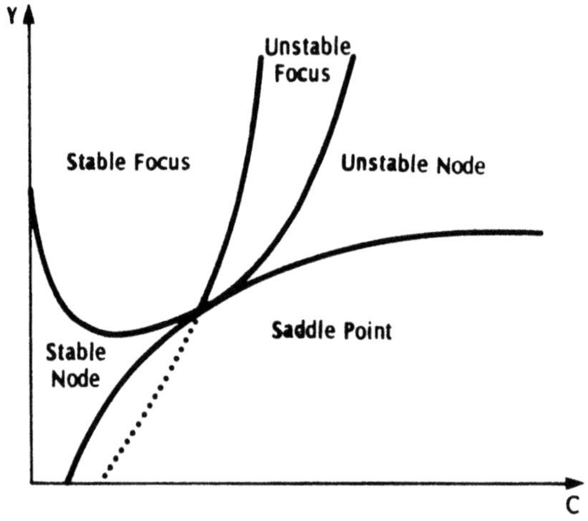

Figure 2 - Changes in Equilibrium as a Function of the Distance Between the Zones, C, and the Vacant Stock Y. Second case: $\alpha < 0$.

Outside the saddle point region, the eigenvalues are either of the same sign or complex conjugate. In order to have stability, one needs either real negative eigenvalues or complex conjugate eigenvalues with negative real part. Outside of the saddle point region, these conditions are equivalent to the single inequality

$$y_1 + y_2 < 0$$

and since it is known from algebra that the sum of the eigenvalues is equal to the coefficient of the first order term in eqn. (34), changed in sign, the stable region is defined by the two inequalities

$$\alpha + 2\lambda f(T+Y) > 0 \qquad (36)$$

$$\lambda f(T+Y)^2 + 2\lambda TY(1-f) + \alpha(T+Y) > 0 \qquad (37)$$

These boundaries determine the union of the regions "stable focus" and "stable node" in Fig. 2. The region of complex eigenvalues, ie., of focusses (both stable and unstable) is defined by the inequality

$$\alpha^2 < 8\lambda^2 + TYf(1-f) \qquad (38)$$

as for the case considered in Fig. 1. The intersection of inequality (38) with inequality (36) determines the region "stable focus" of Fig. 2, and as a difference, also the region "unstable focus". What is left is either a region of unstable nodes (upper right of Fig. 2) or a region of stable nodes (lower left of Fig. 2).

One thus can see that, even for the simple two-zone example, a wide variety of qualitatively different solutions exist, and a simple external control action, like changing the total stock level, might lead to very different results, ranging from stability to oscillations and instability.

CONCLUDING REMARKS

The model structure explored in the paper is admittedly lacking some realistic features, like births and deaths of individuals, household structure, dwelling sizes and so on, which might introduce qualitative differences in the dynamics.

However, the main theoretical goal of the paper was to isolate the pure redistribution process under conditions of capacity shortage from other overlapping processes, and to analyze if and to what extent this process alone might be responsible for nontrivial dynamic behaviour.

Although there is awareness that more general theoretical statements are waited for (this will hopefully be the outcome of ongoing research), the two-by-two example discussed here is felt to be a good point in case, and some general properties can be conjectured, if not proved.

The first interesting property is the role of distance in giving rise to waves. Time lags are known to be often responsible for oscillatory behaviour in many linear and non-linear systems. Here it seems like the friction of distance, which is in a sense a spatial lag, has similar effects. This is indeed a very important property, as long as it introduces a very sharp qualitative difference between systems where the geographic component is absent and systems where it is accounted for.

The second important property is the ease with which changes in the physical setting (eg., housing stock and/or transport network) might cause bifurcations towards instability in the population mobility and value formation.

This rings a warning bell for the otherwise sensible practice of embedding a fast process (the mobility one in our case) into a slow one (eg., housing stock changes), simply by letting the fast one go to equilibrium with negligible adjusting time.

Although the available capacity is held constant in this paper (that is, no explicit dynamics are proposed for it), one can imagine a more general model where the fast mobility process discussed here actually interacts with a slow process of capacity expansion and/or reduction, whose dynamics depend on the state variables of the fast process.

If the overall process is such that critical values of the capacity (that is, values leading to instability in the mobility process) can be realized, then instability is introduced in the whole process, and no equilibrium approximation can be used anymore.

REFERENCES

Ben-Akiva, M. and Lerman, S.R., 1979, Disaggregate Travel and Mobility Choice Models and Measures of Accessibility, in Hensher, D. and Stopher P. (Eds.) Behavioral Travel Modeling, Croom Helm, London.

De Palma, A. and Ben-Akiva, M., 1981, An Interactive Dynamic Model of Residential Location Choice, a paper presented at the International Conference on Structural Economic Analysis and Planning in Time and Space, Umeå, Sweden.

Domencich, T. and McFadden, D., 1975, Urban Travel Demand: A Behavioral Analysis, North Holland, Amsterdam.

Leonardi, G., 1982a, The Structure of Random Utility Models in Light of the Asymptotic Theory of Extreme, WP-82-91, IIASA, Laxenburg, Austria.

Leonardi, G., 1982b, Transient and Asymptotic Behavior of a Random-Utility Based Stochastic Process in Continuous Space and Time, a paper presented at the 3rd Annual Meeting of the Regional Science Association, Italian Section, Venice.

Leonardi, G., 1983a, An Optimal Control Representation of a Stochastic Multi-State-Multiactor Choice Process, in Griffin, D. and Lea, A. (Eds.) Evolving Geographical Structures, Martinus Nijhoff, The Hague, forthcoming.

Leonardi, G., 1983b, A Choice-Theoretical Framework for Household Mobility, and Extensions, final report for the research project Feasibility Analysis of Studies on Transport-Location Interactions, Contract CNR-IRES n. 82.0045.93, Special Project on Transport, CNR, Rome, Italy.

Leonardi, G., 1984, The Use of Random-Utility Theory in Building Location-Allocation Models, in Thisse, J.F. and Zorler, H.G. (Eds.) Location Analysis of Public Facilities, North Holland, Amsterdam, forthcoming.

Leonardi, G., and Campisi, 1981, Dynamic Multistage Random-Utility Choice Processes: Models in Discrete and Continuous Time, a paper presented at the 2nd Meeting of the Regional Science Association, Italian Section, Naples, Italy.

Manski, C.F., 1973, Structure of Random Utility Models, PhD dissertation, MIT, Cambridge, MA.

Smith, T.E., 1982, A Choice Probability Characterization of Generalized Extreme Value Models, WP 66, Department of Regional Science, University of Pennsylvania, Philadelphia, PA.

Williams, H.C.W.L., 1977, On the Formation of Travel Demand Models and Economic Evaluation Measures of User Benefit, Environment and Planning A, 9, 285-344.

Wilson, A.C., 1970, Entropy in Urban and Regional Modeling, Pion, London.

ON THE SENSITIVITY OF MAXIMUM LIKELIHOOD ESTIMATES OF GRAVITY MODEL PARAMETERS

James S. Weber
Department of Management
Roosevelt University
430 South Michigan Avenue
Chicago, IL 60605
United States of America
and
Ashish K. Sen
Department of Urban Planning and Policy
University of Illinois at Chicago
Box 4348, Chicago, IL 60605
United States of America

Abstract. This paper presents a procedure for estimating small changes in maximum-likelihood estimates of gravity model parameters in response to small changes in base period data. The procedure can be used to derive covariance matrices for such parameter estimates from which confidence intervals may be obtained and which may be used for tests of hypotheses. Also the procedure extends a similar procedure for estimating sensitivities, etc., of gravity model forecasts. While this type of problem has been addressed by others, our approach is the only one that is applicable for the large numbers of origin and destination zones one typically encounters.

INTRODUCTION

The Gravity Model

The gravity model may be written in the form

$$T_{ij} = A_i B_j F_{ij} \text{ for } i=1, \ldots, I \text{ and } j=1, \ldots, J \tag{1}$$

where A_i is called an origin factor for each of I origins, B_j is called a destination factor for each of J destinations and F_{ij} is called a separation factor for each origin and destination pair. T_{ij} is the expected flow of people, goods or commodities from zone i to zone j. The form in eqn. (1) is the most general form of the gravity model (Hua and Porell, 1979) and includes the specifications given by Wilson (1967) and Alonso (1976).

Separation Factors

A useful form for the separation factor is given by

$$F_{ij} = \exp\left(\sum_{k=1}^{K} \theta_k c_{ij}^k\right) \text{ for } i=1,\ldots,I \text{ and } j=1,\ldots,J \tag{2}$$

where c_{ij}^k's, for k=1,...,K, are measures of separation or difference between zone i and zone j, such as travel time, travel cost, ethnic or other socio-economic variation, etc., (Sen and Sööt, 1981). $\theta = (\theta_1,\ldots,\theta_K)$ is a vector of parameters relating the F_{ij}'s to these c_{ij}^k measures of separation. The θ_k parameters are estimated from observed trip flows for some base period together with the c_{ij}^k's.

Estimation of Θ

One way of estimating θ_k's is the maximum-likelihood (ML) method summarized in the next section. In the gravity model context, the maximum-likelihood method has been studied by Hyman (1969) and Evans (1971) when K=1 and by Sen and Sööt (1981) and Sen (1982) for more general K. It is particularly valuable when there are many zero valued entries in an observed origin-destination matrix, a situation common in transportation studies and for which linear least squares procedures may not be very suitable (Gray and Sen, 1983; Gray, 1980).

Sensitivity of Observed Flows

In this paper we describe a method for assessing the influence of small changes in observed flows, X_{ij}'s, on these ML theta parameters, θ_1 ,..., θ_K. The procedure can be used to do a sensitivity analysis of the type typically found in engineering studies or it can be used to obtain covariance matrices, which may then be used for confidence intervals and tests of hypotheses. While standard statistical procedures exist for estimating covariance matrices of ML estimates, often they are unusable in a gravity model context since they would involve the inversion of an I+J+K dimensional matrix and for typical gravity model applications the number of zones I and J may be very large. A significant feature of our procedure is that an inverse of a large matrix is not required. Giles and Hampton (1981) have considered a related problem for the ordinary non-linear least squares calibration of the gravity model, however their approach requires a matrix inverse.

Structure of Paper

In the following section of this paper we describe the ML method as it applies here. In the third section we give a detailed account of our procedure and in the fourth section we present a numerical example giving standard errors and confidence intervals for the theta parameters. Appendix A gives details of the linearized DSF (Deming-Stephan-Furness) procedure which is needed to linearize the θ_k's as a function of the observed flows, X_{ij}'s. Appendix B outlines a different but sometimes intractable alternative approach. The DSF procedure involves an iterative scaling of initial gravity model estimates to satisfy prescribed row and column constraints, no matter how the constraints arise, as long as they are consistent. Row and column constraints for a trip matrix are consistent when the sum of the row constraints is the same as the sum of the column constraints. For a more detailed explanation see Sen and Sööt (1981); Evans (1971); Sinkhorn (1964); Deming and Stephan (1940). Apparently

Furness (1962) introduced the procedure into the transportation planning literature. For a discussion of DSF procedure applied when the sum of the row constraints and sum of the column constraints are not equal, see Weber (1981a) and Sinkhorn (1967).

MAXIMUM LIKELIHOOD WITH POISSON RANDOM ERROR

Poisson versus Multinominal Error

Our model of observed flows between zones is that they have expected values, T_{ij}, which may be described by a gravity law in eqn. (1), and a random variation about these expected values which may be described by a Poisson law. Thus

$$\text{Prob}\{X_{ij}\} = \prod_{i=1}^{I} \prod_{j=1}^{J} \frac{e^{-T_{ij}} T_{ij}^{X_{ij}}}{X_{ij}!} \tag{3}$$

gives the probability of an observed trip matrix $\{X_{ij}\}$ over a fixed period of time. This Poisson assumption for fixed time period implies a multinomial assumption with the same expected values for a fixed total number of trips. The Poisson assumption is applicable to methodological procedures which use a fixed time period for observing travel activity (rather than a fixed sample size). Moreover, the ML equations for Poisson distributed cell counts with fixed observation periods and the ML equations for multinomial distributed cell counts with a fixed number of total trips are identical. When the θ_k's and $A_iB_jF_{ij}$'s are constant, then the right hand side of eqn. (3) may be interpreted as the probability of the set of flows, $\{X_{ij}\}$. When the observed X_{ij}'s are held constant, then the right hand side of eqn. (3) may be interpreted as the likelihood function of the A_i's, B_j's, and θ_k's. The values of A_i, B_j, θ_k for which the likelihood function is maximized are the maximum likelihood A_i's, B_j's and θ_k's. Finally, eqn. (3) may look like entropy, but here the interpretation is obviously different.

ML Equations

When the T_{ij} parameters, A_i's, B_j's, θ_k's, in eqn. (3) are unknown, but we have an observed trip table, $\{X_{ij}\}$, then we must estimate the T_{ij}'s. A classical approach is the maximum-likelihood method mentioned above for which good estimates of T_{ij}'s are those which maximize the likelihood given in eqn. (3) of observed flows, X_{ij}'s. The likelihood is denoted by $L(T_{ij}|X_{ij})$ and instead of working directly with the likelihood function, it is usually easier to maximize its logarithm with respect to the unknown statistical parameters.

To do this we begin with eqn. (3) and replace T_{ij} and F_{ij} by the expressions given by eqns. (1) and (2). After taking the logarithm of the resulting expression, we set the derivatives $\partial \ell n L(T_{ij}|X_{ij})/\partial A_i B_j \theta_k$ equal to zero, etc., obtaining

$$\sum_{j=1}^{J} T_{ij} = \sum_{j=1}^{J} X_{ij} = O_i \text{ for } i=1,\ldots,I \tag{4}$$

$$\sum_{i=1}^{I} T_{ij} = \sum_{i=1}^{I} X_{ij} = D_j \text{ for } j=1,\ldots,J \tag{5}$$

$$\sum_{i=1}^{I} \sum_{j=1}^{J} c_{ij}^{k} T_{ij} = \sum_{i=1}^{I} \sum_{j=1}^{J} c_{ij}^{k} X_{ij} \text{ for } k=1,\ldots,K \tag{6}$$

Maximum likelihood estimates of A_i, B_j, θ_k are obtained from the simultaneous solution of eqns. (1), (2), (4), (5), (6), although only the ML θ_k's are of interest here. For a discussion of solutions to these ML equations see Sen and Sööt (1981).

SENSITIVITIES OF ML θ_k PARAMETERS

The Derivatives $\partial\theta_k/\partial X_{ij}$

By sensitivities we mean derivatives of the ML theta parameters with respect to the observed flows, X_{ij}'s. Since the ML thetas are implicitly defined by eqns. (1), (2), (4), (5), (6), we could obtain their derivatives from the implicit function approach. However this leads to an inverse of a large matrix which our linearization procedure avoids. For comparison, notation for the derivatives of the implicitly defined θ_k's is given in Appendix B.

Linearizing the ML θ_k Equations

We obtain $\partial\theta_k/\partial X_{ij}$ by solving the system of linearized maximum likelihood eqns. (1), (2), (4), (5), (6) for $\Delta\theta_k$ in terms of the disturbances ΔX_{ij} and partial derivatives $\partial T_{ij}/\partial F_{rs}$, $\partial T_{ij}/\partial O_p$, $\partial T_{ij}/\partial D_q$ and $\partial F_{ij}/\partial\theta_k$.

The linearizations of eqns. (2), (4), (5), (1) and (6) are given, respectively, by

$$\Delta F_{ij} = \sum_{k=1}^{K} \partial F_{ij}/\partial\theta_k \Delta\theta_k \text{ for } i=1,\ldots,I \text{ and } j=1,\ldots,J \tag{7}$$

$$\Delta O_i = \sum_{j=1}^{J} \Delta X_{ij} \text{ for } i=1,\ldots,I \tag{8}$$

$$\Delta D_j = \sum_{i=1}^{I} \Delta X_{ij} \text{ for } j=1,\ldots,J \tag{9}$$

$$\Delta T_{ij} = \sum_{r=1}^{I} \sum_{s=1}^{J} \partial T_{ij}/\partial F_{rs} \Delta F_{rs} + \sum_{p=1}^{I} \partial T_{ij}/\partial O_p \Delta O_p + \sum_{q=1}^{J} \partial T_{ij}/\partial D_q \Delta D_q \tag{10}$$

for $i = 1,\ldots,I$, $j = 1,\ldots J$

$$\sum_{i=1}^{I} \sum_{j=1}^{J} c_{ij}^{k} \Delta T_{ij} = \sum_{i=1}^{I} \sum_{j=1}^{J} c_{ij}^{k} \Delta X_{ij} \quad \text{for } k=1,\ldots,K \tag{11}$$

Eqns. (7), (8), (9), (11) should be evident. Eqn. (10) is obtained in the following way. Eqns. (1), (4) and (5) are the well-known doubly constrained gravity model equations for expected flows, T_{ij}. Eqn. (10) simply indicates a linear approximation to T_{ij} in terms of the approximate changes ΔF_{rs}, ΔO_p, ΔD_q given by eqns. (7), (8) and (9). The calculation of the derivatives $\partial T_{ij}/\partial F_{rs}$, $\partial T_{ij}/\partial O_p$ and $\partial T_{ij}/\partial D_q$ is accomplished using the linearized DSF procedure which will be discussed shortly and also in Appendix A.

Solving for a Linear Approximation to θ_k

To solve the linear system given by eqns. (7)-(11) for $\Delta\theta$ in terms of ΔX_{ij} we eliminate ΔF_{rs}, ΔO_p and ΔD_q by substituting eqns. (7), (8) and (9) into (10) and then this result into eqn. (11) obtaining

$$\sum_{i=1}^{I} \sum_{j=1}^{J} c_{ij}^{k} \left[\sum_{r=1}^{I} \sum_{s=1}^{J} \partial T_{ij}/\partial F_{rs} \left(\sum_{\ell=1}^{K} \partial F_{rs}/\partial\theta_\ell \Delta\theta_\ell \right) + \sum_{p=1}^{I} \partial T_{ij}/\partial O_p \left(\sum_{q=1}^{J} \Delta X_{pq} \right) + \sum_{q=1}^{J} \partial T_{ij}/\partial D_q \left(\sum_{p=1}^{I} \Delta X_{pq} \right) \right]$$

$$= \sum_{i=1}^{I} \sum_{j=1}^{J} c_{ij}^{k} \Delta X_{ij} \quad \text{for } k=1, \ldots, K \tag{12}$$

Eqn. (12) is a system of K equations in K dependent variables, $\Delta\theta_k$, and this system can be solved for the θ_k's. To express solutions to eqn. (12) we indicate a matrix inverse by $[\ldots]^{-1}$ and the individual entries by $[\ldots]^{-1}_{ij}$. Notice that the matrix for which we need an inverse is of small dimension, K x K, where K is the number of theta parameters in our model of F_{ij} as indicated by eqn. (2). Using this notation the solution to eqn. (12) is given by

$$(\Delta\theta) \tilde{=} \left[\sum_{i=1}^{I} \sum_{j=1}^{J} c_{ij}^{k_1} \left[\sum_{r=1}^{I} \sum_{s=1}^{J} \partial T_{ij}/\partial F_{rs} (\partial F_{rs}/\partial\theta_{k_2}) \right] \right]^{-1} \tag{13}$$

$$\left[\left(\sum_{i=1}^{I} \sum_{j=1}^{J} c_{ij}^{k} \Delta X_{ij} \right) - \sum_{i=1}^{I} \sum_{j=1}^{J} c_{ij}^{k} \sum_{p=1}^{I} \partial T_{ij}/\partial O_p \left(\sum_{q=1}^{J} \Delta X_{pq} \right) - \sum_{i=1}^{I} \sum_{j=1}^{J} c_{ij}^{k} \sum_{q=1}^{J} \partial T_{ij}/\partial D_q \left(\sum_{p=1}^{I} \Delta X_{pq} \right) \right]$$

(in $[\ldots]^{-1}$ in eqn. (13), k_1 distinguishes K rows and k_2 distinguishes K columns).

Properties of The Linearization of The ML θ_k's

Note that in eqn. (13) we are able to express $\Delta\theta$ in terms of the sufficient statistics $(\sum_{i=1}^{I}\sum_{j=1}^{J} c_{ij}^{k}\Delta X_{ij}), (\sum_{p=1}^{I}\Delta X_{pq}), (\sum_{q=1}^{J}\Delta X_{pq})$. Also in eqn. (13) changes to theta, $\Delta\theta$, arise from ΔX_{ij} only after the ΔX_{ij}'s have been adjusted for changes in origin and destination totals, $\Delta O_p = \sum_{q=1}^{J}\Delta X_{pq}$, $\Delta D_q = \sum_{p=1}^{I}\Delta X_{pq}$. To see this, in eqn. (13), factor the c_{ij}^{k}'s to the left in [...]. Thus, subject to certain assumptions, the expected value of $\Delta\theta_k$ is zero if ΔX_{ij}'s are attributable to simply collecting data for a different period of time, for which we expect all the ΔX_{ij}'s would be attributable to ΔO_p's and ΔD_q's. Of course, this also assumes no shift in relative values among O_p's or among D_q's over a different observation period. From eqn. (13) we may obtain explicit formulae for $\partial\theta_k/\partial X_{ij}$ which are given by

$$\partial\theta_k/\partial X_{ij} = \sum_{\ell=1}^{K}\left[\sum_{i=1}^{I}\sum_{j=1}^{J}\sum_{r=1}^{I}\sum_{s=1}^{J} c_{ij}^{k_1}\partial T_{ij}/\partial F_{rs}\, F_{rs}c_{rs}^{k_2}\right]_{k\ell}^{-1} \tag{14}$$

$$\cdot\; c_{ij}^{\ell}\left[1 - \sum_{p=1}^{I}\sum_{q=1}^{J}(\partial T_{ij}/\partial O_p + \partial T_{ij}/\partial D_q)\right]$$

wherein the ij subscripts on the left hand side correspond to the unbound ij's on the right hand side. Eqn. (14) is obtained from eqn. (13) by factoring ΔX_{ij} to the right, expressing $\Delta\theta$ as $(\partial\theta/\partial X).\Delta X$ and identifying the coefficients of X_{ij} as $\partial\theta_k/\partial X_{ij}$.

The Linearized DSF Procedure

To use eqns. (13) and (14) we need values for $\partial F_{rs}/\partial\theta_k$, $\partial T_{ij}/\partial F_{rs}$, $\partial T_{ij}/\partial O_p$ and $\partial T_{ij}/\partial D_{qk}$. By differentiating eqn. (2) we see that $\partial F_{rs}/\partial\theta_k$ is $c_{rs}^{k}F_{rs}$. We obtain $\partial T_{ij}/\partial F_{rs}$, $\partial T_{ij}/\partial O_p$ and $\partial T_{ij}/\partial D_q$ from the linearized Deming-Stephan-Furness Procedure (LDSFP) which is discussed by Weber and Sen (1982), and Weber (1981a, 1981b). We briefly review LDSFP in Appendix A.

ILLUSTRATIVE EXAMPLE

Covariances of Linear Approximations

One objective of the development of the last section is the estimation of the covariances of the ML θ_k's which are collectively denoted by Cov(θ) and defined by

$$\mathrm{Cov}(\theta) = \begin{bmatrix} \mathrm{var}(\theta_1) & \mathrm{cov}(\theta_1,\theta_2) & \dots & \mathrm{cov}(\theta_1,\theta_K) \\ \mathrm{cov}(\theta_2,\theta_1) & & & \vdots \\ \vdots & & & \\ \mathrm{cov}(\theta_K,\theta_1) & & \dots & \mathrm{var}(\theta_K) \end{bmatrix} \tag{15}$$

A well-knnown approach to the estimation of Cov(θ) is by

$$\mathrm{Cov}(\theta) \tilde{=} (\partial\theta/\partial X)\mathrm{Cov}(X)(\partial\theta/\partial X)' \tag{16}$$

where $(\partial\theta/\partial X)$ is the K x IJ matrix of partial derivatives given by eqn. (14). Cov(X) is defined as is Cov(θ) and is an IJ x IJ dimensional matrix. " ' " denotes a matrix transpose. See Clifford (1973) for additional details of this approach to estimating covariances of dependent variables in terms of covariances of independent variables.

Simulated X_{ij}'s

We illustrated eqn. (14) and (16) with simulated data. c_{ij}^k's were specified for i=1, ...,I, j=1,...,J, and k=1,2. Using $\theta_1 = 3.00$ and $\theta_2 = 1.00$, 1.00, F_{ij}'s were computed by eqn. (2). The O_i's and D_j's were chosen arbitrarily and then T_{ij}'s were obtained from the usual DSF procedure. For each of these T_{ij}'s a Poisson error was simulated using a standard algorithm that is given by Naylor et al (1966). This error was added to the T_{ij}'s yielding a set of simulated observed flows, X_{ij}'s. Using these simulated X_{ij}'s we solved the ML equations using the gradient search procedure given in Sen and Sööt (1981) and obtained estimates for θ_1 and θ_2 of 3.16 and .954 (which, incidently are quite close to the true values of 3.0 and 1.0). Then ML F_{ij}'s, T_{ij}'s were computed followed by the derivatives $\partial\theta_k/\partial X_{ij}$ and estimates of covariances, standard errors and confidence intervals. Table 1 gives c_{ij}^k's and the simulated X_{ij}'s.

For these c_{ij}^k's and observed flows, the ML F_{ij}'s are given by

$$F_{ij} = \exp(3.16c_{ij}^1 + .945c_{ij}^2) \tag{17}$$

where 3.16 is the ML estimate of θ_1 and .945 is the ML estimate of θ_2.

Derivatives $\partial\theta_k/\partial X_{ij}$

The derivatives $\partial\theta_k/\partial X_{ij}$ are given in Table 2.

Covariance of observed flows, X_{ij}'s

Consistent with our Poisson assumption we have

$$\mathrm{cov}(X_{ij},X_{pq}) = \begin{cases} \text{ML } T_{ij} & \text{if } (i,j) = (p,q) \\ 0 & \text{if } (i,j) \neq (p,q) \end{cases} \tag{18}$$

TABLE 1

c_{ij}^1, c_{ij}^2 and SIMULATED X_{ij}

c_{ij}^1

	D_1	D_2	D_3	D_4	D_5
O_1	1.0000	0.8000	0.6000	0.4000	0.2000
O_2	0.8000	1.0000	0.8000	0.6000	0.4000
O_3	0.6000	0.8000	1.0000	0.8000	0.6000
O_4	0.4000	0.6000	0.8000	1.0000	0.8000
O_5	0.2000	0.4000	0.6000	0.8000	1.0000

c_{ij}^2

	D_1	D_2	D_3	D_4	D_5
O_1	0.2000	0.4000	1.0000	0.3000	0.6000
O_2	1.0000	0.4000	0.3000	0.7000	0.6000
O_3	0.4000	0.3000	0.3000	0.2000	0.1000
O_4	0.7000	0.2000	0.3000	0.5000	0.2000
O_5	0.3000	0.4000	0.2000	0.1000	0.5000

Simulated X_{ij} Observations

	D_1	D_2	D_3	D_4	D_5
O_1	45.00	17.00	9.00	6.00	6.00
O_2	62.00	26.00	16.00	26.00	12.00
O_3	42.00	22.00	62.00	45.00	26.00
O_4	36.00	19.00	45.00	199.00	77.00
O_5	20.00	16.00	30.00	85.00	258.00

TABLE 2

THE DERIVATIVES $\partial\theta_k/\partial X_{ij}$

$\partial\theta_1/\partial X_{ij}$

	D_1	D_2	D_3	D_4	D_5
O_1	0.003603	-0.002624	-0.010650	-0.012830	-0.019510
O_2	-0.005327	0.002702	-0.002174	-0.009302	-0.014180
O_3	-0.007951	-0.002174	0.003153	-0.001724	-0.006600
O_4	-0.014630	-0.007050	-0.002174	0.002252	-0.001724
O_5	-0.018150	-0.013280	-0.007050	-0.001273	0.002252

$\partial\theta_2/\partial X_{ij}$

	D_1	D_2	D_3	D_4	D_5
O_1	-0.023150	-0.016460	0.001802	-0.017560	-0.007973
O_2	0.000901	-0.017370	-0.019360	-0.006881	-0.008874
O_3	-0.015560	-0.019360	-0.020260	-0.022250	-0.024250
O_4	-0.005980	-0.021350	-0.019360	-0.014470	-0.022250
O_5	-0.016660	-0.014660	-0.021350	-0.025150	-0.014470

Covariances, etc., for θ_1, θ_2

By combining the values given in Table 2 with ML T_{ij}'s (not shown) using eqns. (18) and (16) we obtain the covariances, standard errors and approximate 90% confidence intervals for θ_1 and θ_2. These are given in Table 3.

TABLE 3

COVARIANCES, STANDARD DEVIATIONS, CONFIDENCE INTERVALS AND Z SCORES

Cov(θ)

$$\begin{matrix} \theta_1 \\ \theta_2 \end{matrix} \begin{bmatrix} .0375 & .0230 \\ .0230 & .3820 \end{bmatrix}$$

Standard Deviations

$$\sigma_{\theta_1} \cong .194$$
$$\sigma_{\theta_2} \cong .618$$

Approximate 90% Confidence Intervals

θ_1 : [+2.84, +3.38]
θ_2 : [-.066, +1.97]

Approximate Z Scores

$$z_{\theta_1} = \text{est } \theta_1/\text{est } \sigma_{\theta_1} = 16.3$$
$$z_{\theta_2} = \text{est } \theta_2/\text{est } \sigma_{\theta_2} = 1.54$$

CONCLUSION

As already indicated, this type of problem has been addressed by others including Evans (1971) and Flowerdew and Aitkin (1982). Evans (1971) relies heavily on derivatives for an average cost function which are computed in the special case of $\theta_1=0$ and K=1. The average cost functions which Evans uses are not explicitly relevant here. Flowerdew and Aitkin (1982) apply the unconstrained gravity model using least squares methods and a Poisson assumption of variation about the mean. Sen and Sööt (1981) also address this problem. The discussion of sensitivity in the linear least squares case is a straightforward calculation of standard errors.

Altogether, we have generalized Evans's model and given a method of discriminating between the explanatory power of different cost variables. Certainly which variables explain mean values is as important as which probability law (from, say, the list indicated in the GLIM package referenced in Flowerdew and Aitkin, 1982) to use for variation about the mean. Thus our procedure can address the problem of selection of variables.

Finally, the frequent occurrence of gravity models in planning suggests that we can relate this paper to other contributions in urban modelling. For example Putman (1983) asserts that all models should, eventually, be tested by practical application. We add that in a practical context, especially a continuing application to policy formation, some assessment of individual significance of each of the different cost variables eventually should be carried out. This can be especially pressing in view of the difficulty of obtaining a continuing supply of data, a point which Putman also stresses.

ACKNOWLEDGEMENT

The authors gratefully acknowledge the help of the Computer Centre at the University of Illinois at Chicago for making computer time available for the research presented in this paper

REFERENCES

Alonso, W., 1976, A Theory of Movements: (1): Introduction, WP 266, Institute of Urban and Regional Development, University of California, Berkeley, CA.

Clifford, A.A., 1973, Multivariate Error Analysis, John Wiley, New York.

Deming, W.E. and Stephan, F.F., 1940, On a Least Squares Adjustment of a Sampled Frequency Table When the Expected Marginal Totals are Known, Annals of Mathematical Statistics, 11, 427-449.

Evans, A. W., 1971, The Calibration of Trip Distribution Models With Exponential or Similar Cost Function, Transportation Research, 5, 15-38.

Flowerdew, R. and Aitken, M., 1982, A Method of Fitting the Gravity Model Based on the Poisson Distribution, Journal of Regional Science, 22, 191-202.

Franklin, P., 1944, Methods of Advanced Calculus, McGraw Hill, New York.

Friedman, A., 1971, Advanced Calculus, Holt, Rinehart, Winston, New York 236-242.

Furness, K.P., 1962, Trip Forecasting, a paper presented at a Seminar on the Use of Computers in Traffic Forecasting, London (unpublished), (cited in Evans, S.P. and Kirby, H.R., 1974, A Three-Dimensional Furness Procedure For Calibrating Gravity Models, Transportation Research, 8, 105-122).

Giles, D. and Hampton, P., 1981, Interval Estimation in the Calibration of Certain Trip Distribution Models, Transportation Research B, 15, 203-219.

Gray, R., 1980, Gravity Models: A Conceptually and Computationally Simple Approach, Masters Thesis, School of Urban Sciences, University of Illinois at Chicago, Chicago, IL.

Gray, R. and Sen, A., 1983, Estimating Gravity Model Parameters: A Simplified Approach Based on The Odds Ratio, Transportation Research B, 17, 117-131.

Hua, C. and Porell, F., 1979, A Critical Review of the Development of the Gravity Model, International Regional Science Review, 4, 97-126.

Hyman, G.M., 1969, The Calibration of Trip Distribution Models, Environment and Planning, 1, 105-112.

Lang, S., 1968, Analysis I, Addison Wesley.

Naylor, T.H., Balintfy, J.L., Burdick, D.S. and Chu, K., 1966, Computer Simulation Techniques, John Wiley, New York.

Putman, S.H., 1983, Future Directions for Urban Systems Models: Some Pointers from Empirical Investigations, a paper presented at the International Symposium on New Directions in Urban Modelling, University of Waterloo, Waterloo, Ontario.

Sen, A.K. and Sööt, S., 1981, Selected Procedure for Calibrating the Generalized Gravity Model, Papers of the Regional Science Association, 48, 165-176.

Sen, A.K., 1982, Modeling Spatial Flows: The Generalized Gravity Model, Department of Urban Planning and Policy, University of Illinois at Chicago, Chicago, IL.

Sinkhorn, R., 1964, A Relationship Between Arbitrary Positive Matrices and Doubly Stochastic Matrices, Annals of Statistics, 35, 876-879.

Sinkhorn, R., 1967, Diagonal Equivalence to Matrices with Prescribed Row and Column Sums, American Mathematical Monthly, 74, 402-405.

Weber, J.S., 1981a, Error Propagation in the Gravity Model, PhD dissertation, School of Urban Sciences, University of Illinois at Chicago, Chicago, IL.

Weber, J.S., 1981b, Derivatives of Gravity Models and Statistical Applications, School of Urban Sciences, University of Illinois at Chicago, Chicago, IL.

Weber, J.S., 1981c, A Preliminary Supply and Demand Sensitive Respecification of Constrained Gravity Model, a paper presented at the 28th annual North American Meeting of the Regional Science Association, Montreal, Quebec.

Weber, J.S. and Sen, A.K., 1982, On the Sensitivity of Gravity Model Forecasts, Department of Urban Planning and Policy, University of Illinois at Chicago, Chicago, IL, Journal of Regional Science, forthcoming.

Wilson, A.G., 1967, A Statistical Theory of Spatial Distribution Models, Transportation Research, 1, 253-270.

APPENDIX A

THE LINEARIZED DSF PROCEDURE

DSF Procedure and the Doubly Constrained Gravity Model

The DSF procedure is the well-known doubly constrained gravity model computing algorithm of alternate scaling of rows and columns of an origin-destination flow matrix so that they alternately have row or column sums which satisfy origin or destination total flow constraint eqns. (4) and (5). In the limit, the DSF procedure yields T_{ij}'s satisfying eqns. (1), (4) and (5).

LDSFP and Gravity Model Derivatives

The linearized DSF scalings (LDSFP) is simply the iteration of linearized DSF multiplications and can be used for computing $\partial T_{ij}/\partial F_{rs}$, $\partial T_{ij}/\partial O_p$ and $\partial T_{ij}/\partial D_q$. More specifically, each iteration of a DSF row or column scaling can be written as an explicit formula in terms of the preceding iterated flow estimates and origin or destination totals. These explicit formulae may be differentiated or (equivalently) expanded in a Taylor series at the base point T_{ij} which satisfies the gravity equations for F^o_{ij}, O^o_p, D^o_q. By multiplying matrices of linear coefficients for a sequence of row and column scalings we obtain the linearization for the DSF procedure corresponding to the same sequence of scalings. See Weber and Sen, forthcoming and Weber (1981a) for details,

Notation

We obtain a notation suitable for both the DSF procedure and its derivatives by denoting the set of row scalings by R and the scalings of the ith individual row by R_i. The column scalings are similarly denoted by C and C_j. We may indicate some of the various realizations of the DSF procedure with this R and C notation as

$$R(T^o_{ij}) = T^o_{ij}\frac{O_i}{\sum_{q=1}^{J} T^o_{iq}}, \quad C(T^o_{ij}) = T^o_{ij}\frac{D_j}{\sum_{p=1}^{I} T^o_{pj}} \quad \text{for } i=1,..,I \text{ and } j=1,..,J \tag{19}$$

$$(T^{2n}_{ij}) = (RC)^n(T^o_{ij}) = R \circ C \circ R \circ \ldots \circ R{\circ}C(T^o_{ij}) \tag{20}$$

$$(T_{ij}) = \lim_{n\to\infty} (RC)^n(T^o_{ij}) = \lim_{n\to\infty}(CR)^n(T^o_{ij}) \tag{21}$$

where o denotes composition of functions. In the middle term of eqn. (20) and in eqn. (21) the superscript n indicates repeated compositon. The right hand side of eqn. (20) also can be written as $R(C(R(\ldots R(C(T_{ij}))\ldots)))$. Eqns. (19) and (20) are identities by definition but (21) is true only when the sum of the origin constraints and the sum of the destination constraints are equal.

Since the origin and destination totals O_i, D_j are needed at every step of the procedure, a completely explicit notation will also iterate these variables via identity functions denoted by O and D. Some of these additional notations and DSF procedure derivatives are indicated by eqns. (22)-(27), wherein $\delta_{.,.}$ is the usual Kronecker's delta function.

$$(R,O,D)(T_{ij},O_i,D_j) = [T_{ij}\frac{O_i}{\sum_{q=1}^{J} T_{iq}}, O_i, D_j] \quad \text{for } i=1,..,I \text{ and } j=1,..,J \tag{22}$$

$$\frac{\partial R_i}{\partial T_{rs}} = \frac{O_i}{\sum_{q=1}^{J} T_{iq}} \delta_{ir} \cdot \delta_{js} - \frac{T_{ij} O_i}{[\sum_{q=1}^{J} T_{iq}]^2} \delta_{ir} \tag{23}$$

$$\frac{\partial R_i}{\partial O_p} = \frac{T_{ij} \delta_{ip}}{\sum_{q=1}^{J} T_{iq}} \tag{24}$$

$$\frac{\partial R_i}{\partial D_q} = 0 \tag{25}$$

By using the standard convention of letting juxtaposition of Jacobian matrices of derivatives indicate matrix multiplication and relabelling of variables, we may write

$$\frac{\partial (RC)^n T^o, O, D}{\partial FOD} = [\frac{\partial ROD}{\partial TOD} \cdot \frac{\partial COD^n}{\partial TOD}] \cdot \frac{\partial T^o OD}{\partial FOD} \tag{26}$$

$$[\frac{\partial T_{ij}}{\partial F_{rs} O_p D_q}] \tilde{=} \text{upper left hand IJ x (IJ+I+J) block of } \frac{\partial (RC)^n T^o, OD}{\partial FOD} \tag{27}$$

Eqn. (26) asserts the equality of the iterated coefficients with the partial derivatives of any DSF procedure estimates of T_{ij}.

Specifying Base Points

The reader should note that for computing (T_{ij}) estimates, we may use F_{ij} as the initial estimates, (T^o_{ij}), but that for computing derivatives via the LDSF procedure as expressed by eqn. (26) or as indicated in Weber and Sen (1982), we must use previously computed T_{ij}'s for the base point. Eqn. (26) simply is not true unless T^o = previously computed T_{ij}'s which satisfy eqns. (1), (3) and (4). Weber (1981a, 1981b) gives additional details of the convergence for increasing n of the right hand side of eqn. (27) to the derivative indicated on the left hand side of eqn. (27).

APPENDIX B

IMPLICIT FUNCTION NOTATION FOR THE DERIVATIVES $\partial\theta_k/\partial X_{ij}$

To apply the formulae for derivatives of implicit functions to obtain a formula for $\partial\theta_k/\partial X_{ij}$ when θ_k's are explicitly defined by eqns. (1), (2) (4), (5), (6), these five defining equations should be combined and rewritten as

$$\sum_{j=1}^{J} A_i B_j \exp(\sum_{k=1}^{K} \theta_k c_{ij}^k) - \sum_{j=1}^{J} X_{ij} = 0, \ i=1,\ldots,I \tag{28}$$

$$\sum_{i=1}^{I} A_i B_j \exp(\sum_{k=1}^{K} \theta_k c_{ij}^k) - \sum_{i=1}^{I} X_{ij} = 0, \ j=1,\ldots,J \tag{29}$$

$$\sum_{i=1}^{I} \sum_{j=1}^{J} c_{ij}^k A_i B_j \exp(\sum_{k=1}^{K} \theta_k c_{ij}^k) - \sum_{i=1}^{I} \sum_{j=1}^{J} c_{ij}^k X_{ij} = 0, \ k=1,\ldots,K \tag{30}$$

To be completely explicit, eqns. (28), (29) and (30) may be rewritten as

$$G_m(X_{pq}, A_i, B_j, \theta_k) = \text{left hand side of (28)} = 0 \text{ for } m=1,\ldots,I \tag{31}$$

$$G_m(X_{pq}, A_i, B_j, \theta_k) = \text{left hand side of (29)} = 0 \text{ for } m=I+1,\ldots,I+J \tag{32}$$

$$G_m(X_{pq}, A_i, B_j, \theta_k) = \text{left hand side of (30)} = 0 \text{ for } m=I+J+1,\ldots,I+J+K \tag{33}$$

Then

$$\frac{\partial G}{\partial X} + \frac{\partial G}{\partial AB\theta} \cdot \frac{\partial AB\theta}{\partial X} = 0 \tag{34}$$

So that

$$\left(\frac{\partial A_i B_j \theta_k}{\partial X_{pq}}\right) = \left(\frac{\partial AB\theta}{\partial X}\right) = \left(\frac{\partial G}{\partial AB\theta}\right)^{-1} \left(\frac{-\partial G}{\partial X}\right) \tag{35}$$

that is, $[(I+J+K) \times (IJ)] = [(I+J+K) \times (I+J+K)]^{-1} [(I+J+K) \times (IJ)]$.

Thus we need an inverse of an $(I+J+K)x(I+J+K)$ dimensional matrix. This matrix is necessarily singular, although it can be made non-singular. Making it non-singular requires some explanation which is often lacking. Possibly partitioning of $(\partial G/\partial AB\theta)$ and $(\partial AB\theta/\partial X)$ can be advantageous, since $(\partial AB/\partial X)$ is not of interest. Among many sources, Friedman (1971) and Franklin (1944) give especially comprehensive treatments of differentiating eqns. (31)-(33). [Later we noticed that Lang (1968), p. 310, uses a notation for Jacobian Matrices by derivatives of a composition of functions that is apparently better for stating and proving some of the underlying results, particularly eqn. (26). When this same notation is used to express the derivative of a composition of functions as the composition of the derivatives it less clearly identifies the composition of derivatives as matrix multiplication. Finally we note that the term "Jacobian" seems to be ambigu-ous, meaning a matrix of derivatives in some contexts, the determinant of this matrix in others, and sometimes the absolute value of the determinant. Clearly, we mean the matrix here and in Weber (1981abc).]

PRIOR STRUCTURE AND SPATIAL INTERACTION

Helen Couclelis
Department of Geography
University of California
Santa Barbara, CA 93106
United States of America

Abstract. A rationale for continued interest in simple, static urban models, such as the gravity-type models, is given through the perspective of the notion of prior structure, according to which there is, embedded in every model, a largely non-empirical component resulting from the structural properties of the theoretical language used. It is suggested that the prior structure implicit in gravity models is responsible for the widely observed map effect in spatial interaction as well as for the relative predictive power of these models. A procedure is outlined for deriving that prior structure from first principles. Combined with a minimal amount of behavioural information, that quasi-analytic component can be used as prior information, in the Bayesian sense, to generate familiar forms of the gravity model as the most probable consequences of system specification. The practical significance of the prior-structure effect for model performance is then briefly discussed.

INTRODUCTION

In a collection of papers dedicated to new directions in urban modelling, a contribution on old-fashioned spatial interaction calls for some initial words of explanation. As is abundantly clear from other articles in this volume, over the years the search for more interesting and more useful representation of urban systems has progressed steadily from static to dynamic, from aggregate to disaggregate, from simple to sophisticated, from linear to non-linear, from physicalist to behavioural models. If any two words can capture the present feeling about urban systems, these words should surely be complexity and change.

Moving against the tide, at least in appearance, this paper goes back to the notion of simpler things that never change. Things of this kind, it is argued, are to be sought behind the resilience of the gravity model, which after thirty years of fierce competition, still manages to hold its own. Readers with longer memories may well be reminded of the wild-goose chase for urban-system laws so popular in the early days of social physics; and indeed, in what follows there is more than a hint of the notion of law. The crucial difference with earlier arguments about laws ruling aggregate spatial behaviour is that here the general, simple, invariant patterns sought do not refer to the social phenomena under investigation, but to the chosen mode of representation. However, since the notion of law is charged with connotations incompatible with everything we know about the behaviour of conscious human agents, perhaps the term rules would provide a more appropriate designation for regularities that have little or nothing to say about the nature of the things in themselves, but may drastically constrain the ways such things can appear to the observer-modeller.

A similar distinction between laws and rules is drawn by Pattee (1978), who reserves the term laws for patterns that are rate-dependent, object-specific, and inexorable, and calls rules the regularities that are rate-independent, observer-specific, structure-dependent, and conditional. While for the theorist and the philosopher the distinction may be the basis for endless debate, for the applied modeller it can only mean one thing: namely, that if rules of this kind can be shown to exist, then this is positive knowledge that should be taken into account when modelling urban systems. This paper sets out to explore the existence of such mechanisms mainly dependent on theoretical language and system definition, that may constrain the description of movement in geographic space in certain well defined ways. The discussion focusses on gravity-type models, although in principle it could be extended to models of other kinds.

Despite considerable technical and conceptual advances in other areas of urban modelling, interest in gravity-based spatial interaction models born in the crude social physics of thirty years ago shows no signs of waning. One reason for the continuing popularity of these rather elementary constructs must surely lie in the fact that few other models in social science have ever proved so reliable and robust in repeated applications across space and time: though never too close to actual observation, surprisingly often they come close enough. A further reason for their appeal is that gravity models, despite their simplicity, have been the source of innumerable technical and conceptual problems over the years, some of which remain unsolved and continue to generate lively argument. The present paper addresses one of these problems, the spatial structure versus behaviour controversy in spatial interaction modelling. Clearly, the interest in this question is not merely scholastic, since better understanding of what gravity models really represent will help determine much more reliably than is presently possible the conditions of their transferability across time and space, as well as foster further theoretical developments.

It is argued in this paper that the relative predictive success of the gravity model is largely due to the presence of a built-in prior structure, a quasi-analytic component which, being largely independent of empirical phenomena, retains its validity in changing empirical contexts. Thus the gravity model can be relied upon to represent aggregate spatial behaviour in different situations because of that self-fulfilling factor that ensures at least a rough good fit; at the same time, strictly speaking, the gravity model does not represent aggregate behaviour, since what makes it work seems to be an abstract systemic effect rather than any particular ability to capture the essence of how people behave in space. The notion of prior structure is discussed at length in another paper by the author (Couclelis, 1984). Here this idea will be brought to bear on the problem of distinguishing the spatial structure effect from the effect of human behaviour proper in spatial interaction. This is done by combining certain geometrical properties of bounded surfaces with the method of information minimizing (closely related to entropy maximizing), as proposed by March and Batty (1975) and Batty and March (1976). Some more general implications of the existence of a prior-structure effect in spatial interaction models are discussed in the final section.

MAP, BEHAVIOUR AND STRUCTURE IN GRAVITY MODELS

Ever since Curry (1972) remarked that "the form of the maps over which interaction takes place is an all-important determinant of the pattern of interaction", a debate has flared about whether gravity models reflect spatial structure rather than human behaviour, that is reminiscent, in both substance and intensity, of the notorious nature-nurture controversy in anthropology: is aggregate spatial interaction predetermined by the nature of the underlying map, or does it really reflect the individual choices that motivate human behaviour in space? We have learned enough about spatial interaction by this stage to know that there is truth in both the former and the latter, so that the patterns described in gravity models are now seen to reflect some inextricable mixture of the effects of space and behaviour combined. That much is generally agreed. But judging from the volume of related publications to date (Fotheringham, 1981; Timmermans and Veldhuisen, 1981) for comprehensive bibliographies, this agreement marks only the beginning of the story.

There is a tacit understanding in social science that what is significant and meaningful is what relates directly to human behaviour, as opposed to any other influences sometimes captured in models of social phenomena that constitute noise and are to be treated as such: witness the enormous amount of effort devoted to filtering out cyclical effects from studies in economics, or the war against spatial autocorrelation in geography, notwithstanding Gould's (1970) cautioning that we may be trying to eliminate from the description of spatial phenomena the one thing geographers are really entitled to talk about. In spatial interaction modelling any suspected non-behavioural, or spatial effect is sometimes referred to as the trivial effect (Batty and March, 1976) and the problem is often seen as being one of "obtaining ... estimates that are free of spatial structure effects", (Fotheringham, 1981). Interestingly, the discussion is often confined to the distance-decay parameters of the gravity model, as if the form of the model itself were now well understood and could be taken for granted.

Yet, at the heart of the difficulty in separating the spatial from the behavioural effects in spatial interaction is the fact that no one really knows to this day why the gravity model works. The great mathematical simplicity of not one of the competing alternative versions is indisputably superior to all the others, make any reasonable set of assumptions among those that have been used to justify the model seem almost equally plausible.

The question of what a model really represents does not normally arise in science because the operational answer is given implicitly in the definition of the theoretical entities involved. In gravity modelling this is a different matter. There is on the one hand a size effect, also known as mass effect, attractivity, push and pull, nodal propulsiveness and attractiveness, propensity to generate interaction, and so on. On the other hand, there is a distance effect, also variously referred to as friction of distance, separation factor, distance deterrence, distance discounting, spatial discounting, disutility of travel, distance decay, impedance function, generalized travel cost, least-effect principle, etc. Some of these designations clearly suggest behavioural effects, while others refer to familiar forces in physics, whereby it is not clear whether these are to be understood as convenient labels for undefined terms, as suggestive metaphors, or as analogs of actual social forces in want of a better name. In reaction to the seeming mindlessness of the social physics tradition, other researchers have proposed behavioural rationalizations of the structure of the gravity model, derived from rational choice theory, random utility theory, and psychological theories of choice (for example, Smith, 1975, 1981; Louviere, 1976; Sheppard, 1979). In addition to trying to provide a meaningful basis for modelling movement in space, these models are also thought by their proponents to be relatively independent of spatial structure effects, since evaluations are distinguished from spatial opportunities (Timmermans and Veldhuisen, 1981). However, the problems with such models are well known (Sheppard, 1980; Williams, 1977) not the least of which happens to be a direct consequence of the very reason for their alledged freedom from spatial-structure noise: the inability to establish any systematic relationships between evaluation and overt spatial behaviour.

Between the thoretical naiveté of the relatively successful social-physics derivations and the unsatisfactory practical performance of the more meaningful behavioural attempts, one particular derivation stands out in conceptual elegance and analytical power. This is, of course, Wilson's derivation of the gravity model from first principles using the method of entropy maximizing. That work showed that the model in its various forms is no more and no less than a best guess at the least unlikely state of a spatial system of interest, given only incomplete information. Although Wilson's work "brought a long-awaited sense of closure to the raging confusion about the interpretability and theoretical integrity of the gravity model" (Anas, 1983), sixteen years later the debate is still going strong. There are several reasons why the closure did not take place. First, and rather surprising, is the fact that the entropy-maximizing approach is still seen by a substantial number of modellers as another piece of clever social physics, and is dismissed a priori as such. Second, different derivations sometimes yield models that can fit given data sets more closely than an entropy model (Tobler, 1983) thus encouraging alternative sets of assumptions. Third, the maximum-entropy derivation is subject to the same kind of uncertainty regarding the appropriate measurement of distance and the mass variables as most of its competitors. Fourth, and perhaps most important, is the fact that Wilson's derivation itself is not theoretically flawless. From the beginning there has been some uneasiness concerning the justification of the total-expenditure constraint, often expressed as

$$\sum_i \sum_j T_{ij} c_{ij} = C \tag{1}$$

where T_{ij} is the number of trips between origin i and destination j; c_j is the expenditure of travel between i and j, and C is total expenditure. The problem arises because C is constructed out of the c_{ij}'s rather than being an independently measurable quantity, as is the case in the thermodynamic applications of the maximum-entropy principle, where E, the analog of C, is the average energy in the system (Wilson, 1970; Hua and Porell, 1979).

While all these contrasting tendencies continue to develop and inconclusive debates go on, the more statistically inclined modellers, though restricting themselves mainly to the parameters of distance decay, are busy accumulating evidence of the effect of map pattern on spatial interaction. Fotheringham (1981), for example, presents some results that should make any staunch believer in a purely or mainly behavioural base of the gravity model think twice. According to that study of airline traffic in the United States, it appears that, among other things (i) the value of the distance-decay parameter varies more widely across the country than any socially conditional behavioural differences from place to place could justify; (ii) other things being equal, less accessible origins have stronger negative distance-decay parameters than more accessible ones; and (iii) the most accessible origins even exhibit weak positive parameters, a fact which (if the conventional interpretation of the distance-decay parameter is accepted) any behavioural or traditional social-physics hypothesis would be hard put to explain. On the basis of the above findings Fotheringham concludes that distance-decay parameters seem definitely to be a function of spatial structure, and notes that no theory exists to explain such relationship for all forms of the gravity model, and in particular, for both the constrained and unconstrained case. These recent findings echo conclusions reached several years ago by Gould (1975) who wrote

> "The distance parameters appear to index the relative accessibility of a location ... The supposed effect of distance is not really a distance effect in any traditional or behaviour sense, but rather a matter of where a group is located within the set of information-generating regions."

It will be argued here that despite the difficulties mentioned earlier, the maximum entropy formalism still provides the strongest basis for the hope of cracking the secret of the gravity model, including the question of the part played by each of behaviour and map. For one thing, as evidenced in the specialized literature (Jaynes, 1957, 1967; Tribus, 1969; Levine and Tribus, 1979), the formalism embodies a principle of rational inference more general and versatile than even the supporters of its use in gravity modelling would care to argue. It is significant that what is perhaps the single most successful behavioural model in the field, the multinominal logit model, has recently been proved by Anas (1983) to be formally identical with an entropy maximizing model.

What is of special interest in the present context is the fact that the maximum-entropy formalism seems to be particularly well suited for the operationalization of a very general principle in the theory of models, sometimes referred to as the transfer of structure (Ho, 1979). In a nutshell, the idea is the following: the integers, the reals, the metric and non-metric spaces, formal logic, and in general any formal system used to construct models of empirical phenomena, are highly structured systems in a mathematical sense. In the mapping from an empirical to a formal system that yields a scientific model these structural properties are mostly maintained, so that the fully abstract structures of pure mathematics impart some of their own qualities of atemporal and unconditional validity to the models constructed on their basis. In other words, it is implied that some aspect of the structure of any model, and in particular, the aspect most responsible for predictive success, can be accounted for by properties that have little to do with the empirical phenomena under investigation, but result directly from the structure of the formal language used. If this is so, then a knowledge of that prior structure (prior to any empirical observation, that is) cannot only be extremely valuable in the construction and interpretation of logically consistent models, but can yield useful information about expected empirical performance as well.

Extended to the realm of spatial interaction modelling, this notion suggests a strategy for identifying the spatial structure effect, as opposed to the spatial manifestation of human choice. Indeed, the notorious map effect in spatial interaction should be due to no other than the prior structure entailed by the formal definition of the spatial system at that particular level of analysis. The suggested procedure, which amounts to trying to construct a gravity model from empirical scratch, so to speak, is straightforward: start with just an abstract geometric description and only the most general possible behavioural assumptions (behavioural in a systems sense, not in reference to human behaviour) and try to determine how much structure may already exist in that highly abstract system; then add to that minimal amount of real-world knowledge some more behavioural content, and use the quasi-analytic structure discovered at the previous step as prior information in a Bayesian sense, to obtain a new structure as a posterior estimate; the procedures may be continued for several steps, each time building on the last obtained prior structure.

The first steps of this procedure for deriving the prior structure implicit in the gravity model are sketched in the following. Although the basic argument is very simple, work on the mathematical details is still in progress, so that no claims can be made regarding the practical applicability of the method. With this caveat in mind, let us see how much structure there may be in the isotropic plane of conventional spatial interaction.

THE STRUCTURE OF GEOGRAPHIC SPACE

Consider a 2-dimensional metric space and a population of free-moving particles of finite size. The points in that space will be called locations and it is assumed that at any time a particle will occupy exactly one location. The assumption is equivalent to positioning a discrete space consisting of granules of finite extent rather than dimensionless points, and is meant to reflect the fact that we are dealing with a physical rather than an abstract geometrical space, that is, a space in which physical masses can exist and material events can take place (Carnap, 1956). A fundamental property of such a space is that locations on the plane are countable, so that, whereas a Euclidean area contains the same number of points as the Euclidean plane (infinity), an area in this discrete space contains fewer locations than the unbounded plane. In fact, in this case "the ratio of the sizes of regions is given by the ratio among the number of grains (locations) they contain" (Nerlich, 1976, 1958). The same of course is true of the number of locations along a line segment, so that a segment a that is, say, twice as long as another segment b, will contain twice as many locations. This space can be described by a quasi-Euclidean metric defined over the integers rather than the reals, the unit of which may coincide with the extent of one location or one particle. To distinguish it from abstract Euclidean space, we shall call this space "Space 1" or "geographic space".

Returning to our population of free-moving particles, their position in geographic space on the plane may be identified with locations (i,...j,...). If some particle n is located at i, all the other locations on the plane may be seen to lie on a series of concentric annuli (circles) of centre i. Granted the approximation that the circumference of a circle has a length of $2\pi d$ also in geographic-space, a circle of radius nd will have n times more locations on its circumference than the circle of radius d (Coleman, 1964). Thus if particle n is later found at distance nd from its original position i, it is n times less likely to be at some pre-specified location j than if it had been found only d units away from the origin (objective formulation). In other words, given the information that some particle was observed at distance nd from a location of origin i, the probability of an observer predicting the new location correctly is n times lower (since there are n times more possibilities that are equally probable) than if the event had occurred at distance d from i (subjective formulation).

More generally, it may be said that in Space 1 the a priori probability v_{ij} for any two locations i,j forming an origin-destination pair is inversely proportional to the distance d_{ij} between the two locations

$$v_{ij} = kd_{ij}^{-1} \tag{2}$$

where k is a constant of proportionality. This is of course an expression of the fundamentally important distance-decay effect, and it seems that is can be derived analytically on the basis of an elementary probabilistic argument and the most general possible assumptions. In particular, it is to be noted that no assumptions concerning the behaviour of the particles in the space were made, since a particle starting at i may have covered any path of any length at any velocity before it is observed at the new location j. Thus what is presupposed here is even less commiting than if random walk or Brownian movement had been assumed, in which case some additonal assumptions about unit displacements in space and their temporal sequence would have been needed. On the other hand, the stipulation of a space consisting of points with extent seems to be a relaxation of a taken-for-granted unrealistic assumption, rather than the introduction of a new one: events do not happen on the heads of pins, and conversely, a telephone booth can only hold that many students!

Following the mathematical definition of a potential function in 2-space

$$f(x,y) = \frac{1}{\sqrt{x^2 + y^2}} \tag{3}$$

defined everywhere except at the origin, the equivalent function

$$v_{ij} = kd_{ij}^{-1}, \quad i \neq j \tag{4}$$

given in eqn. (2) may be called the geometric potential of Space 1. The geometric potential gives rise to certain further properties characterizing that space. The most fundamental of these is the fact that its points (locations) can be associated with varying a priori probabilities of being affected by events according to their position relative to a given boundary. A measure of that effect may be derived as follows.

Suppose that a particle that was observed at location j_1 at time t is found at distance d from j_1 at the next moment in time; that particle has equal a priori probability of being anywhere on the circle of radius d, and a probability proportional to $\frac{1}{2\pi d}$ of being at location i in particular. The same is true for any particle starting at distance d from i, at locatons j_2, ... j_n. Since we are dealing with disjoint events, the incidence potential at i for a given distance d may be defined as a quantity proportional to the sum of the corresponding probabilities for all the points j at distance d from i

$$u_{i(d)} = 2\pi d \frac{1}{2\pi d} = 1 = \max \tag{5}$$

However, if the area over which a given set of events may take place is bounded, $u_{i(d)}$ will vary according to the position of i relative to the boundary. Here we must distinguish between two kinds of boundaries, permeable and impermeable. An impermeable boundary delimits spatially a closed system of interactions; in the case of a permeable boundary, outside destinations (but not origins) are allowed.

For a permeable boundary, the approximate value of $u_{i(d)}$ can be easily calculated for any are θ (rad) delimited by the boundary

$$u_{i(d)} = \theta d \frac{1}{2\pi d} = \frac{1}{2\pi} < 1 \tag{6}$$

The case of an impermeable boundary is more complicated because for any distance d, the incidence potential contributed to the origin i by every destination j that is closer than d to the boundary will be greater than $\frac{1}{2\pi}$. Numerical calculations performed on a small number of bounded areas based on a square lattice of points have shown that $u_{i(d)}$ is in general < 1 for locations i that are closer than d units to the boundary.

There is no difficulty in extending the above reasoning to the calculation of the total incidence potential u_i at i for all (discrete) distances d from i within a given boundary. This will simply be the sum of the incidence potentials contributed by each complete or partial annulus of unit width, arc, length θ_d (with $1 \leq \theta_d \leq 2\pi$), surrounding i

$$u_i = \sum_{d=1}^{a} u_{i(d)} \tag{7}$$

where a is the maximum distance of i from the boundary.

Since in the case of permeable boundaries $u_{i(d)}$ will always be smaller than 1 for points i at less distance than d to the boundary, and since this seems to be true in general also for impermeable boundaries, we may accept as a working hypothesis the following proposition: for any location origin i, the greater the number of destinations at any distance d are being cut off by a boundary (that is, the less exposed i is), the smaller on the whole the value of u_i will be for the location. Intuitively, it seems plausible that u_i will reach a maximum over the geometric centre of gravity of the area, but no further use of this conjecture will be made in this paper.

The function $u(x,y) = f(x_i,y_i)$ defined for all locations i inside a given boundary constitutes a discrete scalar field over the bounded region. Because the set of values u_i is finite in this case, we can also define the sum $U = \Sigma u_i$ of the incidence potentials for all the n locations within the region. It is obvious that every bounded area will be characterized by such a positive constant U, the value of which will depend on both the size and the shape of the region.

We thus come to realize that even this minimal spatial system has an intrinsic structure which is very different from that of the isotropic Euclidean plane usually assumed. Whatever empirical phenomena we may wish to describe in a space thus defined, these will be inevitably confounded and distorted by the built-in systemic bias. Responses to that predicament may range from rejecting gravity models altogether, to ignoring the prior structure as a trivial effect conveying no information of empirical interest. It seems to me that the problem of how to deal with this situation was all but solved several years ago in a paper by Batty and March (1976) except that at that time the correct prior structure underlying the gravity model was not identified. The procedure proposed by Batty and March for generating an extended family of spatial interaction models was to start off with a very simple probability distribution based on the Coleman-Zipf model

$$p_{ij} = KO_iD_jd_{ij}^{-1} \tag{8}$$

and treating this as a prior, p_{ij}^o, to derive the next more complex model in the family as a posterior, using the method of information minimizing. As the authors had already shown elsewhere (March and Batty, 1975) information minimizing is consistently and unambiguously related to the method of entropy maximizing. Indeed, it turns out that Shannon's entropy

$$H = -\sum_{ij}\sum p_{ij}\ln p_{ij} \tag{9}$$

which is used as the measure of uncertainty in ordinary entropy maximizing, is only a special case of a more general measure of information, H*, defined in terms of the relative information difference I separating a posterior probability distribution from a prior (Batty and March 1976). The main practical difference between the two methods is that information minimizing allows the explicit encoding of a known prior probability distribution, as opposed to the once-for-all encoding of all the information available required in entropy maximizing. Thus, whereas regular entropy maximization always leads to a general solution of the form

$$p_{ij} = \frac{1}{Z(\lambda_1, \lambda_2, \ldots \lambda_k)} \exp\{-\lambda_1 f^1(x_{ij}) - \lambda_2 f^2(x_{ij}) - \ldots \lambda_k f^k(x_{ij})\} \tag{10}$$

with $f^n(x_{ij})$ being functions of the information x_{ij}, λ_n the associated Lagrangians, and $Z(\lambda_n)$ the partition function, information minimization leads to the general solution,

$$p_{ij} = \frac{p^o_{ij}}{Z(\lambda_1, \lambda_2, \ldots \lambda_k)} \exp\{-\lambda_1 f^1(x_{ij}) - \lambda_2 f^2(x_{ij}) - \ldots -\lambda_k f^k(x_{ij})\} \tag{11}$$

where p^o_{ij} is now also incorporated as a product in the partition function $Z(\lambda_n)$.

The theoretical framework that will allow us to make use of the information contained in the intrinsic structure of Space 1 is thus available. The next problem is to find a probability distribution p_{ij} implied by that structure that may be used as prior information along the lines of the information-minimizing technique. This is attempted in the following.

The possibility of defining a structure of incidence probabilities on the basis of just a boundary and a mode of system definition suggests that some primitive interaction relation may also be present that depends entirely on these non-empirical conditions. It can be easily seen that this is indeed the case. Consider a particle starting at i and arriving at j over some arbitrary path in an arbitrary time. Since we know nothing about the laws of motion of the particle, we can only conjecture about the probability of i and j forming an origin-destination pair, based on our knowledge of the bias of the bounded space as expressed in the field of incidence potentials and any other relations holding in Space 1. To recall the earlier definitions, the incidence potential u_j of a location in Space 1 is proportional to the probability of that location being the destination of a particle. The reasoning as regards origins is exactly symmetric, since what is a destination in one set of observations will be an origin in the next. Applying the rule for conditional probabilities (Tribus, 1969).

$$p(AB|C) = p(A|C) \cdot p(B|AC) \tag{12}$$

where A = location i is an origin; B = location j is a destination; and C = all the other facts in the problems (viz the definition of Space 1 and what follows from it), we have p_{ij} = (probability of i being an origin)·(probability of j being a destination given that i is an origin) = $u_i(v_{ij}u_j)$, where v_{ij} = kd_{ij}^{-1}, the geometric potential defined earlier. Thus,

$$p_{ij} = ku_i u_j d_{ij}^{-1} \text{ in Space 1, with } \sum_{i}\sum_{j} p_{ij} = 1.$$

We now proceed to introduce a small amount of empirical information into the system, moving from the highly abstract Space 1 to a slightly less abstract Space 2, where we shall seek to determine a new p_{ij} distribution. The empirical information now available concerns the actual distribution of origins, O_i, and destinations, D_j. If n origin-destination paths are involved, we can write

$$\sum_j p_{ij} = \frac{O_i}{n} \quad (13)$$

$$\sum_j p_{ij} = \frac{D_j}{n} \quad (14)$$

with

$$\sum_i\sum_j p_{ij} = 1 \quad (15)$$

That knowledge changes the whole field of incidence potentials, since for all the origins i, u_i is now = 1, and new incidence values u' must be calculated accordingly for all the locations in the space. This will be done in a similar manner as before, making use of the geometric potential, and the effect of the boundary. The same recalculation must be performed separately from the point of view of the destinations j. Thus if both the origins and the destinations are known, Space 2 is associated with two distinct incidence potential fields, u_p' for the origins, and u_a' for the destinations, the subscripts standing for production and attraction, respectively.

Once the revised incidence potential fields are calculated, some additonal information about the spatial interaction system becomes available. It is well known that every scalar field f(x,y) has associated with it a vector field, grad f or ∇f. Tobler (1976-1977) and Sheppard (1979b) both interpret that relation to highlight the intimate association between potential and interaction in spatial models. Tobler computes, from the relative net exchanges in a spatial interaction table, a vector field which he calls a flow field or "wind", assumed to facilitate interaction in particular directions. The associated scalar potential is viewed as a pressure which induces the flow. Sheppard, on the other hand, interprets the gradient of a potential function directly as the corresponding interaction function. In addition he shows that the same relation holding for deterministic interaction in continuous space also holds for probabilistic interaction in discrete space. However, it follows from the mathematical definition of gradient that the identification of potential gradient with interaction is not correct unless restricted to neighbouring points. Yet the potential gradient proves directly useful in modelling interaction in a slightly different context. It is known that the movement of a particle on any curve between i and j can be associated with the line integral ${}_i\int^j F.Tds$, where F is a vector field and T the unit tangent vector at any point of the curve (Stein, 1982). If F happens to be the gradient of a scalar field, ∇f, F is a conservative vector field. Now, whenever the vector field F is conservative, the value of the above line integral is the same (constant) for all curves between i and j. Moreover, a related theorem states that in this case

$$ {}_i\int^j \nabla f \cdot Tds = f_{(i)} - f_{(j)} \tag{16}$$

Granted the approximation necessary to define an integral in our discrete Space 2, we may therefore write

$$ {}_i\int^j \nabla u'_p \cdot Tds = u'_{p(i)} - u'_{p(j)} \tag{17}$$

and

$$ \int^j \nabla u'_a \cdot Tds = u'_{a(i)} - u'_{a(j)} \tag{18}$$

These relations, that must hold for every actual origin-destination pair, provide additional information that should be incorporated in the constraints. Rewriting these in the form

$$g(u'_p) = \Delta u'_p$$

and

$$g(u'_a) = \Delta u'_a$$

we have, for the entire system:

$$\sum_i\sum_j p_{ij} g(u'_p) = \overline{\langle \Delta u'_p \rangle} \tag{19}$$

and

$$\sum_i\sum_j p_{ij} g(u'_a) = \overline{\langle \Delta u'_a \rangle} \tag{20}$$

These two sets of equations are formally identical with the energy travel-cost constraint of standard entropy maximizing. The association is in fact a strong one, for the physical interpretation of this kind of line integral is usually given as the work done by a particular force field on a particle traversing a path from i to j, and of course, in physics, work is a quantity very closely associated with energy.

Having identified the prior probability distribution, $\overset{o}{p}_{ij}$, and the constraints (13), (14), (15), (19) and (20) resulting from the new information in Space 2, we can now proceed with the information minimization method. From eqn. (1), the solution to the problem is given by

$$p_{ij} = p^{o}_{ij} \exp\{-\lambda_{i_1} - \lambda_{j_2} - \lambda_3 q(u'_p) - \lambda_4 q(u'_a)\} \tag{21}$$

which can be written as

$$p_{ij} = p^{o}_{ij} K_i K_j O_i D_j \exp\{-\beta_1 q(u'_p) - \beta_2 q(u'_a)\} \tag{22}$$

with

$$K_i = \frac{1}{n \sum_j p^{o}_{ij} K_j \exp\{-\beta_1 q(u'_p) - \beta_2 q(u'_a)\}}$$

$$K_j = \frac{1}{n \sum_i p^{o}_{ij} K_i \exp\{-\beta_1 q(u'_p) - \beta_2 q(u'_a)\}}$$

and $\beta_1 = \lambda_3$, $\beta_2 = \lambda_4$.

Finally, replacing p^{o}_{ij} by its (normalized) value, $u_i u_j d^{-1}_{ij}$, we have

$$p_{ij} = K_i K_j u_i O_i u_j D_j \exp\{-\beta_1 q(u'_p) - \beta_2 q(u'_a)\}\, d^{-1}_{ij} \tag{23}$$

Several things may be said about this gravity model holding for a bounded interaction space. First, the origins and destinations are weighted by a measure of their relative accessibility, and the model is definitely not symmetrical, as it should not be (Tobler, 1976-1977). Second, the impedance function itself clearly reflects the spatial structure of the system (location of origins and destinations relative to each other and to a boundary), as well as the conventional distance effect. Third, for a singly constrained model (say, origin-constrained), the exponential function reduces to

$\exp\{-\beta q(u')\}$, or $\exp\{-\beta(u'_i - u'_j)\}$

which shows that all other things being equal, the most accessible origins (the ones with the greatest u'_is) will have the smallest parameters, as reported by Fotheringham (1981) and Gould (1975). Fourth, it appears that the old controversy about the legitimacy of the total travel cost constraint in standard entropy maximizing is resolved by the substitution of information contained in the geometry of the given spatial system for the rather arbitrary empirical quantities introduced by analogy with energy in the physical applications of the formalism. Fifth, the model is inherently probabilistic (because of the role played by the inherently probabilistic incidence potential field), as seems fit for a representation encoding knowledge that is necessarily very incomplete. Sixth, as suggested by Batty and March (1976) and Couclelis (1982), the posterior probability distribution in (22) can also be seen as the next prior in a recursive sequence reflecting the gradual enrichment of the system under consideration in empirical content. Thus, later steps should involve disaggregaton of the basic variables to any desired degree, and the systematic introduction of economic and other socially relevant concepts and quantities. In principle, the result should be a Chinese-box hierarchy of consistent, increasingly complex spatial models representing most probable states of self-contained abstract worlds, in which the presence of randomness, expressed through the information-minimizing method, testifies for the real-world knowledge that is missing. Among the structures to be rediscovered are the Lowry model, models representing land market and transport system equilibria, and utility maximizing models of spatial choice, thus rejoining Anas's (1983) proof of the formal equivalence of entropy and multinomial logit models. These possibilities are currently being explored, but work along these lines is still too far from completion to warrant any but the broadest conjectures at this stage.

EXTENSIONS AND SPECULATIONS

It is the prerogative of unfinished work to encourage speculation. The same basic argument that was used here to explicate the map effect in spatial interaction could in principle be extended to provide a new perspective on the construction and interpretation of models of other kinds. Implicit in the discussion so far was the idea that, once a system has been formally defined in a particular way, particular forms of system behaviour are necessarily to be expected. Social systems and natural systems are on equal footing in this respect, since the logic of structure transfer cannot discriminate between different empirical interpretations. Provided that the level of analysis is abstract enough, the structure of a model will represent as much, or even more, the formal relations implicit in its mathematical expression, as the empirical phenomena being described. This is why, once an urban system has been defined in terms of a Newtonian system, Newtonian-type laws are bound to be found.

Such a perspective could throw some new light on many familiar macro- and meso- models, whose major present drawbacks are a poor interpretabililty of concepts and terms and the inevitable physicalist stigma. Thus, for example, geographic potentials have preoccupied researchers for several decades, and as the work of Tobler (1976-1977, 1981) and Sheppard (1981) among others testifies powerful mathematical methods can be used for their exploration. The notion of incidence potential presented in this paper could provide a much-needed theoretical justification for turning to geographic potentials once again at this sophisticated age, and at the same time give a new meaning to physical analogies that are rightly resisted as such. Further, noting that incidence potentials as defined here are the results of a particular kind of stochastic process, the recently discovered equivalence of potential theory and Markov processes could begin to bear fruit also in urban science. The theoretical possibilities are many; there remains to see what the practical significance of all this might be.

There is indeed a very practical point to the rather theoretical discussion in this paper. Despite recent disclaimers prompted by the apparent futility of the endeavour, practical urban planning is basically concerned with control; effective control is contingent upon the possibility of (conditional) prediction; prediction in the sciences is closely associated with the presence of certain invariants, sometimes referred to as laws; and the prior structures of models, as defined in this paper, are invariants of a particular sort. Granted prior structures can tell us practically nothing about the way things really are in the world, but this is even more true of the structures of pure mathematics: where would our knowledge of the world be if we had turned away from abstract formalisms on the grounds that they are empirically void?

The rules (rather than laws) embodied in the prior structure of a spatial interaction model do not have, of course, the universal validity of formal invariants, precisely because their existence is contingent upon the introduction in a formal system of some empirical content. In particular, if, as suggested above, a hierarachy of prior structures is considered, it is easy to see from the nature of the probabilistic argument that the prior-structure effect should be expected to weaken gradually, and the accumulated behavioural content to dominate, as we progress from the information-poor to the information-rich models in the sequence. Together with the loss of invariance resulting from the dampening of the prior structure should go a gradual decrease in transferability and predictive power, an inference supported by what we know about the performance of complex versus simple spatial models. Indeed, there is a strong suggestion here that what is invariant and predictable in phenomena may have much more to do with the structure of the language of description than with any immanent properties of the phenomena in themselves.

Be that as it may, what we have here seems to be an indication of the existence of a reliable predictive component in models, one that can be trusted to be at work as soon as the crudest features of empirical phenomena are observed. This is a piece of positive knowledge that we cannot afford to throw away, much though we may deplore its total lack of interst from a human viewpoint. How is that knowledge to be applied in practice, how is it to be combined with other approaches and lines of thought that are more meaningful - and less objective - because they lack the logical necessity of quasi-formal system rules: these are the really important questions, the ones this paper has not even begun asking. The purpose here was much more modest: to show that simple, static physicalist models still allow interesting questions to be raised.

REFERENCES

Anas, A., 1983, Discrete Choice Theory, Information Theory and the Multinomial Logit and Gravity Models, Transporation Research B, 17, 13-23.

Batty, M. and March, L., 1976, The Method of Residues in Urban Modelling, Environment and Planning A, 8, 189-214.

Carnap, R., 1956, Introduction, in Reichenbach, H. (Ed.), 1958, The Philosophy of Space and Time, Dover, New York.

Coleman, J.S., 1964, An Introduction to Mathematical Sociology, Free Press of Glencoe, New York.

Couclelis, H., 1982, Philosophy in the Construction of Geographic Reality, in Gould, P. and Olsson, G. (Eds.), A Search for Common Ground, Pion, London, 105-138.

Couclelis, H., 1984, The Notion of Prior Structure in Urban Modelling, Environment and Planning A, 16, 319-338.

Curry, L., 1972, A Spatial Analysis of Gravity Flows, Regional Studies, 6, 131-147.

Fotheringham, S.A., 1981, Spatial Structure and Distance-Decay Parameters, Annals of the Association of American Geographers, 71, 425-436.

Gould, P., 1970, Is Statistix Inferens the Geographical Name for a Wild Goose?, Economic Geography, 46, 439-448.

Gould, P., 1975, Acquiring Spatial Information, Economic Geography, 51, 87-99.

Ho, Y.S., 1979, Book review of Fundamentals of Measurement and Representation of Natural Systems by R. Rosen, Environment and Planning B, 6, 472-474.

Hua, C. and Porell, F., 1979, A Critical Review of the Development of the Gravity Model, International Regional Science Review, 4, 97-126.

Jaynes, E.T., 1957, Information Theory and Statistical Mechanics, Physical Review, 106, 620-630 and 108, 171-191.

Jaynes, E.T., 1967, Foundations of Probability Theory and Statistical Mechanics, Bunge, 1967 (Ed.), Delaware Seminar on the Foundations of Physics, Springer-Verlag, New York, 77-101.

Levine, R.D. and Tribus, M., (Eds.), 1979, The Maximum Entropy Formalism, The MIT Press, Cambridge, MA.

Louviere, J.J., 1976, Information-Processing Theory and Functional Form in Spatial Behavior, in Golledge, R.G. and Rushton, G. (Eds.), Spatial Choice and Spatial Behavior, Ohio State University Press, Columbus, OH, 211-249.

March, L. and Batty, M., 1975, Generalized Measures of Information, Bayes' Likelihood Ratio and Jayes' Formalism, Environment and Planning B, 2, 99-105.

Nerlich, G., 1976, The Shape of Space, Cambridge University Press, Cambridge.

Pattee, H.H., 1978, The Complementary Principle in Biological and Social Structures, Journal of Social and Biological Structures, 1, 191-200.

Sheppard, E., 1979a, Notes on Spatial Interaction, The Professional Geographer, 31, 8-15.

Sheppard, E., 1979b, Geographic Potentials, Annals of the Association of American Geographers, 69, 438-447.

Sheppard, E., 1980, The Ideology of Spatial Choice, Papers of the Regional Science Association, 45, 197-213.

Smith, T.E., 1975, A Choice Theory of Spatial Interaction, Regional Science and Urban Economics, 5, 137-176.

Smith, T.E., 1981, A Cost-Efficiency Approach to the Analysis of Congested Spatial-Interaction Behavior, Environment and Planning A, 15, 435-464.

Stein, S.K., 1982, Calculus and Analytic Geometry, McGraw-Hill, New York.

Timmermans, H.J.P. and Veldhuisen, K.J., 1981, Behavioural Models and Spatial Planning: Some Methodological Considerations and Empirical Tests, Environment and Planning A, 13, 1485-1498.

Tobler, W., 1976-1977, Spatial Interaction Patterns, Journal of Environmental Systems, 6, 271-301.

Tobler, W., 1981, A Model of Geographical Movement, Geographical Analysis, 13, 1-20.

Tobler, M., 1983, An Alternative Formulation for Spatial-Interaction Modeling, Environment and Planning A, 15, 693-703.

Tribus, M., 1969, Rational Descriptions, Decisions and Designs, Pergamon Press, New York.

Williams, H.C.W.L., 1977, On the Formulation of Travel Demand Models and Economic Evaluation Measures of User Benefit, Environment and Planning A, 9, 285-344.

Wilson, A.G., 1970, Entropy in Urban and Regional Modelling, Pion, London.

INTERDEPENDENCE RELATIONS IN INTERACTION DATA: AN ANALYSIS OF THE STRUCTURE OF THE NIGERIAN ECONOMY

Bola Ayeni
Department of Geography
University of Ibadan
Ibadan,
Nigeria.

Abstract. This paper develops a number of test statistics based on the method of minimum discrimination information to analyze the structural interdependence of the Nigerian economy. The null hypotheses of homogeneity and independence provide adequate basis for comprehending interindustrial relations in a lucid way. Subsequent developments of the methodology could revolutionize classical methods of input-output analysis, the identification of key sectors of an economy and the simulation modelling of intersectoral flows in national, regional and metropolitan economic systems.

INTRODUCTION

Urban and regional systems analysis has within the last two decades developed and perfected a number of techniques not only for mathematical modelling of systems of interest (Wilson, 1970; 1974; Batty, 1976; Ayeni, 1979) but also for the testing and the analysis of the structure of interaction matrices (Macgill, 1977; Bacharach, 1970; Morrison and Smith, 1974; Ayeni, 1976; 1982). Although there is a general appreciation of the possibility of extending these methodological developments into wider areas of investigation, researchers have particularly been wary in such endeavours either because of some philosophical implications of the application of these techniques (Webber, 1975; Beckmann, 1973; Beckmann, et al 1971) or because there is paucity of relevant data for their utilization. The latter reason has been particularly important in the area of the analysis of the structure of economic systems. However, in recent years, there has been a rapid development of input-output tables at national, regional and urban scales (Morrison, 1973) and the exploration of the use of certain techniques of urban and regional systems modelling has become expedient. The present study has thus been designed to further such investigation by the development and utilization of discrete data analysis techniques that are complementary to those log-linear models described by Willekens (1981) and Hutchinson (this volume).

The basis for the approach lies in the fact that a comprehensive representation of an economic system is usually given as an input-output table which essentially is an interaction matrix that may or may not be spatial. As a technique, input-output is itself an analytical scheme that shows the interdependence of economic sectors in a national, regional or urban economy. Nonetheless, very few techniques exist for the determination of the level of importance of interdependence relations expressed in input-output tables. For instance, it is usual to define this importance either by a sequential examination of links on both the input and output sides of input-output tables (Morrison, 1973; Miernyk, 1965) or by expressing interindustry linkages as percentages of total linkages. These same considerations underlie current methods for the determination of the key sectors of an economic system (Hazari, 1970; Hewings, 1974). Nonetheless, the fact that the question of key sector identification could be related to either the sales coefficient matrix or the input coefficient matrix underpins the importance of forward and backward linkages of the economic system (Hazari, 1970; Hewings, 1974; Rasmussen, 1956; Beyers, 1976). Consequently, the input-output table and the associated table of technological coefficients are important representations of the structure of economic systems and are therefore of tremendous importance to policy makers. They could of course be used to make reasonable prognosis of future states of economic systems.

THE 1973 NIGERIAN INPUT-OUTPUT TABLE

The 1973 input-output table is known to be the second interindustrial transactions table ever prepared in the country (Nigeria, 1981). The first table, prepared by Nicholas G. Carter in 1959 had only nine sectors (Nigeria, 1981). On the other hand, the 1973 table had twenty-five main sectors and also identified various categories of final demand, imports and exports in addition to providing a row for value added. Indeed, the twenty-five sectors of the 1973 input-output matrix represent a greater level of disaggregaton of the earlier table as well as the inclusion of new sectors. For instance, the Mining sector was split into Oil Mining and Other Mining and Quarrying to make room for the analysis of the role of the Oil sector in the Nigerian economy (Nigeria, 1981). Furthermore, the ever increasing importance of defence, civil administration and social services makes the inclusion of Producers of Government Services imperative. In addition, the incorporation of such other sectors as Finance and Insurance, Hotel and Catering, Professional and Personal Services have become feasible as more and more data became readily available. Table 1 describes the twenty-five productive sectors of the Nigerian economy.

Furthermore, while the accounting system used in the development of the input-output table is generally consistent with the revised system of National Accounts of the United Nations (1968), efforts have been made to include those characteristics that are peculiar to the Nigerian situation since a basic aim of the development of the table is to use it to meet the needs of the Nigerian development planner and policy-maker. None the less, the system represents "a consolidation of the income and product accounts of the nation in terms of their input from other industries, their use of productive factors, their sale to other industries and their delivery to various final users" (Nigeria, 1981).More details about characteristics of these sectors as well as estimation procedure are described in the National Accounts of Nigeria (Nigeria, 1981).

TABLE 1

THE PRODUCTIVE SECTORS OF THE ECONOMY

No.	Sector	Description of Products
1.	Agriculture	- Crops, eg., yams, cotton, maize, rice, cassava, melon, beniseed, cocoyam, soya bean, palm produce, plantain, millet, guinea corn, groundnut, beans.
2.	Livestock	- Hides, beef, dairy milk, skins, meat, mutton, pork products, eggs and poultry.
3.	Forestry	- Logs, firewood, palm wine, piassava fibre, other vegetable fibres, natural gums and resins.
4.	Fishing	- Products of the commercial fishing sector, ponds and artisanal fishing sectors.
5.	Oil Mining	- Products of existing oil mining companies
6.	Other Mining and Quarrying	- Metaliferous ores, coal, quarrying marble and limestone.
7.	Food, Drinks Beverages and Tobacco	- Meats products, dairy products, fruit canning, vegetable oil, grain mill products, bakery products, sugar, beer, soft drinks and tobacco.
8.	Textile Weaving, Apparel and Leather Products	- Spinning, weaving and finishing of textiles, made up textile goods, knitted goods, cordage rope and twine, weaving apparel, travel goods and leather foot wear.
9.	Wood and Wood Products including Furniture	- Saw-milling, carving, wooden fixtures and furniture.
10.	Paper and Paper products; Printing and Publishing	- Paper and paper products, pulp paper and paper board, container and boxes, printing and publishing.
11.	Drugs and Chemicals	- Fertilizers and pesticides, synthetic resins, paints, varnishes, drugs and medicine, soaps, cleaning agents, toilet goods any by-products of petroleum, petro-chemical and coal.
12.	Rubber and Plastic	- Rubber products such as tyres, tubes and other plastic products.
13.	Basic Metal Products	- Pottery and glass products, bricks and tiles, cement, concrete products, cutlery, hand tools, general hardware, structural metal products, metal furniture fixtures.
14.	Fabricated Metal Products, Machinery and Equipment	- Agricultural machinery and equipment, electrical, radio and communication apparatus, household applicances, ship building and repairing, motor vehicle body building, motorcycles and bicycles, jewelry, etc.

TABLE 1
(continued)

15. Other Manufacturing Products	- Products of activities not elsewhere classified and other manufacturing establishments that employ less than five persons.
16. Electricity and Water	- Generation, transmission and distribution of electricity for sale. The output of water from various water boards and corporations.
17. Building and Construction	- The value of work put in place by contractors and individually constructed buildings in urban and rural areas.
18. Transport	- Revenues from road, rail, air and water transportation modes.
19. Communication	- Products of the post and telecommunications, broadcasting and television services.
20. Distributive Trade	- Products of wholesale and retail trade of goods to industrial, commercial, institutional and household uses.
21. Finance and Insurance	- Activities of the Central Bank, Commercial Banks and Financial Institutions.
22. Producers of Government Services	- The product of Federal, State and Local Governments as well as public non-profit institutions engaged in such varied services as defence, general civil administration, education, health, social security, welfare services and housing.
23. Hotels and Catering	- Operations of hotel, and restaurants.
24. Professional Services and Business Services	- Operation of such fields as services, dentists, lawyers, accounting and auditing, advertising business, recreational facilities, etc.
25. Housing	- Output of rental incomes from office buildings and residential accommodation, letting of industrial buildings.

The Nigerian input-output matrix shown in Table 2 is indeed a rather simple one. A cursory examination shows that out of a possible 625 entries, only 300 or barely 48 percent were filled. By way of contrast, the 42 by 42 input-output matrix of the United States in 1947 had only 393 or 23.4 percent of all its cells unfilled. More recent input-output tables of the United States actually show fewer unfilled cells (Leontief, 1966). Of course there are variations in the number of these entries from sector to sector either by production (rows) or by consumption (columns). For instance, as production sectors, Fishing, Fabricated Metal Products, Building and Construction, Production of Government Services, and Hotels and Catering have very few entries and suggest a poor development of linkages. On the other hand, as consumption or buying sectors, Livestock, Foresty, Producer of Government Services, and Housing have few

TABLE 2

THE INPUT-OUTPUT TABLE OF NIGERIA (Millions of Naira) 1973

	1	2	3	4	5	6	7	8	9	10	11	12	13
1	114.26						144.79	70.82		0.11	0.02	0.01	0.73
2							3.54	15.54			0.02	0.16	
3							0.10	0.02	10.67		5.16	8.55	0.27
4													
5				8.28	5.53	0.64	2.48	2.22	0.54	2.97	1.71	0.35	1.58
6					0.10			0.00					20.25
7		5.00		1.40			55.25				0.07		
8					0.46		2.93	20.28	0.29	4.67	0.04	2.48	0.07
9							0.03	0.08	0.71	1.82	0.79	0.27	0.16
10					1.77		17.32	1.24	0.23	17.58	8.76	1.90	1.88
11	5.76				0.51		1.83	25.56	0.39	1.40	25.15	0.02	0.90
12							0.00	0.57	0.35	0.00	0.80	10.75	0.60
13	28.39				3.57			0.18	0.18		2.10	0.44	33.49
14													0.01
15	13.07						1.77	0.03					
16				2.21	0.62	1.31	4.05	12.31	0.53	2.18	2.15	2.00	4.77
17					2.02								
18			2.30	0.47	48.18	82.04	12.26	20.18	1.84	8.35	16.97	6.14	21.53
19				0.41	0.50		2.45	0.78	0.12	0.28	2.68	1.01	0.57
20	4.61	0.60		1.00	3.81	0.10	19.41	43.06	3.72	13.82	17.57	4.92	37.30
21				5.09	2.26	0.70	4.00	5.15	0.69	1.00	3.43	1.72	3.43
22													
23					0.69								
24				7.00	9.46	14.66	0.16	0.86	0.26	0.68	0.23	0.10	0.22
25				0.77	0.73		0.73	1.21	0.19	0.90	0.76	0.87	0.63
26	2,183.29	488.82	215.02	465.01	1,940.96	198.77	284.09	108.08	18.32	48.30	197.51	59.57	94.81
27	2,349.39	494.4	217.32	491.64	2,021.56	298.23	556.68	328.17	39.02	104.05	285.90	101.26	223.20

TABLE 2
(continued)

	14	15	16	17	18	19	20	21	22	23	24	25	26	27
1		8.22								5.02			2,005.40	2,349.39
2		0.87								1.54			472.75	494.42
3	0.01	3.97		89.18									99.39	217.32
4		0.00								0.97			490.66	491.64
5	0.94	0.43	7.70	1.88	54.70	0.05	8.43						1,920.97	2,021.56
6		1.73		273.84	2.00								0.30	298.23
7		6.49	0.01		0.16	0.01		0.40		3.09	0.50		484.28	556.68
8	0.16	9.10	0.00		0.15	0.09	6.76	0.07			0.29		280.44	328.25
9	3.18	3.65		21.00	0.50		5.04	0.07					1.73	39.02
10	2.86	0.95	0.05	2.67	3.17	0.90	6.20	8.86	0.19	1.80	1.80		25.72	104.05
11	2.88	0.93		27.54	0.05	0.01					1.18		192.32	285.90
12	0.19	2.26			39.89		6.51				0.59		38.75	101.26
13		0.87		53.92									100.05	223.20
14	5.39												139.28	144.67
15		0.44	0.33										86.13	101.77
16	2.13	0.01	0.37	0.02	0.83	0.46	14.82	0.74		0.58	1.58		15.48	69.20
17			1.66		4.65	0.12	258.01					90.31	1,820.26	1,919.02
18	1.91	0.43	1.34	50.89	10.78	2.08	7.39	3.48		0.58	4.50		145.09	699.37
19	0.57	0.00	0.16	5.00	1.84	0.50	19.19	1.60		0.58	2.93		88.34	37.71
20	5.88	1.33	0.86	175.76	53.11	0.20		3.00		5.28	2.68		2,200.11	2,637.32
21	1.00	0.10	0.88	12.22	8.84	0.56							107.38	167.36
22													664.40	664.40
23					1.04	0.72		0.02					49.33	51.80
24	0.57	0.02	10.00	4.34	17.80	6.41	0.30	2.82		0.70	2.16		8.07	87.20
25	0.93	0.09	0.29	13.72	0.95	0.60	36.57	3.37		0.58	3.18		651.26	718.41
26	116.02	59.78	45.55	1,186.99	408.93	25.11	2,268.09	140.63	664.40	32.50	59.22	628.10		
27	144.67	101.77	69.20	1,919.02	699.37	37.71	2,637.32	167.36	664.40	51.80	87.20	718.41		

interactions. By way of contrast are such sectors as Textiles, Wood and Wood Products, Basic Metal Products, Transport, Distributive Trade, and Finance and Insurance, which either as production or consumption sectors show some interdependence relationships. None the less it is difficult to comment meaningfully on these interactions.

The input-output coefficient matrix derived from Table 2 and expressed in inputs per thousand Naira of output is presented in Table 3. It is obvious from this table that many of the coefficients are indeed very small. For example, only 55 of the 300 coefficients have a value that is greater than 0.04; and this number represents only 18 percent of existing interactions or a mere 9 percent of the potentially possible number of interactions. Furthermore, as production sectors of the economy, only Wood, Textiles, Communications and Professional Business have more than five coefficients greater than this threshold of 0.04. On the other hand, only Food, Building and Construction, and Distributive Trade as consumption sectors have more than five coefficients greater than 0.04. Undoubtedly, these deductions are useful but could be grossly inadequate. There is therefore need for the development of a statistical system that determines the significance or otherwise of these coefficients either individually or by sectors.

INTERDEPENDENCE RELATIONS IN INPUT-OUTPUT TABLES

Input-output coefficients constitute viable indicators of the linkage relationships that exist in an economic system. However of equally relevant concern should be the determination of the nature of importance or levels of significance of these coefficients. Thus an analysis of these coefficients must produce inter alia, answers to the following questions. What is the extent of importance or the nature of the linkages in the given input-output table? Are they of any statistical significance whatsoever and have they been developed in crucial sectors of the economy? The answers of these questions are important from many points of view. First, they provide us with some quantitative assessment of a given input-output table and hence may indirectly justify the usefulness or otherwise of the table as well as subsequent derivatives therefrom and deductions therein. Secondly, and considering the fact that an input-output matrix is expensive to construct, quantitative assessments of levels of dependence could serve as precursors to the development of alternative analytical techniques. Furthermore, such analysis as this could also indicate alternative methods for the determination of key sectors of an economic system (Hazari, 1970).

Of course, one must underscore the fact that very few studies have been concerned with the determination of the level of significance of the interdependence relations in input-output tables. To that extent the present study is

TABLE 3

THE INPUT–OUTPUT COEFFICIENT MATRIX IN KOBO INPUTS PER M1,000.00 OF OUTPUT, 1973

	1	2	3	3	5	6	7	8	9	10	11	12	13
1	48.64						61.63	30.14		0.05	0.01	0.01	0.31
2							7.16	31.43			0.04	0.34	
3							0.46	0.09	49.10		23.74	39.34	1.24
4													
5				4.10	2.74	0.32	1.23	1.10	0.27	1.47	0.85	0.17	0.78
6					0.34			0.00					67.90
7		8.98		2.51			99.30				0.13		
8					1.40		8.93	61.78	0.88	14.23	0.12	7.56	0.21
9							0.77	2.05	18.20	46.65	20.24	6.92	4.10
10					17.01		166.46	11.92	2.21	168.96	84.19	18.26	18.07
11	20.15				1.78		6.40	89.40	1.36	4.90	87.97	0.07	3.15
12							0.00	5.63	3.46	0.00	7.90	106.16	5.93
13	127.20				15.99			0.81	0.81		9.41	1.97	150.04
14													0.07
15	128.43						17.39	0.29					
16				31.96	8.97	18.94	58.57	178.02	7.66	31.53	31.09	28.92	68.98
17					1.05								
18			3.29	0.67	68.89	117.31	17.53	28.85	2.63	11.94	24.26	8.78	30.78
19				10.87	13.26		64.97	20.68	3.18	7.43	71.07	26.78	15.12
20	1.75	0.23		0.38	1.44	0.04	7.36	16.33	1.41	5.24	6.66	1.87	14.14
21				30.41	13.50	4.18	23.90	30.77	4.12	5.98	20.49	10.28	20.49
22													
23					13.32								
24				80.63	108.96	168.86	1.84	9.91	2.99	7.83	2.65	1.15	2.53
25				1.07	1.02		1.02	1.68	0.26	1.25	1.06	1.21	0.88
26	147.03	32.92	14.48	31.32	130.71	13.39	18.14	7.28	1.23	3.25	13.30	4.01	6.38

TABLE 3
(continued)

	14	15	16	17	18	19	20	21	22	23	24	25	26
1		3.50								2.14			853.58
2		1.76								3.11			956.17
3	0.05	18.27		410.36									457.34
4		0.00								1.97			998.01
5	0.46	0.21	3.81	0.93	27.06	0.02	4.17	0.00					950.24
6		5.80		918.22	6.71								1.01
7		11.66	0.02		0.29	0.02		0.72		5.55	0.90		869.94
8	0.49	27.90	0.00		0.46	0.27	20.60	0.20			0.88		854.35
9	81.50	93.54		538.19	12.81		129.16	1.77					44.34
10	27.49	9.13	0.48	25.66	30.47	8.65	59.59	85.15		1.83	17.30		247.19
11	10.07	3.25		96.33	0.17	0.03					4.11		672.68
12	1.88	22.32			393.94		64.29				5.83		382.68
13		3.90		241.58									448.25
14	37.26												962.74
15		4.32	3.24										846.32
16	30.80	0.14	5.35	0.29	12.00	6.65	214.32	10.70		8.39	22.85		223.86
17			0.87		2.42	0.06						47.06	948.54
18	2.73	0.61	1.92	72.77	15.41	2.97	368.93	4.98		0.83	6.43		207.46
19	15.12	0.00	4.34	132.59	48.79	13.26	195.97	42.43		15.38	77.70		221.16
20	2.23	0.50	0.33	66.64	20.14	0.08	7.28	1.14		2.00	1.02		841.81
21	5.98	0.60	5.26	73.02	52.82	3.35		12.73		1.14	39.50		641.53
22													1000.00
23					20.08	13.90		0.39					952.32
24	6.57	0.23	115.18	49.99	205.02	73.83	3.46	32.48		8.06	24.88		92.95
25	1.30	0.13	0.40	19.10	1.32	0.84	50.91	4.69		0.81	4.43		906.57
26	7.81	4.03	3.07	79.94	36.29	1.69	152.74	9.47	44.74	2.19	3.99	42.30	187.30

exploratory. Nonetheless, studies by Macgill (1977), Bacharach (1970) among others on biproportional matrices increase our levels of speculation on the potential uses of this analysis especially in the area of the development, improvement and generation of national, interregional and metropolitan input-output models.

Methodology

The methodology we have developed for the measurement of the level of interdependence in an input-output table is that of the minimum discrimination information statistic as outlined by Kullback (1959); Gokhale and Kullback (1978) and Ayeni (1982); for the analysis of multinomial distributions and contingency tables. We argue that the typical input-output matrix $R = \{x_{ij}\}$: 1, 2, ..., m: j = 1, 2, ..., n could be regarded as coming from a multinominal population defined by sectoral levels of activities $x_1, x_2, \ldots, x_n$ such that

$$X_i = \sum_{j=1}^{n} x_{ij} \tag{1}$$

$$X_j = \sum_{i=1}^{m} x_{ij} \tag{2}$$

and

$$X = \sum_{i=1}^{m} X_i = \sum_{j=1}^{n} X_j = \sum_{i=1}^{m} \sum_{j=1}^{n} x_{ij} \tag{3}$$

and

$$x_{ij} \geq 0 \qquad \forall\, i,j \tag{4}$$

The assumption of an input-output table as deriving from a multinomial distribution allows us to regard the m rows or the production sectors of the economy, and the n columns or consumption sectors, as a set of mutually exclusive and exhaustive subsets or populations that have been used to classify the patterns of interdependence of the economy. In this way, we can test such hypotheses that the multinomial probability distributions for each sector are indeed identical; or that certain sectors of the economy do in fact differ in their linkage relationships with others. On the other hand, the assumption of an input-output table as a contingency table allows us to conduct a test of the independence of rows or production sectors and columns or consumption sectors (Marascuilo, 1971). These two sets of hypotheses, ie., of homogeneity and independence may for illustrative purposes be summarized in terms of the probability of occurrence of events A and B with complementary sets $\bar{A}$ and $\bar{B}$ as

$$\text{Homogeneity} : H_o : P(A/B) = P(A/\bar{B}) \tag{5}$$

$$\text{Independence} : H_o : P(A \cap B) = P(A)P(B) \tag{6}$$

For an input-output matrix, the hypothesis of homogeneity necessarily implies two major considerations. The first involves an examination of how the outputs of a particular sector have been distributed among other sectors of the economy; and a comparison of this with some theoretically expected distribution. Such a theoretical distribution might be obtained by assuming that interindustrial or sectoral relations would approach some uniformity. The null hypothesis in such a situation would be

$$H_o : P_{i1} = P_{i2} \dots = P_{in} = P_1 = P_2 \dots = P_n \qquad (7)$$

This is the case of hypothesis testing in a one sample multinomial distribution (Kullback, 1959).

On the other hand, the second approach involves a consideration of the intersectoral relations between each and every sector and an assessment of the extent to which these depart from an expected theoretical distribution. The null hypothesis in this m sample case may be stated as

$$H_o : P_{ij} = P^*_{ij} \qquad \forall_{ij} \qquad (8)$$

where P^*_{ij} is the expected probability distribution function. An acceptance of the hypothesis of homogeneity in either case implies that a reasonable set of intersectoral relations have been developed in the economic system.

The hypothesis of independence in a contingency table involves an examination of the extent to which the intersectoral relations of our input-output table are directly predicted by the row and column totals of the table. The acceptance of a hypothesis of independence implies that the input-output table does in fact possess some structural characteristics that determine to a large extent the intersectoral relations. The null hypothesis for testing this hypothesis is

$$H_o : P_{ij} = P_{i.}P_{.j} \qquad \forall\, i,j \qquad (9)$$

The minimum discrimination information statistic is based on the information gain concept of information theory (Kullback, 1959; Gokhale and Kullback, 1978; Ayeni, 1982) and constitutes some alternative techniques for the testing of hypotheses especially in situations where conventional statistical methods prove inadequate (Ayeni, 1982). The statistic is known to be related to the likelihood ratio test of Neyman and Pearson (1928) while its asymptotic behaviour is that of the Chi-Square distribution (Kullback, 1959). Furthermore, it is both a sufficient and efficient statistic.

For a null hypothesis H_o against an alternative hypothesis H_1, the minimum discrimination information statistic $I(H_o:H_i)$ is defined as

$$I(H_o:H_1) = P_1(x)P_2(y)\ln \frac{P_1(x)\ P_2(y)}{P(x)\ P(y)} \tag{10}$$

where $P_1(x)$ and $P_2(y)$ are probability distributions associated with H_1 and H_o, respectively; and $P(x)$, $P(y)$ are generalized density functions whose parameters are the same values as those of the samples x and y. In testing the three hypotheses described above, these minimum discrimination information statistics are as follows

1. For the hypothesis of homogeneity in the one sample case, the test statistic is

$$2\psi = \sum_k X_k \sum_j P^k_{ij} \ln P^k_{ij}/P_j \qquad \forall_j \quad k = 1,2. \tag{11}$$

where

$$P_{ij} = \frac{x_{ij}}{X_j} \qquad \forall_j \tag{12}$$

and P^k_{ij} are the sets of probabilities associated with the null hypothesis (k=1) and the alternative hypothesis (k=2) respectively:

$$\text{and } P_j = \frac{1}{n} \qquad \forall_j \tag{13}$$

2. For the hypothesis of homogeneity in the m sample case, the test statistic is

$$2\phi = \sum_k \sum_i X_i \sum_j P^k_{ij} \ln P^k_{ij}/P^*_{ij} \qquad \forall\, i, j \quad k = 1,2 \tag{14}$$

where

$$P_{ij} = \frac{x_{ij}}{X} \qquad \forall\, i,j \tag{15}$$

$$\text{and } P^*_{ij} = \frac{1}{n^2} \tag{16}$$

3. For the hypothesis of independence in the contingency table, the test statistic is

$$2\theta = \sum_k X \sum_i \sum_j P^k_{ij} \ln P^k_{ij}/P_{i}.P._{j} \qquad \forall\, i,j \quad k = 1,2 \tag{17}$$

$$\text{where } P_{ij} = \frac{x_{ij}}{X} \qquad \forall\, i,j \tag{18}$$

$$P_i = \frac{X_i}{X} \qquad \forall\, i \tag{19}$$

$$\text{and } P._j = \frac{X_j}{X} \qquad \forall\, j \tag{20}$$

The sets of hypotheses described above as well as the techniques developed for their testing can be seen to focus on the examination of different aspects of the structure of an input-output system. For instance, the hypothesis tested in (i) above focusses on testing for uniformity of entries in each and every row as well as each and every column. On the other hand, the hypothesis in (ii) tests for an overall uniformity of interactions while the hypothesis in (iii) tests for the independence of cell values on rows and columns simultaneously. Consequently, a judicious use of them jointly and severally can be expected to provide valuable insights into the structure of an economic system which the input-output table represents.

INTERDEPENDENCE RELATIONS IN THE NIGERIAN INPUT-OUTPUT SYSTEM

Interdependence relations in an input-output matrix are at least of two major types. The first involves the extent to which the outputs of the production sectors of the economic system are utilized by other sectors of this system while the second involves the extent to which a production sector of the economic system depends on each and every other sector in its production process. In other words, an examination of interdependence relationships involves a study of what are called forward and backward linkages, respectively. Complementing the above procedures is an examination of the extent to which a given set of input-output coefficients reflects expected structural interrelationships. The hypotheses and methodologies described above enable us to make reasonable deductions from input-output tables.

Inter-Sectoral Dependence

Both the hypothesis of homogeneity in the m sample case and the hypothesis of independence in an input-output (contingency) table enable an examination of the structural interrelations that exist between the sectors of the economy. In the former situation, it is possible to examine the extent the input-output coefficient matrix departs from a uniform distribution which would result in a hypothetical situation when all sectors have been uniformly developed. In the latter case on the other hand, one is in a position to examine the extent to which the coefficients are easily predictable by row and column totals ie., total inputs and total consumption. To this extent it is relevant to note that where the coefficients matrix is indeed simple, the coefficients are direct functions of these totals whereas the more complex is the coefficient matrix the greater the failure of row and column totals in predicting interactions.

The testing of the hypotheses of homogeneity and independence is based on the Chi-Square distribution with (m-1)(n-1) degrees of freedom. For the hypothesis of homogeneity, the obsersved χ^2 value using eqns. (14) to (16) is 26,932.56, a value that is greater than the expected value of 709.56 at the α =

0.01 significance level (Yamane, 1973). We therefore reject the hypothesis of homogeneity and conclude that inter-sectoral linkages have not been uniformly developed in the Nigerian economic system. For the hypothesis of independence, the observed χ^2 value using eqns. (17) to (20) is 21,005.04. This value is equally highly significant. Consequently we shall reject the hypothesis of independence to state that existing input-output coefficients are directly predictable by row and column totals because their classifications are not really statistically independent.

The Characteristics of Forward Linkages

The characteristics of the forward linkages in the Nigerian economic system may also be examined under the null hypothesis of homogeneity whereby for each production sector of the input-output matrix, the columns are regarded as n classes of a multinomial distribution. The minimum discrimination information statistic can then be calculated for each sector using eqns. (11) to (13) (see Table 4). In testing the hypothesis, the degree of freedom is 25 if we include the sector of final demand and the value of χ^2 at $\alpha = 0.01$ is 44.30. It is obvious therefore that all the values of the minimum discrimination information statistic are highly significant so that we have to reject the hypothesis of a uniform development of input-output relations.

TABLE 4

VALUES OF THE MINIMUM DISCRIMINATION INFORMATION STATISTIC FOR THE ANALYSIS OF FORWARD LINKAGES

NO.	Sector	MDIS Value*	Ranking
1.	Agriculture	49,520.14	3
2.	Livestock	6,460.19	10
3.	Forestry	3,280.27	12
4.	Fishing	1,280.16	18
5.	Oil Mining	80,627.44	2
6.	Other Mining	2,722.96	13
7.	Food, Drinks, etc.	14,092.36	7
8.	Textiles	10,090.59	8
9.	Wood	617.71	23
10.	Paper and Printing	2,082.29	16
11.	Drugs	7,608.29	9
12.	Rubber	1,219.58	19
13.	Basic Metal	2,602.86	14
14.	Fabricated Metal	674.45	22
15.	Other Manufacturing	821.93	20
16.	Electricity and Water	1,661.63	17
17.	Building and Construction	21,348.46	5
18.	Transport	20,513.27	6
19.	Communications	679.22	21
20.	Distributive Trade	118,890.50	1
21.	Finance and Insurance	4.297.97	11
22.	Government Services	390.02	24
23.	Hotels and Catering	348.63	25
23.	Professional Services	2,202.10	15
25.	Housing	29,530.51	4

*All MDIS values are statistically highly significant

Furthermore, it is known that the larger the value of the minimum discrimination information statistic, the worse is the resemblance between the probability functions being compared (Kullback, 1959). Consequently we can use this notion to evolve a ranking of the levels of discrepancy of existing input-output coefficients with that expected under the null hypothesis of homogeneity. Thus we see that these discrepancies are greatest for Distributive Trade, Oil Mining, Agriculture, Housing, Building and Construction, Transport, Food and Drinks, and Textile Manufacture. An examination of the patterns of interaction in the input-output coefficient matrix of Table 2 indicate that they are all characterized by a situation whereby, out of the usually large number of intersectoral links, many are either very much greater or very much smaller than the expected value of 0.038. Such other sectors as Government Services, Forestry, Hotel and Catering that do not have pronounced deviations have less values for the minimum discrimination information statistic. Thus it is possible to deduce from the above that the statistic is indeed incisive in unravelling the structure of interaction matrices.

The Characteristic of Backward Linkages

As in the case of the analysis of forward linkages, the test of the hypothesis of homogeneity on columns of the input-output table should reveal some latent characteristics of the economic system. In this case, we regard the rows of the m sectors of the input-output matrix as classes of the multinomial distribution and use the same set of equations ie., eqns. (11) to (13) to calculate the minimum discrimination information statistics for the columns of the matrix. The associated results are contained in Table 5. As in the case of forward linkages, existing backward relationships are highly significantly different from what we would except under a null hypothesis of uniform distribution of linkages.

However in terms of the ranking of the values of the minimum discrimination information statistic to identify sectors where the greatest discrepancies exist, we see that while one identifies more or less the same set of sectors the rankings do differ (see Table 5). Thus the Oil, Mining sector shows the greatest discrepancy while the Distributive Trade, Building and Construction, Transport and Agriculture sectors show equally high discrepancies between expected and observed probability distributions. While these sectors are characterized by a large number of backward linkages quite a number of these are very much bigger than 0.038. On the lower end of the scale are such sectors as Government services, Forestry, Housing and Hotels and Catering which have lower values of the minimum discrimination information statistics because they show lower deviations.

TABLE 5

VALUES OF THE MINIMUM DISCRIMINATION INFORMATION STATISTIC FOR THE ANALYSIS OF BACKWARD LINKAGES

No.	Sector	MDIS Value*	Ranking
1.	Agriculture	18,866.79	5
2.	Livestock	2,048.98	16
3.	Forestry	416.41	24
4.	Fishing	8,151.83	9
5.	Oil Mining	73,072.31	1
6.	Other Mining	2,753.85	14
7.	Food, Drinks, etc.	15,494.34	6
8.	Textiles	9,082.56	7
9.	Wood	721.48	21
10.	Paper and Printing	1,514.93	17
11.	Drugs	9,047.05	8
12.	Rubber	2,555.14	15
13.	Basic Metal	6,432.07	10
14.	Fabricated Metal	3,384.05	11
15.	Other Manufacturing	2,865.67	13
16.	Electricity and Water	1,230.81	18
17.	Building and Construction	41,054.92	3
18.	Transport	22,658.28	4
19.	Communications	801.39	20
20.	Distributive Trade	52,171.29	2
21.	Finance and Insurance	3,358.36	12
22.	Government Services	390.02	25
23.	Hotels and Catering	704.42	22
23.	Professional Services	1,157.53	19
25.	Housing	496.80	23

*All MDIS values are statistically highly significant

A further appreciation of the utility of the minimum discrimination information statistic in the examination of the structure of the Nigerian input-output system may be obtained from a formal comparison of the structure unravelled for both forward and backward linkages. This may be achieved by finding the correlation coefficient between the rankings on the analysis of forward and backward linkages (Tables 4 and 5). This rank correlation is only 0.65, a value that is significant at $\alpha = 0.05$. The conclusion then is that neither forward nor backward linkages have been equally developed in the Nigerian economic system.

CONCLUSION

The analysis of interindustrial linkages in an economic system is of practical importance to both planners and policy makers. Indeed it should be of prime interest to planners and policy makers in developing countries where the growth pole theory or concept is an accepted planning methodology and where growth poles are seen in terms of propulsive industries that have well developed backward and forward linkages (Perroux, 1955; Hirschmann, 1958). We have shown in this paper that the minimum discrimination information statistic does provide one reasonable approach to identifying the strength of linkages in an economic system. Thus in the Nigerian situation this technique through tests of the hypotheses of homogeneity and independence could quantitatively assess the low level of intersectoral linkage development. Of course conclusions from these hypotheses are indicative of potential approaches to modelling such interaction within classical entropy maximizing methodology. Furthermore, they could also be useful in bi-proportional adjustments of input-output tables (Macgill, 1977). Consequently, while such excursions as these might be regarded as innovative it is possible that they could open many more doors in particular in the area of key sector identification and the comparison of levels of development depicted in input-output tables.

Although the issues of the analysis of levels of development and the identification of the key sectors of an economic system have not been central to this paper, they cannot be neglected for too long. For instance while one attempts to attribute the underdevelopment reflected in input-output tables to either the level or amount and distribution of productively invested capital; the composition and efficiency of a country's labour force or the country's endowment with natural resources, the issue of key sector identification transcends these considerations. If we illustrate with the fact that a number of methods for key sector identification usually involves the inversion of either the sales coefficient matrix or the production coefficient matrix (Beyers, 1976; Rasmussen, 1952) a number of pertinent questions do arise. First, to what extent can such methods be justified at least in the Nigerian case, given our earlier observations and deductions? Secondly, how can these methods of key sector identification be improved or new sets of techniques developed through the notion of the minimum discrimination information statistics and bi- and multi-proportional matrix analysis (Bacharach, 1970)? Finally, given an input-output matrix that shows limited structural interdependence, what are the limitations of such methods of input-output analysis as triangulation and the inverse coefficient matrix in the forecasting of levels of economic activities? These undoubtedly are some of the numerous issues about which this paper provides a framework of analysis and investigation.

Although the analysis of discrete data has become a major research theme in urban and regional systems modelling as typified by the emergence of a number of approaches (Bacharach, 1970; Macgill, 1977; and Hutchinson, this volume), our approach provides a complementary technique for the evaluation of interaction data in terms of the strength of the linkages they represent. The adaptation of well known principles of information theory to such analysis as this as well as to other situations described elsewhere (Ayeni, 1982) is considered some of the more fruitful directions for urban systems modelling in the next few years.

REFERENCES

Ayeni, M.A.O., 1976, The City System and the Use of Entropy Urban Analysis, Urban Ecology, 2, 33-53.

Ayeni, B., 1979, Concepts and Techniques in Urban Analysis, Croom Helm, London.

Ayeni, B., 1982, The Testing of Hypotheses on Interaction Data Matrices, Geographical Analysis, 14, 79-84.

Bacharach, M., 1970, Biproportional Matrices and Input-Output Change, Cambridge University Press, Cambridge.

Batty, M., 1976, Urban Modelling: Algorithms Calibrations Predictions, Cambridge University Press, Cambridge.

Bechmann, M.J., 1973, Entropy, Gravity, Utility and All That. Manuscript.

Beckmann, M.J. and Golob, T.F., 1971, On the Metaphysical Foundations of Traffic Theory: Entropy Revisited, Fifth International Symposium on the Theory of Traffic Flow and Transportation, Berkeley, CA.

Beyers, W.B., 1976, Empirical Identification of Key Sectors: Some Further Evidence, Environment and Planning A, 8, 231-236.

Gokhale, D.V. and Kullback, S., 1978, The Information in Contingency Tables, Marcel Dekkar, New York.

Hazari, B.R., 1970, Empirical Identification of Key Sectors in the Indian Economy, Review of Economicis and Statistics, 52, 301-305.

Hewings, G.J.D., 1974, The Effect of Aggregation on the Empirical Identification of Key Sectors in a Regional Economy: A Partial Evaluation of Alternative Techniques, Environment and Planning A, 6, 439-454.

Hirschman, A.G., 1958, Strategy of Economic Development, Yale University Press, New Haven, CT.

Hutchinson, B.G., 1983, Contingency Table Analysis and Urban Travel Accounts, this volume.

Kullback, S., 1959, Information Theory and Statistics, John Wiley and Sons, New York.

Leontief, W., 1966, Input-Output Economics, Oxford University Press.

Macgill, S.M., 1977, Simple Hybrid Input-Output Models: A Graphical Approach, Environment and Planning A, 9, 1032-1042.

Marascuilo, L.A., 1971, Statistical Methods for Behavioral Science Research, McGraw Hill, New York.

Miernyk, W.H., 1965, The Elements of Input-Output Analysis, Random House, New York.

Morrison, W.I., 1973, The Development of an Urban Inter-Industry Model: 2. The Structure of Peterborough Economy 1968, Environment and Planning, 5, 433-460.

Morrison, W.I. and Smith, P., 1974, Nonsurvey Input-Output Techniques at Small Area Level: An Evaluation, Journal of Regional Science, 14, 1-14.

Neyman, J. and Pearson, E.S., 1928, On the Use and Interpretation of Certain Test Criteria for Purposes of Statistical Inference, Biometrika, 20A, 175-240 and 263-294.

Nigeria, Federal Ministry of National Planning, 1981, The National Accounts of Nigeria 1973-1975, Lagos, Nigeria.

Perroux, F., 1965, Note Sur la Notion de Pole de Croissance, Economic Appliques, 7, 307-320.

Rasmussen, P., 1952, Studies in Intersectoral Relations, North Holland, Amsterdam.

Webber, M.J., 1975, Entropy Maximising Location Models for Non-Independent Events, Environment and Planning A, 1, 99-108.

Willikens, F., 1981, Multi-Dimensional Population Analysis with Incomplete Data, WP 20, Netherlands Inter University Demographic Institute, Voorburg, The Netherlands.

Wilson, A.G., 1970, Entropy in Urban and Regional Systems Modelling, Pion, London.

Wilson, A.G., 1974, Urban and Regional Models in Geography and Planning, John Wiley, London.

Yamane, T., 1973, Statistics: An Introductory Analysis, Harper and Row, New York.

Discrete Choice

RANDOM UTILITY MODELS OF SPATIAL CHOICE

Steven R. Lerman
Department of Civil Engineering
Massachusetts Institute of Technology
Cambridge, MA 02139
United States of America

Abstract. Random utility models are now in widespread use for analyzing decisions such as mode to work. However, their application to problems of spatial choice have been far fewer and have faced some methodological obstacles specific to choices among numerous alternatives. This paper reviews both the major problems and the alternative solutions which have been developed. Particular attention is given to uses of multinomial logit analysis and its variants primarily because of their potential for dealing with large choice sets without imposing unrealistic computational burdens on the model estimation process.

INTRODUCTION

In the past decade, researchers from a variety of disciplines have focussed their attention on the application of random utility models to problems of spatial choice. Stated succinctly, random utility models assume the existence of a utility maximizing decision maker confronted with a set of mutually exclusive, collectively exhaustive alternatives, only one of which can be selected. This decision maker is further assumed to associate some utility with each alternative. This utility is random for two possible reasons. Either some aspects of the decision problem or decison maker lead to variability in the evaluation of the alternatives that cannot be explained by any measurable factors, or the analyst, when attempting to explain the observed choices, cannot fully characterize the decision maker's choice criterion.

The assumptions underlying random utility theory have led to a very rich class of model forms and a now well-developed statistical theory for estimation of these model forms. By far the most widely known member of this class of models is the multinomial logit model, derived from the assumptions that the utilities are independent and identically distributed across decision makers and their alternatives, and that the probability density function of any one of the utilities is Type I Extreme Value, also referred to as Gumbel.

We can formalize the above verbal statement of random utility models as follows. Let C_n denote the set of alternatives available to some decision maker n, and let U_{in} denote the utility of any alternative i to decision maker n. The probability that n chooses alternative i from the C_n can be derived from the following statement

$$P_n(i) = \text{Prob}(U_{in} > U_{jn} \text{ for } i \neq j,\ i,\ j \in C_n) \quad (1)$$

To make the above probability statement useful, we must typically assume that we know the distribution function of the utilities and the systematic portion of the utilities at least up to some finite vector of coefficients. In this case, we can write the total utility as

$$U_{in} = V_{in} + \varepsilon_{in} \quad (2)$$

where V(•) is the systematic utility of and ε is the random component of utility. The value of V(•) is typically a function of both the attributes of alternative i and those of decision maker n.

In most applied work, it is assumed that the systematic portion of the utilities is a linear in parameters function, and that the probability function for the utilities is fully known. However, alternative assumptions for both of these are possible and in some cases justified. In the case of a multinomial logit model in which the systematic utilities are linear in parameters, the choice probabilities are given by

$$P_n(i) = \exp(b'x_{in}) / \sum_{j \in C_n} \exp(b'x_{jn}) \quad (3)$$

where b = a vector of unknown coefficients; and x_{in}, x_{jn} = vectors of known, independent variables describing alternatives i and j.

There has been a great deal written about a specific aspect of the logit model termed the independence of irrelevant alternatives property. Stated briefly, this property is that the ratio of two choice probabilities is independent of the attributes or even the existence of any other alternatives. Whether this property is good or bad is highly context-dependent, though most commentary regarding it refers to its unrealistic predictions in specific circumstances.

Other random utility models can be derived from different assumptions on the distribution of the random components of the utilities. The most widely discussed option is the multinomial probit model, derived by assuming that the disturbances are independent across decision makers but jointly normally distributed across alternatives for any one decision maker. This model has a considerably larger set of unknown coefficients because some or all of the variance and covariance terms characterizing the normal distribution functions are typically unknown. Moreover, there are enormous computational problems associated with applying multinominal probit to large choice sets. Readers interested in this area are referred to Daganzo (1979) for a complete discussion of both the theoretical and computational issues.

The unknown coefficients of random utility models are typically inferred using maximum likelihood, though in some instances variants of least squares estimation can be used. Readers interested in a review of the range of estimation techniques for various sample designs now available should consult Manski and McFadden (1981) or Cosslett (1981).

In this paper, we will explore how the random utility paradigm has been adapted and used to analyze problems of spatial choice. To begin, however, it is important to first establish the extent to which the analysis of decision makers' choices across sets of spatial alternatives differs from other choices that have been widely analyzed using random utility models. For example, the early applications of logit analysis were to choice of mode for work trips. A number of researchers have applied random utility models to a host of choice situations, including choice of auto ownership level, auto type, coffee and soft drink brands, vacation mode of travel, housing type, whether to participate in specific public welfare programs, use of health maintenance organizations, labour force participation and many other diverse problem areas. The factors which tend to make these applications distinct from many spatial choice problems are as follows

1. Most, but not all, applications of random utility models have been to situations in which the elements of C_n, the choice set are well-defined. In contrast, many spatial choice problems involve choice elements that are difficult to define. For example, when a household chooses where to live, are they selecting a political jurisdiction, a city, a neighbourhood, a block or some other spatial unit? Similarly, firms choosing a site from which to do business may be selecting among one or more different geographical levels. In many applications of random utility theory to spatial problems, the definition of the elements in C_n is far from trivial.

2. Most spatial choices are made from very large sets of feasible alternatives. For example, the number of possible places a person with reasonable income and assets might live in a large city numbers in the thousands. The physical size of the potential choice set makes it difficult to sustain the hypothesis that any one decision maker is fully cognizant of all the potential options he or she has available at any one time.

3. Because the potential choice set is so large, we most often do not have data characterizing all elements of the choice set. This is particularly true when we, as analysts, choose to work with very small spatial units as the underlying elements of C_n. Thus, some operational theory about how to

aggregate geographical units and still preserve the integrity of the underlying random utility assumptions is often essential in actual applications.

Given the above distinctions that make spatial choice analysis somewhat distinct from the mainstream of random utility theory, this paper will summarize four main areas in which progress has been made.

1. How can the theoretical and computational problems associated with large choice sets be managed?
2. How can the process of choice set formation be incorporated into random utility models?
3. How can the relationships between endogenous variables which are spatial and related, non-spatial choices be incorporated into random utility models?
4. Are there alternative formulations similar to random utility models that can be useful in spatial choice analysis?

Each of these questions will be considered in a separate section below.

THE PROBLEM OF CHOICE SET SIZE

The large number of potential alternatives that characterize most spatial decisions made by firms and households presents particular problems in the use of random utility models. Assuming for the moment that the true choice set C_n has a large number of choice elements, analysts attempting to apply random utility models have adopted four distinct approaches.

Brute Force. Even when the choice set is quite large, it is often possible to apply at least the multinomial logit model. It should be emphasized that doing this requires acceptance of the assumption that all the utilities for all the alternatives are independent random variables; however, as we shall discuss later, there are in fact few alternative tractable forms of random utility models that can be used for choice sets with any reasonable number of spatial alternatives. To date, the largest choice set used in any single logit model was for a study of residential location decisions by Lerman (1975), who used as many as 300 alternatives in a single choice model for each household in a sample of nearly 200.

The critical shortcoming of the brute force approach is that it imposes enormous computational costs during the model estimation process. As a rough rule of thumb, for a given number of coefficients and a given sample size, the costs of estimating a multinomial logit model grow roughly linearly with the average choice set size. Unfortunately, while each of the added alternatives implies some increase in the precision of parameter estimates, the incremental precision gained by increasing the choice set beyond about 10 to 20 alternatives is quite small and declines further as the choice set size increases. Thus, while estimation costs continue to grow as one uses ever larger choice sets, there is little gained in terms of the precisions of the estimated coefficients.

Sampling from Choice Sets. Given the obvious inefficiencies of using very large choice sets, analysts sought ways of reducing the choice set used in estimation while still retaining the useful properties of available estimation procedures. One logical approach is to take the large true choice set, C_n, and draw a smaller choice set, D_n from it at random according to some known probability rule. After drawing such a choice set for each observation in a sample, the analyst would then proceed as though the randomly drawn subset were in fact the full set, applying conventional maximum likelihood estimation. This procedure was first applied by Ben-Akiva (1973), relying on a heuristic argument that the independence from irrelevant alternatives property of the multinominal logit model made this procedure valid for any such subset. In his case, he was analyzing choice of shopping destination, and he included all shopping zones selected by any resident of the origin zone as alternatives in D_n. Thus, people who resided in a zone where there was a large number of alternative destinations chosen by neighbours in the sample were assigned large choice sets, while those living in zones where other residents selected only a small number of shopping sites were given choice sets with only a few elements. All members of the sample were given the CBD as an alternative. Lerman (1975) applied essentially the same procedure in a multinominal logit model of residential location decisions.

In the only formal analysis of this problem, McFadden (1978) developed a set of conditions under which this above heuristically derived procedure will in fact lead to consistent estimates of the unknown parameters. These conditions require that the probability rule for drawing D_n from the full choice set C_n meet certain specific mathematical criteria. The most stringent of these conditions states basically that if two alternatives, i and j, are both elements of some sampled choice set D_n, then the probability of drawing D_n from the complete choice set be the same regardless of whether i or j was in fact chosen and regardless of the values of the independent variables for observation n. This requirement, which McFadden terms the uniform conditioning property is sufficient for standard maximum likelihood estimation to yield consistent estimates when the sampled choice set is treated as though it were in fact the complete choice set. As a practical matter, the simple sampling rule of taking D_n as the union of observation n's chosen alternative and a simple random example of the non-chosen elements in C_n is the most widely applied method meeting these conditions. However, it can be shown that the original method used by Ben-Akiva and later by Lerman of using observed patterns of choices for similarly situated members of the sample is only valid asymptotically as the sample size gets large. The intuitive reason for this is that this rule for constructing D_n from a large choice set tends to over-sample alternatives with high choice probabilities and undersample those with small choice probabilities.

McFadden also develops a correction technique that allows use of probability rules for drawing reduced choice sets when the uniform conditioning property is in fact not met. This technique is straightforward to implement and requires only that the rule for sampling choice sets meets the positive conditioning property, a weaker requirement than the uniform conditioning property. Let i and j be elements of some sampled subset of the full choice set C_n. The positive conditioning property requires that if the probability of the analyst sampling subset D given i was chosen by the decision-maker is positive, then the probability of sampling D given j was chosen must also be positive. Note that the uniform conditioning property implies the positive conditioning property, but not vice versa.

Given the tremendous value of McFadden's theoretical results in applying logit analysis to spatial choice problems, it is natural to speculate whether there are parallel, or in fact identical, properties for other random utility models. To date, the only results available are negative (Manski, et al, 1977) and there is reasonable basis for speculation that logit may be the only model for which such simple and useful results on sampling from choice sets will be developed.

Aggregation Across Alternatives. Another strategy for coping with the extremely large choice sets often encountered in spatial choice analysis is to aggregate choice elements into a smaller number of groups. In many instances, this type of aggregation is forced on the analyst simply because data are not available for all the alternatives at the original level of what we shall term elemental alternatives. Lerman (1975) analyzed this problem in the context choice of residential location, where the number of potential elements in C_n is unmanageable if one works with housing units as elemental alternatives. In addition, data are rarely available for individual housing units; rather, one is forced to work at some level of spatial aggregation such as census tracts or traffic analysis zones. Lerman derived an approximation that allows use of aggregated alternatives which is essentially as follows.

Let C denote the full set of alternative housing units with elements c_1, c_2, c_3, etc. Let x_1, x_2, x_3, ... be the vectors of indpendent variables associated with elements in C. Note that for the sake of notational clarity the subscript n denoting the specific decision maker has been suppressed. We now aggregate and partition the elements in C into L subsets that are mutually exclusive and collectively exhaustive, and denote these elements as C_1, C_2, C_3, ... C_L. Let M_k denote the number of elements in C that belong in aggregate set C_k, and let Z_k denote the mean of the independent variables taken over all alternatives in C_k. Lerman demonstrates that if the assumptions of the logit model hold, then as an approximation, the aggregated alternatives can be used as though it were the true choice set (and the mean independent variables for the aggregate used in the systematic utility function) if an additive correction term equal to $\ln(M_k)$ is placed on each aggregated systematic utility. Thus, the logit model to be estimated for aggregated alternatives is as

$$P_n(I) = \exp(V_I + \ln M_I) / \sum_{J=1}^{L} \exp(V_j + \ln M_j) \tag{4}$$

where I and J denote sets of aggregated alternatives.

This result is accurate when the elements within each aggregated set are nearly homogeneous in their independent variables. Some simple numerical experiments suggest that the approximation is quite robust as long as the degree of variability within aggregated choices is not too large or the degree of variability is nearly uniform across aggregations. McFadden (1978) has extended this analysis from what is essentially a first order expansion to a considerably more accurate second order series, and derived some interesting closed form results for the situation where the distribution of independent variables within each aggregated unit can be assumed normal. To date, however, these results have at least to this author's knowledge not been used in actual applications.

<u>Assumption of Continuity of Alternatives.</u> A natural extension of random utility theory applied to very large choice sets is to permit the set C_n to be a continuous rather than a finite set. This extension, first suggested for the multinomial logit model by Ben-Akiva and Watanatada (1977), was subsequently derived more formally by McFadden (1979) by generalizing the independence of irrelevant alternatives property to continuous choice subsets. The basic form of this model is as follows

$$f_n(i) = \exp(V_i) / \int_{j \in C} \exp(V_j) d_j \tag{5}$$

where $f_n(i)$ = the choice probability density; C = the continuous choice set (in many cases the points on the real plane); and V_i = the systematic utility associated with point i.

A formal derivation of the continuous logit model directly from a set of postulates about maximization of random utility was developed by Litinas (1980).

One of the more interesting aspects of the continuous form of the logit model is that by assuming tractable forms for the distribution of the systematic utilities over space, one can derive closed form solutions for specific quantitites of interest. Many interesting examples for the case of residential location in a monocentric city are derived in Ben-Akiva and Watanatada (1981). For example, if one assumes some reasonably simple form for the distribution of residential opportunities over space and a travel time disutility that is linear in distance from the city centre, one can derive quantities such as the mean work trip length or total vehicle miles travelled directly as a function of parameters of the logit model.

THE PROBLEM OF CHOICE SET FORMATION

In part as a consequence of the potential choice set for spatial decisions being so large, it is often unrealistic to assume that decision makers are fully aware of the existence and attributes of all possible alternatives. To be sure, this problem is not unique to spatial analysis; it is simply more likely to be a problem when the choice set is large. Given that the actual set of choices from which the decision maker is selecting may contain far fewer elements than the full set of potential options, the problem for the analyst becomes one of inferring in some fashion the decision makers' choice sets.

Before describing the various approaches that exist for dealing with this issue it is important to emphasize the potential consequences of a mis-specification of the choice set by the analyst. In theory, if the true choice set (ie., the one upon which the decision maker is actually making a choice) is a superset of the set imputed by the analyst, then in a formal sense the analyst can be thought of as sampling alternatives; McFadden's results outlined in the first section apply directly to this situation. Under specific assumptions about how the imputed choice set is created by the analyst from the larger, true set, one can at least in theory demonstrate whether logit parameter estimates will be consistent. The problem is considerably more severe if the analyst uses a choice set that includes elements never actually evaluated by the decison makers. In this case, the logit model will assign some positive probability to alternatives which in fact have zero probability of being selected. In theory, this will lead to entirely inconsistent parameter estimates.

The more practical issue is whether the observed attributes of the alternative which is erroneously included in the choice will, assuming the true parameter values for the model, result in predicted choice probabilites close to zero. If this is the case, there is reasonable basis for assuming that the impact of the mis-specification of the choice set on the parameter estimates will be small. For example, if we mistakenlv include an alternative place to live which is far from work and has values of neighbourhood and other variables that would make it undesirable in a residential choice model, empirical experience suggests that it will not affect the coefficients profoundly. However, if the erroneouslv included alternative has relatively favourable attributes, then it can radically alter the resulting estimated coefficients, potentially rendering the resultinq model almost useless for many applications.

Given the possible importance of correctly specifying the choice set, users of random utility models have employed a number of strategies to at least approximate the true choice set. The methods used include those in the following paragraphs.

Heuristic, Deterministic, Choice Set Generation Rules. There are many practical situations in which the analvst is willinq to impose specific restrictions on the availability of certain alternatives. In fact, the simplest such restriction is the result of defining a bounded studv area for the analysis. In doing so all spatial alternatives outside that boundary are automatically excluded from all decision makers' choice sets. Other tvpes of restrictions mav result from hvpotheses such as a maximum travel time to work for residential location models, or the restriction of certain residential areas from households with insufficient income to afford the existing housing stock.

There are frequently instances in which a priori restrictions arise directly from some theory underlyinq the model. For example, Miller and Lerman (1979) draw on central place theory to argue that the set of feasible locations for a specific tvpe of clothinq retail store was limited to seven specific major retail centres in the area they studied. This argument was supported by an analysis of retail sales data.

Deterministic restrictions on the availability of alternatives are inevitably approximations when applied in actual practice. Nevertheless, they often serve to reduce the choice set, and since they usually delete alternatives with low choice probabilities, it is unlikely that any severe problems result from their application. It should be noted, however, that in a large sample one will usually find a small number of decision makers who actually select an alternative which the analyst has deemed infeasible. Such observations can be dropped from the sample, included as having special choice sets that do not reflect the a priori constraints or can serve as a basis for simply alterinq the previous restriction.

Obtain Choice Set Information for Sample. Given the potential importance of using the correct choice set, one possible approach is to design survey procedures to elicit information not only about the chosen alternative but also the options that were considered by the decision maker in making a choice. This approach usually requires that a special data collection effort be undertaken, and it is therefore often prohibitively expensive. Moreover, there has been some evidence to suggest that simply asking respondents directly for a list of their alternatives proves unsatisfactory; they usually provide only a very small number of options which do not include obvious alternatives. While this may be in fact the way they consciously think about their alternatives in the very short run, their longer run behaviour probably reflects a wider set of options.

The use of reported choice sets also creates some difficulties in the application of random utilities to forecast future decisions when conditions may have altered sufficiently for new choice alternatives to be considered by substantial portions of the population. In this case, the analyst will have to predict how choice sets have shifted, a task which may be far more difficult than the prediction of choice conditioned on a given choice set.

Random Choice Sets. Perhaps the most theoretically satisfying approach to the problem of choice set generation was first suggested by Manski (1977), who proposed that choice probabilities be considered as the result of two distinct processes, each of which was random due the analyst's inability to observe fully some aspect of the decision process. The first part is what he termed the choice set generation process, which defines a probability distribution over all possible choice sets. The second part is the choice model itself, which is conditional on a specific choice set and produces a probability of choice for each alternative. If we denote B_n as the set of all non-null subsets of the full choice set C_n, and let B_1, B_2, ... be elements of B_n, then Manski's formulation can be written as

$$P_n(i) = \sum_{B_k \varepsilon B_n} P_n(i|B_k) P_n(B_k) \qquad (6)$$

where $P_n(i)$ = the total choice probability for decision maker n choosing alternative i; $P_n(i|B_k$ = the probability n chooses i given that the true choice set is B_k; and $P_n(B_k)$ = the probability of the choice set being B_k.

Manski's formulation was first implemented by Pitschke and Lerman (1980) in the context of modal choice. In their formulation, logit models are used for both the choice set generation and choice models. The key problem in extending their work to spatial choices is the combinatoric growth in the number of subsets of C_n as the number of elements in C_n increases. One potential solution is to place far more structure on the choice set generation model.

For example, the dogit model proposed by Gaudry and Dagenais (1977) can be interpreted as a choice model in which the feasible choice sets are restricted to either all subsets of C_n with only one element or the full set C_n. Ben-Akiva (1981) provides a richer variety of potentially practical choice set generating rules with similar restrictions.

RELATIONSHIPS AMONG CHOICES

As discussed in the introduction, it is not unusual for problems in spatial analysis to involve non-spatial decisions. It is difficult to think of households choosing locations in the abstract without also dealing with the attributes of the housing they are choosing. Similarly, firms selecting locations from which to operate must often also choose a production technology consistent with the location. For example, retail firms choosing central city locations may adopt entirely different floorspace/employee mixes than suburban firms because of the large differences in rents.

The approaches available for incorporating complex relationships among spatial and non-spatial choices have been somewhat restricted by the size of typical spatial choice sets. The major lines of research fall into the general categories, each described below.

Joint Choice Analysis. The simplest approach to incorporating other choices in a random utility model of a spatial decision is to treat the non-spatial choice dimensions as discrete, and form a large, but still finite, super choice set as the Cartesian product of the original choice set with the other, non-spatial choices. For example, if one were incorporating housing choice into a model of residential location decisions, the various types of housing would first be discretized, and all possible combinations of housing type and residential location would become the full choice set. Some care must be exercised to eliminate infeasible combinations from this large choice set. For example, some housing types will not be available in certain locations. Given this newly generated choice set, it is then possible to use any exisitng discrete choice model. As a practical matter, however, the large size of the choice sets that result from this approach generally make logit analysis the only feasible option.

This approach was first developed by Ben-Akiva (1972) in a model of shopping destination and mode choice. It was later applied by Lerman (1975) to model choice of residential location, housing type, auto ownership level and mode of travel to work. Subsequent applications have included a great number of decisions such as choice of region to migrate into and housing type (Weisbrod, et al, 1980) and a variety of travel demand problems. Its key disadvantage lies in the fact that it can vastly enlarge the choice set, potentially taxing even the multinomial logit models unless some of the techniques described in the second section are used.

Nesting of Choice. An alternative to treating large multidimensional choice sets within a single, joint model structure is to construct what has been termed a nested choice model. This form, usually depicted in terms of a decision tree, often allows a complex choice model to be decomposed into a sequence of simpler models each with a smaller choice set. For logit models, this type of decompositon was first derived by Domencich and McFadden (1975) and later formalized in terms of random utility theory as a subset of a more general model termed the generalized extreme value, or GEV model.

This form permits estimation of the complete model structure as a sequence of logit models, each of which represents a decision at another level of the decision tree. For example, a two level tree of location choice followed by housing choice would be depicted as shown in Fig. 1.

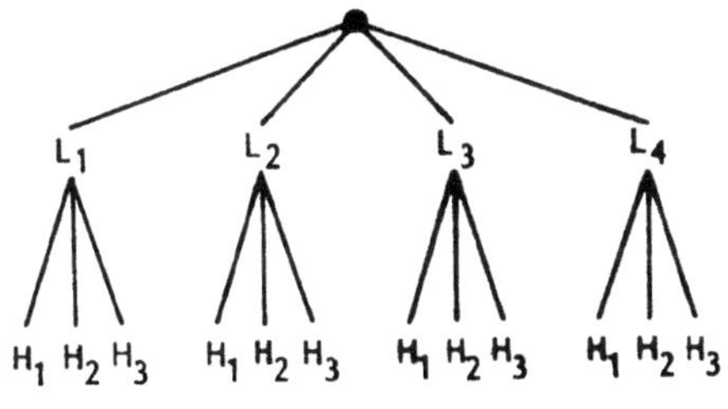

Figure 1 - Location and Housing Choice

In this figure, the first level represents a choice of location among four possible sites denoted as L_1, L_2, L_3, L_4. Then, in the second level, there are three possible housing types assumed to be available in each location denoted as H_1, H_2 and H_3 in Fig. 1. The lower level in this type of tree is termed the conditional choice because it is modelled conditional on the location decisions.

In applying the nested choice model, one would represent each of the choice levels as a logit model. At the housing choice level, the attributes of the conditioning decision, in this case the location decision, are treated as fixed, ie., as though location were exogenous. In the model of location decision, an additional variable is added to the utility function reflecting what can be interpreted as the utility of the lower level decision. Mathematically, this expected utility is the natural logarithm of the denominator of the lower stage logit model.

It should be emphasized that one need not interpret nested logit models as reflecting a behaviourally sequential decision process. One can simply view the entire decision tree as a complete random utility model that has the convenient property of decomposing into a sequence of simple logit models. One can demonstrate that the simple logit model is in fact a special case of the nested logit form, and that there are a priori restrictions on the coefficient of the expected utility that are required if the nested model is to be consistent with random utility theory. Specifically, the coefficient on the expected utility term must be between zero and one for a nested form to be a random utility model. In addition, extension of nesting to any number of levels is straightforward.

While it is usual practice to estimate nested logit models in a sequence, it is also feasible to estimate all the parameters of the entire model simultaneously. This, however, destroys the most useful aspect of the models since it does not permit decomposition of the estimation process into a series of smaller, easier to manage models. It does, however, yield parameter estimates that are somewhat more efficient than those developed by sequential estimation. A usual practice when estimating the parameters jointly is to use the sequential estimation technique as a starting point in whatever optimization algorithm is being employed to solve for the maximum likelihood estimates.

Mixed Continuous Discrete Choice Models. There are many instances in which the choices related to the spatial dimension are not naturally discrete. Rather than articifically discretizing such decisions in order to fit them in the random utility framework, it is often feasible to construct models that permit both discrete and continuous endogenous variables. The first such work in this area was by Heckman (1978), who was principally interested in adding a binary, discrete variable to a system of continuous dependent variables. His work, which was focussed on problems in labour force participation, was closely followed by Westin and Gillen (1978), who modelled choice of mode to work, discrete variables, and distance walked by auto users from their parking place to their place of work, a continuous variable.

Both these early mixed continuous/discrete models used probit analysis for the discrete choice model. Given the extremely large computational requirements of multinomial probit, this made their techniques impractical for situations with large choice sets. Dubin and McFadden (1980) developed comparable models using multinomial logit for the discrete part. To the author's knowledge, their results have to date never been applied to spatial decisions.

Miller and Lerman (1981) developed a specific mixed/continuous model for analyzing decisions of retail firms on where to locate, a discrete choice among major retail activity centre, and the continuous choices of amount of retail floorspace and number of employees. Because of the particular forms used, they were able to incorporate the continuous portion of the model into the discrete part, producing a multinomial probit model. The parameter estimates from the continuous sub-model were derived directly from the discrete model's coefficients. In actual application, Miller and Lerman found it necessary to discretize the size of the retail establishment, leaving the number of employees used as the continuous dimension of choice.

ALTERNATIVE FORMULATION

The last topic to be considered in this review is whether there may be formulations of spatial choice problems that are more useful than standard random utility models. Two recently developed approaches, both of which are closely related to random utility models as presented in the first section, offer considerable promise for practical application. These are the development of sequential search models and what have been termed random bid models. Each of these is considered briefly below.

Sequential Search Models. The general theory of sequential search has been widely discussed as a potentially useful way of viewing the search for a residence. The theory has the advantage of viewing the decision maker as examining one alternative at a time. When each alternative is viewed, the decision maker has the option of taking that alternative or continuing the search.

This straightforward general structure allows for innumerable variants. Different sequential search models have been derived allowing for different objectives of the searcher, assumptions about the cost of viewing each successive option, assumptions about the distribution of the attributes of the alternatives, whether the decision maker is allowed to recall previously rejected alternatives (with and without certainty) and whether the full set of alternatives is finite or infinite. Virually all of this extensive literature deals exclusively with the problem of theoretical model structure, and almost not at all with the practical problems of model estimation on the part of the analyst who observes a sequence of searches and wishes to infer some unknown model parameters. The major exception to this is Hall (1980), who examines the search for housing in a metropolitan area. In his empirical work, each stage of the search sequence is in fact viewed as the outcome of a random utility model, where the two alternatives are to take the current housing unit being examined or to continue searching. The probability of any given search pattern occurring is the product of a series of binary events.

Lerman and Mahnassani (1984) have extended Hall's work to develop the theory of search model estimation in greater detail. They examine a wide range of possible informational situations the analyst might encounter when estimating a sequential search model and consider both the case where rejected alternatives can and cannot be recalled for further consideration. Among the more interesting informational situations is where only the searcher's original and final locations are actually observed by the analyst.

Random Bid Models. An alternative formulation of spatial decisions was proposed independently by Ellickson (1981) and Wolfe (1981). In their model each alternative is viewed as implicitly a commodity for which different potential buyers are bidding. The bids of the potential buyers, rather than the utility each buyer associates with each alternative, is viewed as a random variable. In contrast with random utility theory, the basic unit of observation in a random bidding model is the spatial alternative rather than the decision maker. The random bidding model assumes that the highest bidder will in fact receive the location. Readers familiar with conventional bid rent theory will recognize this way of looking at locational decisions as having its roots in Alonso's (1964) original theory of residential and retail firm location.

It is interesting to note that Ellickson and Wolfe derived the same basic model form while examing two entirely different applications. Ellickson's empirical work was on housing choice, while Wolfe's was on retail firm decisions. In both cases, they derived models that are essentially logit forms. However, rather than predicting the probability that each alternative will be selected, the models predict the probability that each bidder will in fact make the highest bid. Neither Ellickson nor Wolfe consider the case where the highest bid itself is actually observed by the analyst. This case is analyzed by Lerman and Kern (1983) who derive a model that jointly predicts the probability any bidder makes the highest bid and the value of that bid. This type of model is essentially a mixed continuous/discrete model, but differs in its interpretation from those discussed above in the fourth section of the paper.

The advantage of Lerman and Kern's extension is that it provides a direct means of inferring willingness-to-pay for various attributes of alternatives. As Ellickson notes, without explicitly using the observed price information, both random utility and random bid models only allow estimates of willingness-to-pay up to an arbitrary scaling; thus it is possible only to infer ratios of substitution for various attributes from these formulations unless one of the attributes is price. The extension allowing price paid by the highest bidder to be endogenous to the model makes estimation of the scaling part of the model itself.

To date there has only been one pilot application of Lerman and Kern's model. However, an efficient estimation code has been developed and further applications are in progress.

CONCLUSION

There is obviously significant potential in the use of random utility models for analyzing spatial choices. The considerable advances in econometric theory that have occurred recently have made the actual application of these models feasible. In a few cases, models of destination choice have been estimated and applied in actual practice.

As with any new technique, there are a series of questions which must be resolved before widespread use in planning practice can be recommended. First, there must be further efforts on validating forecasts derived from spatial choice models. The evidence which exists suggests that validation produces new insights into the appropriate specification of utility functions for spatial decisions.

Second, we must develop a clearer understanding of whether simpler choice models such as multinominal logit are useful for modelling spatial choices, or whether more complex functional forms are required. This issue will be difficult to resolve in any concrete way; in large measure, the appropriateness of a particular choice model depends crucially on how the systematic component of the utility function is specified.

The final question to be resolved is the domain of modelling situations for which the random utility framework is most appropriate. As more evidence accumulates, we will come to understand better the appropriate niche choice models should occupy in the spectrum of available analysis tools.

REFERENCES

Alonso, W., 1964, Location and Land Use, Harvard University Press, Cambridge, MA.

Ben-Akiva, M., 1973, Structure of Passenger Travel Demand Models, PhD dissertation, Department of Civil Engineering, MIT, Cambridge, MA.

Ben-Akiva, M., 1981, Choice Models with Simple Choice Set Generating Processes, working paper, MIT, Cambridge, MA.

Ben-Akiva, A. and Watanatada, Thawat, 1981, Application of a Continuous Spatial Choice Logit Model, in Manski, C. and McFadden, D. (Eds.), Structural Analysis of Discrete Data with Econometric Applications, MIT Press, Cambridge, MA.

Cosslett, S.R., 1981, Efficient Estimation of Discrete Choice Models, in Manski, C. and McFadden, D. (Eds.), Structural Analysis of Discrete Data with Econometric Applications, MIT Press, Cambridge, MA.

Daganzo, C., 1979, Multinomial Probit: The Theory and its Applictions to Demand Forecasting, Academic Press, New York.

Domencich, T. and McFadden, D., 1975, Urban Travel Demand: A Behavioral Analysis, North Holland, Amsterdam.

Dubin, J.A. and McFadden, D., 1980, An Econometric Analysis of Residential Electric Appliance Holdings and Consumption, Department of Economics, MIT, Cambridge, MA.

Ellickson, B., 1981, An Alternative Test of the Hedonic Theory of Housing Markets, Journal of Urban Economics, 9, 56-79.

Gaudry, M.J.I. and Dagenais, M.G., 1978, The Dogit Model, Transportation Research B, 13B, 105-111.

Hall, P., 1980, Search Behavior in Urban Housing Markets, PhD thesis, MIT, Cambridge, MA.

Heckman, J.J., 1978, Dummy Endogenous Variables in a Simultaneous Equations System, Econometrica, 46, No. 4.

Lerman, S.R., 1975, A Disaggregate Behavioral Model of Urban Mobility Decisions, PhD disseration, MIT, Cambridge, MA.

Lerman, S.R. and Kern, C.R., 1983, Hedonic Theory, Bid Rents and Willingness to Pay: Some Extensions of Ellickson's Results, Journal of Urban Economics, 13, 358-363.

Lerman, S.R. and Mahnassani, H., 1984, The Econometrics of Search, Environment and Planning, forthcoming.

Litinas, N., 1950, Simplified Methods for Transportation Policy Analysis: A Continuous Modeling Approach, ScD thesis, MIT, Cambridge, MA.

Manski, C.F., 1977, The Structure of Random Utility Models, Theory and Decision, 8, 229-254.

Manski, C.F. and McFadden, D., 1981 (Eds.) Alternative Estimators Sample Design for Discrete Choice Analysis, in Structural Analysis of Discrete Data: With Econometric Applications, MIT Press, Cambridge, MA.

Manski, C.F., Lerman, S.R. and Albright, R.L., 1977, Technical Memorandum on the Development and Testing of a Multinomial Probit Estimation Procedure, series of technical memoranda prepared for the Federal Highway Administration, Washington, D.C.

McFadden, D., 1978, Modelling the Choice of Residential Location, in Karlqvist, et al (Eds.), Spatial Interaction Theory and Planning Models, North Holland Press, Amsterdam.

McFadden, D., 1979, Quantitative Methods for Analyzing Travel Behavior of Individuals: Some Recent Developments, in Hensher, D. and Stopher, P. (Eds.), Behavioral Travel Modelling, Croom Helm, London.

Miller, E.J. and Lerman, S.R., 1979, A Model of Retail Location, Scale and Intensity, Environment and Planning A, 11.

Pitschke, S. and Lerman, S.R., 1980, Choice Set Formation for Low Income Households: A Methodology for Analysis, working paper, Department of Civil Engineering, MIT, Cambridge, MA.

Watanatada, Thawat, 1977, Application of Disaggregate Choice Models to Urban Transportation Planning, PhD disseration, Department of Civil Engineering, MIT, Cambridge, MA.

Weisbrod, G.E., Lerman, S.R. and Ben-Akiva, M., 1980, Tradeoffs in Residential Location Decisions: Transportation versus other Factors, Transport Policy and Decision Making, 1, 12-25.

Westin, R.B. and Gillen, D.W., 1978, Parking Location and Transit Demand: A Case Study of Endogenous Attributes in Disaggregate Mode Choice Models, Journal of Econometrics, 8, North Holland, Amsterdam.

Wolfe, R., 1981, An Econometric Bid Rent Model of Urban Retail Store Entry and Location, PhD dissertation, MIT, Cambridge, MA.

THE APPLICATION OF AN ELIMINATION-BY-ASPECTS MODEL TO URBAN LOCATION DECISIONS

William Young
Department of Civil Engineering
Monash University
Clayton, VIC 3168
Australia

Abstract. Until recently, models of the relationship between the demand for urban space and the attributes influencing this demand have relied on empirical comparisons and few have contained a solid behavioural base. The Elimination-by-Aspects model presented in this paper has its origins in the behavioural sciences. This paper briefly outlines the theory underlying the model and describes applications to the choice of residence of a group of people in Melbourne and the freight facility location choice of a number of firm managers.

INTRODUCTION

The evolution of urban areas and their transport systems are inextricably interrelated. Changes in land use influence the demand for and construction of transport infrastructure and the creation of transport systems influences urban development. Knowledge of the components of this interaction is essential before good planning decisions can be made.

Much of the research into this aspect of urban planning concentrates on the development of mathematical models to replicate the evolution of urban areas. These models range from the simple descriptive models of Hoyt (1939) and Burgess (1929) to the more complex economic theories of Alonzo (1964) and Muth (1969). Application of these models have often focused on zonal aggregations of people within an urban area and until recently few models have been built to investigate the location decisions of individuals.

Over the last decade a number of modellers (Lerman, 1975; Quigley, 1973) have realized that there is a deficiency in the tools available to urban planners and have begun to develop behavioural models. Unfortunately many developments in applying choice models to location decisions have taken models of transport mode choices and applied these to location choice.

These initial applications of choice models to location decisions attempted to apply a compensatory logit model. However as will be discussed later the appropriateness of the behavioural assumptions made in applying this model may be questioned. Possibly a more appropriate model form can be based on an elimination procedure where the decision maker considers the attributes describing an alternative in order of importance and eliminates alternatives as they are found to be unsatisfactory with respect to each attribute. This model has been called an Elimination-by-Aspects (EBA) model.

This paper presents an outline of the EBA model and its application to two location choices and these are (i) residential location choice; and (ii) freight facility location choice. Initially the paper discusses the deficiencies in existing models of location choice. The mathematical form of the EBA model and its ability to overcome these deficiencies are discussed next. The application of the model to residential location choice and freight-facility location choice are described in the third and fourth sections.

REVIEW OF EXISTING LOCATION CHOICE MODELS

To determine the factors affecting location decisions it is first necessary to propose an appropriate model of this decision. Two distinctly different choice structures can be identified in the literature on choice models and these are compensatory and non-compensatory models. Compensatory models assume that an individual can trade-off high levels of satisfaction in some attributes with low levels in others. Non-compensatory models do not allow this trade-off between attribute levels.

Most choice models have been applied to land use studies (Quigley, 1973; Lerman, 1975; Anas, 1975) and can be classed as compensatory since they use a linear additive procedure for combining the attribute satisfaction levels into an overall measure of satisfaction with each alternative. In the case of Lerman's (1975) model this results in an individual combining sixteen attributes into a composite evaluation for its alternatives. This seems to be beyond the mental capabilities of any individual.

Another characteristic of many existing location choice model results from the historical development of choice models in transport planning. Most applications of choice models to transport problems have used the logit model and many location choice models have followed this tradition, (Mayo, (1973; Quigley, 1973; Lerman, 1975; Friedman, 1975; Anas, 1975).

There is one major problem in applying the logit model to location choice and this results from the violation of the basic premise of the model which is the case of residential location choice. This assumption is the Independence from Irrelevant Alternatives (IIA) axiom. It states that the odds of choosing an alternative over another are constant irrespective of the other alternatives in the choice set.

To illustrate the problems associated with the IIA assumption, take two suburbs, one near the centre of the city, x, and one in the outer suburbs, y. The probability of choosing x is 0.60 and the probability of choosing y is 0.40. Suburb y is now subdivided into two smaller suburbs. The second suburb becomes known as location z. If the supply of housing has no influence on choice and the new residents are indifferent to the two outer suburbs, the probability of choosing y from a choice between y and z is 0.50. However the probability of choosing y from locations x, y, z given the IIA axiom holds is now 0.29. Hence the probability of choosing y or z is 0.58. Thus the subdivision of a suburban area means a developer can capture 58 percent of the market compared with his previous share of 40 percent. In fact, if a third outer suburban area were introduced by further subdivision, the model would predict that the developer's share of the market would rise to 67 percent and so on. The full derivation of these percentages may be found in Young (1982).

The paradox outlined above is commonly referred to as the "red bus/blue bus" problem in the mode choice literature. It highlights a serious deficiency in applying the logit model to location choice. This deficiency is not present in the EBA model since it incorporates similarities between alternatives into the model structure.

It should be noted at this point that many of the more commonly used macroscopic land use models such as the gravity model (Lowry, 1964) the accessibility model (Patton, 1970) and the intervening opportunities model (Brindle, 1970) have a mathematical form similar to the logit model (Young and Richardson, 1981). The paradox discussed in the last few paragraphs therefore influences the predictions given by these models.

An attempt to overcome the IIA problem in the logit model could be made by grouping the alternatives with similarities and forming a hierarchy of choices. This model is called a nested logit and was first discussed by Daly and Zachary (1978) but there are two problems with this approach. The first problem is that there is no clear distinction between one location in an urban area and another. Rather every area within an urban region is related to the others due to their spatial proximity. It is therefore necessary to adopt a trial and error procedure for determining the most appropriate groupings of areas and then determine the hierarchial order of these groupings. This is a complicated, time consuming and expensive task.

The second problem with the nested logit would result when the model is applied. Application of the nested logit would use the same hierarchy as that developed at the calibration stage. However there can be no certainty that if a change in the urban system is made that change does not result in new groupings and a new hierarchy of choice, hence making the old hierarchy of choice inappropriate. The building of a road bridge would for instance make two areas which were distinctly different before its construction much more similar in their spatial proximity to activities after its construction. Both of these problems cast doubt on the usefulness of the nested logit model for modelling location choice.

THEORETICAL FOUNDATIONS OF THE EBA MODEL

Two features of the EBA model are fundamental. The first assumption is that rather than considering all attributes describing a location simultaneously in order to generate an overall composite evaluation of the alternative, the individual conducts a mental search of the attributes in a sequential fashion proceeding from that attribute which is considered most important through to that attribute which is considered least important. It may well occur, however, that this search is not completed and that the individual will make a choice before all attributes have been considered. The method by which this attribute-search is terminated is the second feature of such a model. It is assumed that at each stage of the search when a new attribute is considered, the level of the attribute for each location is compared to a minimally acceptable level of that attribute. If a location fails this test then that location is eliminated from further consideration. If it passes the test, it continues in the attribute-search to be compared with other remaining locations with respect to the next most important attribute. The search continues until all except one of the locations have been eliminated. The remaining location is then considered to be the chosen alternative. Both the importance and acceptance level associated with each attribute need to be determined prior to application of the EBA model.

The model developed in this study is based primarily on the EBA model described by Tversky (1972) which assumes that more important attributes have a greater probability of being considered earlier in the attribute-search process. By allowing for individual differences, the probability of selection of each attribute for examination is in proportion to a function of the importance of each attribute. The most important attributes are likely to be examined first, but not necessarily so for any one individual. Because of the probabilistic nature of the attribute ordering procedures, repeated applications of the model for each individual will not result in the same choice every time but rather will result in a set of probabilities of selection of each location.

To avoid simulating this decision process on repeated occasions in order to obtain choice probabilities, it is possible to express this model structure in the form of a general mathematical equation as shown by Tversky (1972). The derivation starts with the representation of a three-alternative choice problem in the form of a Venn diagram as shown in Fig. 1. In location choice each location is represented by a circle encompassing those attributes for which the location provides a minimally acceptable level of satisfaction. The area which each attribute contributes to the circle is given by a function of the importance of that attribute. Thus the total area of each circle is given by the sum of the importance of those attributes for which the location provides a minimally acceptable satisfaction level.

Areas of overlap between the circles represent attributes which are satisfactory for two or more locations while areas occupied by only one circle represent attributes which are satisfactory for only that location. The sets of satisfactory attributes may be represented by set notation, such that $\bar{x}$ represents the set of attributes which are satisfactory for location x alone, $\overline{xy}$ represents the set of attributes which are satisfactory for location x and y (but not others) while $\overline{xyz}$ represents the set of attributes which are satisfactory for all three locations. The area of each part of the circles is given by the sum of the importances over the relevant attributes and may be denoted by (eg., $I(\bar{x})$, $I(\overline{xy})$ etc.) In addition to those satisfactory attributes actually specified for each of the locations, it is assumed that there also exists one set of unspecified satisfactory attributes for each of the locations. These location-specific attributes are mutually exclusive and non-zero. The size of these sets may be obtained through the calibration process in the form of location specific constants. These constants (or attribute sets) are represented by C_x, C_y and C_z.

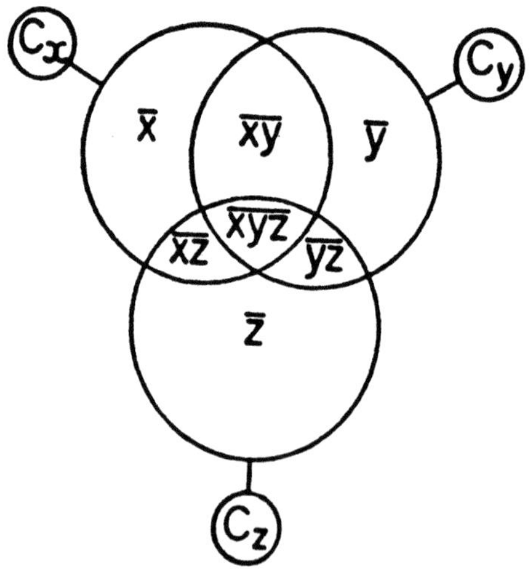

Figure 1 - Venn Diagram for EBA Model

The probability of selection of x is given by

$$P(x/xyz) = \frac{C_x + I(\bar{x}) + I(\overline{xy}).P(x/xy) + I(\overline{xz}).P(x/xz)}{K} \qquad (1)$$

where P(x/xyz) = probability of choosing x given a choice between x, y and z; and $K = C_x + C_y + C_z + I(\bar{x}) + I(\bar{y}) + I(\bar{z}) + I(\overline{xy}) + I(\overline{xz}) + I(\overline{yz})$.

A more complete derivation of the mathematical expression can be found in Young (1982) or Young, Richardson, Ogden and Rattray (1982).

Another problem to be addressed is the method by which minimally acceptable satisfaction levels are to be set. The present study uses a minimum regret criterion whereby attribute satisfaction levels are considered to be acceptable if they lie within a specific fractional tolerance of the maximum satisfaction level for that attribute over all locations for that individual.

$$\text{Acceptable } S_{kjq} > (1 - T_k)\max_j\{S_{kjq}\} \qquad (2)$$

where S_{kjq} = satisfaction with kth attribute of the jth location for the qth individual; T_k = tolerance for the kth attribute; $\max_j\{S_{kjq}\}$ = the maximum satisfaction with the kth attribute for the qth individual over all j alternatives.

The calibration process involves the determination of the most appropriate set of critical tolerances and importance ratings wherein the importances and tolerances are selected such that a specified objective function is maximized. The subjective level of satisfaction associated with each of the attributes describing each location is input into the model. Because the output of the EBA model in eqn. (1) is a probability of selection a maximum likelihood method is used to estimate these parameters.

It is necessary to discuss the EBA model in the context of the criticisms levelled at existing location choice models in the previous section. The first criticism relates to the complexity of the choice process. The EBA model allows the individual the opportunity of reducing the complexity of the choice by eliminating many locations early in the choice process. The few locations left can be compared using a more comprehensive set of attributes.

The second criticism related to the IIA axiom and which was illustrated by references to a developer subdividing land and increasing his market share. The EBA model overcomes this problem since it allows for similarities between locations as shown in Fig. 1 and any location which is the same as any other will be considered as such. The probability of being attracted to an outer suburban location will not be increased by subdividing that suburb.

The final criticism relates to the application of the choice model and the need for the model to be sensitive to changes in the similarities between locations. Unlike the nested logit model the EBA model allows the degree of interdependence between locations to vary with changes in the satisfaction levels associated with the attribute describing each location. The EBA model is a more appropriate model for studying the factors affecting location choice.

THE APPLICATION OF THE EBA MODEL TO RESIDENTAIL LOCATION CHOICE

The location decisions of new home owners have been investigated using data collected in a survey of residential location choices in Melbourne by Young, Morris and Ogden (1978). The survey was conducted in 1977-78 and provided measures of the attitudes and behaviour of a sample of new residents in Burwood, Wantirna and Belgrave, three outer suburban areas of Melbourne. These three areas were not very different in social and physical characteristics and were located along the same transport corridor and it was assumed that the residents in the study would have reasonable knowledge of the character of each area.

Residents in the three areas were interviewed as soon as possible after moving into their new homes. Measures of their perception of the satisfaction they would obtain from each of the attributes shown in Table 1 for each of the three areas were obtained through 100 point semantic scales to obtain the satisfaction ratings and 716 male decision makers were interviewed.

Model Calibration

The model calibration procedure consisted of first removing attributes that were correlated with other attributes. Secondly, those attribute parameters that had no significant influence on the overall fit of a model were removed, Young (1982). This process resulted in the removal of thirteen attributes and the ten remaining attributes and their parameter estimates are shown in Table 1.

It may be seen that with thirteen attributes removed the model was found to be highly significant as shown by the values of $-2\ln\lambda_T$ and ρ^2. Of the attributes removed, closeness to present workplace is the most noticeable and this attribute is a commonly used attribute in most land use models. In the context of the EBA model, however, all that is being said is given the spatial relationship between each of the three areas and the respondents' workplaces, most respondents are insensitive to or satisfied with this separation. Put another way, the proximity to workplace provides an outer limit to where people will locate and within this limit the cost and standard of housing, provision of schools and shops, and the quality of the physical environment have a large role in determining the actual location.

TABLE 1

PARAMETERS FOR REFINED EBA MODEL OF RESIDENTIAL LOCATION CHOICE

ATTRIBUTE	PARAMETERS	
	IMPORTANCE	TOLERANCE
Closeness to present workplace	*	*
Closeness to bay beaches	+	+
Closeness to open country	50	0.45
Closeness to parks, play areas, golf courses	*	*
Closeness to entertainment	*	*
Closeness to friends	70	0.20
Closeness to relatives	100	0.60
Closeness to people of same age	*	*
Closeness to people of same social level	*	*
Closeness to people of same social nationality	+	+
Availability of suitable shops	90	0.20
Availability of suitable schools	65	0.10
Public transport	*	*
Pedestrian safety	*	*
Traffic noise	+	+
Traffic congestion	*	*
Tidiness of area	55	0.05
How well buildings are maintained	*	*
How clean the air is	100	0.35
Presence of trees, shrubs, grass	80	0.20
Dwelling type in the area	100	0.25
Type of dwelling you can afford	100	0.15
Expected financial gain from reselling dwelling	*	*
CONSTANTS		
Burwood	5	
Wantirna	5	
Belgrave	5	
$-2\ell n\lambda_T$	947	
ρ^2	0.60	

* Parameters not significant at 5% level
\+ Attributes satisfaction ratings correlated with that of other attributes

This finding has general support from a number of studies such as Highway Research Board (1969); Stegman (1969); Catanese (1971); Richardson (1971); O'Farrell and Markham (1975); and Guest and Cluett (1976).

The Highway Research Board report on moving behaviour and residential choice concludes that the "accessibility to a number of regular, out-of-home activities, including workplace was found to be a relatively unimportant factor in household residential mobility and in a household's choice of new residence". The report does however, state that households living at more than 40 minutes distance from work have a greater tendency to move than households that lived nearer to work.

Stegman (1969) investigated the influence of workplace on location choice suggested that residential environment plays a much more important role than does the work trip. Moriarty (1974) and Troy (1972) support this general hypothesis. Stegman does state that these priorities may be the result of people not paying directly for transport facilities and hence not giving them due weighting in the location decision.

Catanese (1971) observed that home to work place distances increase with income. O'Farrell and Markham (1975) came to a similar finding but went further and stated that the majority of car owners did not even know their running cost, let alone their total travel cost. Richardon (1971) contends that home to work expenses are considered only in determining an outer constraint to location choice. Within this constraint the residential environment, household quality and cost as well as the accessibility to other facilities plays a major part in influencing location choice. Guest and Cluett (1976) confirm this finding in their study of the interrelationship between home and workplace location decisions.

Further research is required before the outer constraint of work trip duration can be confirmed. However, if closeness to workplace does provide this outer constraint then improvements to the traffic system, such as freeways and area traffic control may influence where people live. These improvements will allow people to travel more quickly between their home and workplace. In turn, this decreased travel time to work increases the area of suitable locations and may result in people living a greater distance from their work than at present. The energy consumption savings from these road improvements may therefore be reduced by the tendency of people to travel further to work.

Many of the attributes that remained in the model related primarily to aspects of the local area. Accessibility to schools and shops were found to have significant parameter estimates. The quality of the local environment was measured by the presence of trees and shrubs, the tidiness of the area, closeness to open country, the cleanliness of the air and the dwelling type in the area. The social environment was influential through access to friends and relatives. Finally, the cost dimension was introduced through the type of dwelling the respondent could afford.

It is interesting to note that with these attributes in the model the values of the constants are very low. This indicates that the model is well specified and that most of the attributes influencing the choice are included in the model.

Elasticities

In order to test the effect of policy initiatives it is necessary to test the response of the model to changes in attribute satisfaction. Elasticity is often defined as the percentage change in model prediction consequent on a one percent change in satisfaction. For the EBA model it is unlikely that a one percent change in satisfaction will illustrate the influence of the tolerances. Hence larger changes in satisfaction ratings are required. Specifically, changes in satisfaction with Burwood between -100% and +100%, using 5% increments were input into the model and the percentage change in model prediction consequent upon these changes calculated. The ratio between the percentage change in model prediction and the change in satisfaction is referred to as the arc-elasticity. Both direct-arc and cross-arc-elasticities were calculated and are discussed in the following sections.

The results of the direct-arc-elasticity calculations for five attributes are shown in Fig. 2. Fig. 2 shows that the direct-arc-elasticity is not a smooth function of the change in attribute satisfaction and this is mainly because the EBA model is inherently discontinuous in nature. Changes in prediction can only occur when the satisfaction level for that attribute crosses the minimally acceptable satisfaction level for that attribute. Location changes from unsatisfactory to satisfactory with respect to that attribute when satisfaction is rising and hence the probability of selection of that location increases in a discontinuous way.

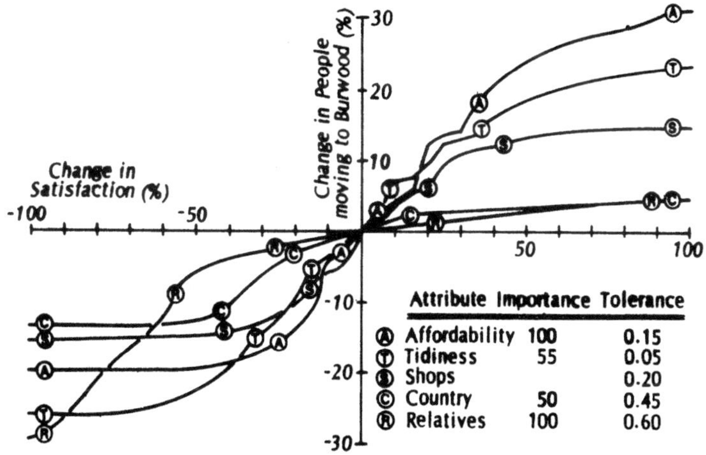

Figure 2 - Direct-Arc-Elasticities for EBA Model

This tolerance effect can be seen by comparing the rate of change of the model predicion with the value of the tolerance. For instance, tidiness of the area has a sharp change in model prediction between +5 and +10%, and -0 and -5% change in satisfaction and its tolerance is 0.05. The threshold effect illustrated in Fig. 2 would provide quite a different model prediction from those obtainted from the more conventional compensatory logit or regression models.

It is also of note that depending on the percentage change in satisfaction, different attributes will have the greatest influence on choice. A +100% change in the satisfaction with the type of dwelling one could afford will result in a larger change in people moving to Burwood than will any other attribute. However, for a 10% change in tidiness of the area will have the greatest impact while for a -100% change in closeness to relatives will have the largest impact on choice. It is therefore necessary to determine the level of change that can be made in any satisfaction level before the most efficient strategy for attracting people to any location can be determined.

Table 2 presents the cross-arc-elasticities consequent upon a +50% change in Burwood satisfaction ratings and shows that for changes in most attributes more people are drawn from Wantirna than Belgrave. This is obviously the result of a greater similarity between Burwood and Wantirna for these attributes. However, a +50% change in satisfaction for dwelling type in the area, maintenance of the buildings, and closeness to relatives, result in more people being drawn from Belgrave to Burwood and for these three attributes there is more similarity between Belgrave and Burwood. In a policy sense the EBA model states that more people can be drawn from one area to another by selection of the appropriate attribute. Young (1982) has noted that this is not consistent with the compensatory logit model which always draws more people from one area for all attributes.

TABLE 2

CROSS-ARC-ELASTICITIES FOR EBA MODEL FOR A +50% CHANGE IN SATISFACTION RATINGS IN BURWOOD

	CROSS-ARC-ELASTICITY	
ATTRIBUTE	Wantirna	Belgrave
Availability of suitable schools	-0.150	-0.096
Type of dwelling you can afford	-0.144	-0.066
Availability of suitable shops	-0.126	-0.086
Closeness to friends	-0.126	-0.060
Presence of trees and shrubs	-0.114	-0.074
How clean the air is	-0.012	-0.078
Closeness to open country	-0.084	-0.064
Dwelling type in the area	-0.080	-0.086
How well buildings are maintained	-0.034	-0.072
Closeness to relatives	-0.004	-0.014

FREIGHT-FACILITY LOCATION CHOICE

Both passenger and freight transport systems have important spatial ramifications. Transport effects, for instance, often influence the location decisions and viability of industry (Weber, 1929; McMillan, 1965; Rimmer, 1970). However, the extent of this influence and the nature of the relationship are as yet generally not well understood.

Although the amount of urban land occupied by freight distribution facilities is relatively small, such land uses are amongst the most volatile from the community viewpoint, especially where large, heavy trucks are involved. Data from the United Kingdom (Wigan, 1979) have shown that freight depots and warehouses in London are highly footloose. If this is so in other cities it may be possible to influence the location of such freight-generating land uses throughout the planning process to reduce transport costs and the broader community costs associated with environmental and social impacts. Ogden (1979) has suggested that control of the location of freight generating activities is one of the main influences that the planner can exert on the urban freight system.

Although a large body of theoretical and empirical work on the location of manufacturing industry already exists comparatively little has been reported on the location of freight-distribution activities which mostly fall within the service industry sector. Before predictions about the spatial impact of policy initiatives on urban goods movement can be attempted it is necessary to investigate further the location characteristics of such freight firms. The successful derivation of an explanatory capability for the location preference of individual freight firms could ultimately lead to the development of disaggregate behavioural models of freight-facility location for use in transport and land use planning of urban systems (Watson, 1975).

Sample Selection

In selecting a sample from which to obtain data for location choice models two criteria should be met. The first is that the sample should be homogeneous with respect to location choice. This criterion was partly met in this study by selecting only firms that were (i) involved in the distribution of freight; and (ii) located in Melbourne. Since the distribution sector is large, different firms have different market and location characteristics and therefore the sample could not be said to be truly homogeneous.

The second criterion is that the firms should be in equilibrium so that the factors which affect the decision to locate will be the same for all firms in the study. It is unlikely that this criterion will be satisfied since different firms in the sample had been at their present locations for different lengths of time, and each firm was probably faced with a unique set of attributes when it made its latest location decision. However, after that decision was made, changes in the firm's circumstances, or in the urban and economic environment, may have resulted in another location being more appropriate. To overcome this problem of lack of equilibrium, respondents to the survey were asked to compare their existing location with one other possible location as of the time of the study, and not as of the time when their last location decision was made. They were also asked which of these two locations they would select if they were making their location decision now. This preferred location, rather than the firm's actual current location, was used in the development of the models presented in this paper.

It is important to note the distinction between the preferences of a decision-making unit and its final decision, since even if it is assumed that a firm's location behaviour is rational and that the choice set for the firm is completely specified, a firm's preference for a location other than its current one need not necessarily lead to a relocaton. The preferences of individual firms for alternative locations can be viewed as a measure of the demand for alternative locations, but before a choice decision will result, and interaction of demand and supply must be considered. Moreover, unless the perceived benefit to the firm in moving to an alternative location exceeds the cost of that move, perhaps by some threshold amount, the firm is unlikely to relocate regardless of its stated preferences.

Questionnaire

Data were obtained by using a questionnaire completed during interviews with senior management personnel of a sample of firms in Melbourne (Ritchie and Ogden, 1979). These firms covered a range of activities in the transport and distribution sector and a total of 71 questionnaires were completed satisfactorily.

Each respondent was first asked to rate on a 100 point semantic scale how satisfactory two locations were with respect to the 19 locational characteristics shown in Table 3. The two locations were the firm's current location and one other possible location nominated by the respondent. It should be noted that not all areas in the urban region can be considered alternative locations. For example, land use planning regulations may prohibit freight activity in certain localities and if all locations were considered in the estimation of model parameters, a biased result may be obtained.

TABLE 3

PARAMETER ESTIMATES FOR REFINED EBA MODEL OF FREIGHT-FACILITY LOCATION CHOICE

	PARAMETERS	
ATTRIBUTES	IMPORTANCE	TOLERANCE
Closeness to existing markets	50	0.40
Closeness to expanding markets	+	+
Closeness to other facilities of firm	*	*
Closeness to firms providing services	+	+
Closeness to arterial roads	*	*
Closeness to freeways	+	+
Access to country highway	+	+
Closeness to rail freight facilities	+	+
Closeness to port facilities	+	+
Closeness to public transport	*	*
Traffic congestion and delay	*	*
Availability of suitable suites	*	*
Investment potential	*	*
Company prestige	10	0.05
Cost of land and buildings	10	0.10
Cost of council rates	+	+
Cost of operating the respondents vehicle fleet	+	+
Availability of labour	45	0.35
Environmental impact of the facility	+	+
$-2\ell n\lambda_T$	35.78	
ρ^2	0.49	

+ Parameters not significant at 5% level
* Attributes satisfaction ratings correlated with that of other attributes

Model Calibration

The model calibration was carried out in the same manner as that described for the residential location choice model. The attributes that were correlated were removed from the model specification and then the attributes with parameter estimates that did not have a significant impact on the overall fit of the model were removed. This process resulted in a model with four attributes as shown in Table 3. These are (i) closeness to existing customers; (ii) company prestige; (iii) cost of land and buildings; and (iv) availability of labour. The tests of significance do suggest that the model is highly significant ($\chi^2_{0.05,8}$ = 15.51 > 35.78 = $-2\ell n\lambda_T$ of ρ^2 = 0.49).

The sensitivity of the attributes to changes in the level of satisfaction have been shown to be related to the size of the tolerance, (Young, 1982). Attributes with small tolerance estimates are more sensitive to changes in attribute satisfaction than are those with large tolerances. The attributes which are most sensitive to changes in satisfaction level are company prestige and land cost. The closeness to existing customers and the availability of labour are the least sensitive.

CONCLUSIONS

Conclusions may be grouped into those related to the use of the EBA model in analyzing location choice and those relating to the factors found to influence that choice. Because of the relatively small sample size and the explanatory nature of the study of freight-facility location choice the results should be treated with caution. The residential location choice study has a larger sample size but it too is limited in that it considers only three alternatives. Nevertheless the results are encouraging. The EBA model not only provided a behaviourally acceptable theoretical foundation for this sort of analysis but it also provided a satisfactory fit to the data.

In the residential location choice study ten attributes were found to have significant parameters with the price of housing and closeness in amenities such as schools and shops having a large influence on the decision. The model implied that an individual's proximity to workplace provides an outer constraint on location. A location is then chosen within this outer constraint that provides acceptable levels of house quality, physical and social environment. Major investments in freeways, public transport and area traffic control have a large influence on the distribution of land use since they influence how quickly individuals can get to and from work and therefore the range of possible locations open to this individual.

Four attributes were found to be important to freight facility location with accessibility to labour and customers playing an important part in the location decision of freight-facility firms along with the land cost and the prestige gained from particular sites.

ACKNOWLEDGMENT

The data used in this study were collected as part of a research study funded by the Australian Road Research Board. This support is very gratefully acknowledged. The author would also like to thank Tony Richardson, Peter Gipps and Ken Ogden for their aid in preparing this paper.

REFERENCES

Alonso, W., 1964, Location and Land Use, Harvard University Press, Cambridge, MA.

Anas, A., 1975, The Empirical Calibration and Testing of a Simulation Model of Residential Location, Environment and Planning A, 7, 899-920.

Brindle, R.E., 1970, The Effects of Transport Improvements on Urban Development: Tests on an Intervening Opportunities Model, Special Report 6, Transport Section, Department of Civil Engineering, University of Melbourne.

Burgess, E.W., 1929, Urban Area in Chicago, Smith, T.V. and White, L.D. (Eds.), Chicago: An Experiment in Social Science Research, University of Chicago Press, Chicago, IL.

Cantanese, A.J., 1971, Home and Workplace Separation in Four Urban Regions, Journal of the American Institute of Planners, 37, 331-337.

Daly, A.J. and Zachary, S., 1978, Improved Multiple Choice Models, in Hensher, D.A. and Dalvie, Q. (Eds.), Determinants of Travel Chocie, Saxon House, 335-357.

Friedman, J., 1975, Housing Location and the Supply of Local Public Services, PhD dissertation, Department of Economics, University of California at Berkeley, CA.

Guest, A.M. and Cluett, C., 1976, Workplace and Residential Location: Push-Pull Model, Journal of Regional Science, 16, 399-410.

Highway Research Board, 1969, Moving Behaviour and Residential Choice: A National Survey, NCHRP Report 81, Washington, D.C.

Hoyt, H., 1939, The Structure and Growth of Residential Neighbourhoods in American Cities, Federal Housing Administration, Washington, D.C.

Lerman, S.R., 1975, A Disaggregate Behavioural Model of Urban Mobility Decisions, PhD dissertation, Massachusetts Institute of Technology, Cambridge, MA.

Lowry, I.S., 1964, A Model of Metropolis, RM-4035-RC, Rand Corporation, Santa Monica, CA.

McMillan, T.E., 1965, Why Manufacturers Choose Plant Locations, Land Economics, 41,

Mayo, S., 1973, Local Public Goods and Residential Location: an Empirical Test of the Tiebout Hypothesis, Metropolitan Governance Committee on Resources for the Future, Washington, D.C.

Moriarty, B.M., 1974, Socioeconomic Status and Residential Location Choice, Environment and Behaviour, 6, 448-469.

Muth, R.F., 1969, Cities and Housing: The Spatial Pattern of Urban Residential Land Use, University of Chicago Press, Chicago, IL.

O'Farrell, P.N. and Markham J., 1975, Commuting Costs and Residential Location: A Process of Urban Spatial, Tijdschrift voor Economische en Sociale Geografic, 66, 66-74.

Ogden, K.W., 1979, Goods Movement Processes and Policies, Proceedings Freight Symposium, University of Newcastle-upon-Tyne, UK.

Patton, T.A., 1970, The Effect of Accessibility on Residential Density, Special Report 7, Transport Section, Department of Civil Engineering, University of Melbourne, Australia.

Quigley, J.M., 1973, Housing Demand in the Short Run: An Analysis of Polytomous Choice, paper presented at the Winter Meeting of Econometric Society, New York.

Richardson, H.W., 1971, Urban Economics, Penguin Books, UK.

Rimmer, P.J., 1970, Manufacturing in Melbourne, Publication GC/2, Department of Human Geography, Australian National University, Canberra, Australia.

Ritchie, S.G. and Ogden, K.W., 1979, Analysis and Appraisal of Freight Generation Characteristics: Part 1 - Data Report, Australian Road Research Board, Melbourne, VIC, Australia.

Stegman, M.A., 1969, Accessibility Models and Residential Location, Journal of the American Institute of Planners, 35, 22-29.

Troy, P.N., 1973, Environmental Quality of Four Melbourne Suburbs, Urban Research Unit Monograph, Australian National University, Canberra, Australia.

Tversky, A., 1972, Elimination by Aspects: A Theory of Choice, Psychological Review, 79, 281-299.

Watson, P., 1975, Urban Goods Movement, Lexington Books, Lexington, MA.

Weber, A., 1929, Theory of Location of Industry, University of Chicago Press, Chicago, IL.

Wigan, M.R., 1979, Indicators of Urban Commodity Movements, in Hensher, D.A. and Stopher, P.R. (Eds.), Behavioural Travel Modelling, Croom Helm, London, UK.

Young, W., 1982, The Development of an Elimination-by-Aspects Model of Residential Location Choice, PhD dissertation, Department of Civil Engineering, Monash University, Melbourne, VIC, Australia.

Young, W., Morris, J.M. and Ogden, K.W., 1978, Developing and Administering a Home Interview Survey, AIR 301-1, Australian Road Research Board, Melbourne, VIC, Australia.

Young W. and Richardson, A.J., 1981, Macroscopic Location Models Revisited, Transportation Research, 4B, 261-269.

Young, W., Richardson, A.J., Ogden, K.W. and Rattray, A.L., 1982, A Freight Mode Choice Model, Transport Research Board Record, 838, 38-44.

RESIDENTIAL MOBILITY WITH A PROBIT MODEL

Wal van Lierop
Department of Economics
Free University
PO Box 7161
1007 MC Amsterdam
The Netherlands

Abstract. Residential mobility patterns of individual households in The Netherlands are studied by means of a probit model. Two surveys were available for this study: one held at the end of 1977 sampled data on the previous dwelling, the willingness to move, dwelling preferences and a variety of household characteristics; a second held a year later in 1978 to assess differences between the actual moving behaviour and the earlier formulated willingness to move house and dwelling preferences. Much attention is paid in the paper to the entire strategy of the research. Some empirical results are presented illustrating the potential of this method of housing market analysis.

INTRODUCTION

Recently behavioural and disaggregate models of choice have become increasingly popular for the analysis of various spatial interaction patterns and processes. This paper reports on an attempt to use a probit model within the framework of a bigger housing market model focussing on both residential mobility and dwelling choice. This housing market model was developed to study moving behaviour of individual households in The Netherlands.

The paper is organized as follows. In the next section some insight is given into the complex mechanisms of the housing market. The choice of model type and the theoretical concept of the multinomial probit (MNP) model are discussed in the third section. The fourth section gives a short description of the data used while the fifth section presents an overview of the research strategy. The paper ends with the presentation of some empirical results illustrating the potential of this method of housing market analysis.

The paper is part of a bigger housing market research project of the Department of Spatial Economics, Free University, Amsterdam (van Lierop, 1984).

THE HOUSING MARKET

Human settlement patterns in a dynamic society are always characterized by a state of flux. They do not display a static pattern but reflect changes in economic conditions, technological developments, demographic changes, social developments and the impact of public policy. In consequence, an analysis of the housing market and of related settlement patterns is an extremely important issue, as it focusses attention on one of the central elements of a society in transition. In the light of the foregoing remarks, the housing market may be characterized as a multidimensional phenomenon marked, among other things by (i) complex search and choice processes of individual households due to multiple motives; (ii) the emergence of drastic shifts in locational behaviour due to structural economic changes; (iii) the presence of positive and negative social spill-over effects (bandwagon effects, Veblen effects, segmentation effects); (iv) a high public policy impact due to a strong institutional concern with living conditions of families; and (v) the occurrence of several disequilibrium situations between supply and demand for dwellings, due to land use competition, rigid decision procedures, demographic changes and resource constraints.

The lack of insight into the direct consequences of public policy measures on urban housing markets and on the city in general, has led to the development of urban impact analysis (Glickman, 1979; Nijkamp, 1981). Though this may be a meaningful instrument in the public policy domain, especially to study longer term impacts, it does neither offer a profound insight into the complex mechanism of the housing market nor in the way this market can be controlled by public policy.

In the 1970s a wide variety of mainly urban housing market models were developed (Anas, 1976; Bird, 1976; Evans, 1973; Kain and Quigley, 1970; Putman, 1979; Richardson, 1973; Stahl, 1980; Wilkinson, 1973). A recent extensive bibliography may be found in Porell (1981) and van Lierop (1984). Usually the choice of a specific type of model will depend on the research aims, the availability of data, the presence of suitable computer programs and data storage capacity, the research budget and so forth. Consequently, the search for an ideal housing market model is illusory.

Only within given limits, an attempt can be made to construct a most appropriate model which is able to cope with the complexity of the housing market. The rest of this paper describes such attempts to build an operational disaggregate choice model for the Dutch housing market.

THE PROBIT MODEL

Choice of Model Type

The nature of the housing market is too complicated to be analyzed by means of a standard aggregate method for analyzing discrete choices. Especially if one tries to focus on several household classes and dwelling types and also wants to study dwelling preferences, this causes a need for a more disaggregate model. Furthermore, because it is realistic to assume the existence of interrelations between many dwelling types on the housing market, a model should be chosen which is able to cope with interdependencies between the various relevant alternatives.

In this respect the multinominal probit (MNP) model with a variance-covariance matrix of the Hausman and Wise form was judged to be most promising from a theoretical point of view. Evaluating this model in a first simple empirical case together with a MNP model with the same variance-covariance matrix for all individual households and a multinominal logit (MNL) model gave support to this theoretical assumption and van Lierop (1984) provides a more detailed discussion.

Description of the Probit Model

The theoretical background of the probit model is based on utility theory. It is assumed that any individual or household n selects an alternative i from a set of available discrete alternatives on the basis of the utility (u_{in}) the individual or household expects to get from that alternative i in comparison to all other alternatives. Consequently, the probability P of a household n choosing an alternative i can be written as

$$P_{in} = Pr(u_{in} \geq u_{i'n}) \qquad i,i' = 1,\ldots,I, \qquad i \neq i', n = 1,\ldots,N \tag{1}$$

The utility u_{in} can approximately be described as the sum of an average (measurable) utility v_{in} and a disturbance term ε_{in} for unknown individual differences (individual preferences etc., see eg., Domencich and McFadden, 1975). The average utility v_{in} can be expressed as a linear function of a vector $\bar{x}$, consisting of known attributes of individual households. The utility of an alternative i for a household n can then be defined as

$$u_{in} = \vec{v}(x'_{in}\ \beta) + \varepsilon_{in} \qquad i = 1, \ldots, I \qquad n = 1, \ldots, N \tag{2}$$

Substitution of eqn. (2) into eqn. (1) gives

$$\begin{aligned} P_{in} &= Pr\ [v(\vec{x}'_{in}\ \beta) + \varepsilon_{in} \geq v(\vec{x}'_{i'n}\ \beta) + \varepsilon_{i'n}] \\ &= Pr\ [\varepsilon_{i'n} \leq v(\vec{x}'_{in}\ \beta) + \varepsilon_{in} - v(\vec{x}'_{i'n}\ \beta)] \end{aligned} \tag{3}$$

with the logical condition that $\sum_{i=1}^{I} P_{in} = 1$ (4)

The MNP model can be derived from eqn. (3) by assuming that the disturbances are normally distributed (Daganzo, 1979). This leads to the following probability function

$$P_{in} = \int_{\varepsilon_{in}=-\infty}^{\infty} \int_{\varepsilon_{1n}=-\infty}^{v(\vec{x}'_{in}\beta) - v(\vec{x}'_{1n}\beta) + \varepsilon_{in}} \cdots \int_{\varepsilon_{i'n}=-\infty}^{v(\vec{x}'_{in}\beta) - v(x'_{i'n}\beta) + \varepsilon_{in}} \cdots \int_{\varepsilon_{In}=-\infty}^{v(\vec{x}'_{in}\beta) - v(\vec{x}'_{In}\beta) + \varepsilon_{in}} . N(\varepsilon|0,\Omega) d\varepsilon_{In} \, .. d\varepsilon_{i'n} .. d\varepsilon_{1n} d\varepsilon_{in} \quad (5)$$

in which the number of integrals equals the number of alternatives and $N(\varepsilon|0,\Omega)$ is a multivariate normal density function with mean vector 0 and variance-covariance matrix Ω.

The estimation of the coefficient-vector β can be done in an iterative way, but only if beforehand, specific assumptions are being made about the structure of the variance-covariance matrix Ω. Two specifications are possible in this respect.

1. A variance-covariance matrix, which is the same for all individuals ($\Omega_n = \Omega, \forall_n$) and for the binominal case this variance-covariance matrix takes the following form

$$\Omega = \begin{bmatrix} \theta_1 & \rho \\ \rho & \theta_2 \end{bmatrix} \quad (6)$$

   where the values of θ_1, θ_2 and ρ can be estimated simultaneously with the influences of the specified explanatory variables by means of a single numerical approximation method.

2. A variance-covariance matrix of the Hausman and Wise form (Hausman and Wise, 1978) and for the binomial case this variance-covariance matrix has the following form

$$\Omega_n = \theta \begin{bmatrix} E(alt.1) & \rho\sqrt{E(alt.1)E(alt.2)} \\ \rho\sqrt{E(alt.1)E(alt.2)} & E(alt.2) \end{bmatrix} \quad (7)$$

   in case of three exogenous variables and a constant term E(alt.1) and E(alt. 2) are defined by

$$E(alt.1) = \beta_0 + \beta_1 X_1 + \beta_2 X_2 + \beta_3 X_3$$

$$E(alt.2) = \gamma_0 + \gamma_1 X_1 + \gamma_2 X_2 + \gamma_3 X_3 \quad (8)$$

Eqn. (8) implies that the variances and the alternatives are proportional with the expectation for the alternatives (the expectations for the disturbances are 0) and that the covariances are proportional with the root of the product of the means. Also here θ and ρ can be derived simultaneously within the framework of the entire estimation procedure.

The benefit of the latter form compared with the first one is that different variance-covariance matrices can be defined for different individual households without a loss of degrees of freedom (caused by the introduction of additional parameters). The appearance of differences of variances of alternatives and of covariances between alternatives for individual households seems intuitively very realistic. It means that taste variations can exist among the individual households concerning various dwelling alternatives (Daganzo, 1979).

DATA

The data used here have not been sampled specifically for this study. They were sampled for the sake of a study into dwelling unit preferences in The Netherlands by means of economic-psychological methods (Kuylen, 1980) and consist of the results of two home-based surveys. The information has not been derived from one specific and clearly described regional or urban housing market, but has been sampled in a large number of municipalities throughout the country. The municipalities did not only differ in geographical location, but also in size, degree of urbanization, growth pattern, tension between demand and supply, and regulations of the housing market. The purpose of this variety was to give a representative description of the entire Dutch housing market.

In the first survey, held at the end of 1977, information was gathered on a large number of characteristics for almost 2000 households including attributes of their current housing situation and their housing preferences. It included many elements which could give a better understanding of the priority schedules of households concerning all kinds of housing properties.

The second survey was held one year later, at the end of 1978, in order to examine the stability of the household's judgment on housing attributes and to examine the discrepancies between the actual moving behaviour and the dwelling preferences which had been reported in the first inquiry. Those households which were willing to move at the time of the first inquiry have been interviewed again in the second inquiry, as well as those which were not inclined to move but yet had been moved at the time of the second inquiry.

With the help of a housing scoring system, developed by the Ministry of Housing and Physical Planning and the Ministry of Justice (1979), an objective qualitative evaluation of each dwelling was derived. With this system objectively defined quality points can be given to a large set of housing characteristics such as number of rooms, distance to the nearest shopping centre, etc. The sum of the quality points for a dwelling indicates its total quality. In this way a balanced overview may be given of all dwelling types at the housing market. For the exact calculation and definition of the data see van Lierop (1984).

It should still be remarked that the possibility to divide the housing market into dwelling quality score classes simplifies the analysis very much. It becomes quite easy to extend the analysis from a case with few alternatives to more complex dwelling choice situations. Assuming that most households and especially those who are planning to move, have a reasonably good idea about relative quality differences on the housing market a subjective quality evaluation for each relevant dwelling has been defined in the present study. This was done by correcting the objective scores with perception weights of the individual households for 12 preselected important (preferred) housing characteristics. This subjective quality was judged to be an extremely important variable to explain moving behaviour from and to objectively defined dwelling quality classes. Consequently, the price/quality ratio used in the empirical part of this study has been determined with the help of subjective scores.

Table 1 gives a brief impression of the 1134 survey records which were suitable for use in the present study after screening. The figures between brackets represent the so-called forced moves, that is households which had or still have to move because of labour market reasons, due to demolition of their old dwelling units, etc.

A special drawback of the data that should be mentioned is that starting households have not been taken into account. This might qualify the importance of our results a bit as starters form a considerable part of the annual demand for housing (Ministry of Housing and Physical Planning, 1979).

TABLE 1

HOUSEHOLDS WILLING TO MOVE AND ACTUAL MOVERS
IN THE SCREENED SAMPLE POPULATION

		Willingness to move in 1977		
		yes	no	
Actual moves in 1978	yes	37 (+8)	5	42 (+8)
	no	102 (+19)	963	1065 (+19)
	Total	139 (+27)	968	1107 (+27)

RESEARCH STRATEGY

Fig. 1 gives a short overview of the structure of our research strategy to model the Dutch housing market. The various blocks of Fig. 1 are explained in the following paragraphs. In the first phase of the research process only the willingness to move house is analyzed. The probability P_{tin}, that a household n is willing to move is assumed to be equal to the probability that the expected utility of moving minus the transition costs exceeds the expected utility of staying (ie., conform to eqn. (1)). Expectations are in this respect considered to be much more important than current values of utilities. It should be remarked, however, that the possibilities to include expectations in actual analyses are still rather limited at present.

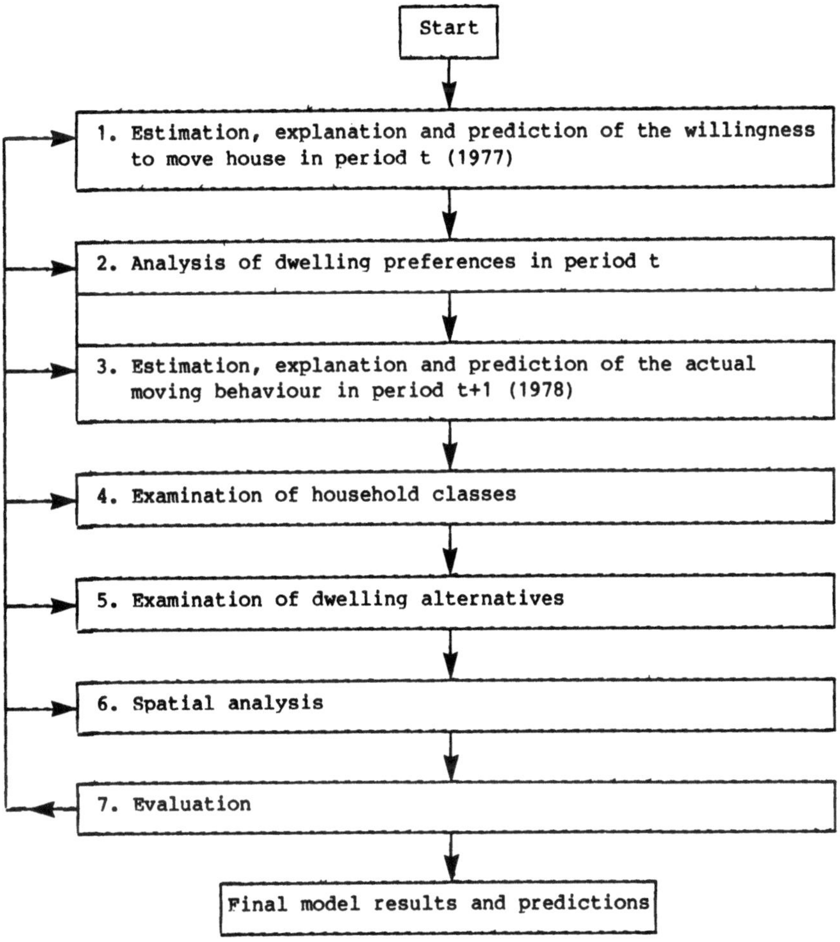

Figure 1 - Structure of the Research Strategy for the Dutch Housing Market Model

The relevant utilities of moving versus staying may be specified as a function of, among others

1. The price/quality ratio of the current dwelling i for household n.
2. The income/current housing costs ratio of household n.
3. The family size/number of rooms ratio of the current dwelling i.
4. Information on whether the household has to move due to demolition of its current dwelling or a change of workplace.

5. The perception the household has of the strain (vacancy rate) on the relevant part of the housing market. This factor should give an indication of possibilities people expect to have in actualizing their desired move from i. One could suppose that in this phase of defining the willingness to move, individual households do not yet have a clear idea of the utilities they may get from specific alternative dwellings. The expected utility of moving from i can in such cases be mainly influenced by the availability of desired dwellings. Then consequently, relevant vacancy-rate perception indices have to be included in the explanation of the willingness to move.
6. Feelings about present distance to work or to school.
7. The desire of household n to own a dwelling instead of renting one.
8. The transition costs or disutilities of moving from i (including the evaluation of the search time). It should be noticed that this variable has a special character. Some evidence exists (Meyer, 1981) that transition costs (or, even more perceptions of these costs) play an important role at the beginning of the process of searching for another dwelling, while, after more information has been gathered, in later phases of the process its influence seems to be marginal or even zero.

In the second phase of the analysis of the dwelling preferences, the integral probability is calculated with which a random household from the population prefers in period t to move in period t+i into a specific type of dwelling. This probability equals the product of (i) the probability of willingness to move for households from the same class; and (ii) the probability of preferring a specific type of house if the household is indeed willing to move. Comparison of the preferences from period t and the forecasts of the actual moving behaviour for period t+1 should give an overview of the most important bottlenecks between housing demand and supply. Due to the non-response to many of the relevant preference questions in the available questionnaires, it was rather impossible to complete this research phase in the way planned (van Lierop, 1984). An alternative more practical approach was adopted in order to still obtain some preference information. It should be remarked that the above mentioned data problems prohibited also a full integration of all the phases of Fig. 1. Consequently these problems frustrated part of the empirical side of our new Dutch housing market model considerably.

The third part of the research consists of the analysis of the probabilities with which households (willing to move in period t) actually move in period t+1. Explanatory variables in this phase are, among others (i) the willingness to move house, alternatively also used as classification criterion; (ii) the above mentioned ratios (1-3); (iii) an integral suitability index for the old dwelling; (iv) the net monthly income; and (v) the subjective evaluation score for the old dwelling.

Beginning with the fourth stage the analysis does not focus any longer on the entire population, but rather on various distinct household classes. This more detailed anlaysis can be initiated by among others (i) a special interest for certain classes of households (income classes, age classes, etc.); (ii) the fact that the predicted choice probabilities of a model which explains well for the entire population do not fit the realized choices from the available data-sample in a satisfactory way; and (iii) an unsatisifactory explanation of a model developed for the entire population. After the splitting process the previous research phases should be repeated for each individual class.

The fifth research phase makes a more specific distinction among the dwelling alternatives which can be chosen. This is done by dividing the scale on which the objective dwelling quality scores are ranked into an increasing number of parts. Each part representing a class of dwelling quality or type.

The sixth part of the research process concentrates the analysis of the foregoing phases explicitly on the regional level. Only in this phase complete attention is paid to the spatial element such as differences between the Western, Northern, Eastern and Southern regions of The Netherlands, differences between big cities, medium size cities and rural municipalities, etc.

In the last phase a complete evaluation of the modelling process should take place with separate attention for (i) the more technical aspects of the new housing market model; (ii) several data issues; and (iii) the actual empirical results.

SOME EMPIRICAL RESULTS

In this section of the paper only some illustrative empirical results are presented, mainly considering research phases 1 and 3.

Willingness to Move

Initially the willingness to move for the entire sample population, excluding forced moves in order to avoid distortions, was calculated by means of a binary probit model with, apart from a constant term, the following explanatory variables (i) the price/quality ratio of the current dwelling i for household n; (ii) the income/current housing costs ratio of household n; and (iii) the family size/number of rooms ratio of the current dwelling i for household n.

The estimation results and the predicted probabilities are presented in Table 2 under model number 1. The estimations were calculated by means of an adapted version of the computer program CHOMP (Daganzo and Schoenfeld, 1978) and the predicted probabilities were calculated by means of an adapted version of the computer program CONFID (Sparmann and Daganzo, 1979). The interpretation of the estimation results is not very easy as their calculation did not take place in a straightforward way and the usual standard errors are not included in Table 2 for model 1. The reason for the latter is that computation of correct standard errors with the computer model at hand was quite expensive. van Lierop (1984) has described an alternative method of obtaining information about the statistical significance of the estimations.

TABLE 2

ESTIMATION AND PREDICTIONS OF WILLINGNESS TO MOVE

Model No.	No. of Respondents	Options	Constant	Price/ Quality	Income/ Current Housing Costs	Family Size/ Number of Rooms	θ	ρ	max.log-likelihood	$\Sigma d_i^2/npar$	Realized choices	Predicted Probabilities
1	1107	not-willing to move	1.45801	1.75322	0.07028	0.70010	0.43327	0.43284	-408.69	94.4857	0.87444	0.86987
		willing to move	-0.09344	1.58508	0.06827	0.94924					0.12556	0.13013
2	1107	not-willing to move	0.33242 (0.00288)	1.23835 (0.05694)			0.13097	0.78493	-412.75	0.00027	0.87444	0.85927
		willing to move	0.11262 (0.00304)	1.15480 (0.02957)							0.12556	0.14073

The interpretation of the estimation results of a probit model should always take place in combination with an interpretation of the predicted probabilities. The probabilities for Model 1 fit the realized choices reasonably although an optimum connection has not been reached yet.

A high correlation was expected between the three dwelling related ratios. If that held true a high multicollinearity should exist between the exogeneous variables of Model 1. This assumption of expected multicollinearity has been studied by including into the specification of Model 1 just one of the three ratios as single explanatory variable next to a constant term. The model with only the price/quality ratio scored the best in this respect. Its results are presented in Table 2 under model number 2 and the standard errors are shown in parentheses.

The explanatory power of the model is not significantly different from model 1 which includes all three dwelling related ratios. Only the predicted probabilities give less adequate connections with the realized choices. The superior characteristics of model 2 can be proved by splitting the sample population into 10 classes of the price/quality of the old dwelling. The predictions of the probabilities for each of these classes separately gave very good results. It may be concluded that it is possible to explain and predict the willingness to move of individual households in a very satisfactory way, by means of a fairly simple model including only the price/quality ratio as exogenous variable.

Actual Moves

For the analysis of the probabilities in period (t) with which households will actually move in one period later (t+1), several specifications have been tested. Table 3 presents the results of the three most important. Model 3 contains a single explanatory variable, a dummy for the willingness to move in period t (in addition to a constant term). The coefficients for this dummy have the correct signs for both alternatives and connections between the generated and realized choices are reasonable. Model 4 shows the results of the same specification plus the price/quality ratio of the old dwelling. It can be seen that this push-factor did not really improve the results. The same is true for model number 5 with the price/quality ratio as the only exogenous variable. The maximum log likelihood value of this model is worse than that for model 3.

TABLE 3

PROBIT-ESTIMATIONS AND PREDICTIONS CONCERNING
THE PROBABILITY OF ACTUALLY MOVING

Model No.	No. of Respondents	Alternatives	Constant	Price/ Quality Ratio	Dummy for Willingness to Move	θ	ρ	Max.Log-Likelihood	Σd_i^2/npar	Realized Choices	Predicted Probabilities
3	1107	1. not moved	0.62894		-0.11950	0.03876	0.50654	-111.86	0.0008	0.96206	0.99014
		2. moved	0.27795		0.14782					0.03794	0.00986
4	1107	1. not moved	0.63242	0.62316	-0.12314	0.01998	0.51173	-110.93	0.5424	0.96206	0.99051
		2. moved	0.27441	0.61350	0.15158					0.03794	0.00949
5	1107	1. not moved	0.47503	0.71288		0.02089	0.47510	-171.64	3.1878	0.96206	0.96051
		2. moved	0.24736	0.67739						0.03794	0.03948

It may be concluded, that information on the willingness to move provides a reasonable explanation for actual moving behaviour.

In order to get a better connection of the predicted probabilities with the realized choices the willingness to move or not was used as a classification criterion. The sample population was split into two groups: 139 households willing to move in period t and 968 households not willing to do so. Table 4 gives the probit results for each of these groups. It is interesting to notice that the influence of the price/quality ratio in model 6 is bigger on alternative 1 (not moving) than on alternative 2 (moving), whereas the reverse holds true for model 7.

TABLE 4

THE SPLIT-PROBABILITIES TO ACTUALLY MOVE FOR HOUSEHOLDS WILLING TO MOVE AND HOUSEHOLDS NOT WILLING TO MOVE

Model No.	No. of Re-spondents	Alter-natives	Constant	Price/Quality Ratio	θ	ρ	Max. log-Likelihood	$\Sigma_i^2/npar$	Realized Choices	Predicted Probabilities
6	968 not willing to move	not moved	0.47492 (8.08241)	0.67547 (0.03529)	0.01151	0.58421	-30.02	0.000029	0.99483	0.99457
		moved	0.27619 (0.00339)	0.62383 (0.05340)					0.00517	0.00543
7	139 willing to move	not moved	0.28664 (0.00310)	0.59175 (0.20119)	0.09947	0.44257	-77.83	0.000093	0.73381	0.72538
		moved	0.05333 (0.00085)	0.64614 (0.18046)					0.26619	0.27462

While the explanatory power hardly improved with this process of splitting of the population (using a comparison of the total of the maximum log likelihood values of the models 6 and 7 with the value of the unsplit analysis), the predicted probabilities for both groups were considerably closer to the actual choices. Various alternative model forms were studied in order to try to improve the explanatory power but the results for models 6 and 7 were the best that could be obtained. The integral probabilities in period t of moving or not in period t+1 have been calculated by connecting the results of models 6 and 7 with those of model 2 and these are shown in Table 5.

TABLE 5

CALCULATION OF INTEGRAL PROBABILITIES TO MOVE OR NOT

	Predicted Probability Model 2	Predicted Probability Model 6	Predicted Probability Model 2	Predicted Probability Model 7	Integral Probability
Prediction in t not to be moved in t+1	0.85927 x	0.99457 +	0.14073 x	0.72538 =	0.95669
Prediction in t to be actually moved in t+1	0.85927 x	0.00543 +	0.14073 x	0.27462 =	0.04331

Usually it is quite easy, although perhaps expensive, to derive information on the willingness to move in period t, in the period itself in which the forecasting is done through say, a household survey. This additional information would provide the calculations of Table 5 with a better perspective of reality.

CONCLUSION

The few empirical results presented in this paper give a first impression of the use of the probit model within the framework of a newly developed Dutch housing market model. They show that it is possible to model the demand side of the complex housing market with a rather simple stepwise approach consisting of an analysis of the willingness to move followed by split research of actual moving behaviour for households willing to move and of those which are not willing to do so. The price/quality ratio of the old dwelling unit is the most important explanatory variable in this split analysis which provides good insight into the decision processes of individual households of the housing market.

REFERENCES

Anas, A., 1976, Short-Run Dynamics in the Spatial Housing Market, in Papageorgiou, S.J. (Ed.), Mathematical Land Use Theory, Lexington Books, 262-275.

Bird, H., 1976, Residential Mobility and Preference Patterns in the Public Sector of the Housing Market, Transactions of the Institute of British Geographers, 1, 20-33.

Daganzo, C., 1979, Multinomial Probit, The Theory and its Application to Demand Forecasting, Academic Press, New York.

Daganzo, C. and Schoenfeld, L., 1978, CHOMP User's Manual, Research report UCB-ITS-RR-78-7, Institute of Transportation Studies, University of California at Berkeley, CA.

Domencich, F.A. and McFadden, D., 1975, Urban Travel Demand, A Behavioural Analysis, North Holland, Amsterdam.

Evans, A.W., 1973, The Economics of Residential Location, MacMillan, London.

Glickman, N.J. (Ed.), 1979, The Urban Impacts of Federal Policies, The John Hopkins Press, Baltimore, MD.

Hausman, J.A. and Wise, D.A., 1978, A Conditional Probit Model for Qualitative Choice: Discrete Decisions Recognizing Interdependence and Heterogeneous Preferences, Econometrica, 46, 403-426.

Kain, J.F. and Quigley, J.M., 1970, Evaluating the Quality of the Residential Environment, Environment and Planning, 2, 23-32.

Kuylen, A., 1980, Prioriteiten in het Wonen: een Ekonomisch-Psychologische Benadering, Werkverslag IVA-Tilburg.

Lierop, van, W.F.J., 1984, Spatial Interaction Analysis and Housing Choice Modeling, (forthcoming).

Meyer, R.J., 1981, A Descriptive Model of Consumer Information Search Behaviour, WP 47-80-81, Carnegie-Mellon University, Pittsburgh, PA.

Ministry of Housing and Physical Planning and the Ministry of Justice, 1979, Nieuwe Regels voor Huur en Verhuur van Woonruimte, Den Haag.

Ministry of Housing and Physical Planning, Centrale Directie van de Volkshuisvesting, afdeling sociaal-economisch onderzoek, Woningbouwprogrammering, Deel 1, 1979, deel 3, 4, 5, 1981.

Nijkamp, P., 1981, Urban Impact Analysis in a Spatial Context, Research Memorandum 1981-5, Department of Economics, Free University, Amsterdam.

Porell, F.W., 1981, Models of Intra-Urban Residential Relocation, PhD dissertation, University of Wisconsin, Milwaukee, WIS.

Putman, S.H., 1979, Urban Residential Location Models, Martinus Nijhoff, Boston, MA.

Richardson, H.W., 1973, The Economics of Urban Size, Saxon House, Farnborough.

Rima, A., 1982, Een Probit-model voor de Woningmarkt: een Gedesaggregate Analyse van de Verhuisgeneigdheid van Individuen, Department of Economics, Free University, Amsterdam.

Sparmann, J.M. and Daganzo, C., 1979, CONFID User's Manual, Research Report UCB-ITS-RP-79-5, Institute of Transportation Studies, University of California at Berkeley, CA.

Stahl, K., 1980, Externalities and Housing Unit Maintenance, WP 8001, University of Dortmund, Federal Republic of Germany.

Wilkinson, R.K., 1973, House Prices and the Measurement of Externalities, Economic Journal, 83, 72-86.

MODAL CHOICE MODELLING FOR SEVERAL ALTERNATIVES: APPLICATION OF DISAGGREGATE DEMAND MODELS IN SANTIAGO, CHILE

Juan de Dios Ortúzar and Patricio Donoso
Department of Transport Engineering
Pontificia Universidad Catolica de Chile
Casilla 114-D
Santiago
Chile

Abstract. Disaggregate choice models estimated with a 1977 data base are used to evaluate the economic feasibility of several alternatives for extending the Santiago underground system. More sophisticated models developed with a 1981 data base for a particular urban corridor in the city are compared with models calibrated for a similar situation in England. Finally, the models estimated in 1981 are used to predict the impact of an increase in Metro fares that was actually implemented in 1982 and a comparison is made with the actual impact observed.

INTRODUCTION

The population of Santiago has grown during the present century from about 260,000 inhabitants in 1900 to some 4,300,000 in 1982. In the last few years car ownership has increased tremendously from about 0.06 vehicles per person in 1977 to about 0.09 vehicles per person in 1982. However some of the Municipalities of Santiago already had car ownership figures higher than 0.20 vehicles per person in 1977 but unfortunately there are no such disaggregate figures available for 1982. The main reason for this surge can be traced back to the policy started in 1977 of lowering import duties for small cars (ie., of less than 850 cc) from an average of over 12 percent to only 10 percent.

There are several means of transport available in Santiago, including (i) various types (size, age and operating characteristics) of public transport buses, totalling some 10,000 at present; (ii) taxis and shared-ride taxis, totalling some 35,000; (iii) an underground with two lines totalling 25 km, in operation; (iv) private car; and (v) combination of the above modes.

The Metro system was started in 1969 and the first section of line 1, from the low income west to the CBD, was opened in 1975. In 1977 the second section, from the CBD towards the high income district to the east of the city, was completed and in 1978 the line, from the middle income south to the CBD, was also finished. Finally, in 1980 the last section of line 1, to the high income district was put into service thus completing the 25 km approved for the first stage of the system (DGM, 1982). It is important to mention that the original plan, made in 1968, contemplated five lines and 105 km of rail. However a revision made in 1975 showed that the construction costs had been grossly underestimated and it was also quickly realized that the demand figures projected for line 2 were heavily overestimated.

In 1980 the Ministry of Transport asked the Department of Transport Engineering of the Pontificia Universidad Catolica de Chile (UC) to assess the economic feasibility of extending the underground system. The tasks to be performed in this study were (i) to determine the investment cost of every alternative where these varied from a small addition to line 2 from the CBD to the north, to a rail ring way around the CBD, with extensions to the northeast and southeast, but using a different rail technology (tram or semi-metro rather than rubber wheeled Metro as in the current system); (ii) to estimate the demand for each alternative network under different operating conditions; and (iii) to evaluate each alternative both from the social and private points of view.

The following section of the paper summarizes the main results of the demand modelling exercise carried out in 1980, as part of the aforementioned study, using 1977 data for the whole of Santiago. Section 3 presents some improved models obtained with data gathered in 1981 for a corridor between the CBD and the high income district and compares them with similar models developed for an urban corridor in England. Finally the aggregate response properties of these models are analyzed using as a case study an increase in the Metro fares which was actually implemented in 1982.

USE OF DISAGGREGATE CHOICE MODELS FOR EVALUATING UNDERGROUND EXTENSIONS

Alternatives Considered

Apart from a do-nothing option four Metro extension alternatives were analyzed in the 1980 UC study where the current concern here is only with the one described in Table 1 which is also depicted in Fig. 1.

TABLE 1

CHARACTERISTICS OF THE ALTERNATIVES STUDIED

Alternative	No. of Stations	Length of Track (km)	Investment Cost* (1,000$)
Present Metro (do nothing option)	35	24.4	-
Rail ringway and suburban extensions plus extension of line 2 to the ringway	87	82.9	7,329,860

*In 1980 the exchange rate was $US1 = $39

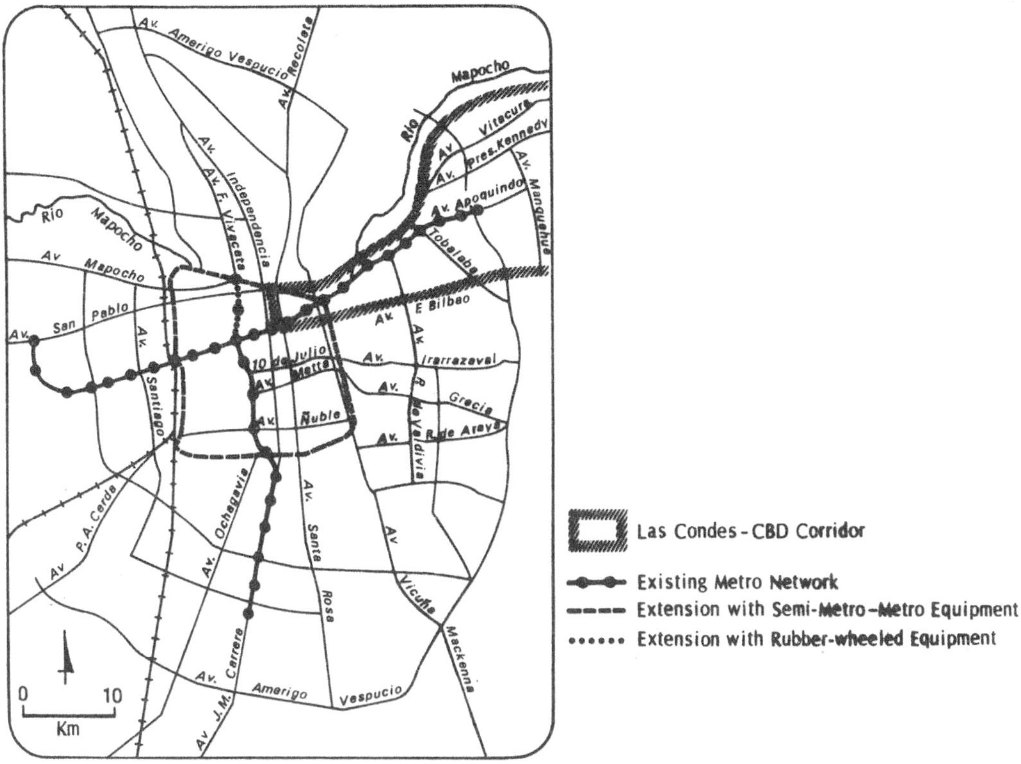

Figure 1 - Extension Alternative and Las Condes-CBD Corridor

Demand Estimation

The demand estimation phase of the study (Fernandez, et al 1981), consisted of the application of the usual four-step transport models of generation, distribution, modal choice and assignment. It incorporated, however, the following differences from a traditional study (i) the modal choice stage involved the calibration of multinomial logit (MNL) models using disaggregate information synthesized from the 1977 O-D survey data base (DICTUC, 1978); and (ii) detailed assignment was only performed for the Metro network with the impact of the alternatives on the road network analyzed using an aggregate model of network behaviour (Zahavi, 1972).

Demand Projection

After the demand models were calibrated for 1977 (the base year), they were validated by comparing the estimated passenger loadings on the Metro network in 1980, before and after the final extension of line 1, and the observed figures. The comparison was very satisfactory. Demand projections were made for the years 1982, 1987 and 1995, for each alternative and study period. The results for 1982 and 1995 are summarized in Table 2.

TABLE 2

TOTAL TRIPS BY MODE AND PERIOD

		Do-Nothing Alternative	Rail Ringway Alternative
Year 1982			
PEAK			
	Car	211,682	210,849
	Bus	691,995	622,462
	Metro	81,678	156,459
OFF PEAK			
	Car	40,693	37,453
	Bus	197,559	159,158
	Metro	58,207	99,823
Year 1995			
PEAK			
	Car	523,933	517,063
	Bus	725,808	664,080
	Metro	91,116	166,048
OFF PEAK			
	Car	146,644	143,949
	Bus	217,993	173,572
	Metro	72,244	119,381

Estimation of Benefits

Benefit estimation considered both the changes in consumer surplus experienced by those users that would be affected by the implementation of the projects, and the changes in the social costs or benefits derived from the projects but which would not be perceived by the users of the system. The changes in consumer surplus considered the following benefits (Fernandez, et al 1981) (i) time savings, (ii) savings in operating costs, (iii) savings in the size of the public transport fleet, (iv) savings in accidents, and (v) savings in road infrastructure investment.

Social Evaluation

The computation of costs and benefits for each extension alternative, when compared with the do-nothing option, was done using the estimated figures for 1982, 1987 and 1995. Table 3 shows a summary of the discounted values for each benefit and cost item considered in the evaluation and the internal rate of return of the project. As the implementation of the project produces a shift from cars and buses to the Metro system, travel times, operating costs and accidents should decrease for these modes and the differences with the base alternative appear as benefits of the project. However, and as a consequence of the increase in Metro trips, the total amount of time spent in this mode should increase with the implementation of the project. Therefore the items travel time and access time savings for Metro appear with a negative value in the table.

TABLE 3

SOCIAL BENEFITS AND COSTS

Item	Project less do-nothing* (1,000$)
Benefits	
Savings in car operating costs	1,470,129
Car travel time savings	596,534
Car accident savings	522,174
Savings in bus operating costs	6,501,041
Bus travel time savings	16,963,458
Bus access time savings	3,009,794
Bus accidents savings	278,867
Bus fleet investment savings	634,689
Metro travel time savings	-9,551,400
Metro access time savings	-8,587,272
Savings in road investment	806,695
Costs	
Infrastructure investment	6,937,189
Investment in equipment	5,799,088
Fixed operating costs	1,818,831
Variable operating costs	1,473,719
Internal Rate of Return	8.84%

*Values correspond to the 1980 present value of each series of costs and benefits, discounted at the 12% social rate.

As the government required a 12 percent minimum social discount rate, none of the projects were judged economically feasible. However, a sensitivity analysis considering reasonable variations in the hypotheses used to represent (i) the behaviour of congestion in the road network; and (ii) the relative value of access time as compared to travel time, showed that the project could reach an internal rate of return of 12.2 percent. It is also fair to mention that all the projects considered could pay for their operating cost and contribute an important part to their investment costs both in infrastructure and equipment.

FURTHER EXPERIENCE WITH DISAGGREGATE CHOICE MODELS

A Comparison of Chilean and English Models

In 1981 funds were granted to study among other things the transferability of disaggregate choice models. The idea was to compare models calibrated for a suburban corridor in England with models calibrated for a similar corridor in Santiago. The Las Condes-CBD corridor, see Fig. 1, was chosen because it had a reasonable similarity with the English corridor. The main characteristics of both corridors and of the data available in each case are shown in Table 4. As it can be seen, the setting seems ideal for a transferability analysis.

TABLE 4

COMPARISON OF THE TWO CORRIDORS AND DATA SETS

Characteristic	Garforth-Leeds f/	Las Condes-CBD
Of the Corridor		
Main city population a/	500,000	4,000,000
Travel pattern	suburban to urban	intraurban bus,
Pure modes available	train, bus, car	car, taxi, shared taxi, Metro,
Length of railway line b/(km)	11.5	8
No. of railway stations b/	3	11
Train frequency (trains/hour)	5	30
Train fare c/ (Chilean $)	25.5	9
Bus fare d/ (Chilean $)	16.5	10
Average car operating cost (Chilean $/km)	2.9	2.2
Of the Sample		
Sample size	724	637
Year of survey	1975	1981
Is there income information?	no	yes
Is there information about alternatives to the chosen mode?	no	yes
% of trips going to the CBD	67.7	100
% of households with one or more cars	79.3	88.3
Average parking charge e/ (Chilean $/hour)	11.5	8

Notes: a/ Leeds and Santiago, respectively; b/ underground in the Chilean case; c/ fixed in the Chilean case; d/ fixed in both cases; e/ calculated as a weighted (by the corresponding proportions) average of the different amounts paid by the individuals in the sample; f/ in all cases the British cost in £ of 1975 were converted first to 1981 equivalent using a factor of 2.181 (given by the British Embassy in Santiago) and then converted to Chilean $ using the 1981 rate of $75 per £.

In this part of the paper the same model structure, except for the number of alternatives, is estimated for both the Leeds and Santiago data sets, and some conclusions about model transferability are drawn from the comparison of results.

The statistical measures used as one of the ways of comparing the models are briefly presented in Table 5. A fuller description of all the statistics and tests employed can be found in McFadden (1976), Tardiff (1976) and Gunn and Bates (1982). The variables used in the specification searches are defined in Table 6. Because all the level-of-service variables are generic, the models will in addition contain a number of mode specific constants. The criteria used in the search for the best model specification was a class of stepwise analysis (Ortuzar, 1982), where those variables judged not significant (a t-ratio smaller than 1.96) or incorrectly specified (wrong sign) were eliminated.

TABLE 5

STATISTICAL MEASURES AND TESTS USED IN MODEL COMPARISONS

For Estimation Data Set	
L(O)	= log-likelihood at zero, ie., for the equally likely model
L(C)	= log-likelihood of a model with only mode-specific constants
L(θ)	= log-likelihood at convergence
LR(O)	= likelihood ratio statistic with respect to the equally likely model = $-2\{L(O) - L(\theta)\}$
LR(C)	= likelihood ratio statistic with respect to the constants only model = $-2\{L(C) - L(\theta)\}$
ρ^2	= rho-squared index = $1-L(\theta)/L(O)$
$\bar{\rho}^2$	= corrected rho-squared index = $1-L(\theta)/L(C)$
% Right	= percentage correctly predicted according to a maximum utility classification

TABLE 6

EXPLANATORY VARIABLES USED IN THE SPECIFICATION SEARCHES

Variables	Definition
Socio-Economic	
NAUT	- number of cars in the household
CO_1	- car ownership dummy, takes value of 1 for one car owning households and 0 otherwise
CO_2	- car ownership dummy, takes a value of 1 for multiple car owning households and 0 otherwise
CBD	- destination dummy, takes a value of 1 if trip goes to CBD and 0 otherwise
Level-of-Service	
OVT	- out-of-vehicle time (walking and/or waiting, including transfers) (min)
COST	- out-of-pocket and/or operating cost (1981 Chilean $)
COSINC	- cost divided by income (Chilean $/min)
IVT	- in vehicle time (min)
WAIT	- waiting time (min)
WALK	- walking time (min)
Mode Specific Constants	- one for each mode excluding car passenger (which was arbitrarily set to zero)

Table 7 presents the best MNL models found using both data sets. It is important to remember that the English data set contained information about six alternatives while the Chilean one considered a total of nine. In addition the variable CBD included in the Leeds case was irrelevant for the Santiago case, as all the trips considered in the latter have their destination in the CBD area. It is also very important to mention that the estimation process in the Chilean case was constrained in the sense that only variables that had been used in the English study (Ortuzar, 1983) were employed, as the main objective was to examine model transferability. For this reason the full richness of the Santiago data was not exploited and the models are not necessarily good representations, indeed they are rather bad!

TABLE 7

MNL MODELS WITH ENGLISH AND CHILEAN DATA

Variables (alternative entered) a/	Coefficient (t-ratios)	
	English Model	Chilean Model
CBD (4-7)	1.015 (3.17)	-
CO_1 (1,2,6,7)	2.471 (6.01)	0.904 (-2.95)
CO_2 (1,2,6,7)	2.970 (5.83)	-0.001 (-0.41)b/
OVT (1-9)	-0.161 (-7.06)	-0.372 (-2.89)
IVT (1-9)	-0.076 (-2.87)	-0.070 (-2.54)
COST (1-9)	-0.049 (-3.68)	0.023 (0.90)b/
CAR (1)	2.623 (9.08)	1.400 (6.02)
TRAIN/METRO (4)	6.734 (7.27)	2.980 (6.91)
BUS(5)	5.781 (9.01)	0.650 (1.24)b/
P & R (6)	1.472 (2.27)	2.082 (6.87)
K & R (7)	0.958 (1.69)	0.465 (1.35)b/
SHARED TAXI-METRO (8)	-	0.840 (1.54)b/
BUS-METRO (9)	-	2.065 (3.17)
LR(0)	572.52	376.05
(Degrees of Freedom)	(11)	(12)
% Right	65.8	47.6
ρ^2	0.378	0.219
$\bar{\rho}^2$	0.148	0.025
Sample Size	600	517

a/ Alternatives are: (1) car driver; (2) car share; (3) shared taxi (4) Metro; (5) bus; (6) park and ride; (7) kiss and ride; (8) shared taxi-Metro; (9) bus-Metro.

b/ Not significant at 95% level.

As we can see in Table 7 the English model is quite satisfactory. On the other hand most parameters obtained with the Chilean data are statistically significant at the 95 percent level and present correct signs, with the exception of that corresponding to the cost variable which is not significant and has the wrong sign. In addition, the general statistical measures for the Chilean specification present values that are within the normal range for this type of model. However it is interesting to note that the relative magnitudes of the dummy variables CO_1 and Co_2 are not in accordance with a priori intuition and evidence. The latter should be larger than the former and both should have positive signs.

In Table 8 a comparison is made of the frequency of choice of each alternative, and also of the number of people that had each alternative available in both samples. As can be seen the importance of several alternatives vary significantly in both cases. For example, the bus mode changes from being the most popular alternative in the English case, with 43.8 percent of the people choosing it, to being chosen by only 9.7 percent of the Chilean sample. The reverse occurs with the train mode which jumps from 3.5 percent in the English case to Metro being the second most popular option (20.9 percent) in the Chilean case. The car passenger mode also decreases significantly, 16.7 percent in England to only 6.2 percent in Chile, and P & R shows a spectacular increase from 1.7 percent in England to 17.5 percent in Chile. These changes, together with the evidence about the availability of each alternative, help to understand the conclusions we present below.

TABLE 8

DISTRIBUTION OF CHOICES IN BOTH SAMPLES

Mode	English Case		Chilean Case	
	Frequency of Choice	Available To	Frequency of Choice	Available To
Car driver	185 (30.8)	313 (52.2)	112 (20.9)	412 (79.6)
Car passenger	100 (16.7)	600 (100.0)	33 (6.2)	464 (86.6)
Taxi	-	-	14 (2.6)	470 (87.7)
Shared taxi	-	-	29 (5.4)	461 (86.0)
Train/Metro	21 (3.5)	120 (20.0)	109 (20.3)	158 (29.5)
Bus	263 (43.8)	600 (100.0)	52 (9.7)	379 (70.7)
P & R	10 (1.7)	240 (40.0)	94 (17.5)	313 (58.4)
K & R	21 (3.5)	500 (83.3)	22 (4.1)	330 (61.6)
Taxi-Metro	-	-	5 (0.9)	340 (63.4)
Shared Taxi-Metro	-	-	27 (5.0)	244 (45.5)
Bus-Metro	-	-	39 (7.3)	173 (32.3)
TOTAL	600		536	

Note: The numbers in parentheses are percentages over the total.

CONCLUSIONS

As it is well known, the mode specific constants of a MNL model represent those characteristics of the alternative not considered by the socio-economic and level of service variables included in the specification. Thus it can be said that they are affected by the modal perceptions of the users with respect to comfort, privacy, environment, safety, reliability, etc. They are also affected by the way in which the availability of each mode is defined for the individuals included in the data set. Therefore, the differences observed between the values obtained for the mode specific constants in the Leeds and Santiago cases should be mainly due to differences in those factors. However as was already noted, choice set availability was defined in both cases in the same objective manner (the only difference was that in Santiago the empirically found constraint that no individual with a high income had BUS available was added). It is interesting to note that in both cases the preferred mode (ceteris paribus) is TRAIN/METRO and the less preferred one, CAR PASSENGER. In this sense also BUS comes second in England and third in Chile (after BUS-METRO). The rest of the ordering however is not so similar. It is not clear whether this is just a coincidence or if there is some similarity in the unexplained factors that determine the size of the mode-specific constants in both cases.

The importance and behaviour of the car ownership variable was very different in both cases. Besides, the coefficient of the variable COST was not significant and of incorrect sign in Chile (this is not new, see for example Fernandez et al, 1981).

In general then, it is safe to conclude that results obtained do not grant the transferability of MNL models between different cultural settings. There are several reasons why this should have been expected. The main ones are related to the kind of model used and the variables included in its specification. Firstly, it is well known that the use of the MNL is bounded to the limitations imposed by the independence of irrelevant alternatives property of the model. Both in the Leeds and Santiago cases the set of alternatives used were far away from being totally independent, therefore violating a basic assumption of the model; this should have important consequences for the correct calibration in each case and therefore could reduce transferability. Secondly, the specification used in the Leeds case, on which the comparison was based, was (as usual in practice) limited by the information available and does not necessarily correspond to the ideal correct specification of the true model behind the situation studied. In particular this is true of the socio-economic variables used and the specification of the COST variable. It is difficult to compare cost figures without reference to income.

AGGREGATE RESPONSE PROPERTIES OF THE CHILEAN MODEL

The Chilean model in Table 7 is, as was discussed above, a rather poor specification. However after relaxing the constraints imposed by the English data set, actually we only decomposed some of the variables and introduced income information, we found a more satisfactory form which is shown in Table 9. Firstly we disaggregated the variable OVT into its components walk and wait. Model MNL-1, which was judged to be the best, eliminated the walk variable as it was found during the coding and validation of the data that several individuals exhibited an unusual behaviour in terms of this variable; that is, they walked normally far more than the assumed maximum of 500 metres because they "did not have another opportunity during the day to exercise" and this had the effect of improving the statistical indices of the model. It is interesting to note that the only parameter which is significant at the 90 percent level (all the others are strongly significant at the 95 percent level) is COSINC. This would suggest that for the population of the corridor money matters less than the rest of the ingredients of the level of service.

TABLE 9

BEST MNL MODEL FOR LAS CONDES - CBD CORRIDOR

Variables (alternatives entered) a/	Coefficients (t-Ratios) MNL-1
NAUT (1,6)	0.302 (3.78)
IVT (1-9)	-0.023 (-2.01)
COSINC (1-9)	-0.017 (-1.81) b/
WAIT (3-9)	-0.354 (-3.75)
CAR DRIVER (1)	0.671 (2.39)
CAR PASSENGER (2)	-0.327 (-0.69) b/
METRO (4)	2.605 (6.28)
BUS (5)	0.613 (1.97)
P & R (6)	1.407 (3.79)
K & R (7)	-0.239 (-0.48) b/
SHARED TAXI-METRO (8)	1.336 (2.52)
BUS-METRO (9)	1.897 (5.32)
LR(0)	393.9
(Degrees of Freedom)	(12)
$\bar{\rho}^2$	0.037
Sample Size	517

Note: a/ (1) car driver; (2) car share; (3) shared taxi; (4) Metro; (5) bus; (6) park & ride; (7) kiss & ride; (8) shared taxi-Metro; (9) bus-Metro

b/ not significant at 95% level.

On October 23, 1982, the Metro raised its fares from \$10 to \$14 in the case of single tickets and from \$80 to \$130 in the case of carnets (a set of 10 tickets).

Table 10 shows the figures for monthly entries to the Metro system between August and November at the nine boarding stations in the Las Condes-CBD corridor. Note that these are total-day (not AM peak) figures and that no adjustment has been made for travellers that exit from the system before or after the CBD.

TABLE 10

MONTHLY METRO PATRONAGE AT BOARDING STATIONS OF THE LAS CONDES-CBD CORRIDOR

Station	August	September	October	November
No. of working days	22	22	20	22
Escuela Militar	676,430	659,436	622,521	571,611
Alcantara	117,860	112,362	109,553	108,389
El Golf	123,890	123,268	116,484	114,336
Tobalaba	451,975	430,538	410,986	388,474
Los Leones	361,449	359,787	348,447	328,114
P. de Valdivia	426,495	410,900	395,273	371,079
Manuel Montt	287,392	284,423	276,675	255,935
Salvador	371,645	359,095	353,759	314,764
Baquedano	504,564	491,182	471,851	414,363
TOTAL	3,321,700	3,230,991	3,105,659	2.867,065

In order to estimate the observed impact of the fare increase we calculated the demand-price elasticity using as the before the change point an estimation of the November figures regressed from the previous months data on the assumption that the tendency thereby shown would be maintained. This was done using weekly data of trips per working day (in order to account for the fact that October had only 20 working days, see Table 10), and obviously leaving out the figure for the week starting October 25. The figure thus obtained from November was 3,010,000 monthly trips. It is interesting to mention that the estimated figure for the whole of October using this process was actually higher than the observed figure given in Table 10, so we used the latter for the November extrapolation. For calculating the elasticity we used the well known approximation

$$\varepsilon_{D/p} = \frac{\Delta Q/Q_1}{\Delta p/p_1} \tag{1}$$

where Q_1 = number of monthly trips in November without a change in fares (ie., the regressed figure); ΔQ = difference between observed monthly trips in November and Q_1; p = Metro fare before the change ($8), (the majority of AM peak travellers in the corridor use carnet); and Δ_p = variation in the fare ($5).

The elasticity obtained was

$$\varepsilon_{D/P} = \frac{(2,867,065 - 3,010,000)/3,010,000}{5/8} = -\ 0.076$$

To estimate the modelled elasticity we calculated the sample enumeration number of individuals choosing the Metro, according to model MNL-2, with the old and new fares, applied to eqn. (1) and obtained the value

$$\varepsilon_{D'/P} = -\ 0.043$$

Although this value is obviously much smaller than the observed one, we feel it would be unrealistic to think it could be higher; in effect, we would expect that a change in fares should have a lesser impact on people travelling to work (which is the majority of those travelling in the AM peak).

ACKNOWLEDGMENTS

The authors wish to thank Gloria Hutt for her help throughout the project as well as DIUC, the University's Research Division, for funding the project.

REFERENCES

DGM, 1982, Metro de Santiago 1981, Direccion General de Metro, Ministerio de Obras Publicas, Santiago, Chile.

DICTUC, 1978, Encuesta de Origen y Destino de Viajes 1977 para el Gran Santiago, final report to the Ministerio de Obras Publicas, Santiago, Chile.

Fernandez, J.E., Coeymans, J.E., Diaz, J. and Ortúzar, J.D., 1981, Evaluacion de Alternativas de Ampliacion de la Red de Transporte Colectivo Independiente en el Gran Santiago, final report to the Ministerio de Transporte y Telecomunicaciones, Department of Transport Engineering, Pontificia Universidad Catolica de Chile.

Gunn, H. F. and Bates, J.J., 1982, Some Statistical Considerations in Fitting Travel Demand Models, Transportation Research, 16A, 371-382.

McFadden, D., 1976, The Theory and Practice of Disaggregate Demand Forecasting for Various Modes or Urban Transportation, WP 7623, Institute of Transportation Studies, University of California at Berkeley, CA.

Ortúzar, J. de D., 1982, Fundamentals of Discrete Multimodal Choice Modelling, Transport Reviews, 2, 47-78.

Ortúzar, J. de D., 1983, Nested Logit Models for Mixed-Mode Travel in Urban Corridors, Transportation Research, 17A, 283-299.

Tardiff, T.J., 1976, A Note on Goodness-of-Fit Statistics for Probit and Logit Models, Transportation, 5, 377-388.

Zahavi, Y., 1972, Traffic Performance Evaluation of Road Networks by the Alpha Relationship, Traffic Engineering and Control, 14, 228-231.

CHOICE OF URBAN TRANSPORT MODES FOR WORK TRIPS

H. K. Sinha
Department of Civil Engineering
Bihar College of Engineering
Patna, India

S. K. Khanna and M. G. Arora
Department of Civil Engineering
University of Roorkee
Roorkee, India

Abstract. Choice of modes for work trips in medium size cities in India is a difficult one due to the constrained travel budget and characteristic large separation of homes and work places. Multiplicity of modes for urban travel is also a particular phenomena. In this paper a modelling effort for mode choice selection in Patna is reported where MNL and EBH techniques have been used. The models reproduce the observed behaviour very closely and revealed other travel characteristics of commuters in Patna.

INTRODUCTION

Developing countries are facing serious problems of congestion on transportation facilities due to continued growth and increased population migration to cities. The fact that only a fraction of the urban commuters in India can afford to own mechanized private transport further aggravates the mobility problem in urban areas. Private vehicle owners are also discouraged due to increased operating costs, congestion and high accident rates. The result is obviously an increased demand for public transport which is grossly inadequate in most cities in terms of quality and quantity of services.

Due to the wide spectrum of socio-economic status of the population affordability of transport has a very large range. This has resulted in a multiplicity of available modes for urban travel. These may broadly be classified as private transport, public transport and intermediate public transport. In spite of this categorization, the mode choice is a very complex process ranging from the private car mode to animal drawn intermediate public transport modes. Many of the lower level slow modes are present because of the fact that some portions of the network are not accessible by the fast moving modes. Unlike developed countries, urban travel choice is not a simple one between private automobile and transit, but involves a choice among variety of modes. Further, owing to the low level of income, slight changes in the cost of travel have great impacts on travel behaviour and therefore in the shares of various modes.

This paper examines the various factors which influence the choice of modes for home based work trips in a medium size city in India. Utilities derived from the choice of individual modes could be assessed by estimating the value of time. The mode choice process was modelled in two ways. Firstly in the conventional way using a multinominal logit (MNL) function, and secondly by using and equivalent binary hierarchy (EBH) of mode choice. The utility in each case has been defined in terms of generalized cost. Also the work reported here demonstrates the application of MNL and EBH approach in modelling mode choice for a typical Indian city with multiple modes with their extreme characteristics.

THE DATA

Patna, a typical medium size city, which is state capital of Bihar, has a population of nearly one million was used for the study. Over the past two decades Patna has grown tremendously in terms of employment opportunities necessitating migration of people to the city. At the present time the eastern part of Patna city has developed as a highly commercial area with high population density and narrow roads. The central part is of mixed land use with some government offices, hospitals and Patna University. The western sector mainly includes the government and semi-government offices. Since the housing opportunities are not distributed like the jobs, a large amount of home-to-work travel is necessitated by the separation between the two. A wide variety of modes are used by the commuters where these modes suit their particular travel budgets.

All the work trips internal to Patna city and those trips made from vicinity to Patna for the purpose of work are accounted for in the travel survey. Fourteen major work places located all over the city were identified for interviewing commuters. A sample of 418 persons was selected for personal interview. A choice-based sampling procedure was adopted to ensure sufficient sample units for various modes. Such a technique has been recommended specially for the development of mode choice models (Stopher, 1979). The layout of Patna city and the major work places selected for the study are shown in Fig. 1.

SURVEY ANALYSIS

Socio-Economic Condition

Household income is an important indicator of travel activities particularly mode choice. The income distribution and motorized vehicle ownership data available from the 1971 census is shown in Fig. 2. The distribution is skewed towards the lower income group and more than 85 percent of the households earn less than Rs.750/- per month. The relationship of motorized vehicle ownership to income level is perfectly linear and given by

$$y = 0.054(x - 289), \text{ for } x > 289 \qquad (1)$$
$$= 0, \text{ otherwise}$$

The seriousness of the mobility problem in the Patna urban area is further revealed by the fact the 90 percent of the households own only five motorized vehicles per 100 households. Thus, a large fraction of the public depend on public and intermediate public transport available, including the walk mode.

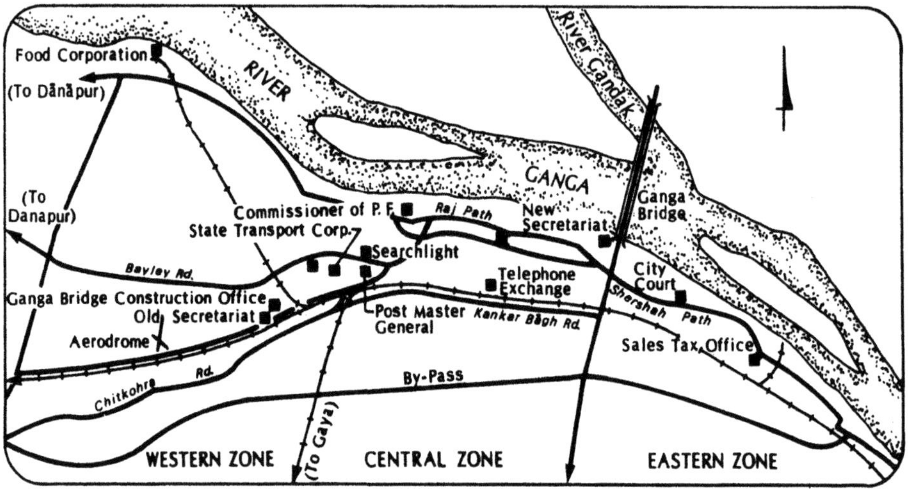

Figure 1 - Location of Work Places Shown With DOT on Map of Patna City

Choice of Modes

If cities are allowed to grow without check, the non-motorized modes will not be able to cope with the requirements of urban travel. On the other hand, due to increases in fuel prices, there is a gradual shift towards motorized public transport as well as other non-motorized modes. This study has attempted to bring out these issues which are becoming serious problems in relation to mode choice in medium size cities in India.

The choice of various modes in Patna city as revealed in the sample survey is shown in Table 1 disaggregated by income group. It may be seen that the choice of mode varies significantly with income level. In order to find out the preferences of a particular mode over another, ranking analysis was done.

It was concluded that the usage of car, scooter and rickshaw (non-motorized three wheeler) decreases and that of public transport bus, minibus and trains increases as the income level reduces from Rs.2,500/- to Rs.800/- per month. Commuters in the lower income groups use primarily the cheaper modes like walk, bicycle, trains and minibus.

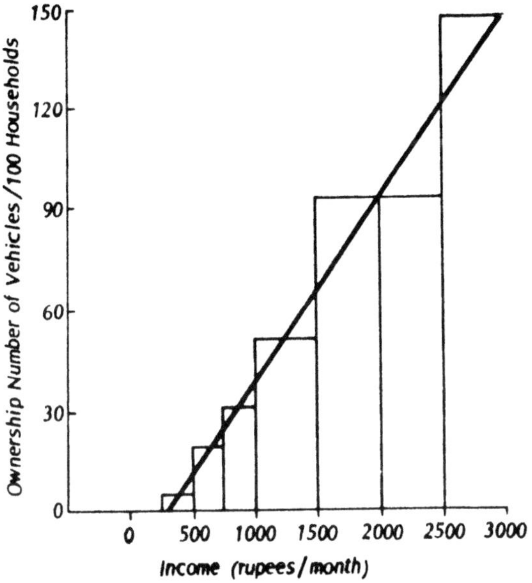

Figure 2 - Number of Motorized Vehicle/100 Households With a Given Income

TABLE 1

CHOICE OF MODE BY DIFFERENT INCOME GROUPS

Income Group (Rs.)	Bus	Mini-Bus	Three Wheeler	Scooter	Motor Cycle	Cycle	Train	Walk	Car	Rickshaw	Tonga
< 400	5.53	6.63	1.10	0.0	1.10	14.37	14.37	16.58	0.0	0.0	0.0
400-600	1.68	3.35	0.93	0.37	0.19	4.28	4.10	2.61	0.0	0.37	0.19
600-800	0.47	1.41	0.37	1.03	1.03	1.50	1.31	0.94	0.0	0.47	0.09
800-1000	0.29	0.73	0.22	0.44	0.22	0.15	0.37	0.44	0.07	0.66	0.0
1000-1500	0.37	0.37	0.28	1.11	0.74	0.55	0.09	0.28	0.18	0.92	0.0
1500-2000	0.12	0.12	0.06	0.58	0.29	0.0	0.06	0.17	0.47	0.29	0.0
2000-2500	0.07	0.13	0.0	0.20	0.0	0.0	0.0	0.07	1.00	0.13	0.0
> 2500	0.0	0.0	0.0	0.0	0.0	0.0	0.0	0.0	0.0	0.0	0.0
Modal Share	8.53	12.74	2.96	3.73	3.57	20.85	20.30	21.09	2.00	2.96	0.28

Various modes have characteristic distances within which they are used the most. It was observed from the survey data that even for the same income group the set of alternative modes chosen changes with the trip distance. However, the lower income groups were found to travel to work only up to a distance of about 16 km where this characteristically represents the constrained travel and housing budget of these income groups.

Table 2 shows the comparative travel cost and time for various modes in relation to certain characteristics of the traveller and it is apparent from the data that cycle and walk are the cheapest modes as they do not have direct travel costs. Other cheaper modes are train, bus and minibus, while the cost increases sharply for motorized three wheeler, scooter and motorcycle. As expected, the cost is found highest for the private car which is generally chosen by upper middle and high income groups because of lower travel time, more comfort and privacy. The age of the traveller was not related to mode choice in any of the income groups. The only deviation from this was that the older people of high income groups preferred those modes which have privacy such as rickshaw and car. The survey also revealed the obvious fact that lower income groups use generally the less comfortable modes which are cheaper.

TABLE 2

AVERAGE CHARACTERISTICS OF THE MODE AND USER

Mode	Monthly Income (Rs)	Age of User (years)	Travel Cost (paisa)	Travel Time (mins)	Travel Distance (kms)
Bus	754	37.0	32	40.0	10.0
Minibus	738	36.1	45	34.8	6.0
Three Wheeler	795	40.5	106	20.0	6.2
Scooter	1145	38.9	123	17.0	5.8
Motorcycle	947	38.6	161	17.6	4.8
Tonga	575	30.5	50	45.0	6.5
Cycle	562	34.0	0	27.4	4.4
Train	548	35.0	32	74.0	28.0
Walk	645	35.3	0	21.6	2.0
Car	2426	45.2	275	25.9	4.7
Rickshaw	1159	41.3	129	25.0	3.5

Housing and Travel Budget

Combined expenditure on housing and travel for commuters using different modes are shown in Table 3 as percent of total income. It is also emphasized in the table that 23 percent of the commuters belong to the middle and high income groups, whereas 73 percent in the lower income group can afford to spend only 11 to 13 percent of their income for housing and transport. Thus a commuter seems to adjust his location of housing depending on the budget for travel cost, keeping the total expenditure as a constant proportion of income.

Table 2 shows that middle and high income groups located within about 6 kms of their place of work and use a costlier mode. On the other hand, poor urban dwellers live at the outskirt to save on housing cost as well as use less comfortable and cheaper modes such as bus and train. Travel time is another important factor to be considered in the process of mode choice. It was found to vary from 34 minutes for those using scooter/motorcycle to 148 minutes for train users. Only the low income groups were found to tolerate high travel time. Thus, the concept of United Mechanism of Travel (UMOT) introduced by Zahavi (1977) is supported by the survey results.

TABLE 3

COMBINED EXPENDITURE OF HOUSING AND TRAVEL FOR VARIOUS MODE USERS

Mode Group	Combined Housing and Travel Budget (percent of income)	Percent of Population in the Group
Motorcycle Scooter Car Three Wheeler Rickshaw Minibus	21 to 26	23
Cycle Bus Walk Train	11 to 13	73

Captivity and Multi-Modal Choice

Information about transport mode captivity was also obtained during the interview by asking whether the use of the particular mode was by choice or by compulsion. The possible alternative choice was also asked which gave an idea of the range of choices considered by a commuter. It was found that in most cases the choice of alternatives were in the group of similar modes. Table 4 shows the level of usage of alternative modes by the normal user of a primary mode.

In the sample survey it was observed that there were certain proportions of users in each mode who did not have any alternative to the primary mode, implying captivity. Thus, it was found that 10.6 percent of car users, 14.7 percent of rickshaw users, 21.4 percent of train users and 25 percent of those walking were captive travellers.

It was also observed during the interview that questions relating to the characteristics of the first alternative mode of choice could not be answered by the respondent because of inadequate knowledge of it. While this is true, any one will have less information about the second alternative mode and so on. It is asserted therefore, that the procedure of mode choice modelling may be constructed as a hierarchy of binary choices in series, in place of the multiple choice approach.

TABLE 4

CHOICE OF ALTERNATIVE MODES IN CLASSIFIED CATEGORIES

Primary Mode	Percent Using Alternative Mode		
	PT	IPT	OM
Bus (PT)	46.6	36.9	16.5
Minibus (PT)	8.7	61.3	30.0
Three Wheeler (IPT)	47.1	41.2	11.7
Scooter (OM)	22.7	54.5	22.8
Motorcylce (OM)	17.2	62.3	20.5
Cycle (OM)	40.0	38.5	21.5
Train (PT)	73.1	25.3	1.6
Walk (OM)	7.7	59.6	32.7
Car (OM)	2.7	73.0	24.3
Rickshaw (IPT)	14.7	26.4	58.9
Tonga (IPT)	50.0	-	50.0

PT : Public Transport
IPT : Intermediate Public Transport
OM : Personally Driven (Own) Mode

Value of Time

The willingness to pay technique of Hensher (1976) to the value of travel time was intended for use and accordingly the survey included an appropriate question. But, the people were not able to estimate their behaviour under a hypothetical situation and therefore sufficient data could not be collected for the use of the technique. Instead, the value of time has been estimated from the concept of the time-cost trade-off behaviour of the travellers.

The details of the estimation are given elsewhere (Sinha, 1981). It was found from the analysis that the value of time to urban commuters varies from a minimum 0.17 paisa per minute for the train users to a maximum of 11.8 paisa per minute for the car owners. In relation to the commuters' income, a train user assigned a value to the time spent in a train as 4 percent of income, whereas a car owner's value of time was found to be as high as 98 percent of the income. The users of other modes were found to have assigned intermediate values to their travel time and thus income has been found to affect the value of travel time judgment and reflecting in the actual choice of modes.

MODEL DEVELOPMENT AND CALIBRATION

Models describing travellers' behaviour are generally based on the principle of utility maximization (Domencich and McFadden, 1975), subject to resource constraints. A traveller's choice of mode is dependent of his perception of the level of service attributes under the influence of his own socio-economic characteristics. Due to the uncertainty of the behaviour the choice becomes probabilistic. Assuming that the random error has the Weibull distribution (McFadden, 1973), it can be shown that the choice model takes a multinomial logit form

$$P_i^j = \frac{\exp U(x_j, s_i)}{\sum_{k=1}^{M} \exp U(x_k, s_i)} \tag{2}$$

where P_i^j = the probability of choosing mode j by the traveller i; $U(x_j, s_i)$ = the utility of mode j to the traveller i; M = the number of alternative modes including the chosen one.

The utility is a function of the variables which characterize the attributes of mode j, denoted as x_j and the socio-economic variation describing the traveller i, denoted by s_i.

The functional form of utility x_j, s_i may be assumed to be linear as

$$U(x_j, s_i) = \alpha_j + \sum_S \alpha_s x_{sj} + \sum_t \alpha_{tj} s_i \tag{3}$$

where s = the number of attributes related to the urban transport mode; and t = the number of attributes related to the socio-economic characteristics of the traveller. The values of the coefficients α_j, and α_{tj} are estimated as a part of calibration by maximum likelihood estimation of the model.

The analysis of survey data revealed that the commuters of various income levels in Patna use definite sets of modes for their travel to work. Further, it has been argued earlier that the choice sets for each income group can be arranged in an hierarchy of binary choices. Accordingly, the commuters are believed to have first experienced choice between the preferred mode and the immediate alternative and then between the preferred of the first two and the third and so on. A similar equation system to eqns. (2) and (3) can be developed for the equivalent binary choice case and coefficients in binary logit function may be determined by maximum likelihood using the Newton-Raphson method.

For the purpose of calibration, the utility of the selected mode has been calculated in terms of generalized cost which is a function of the value of time and travel cost

$$G_j = V_j T_j + C_j \tag{4}$$

where Vj = the value of time; T_j and C_j = travel time and cost of travel, respectively.

The generalized cost for alternative modes for comparison with the selected mode were obtained from a similar relationship using the travel time and cost per unit distance values in conjunction with the actual distance travelled. Thus the functional form of utility has been expressed as

$$U(x_j, s_i) = \alpha_0 + \alpha_1 (\text{Generalized Cost}) \tag{5}$$

CALIBRATION RESULTS

The model was calibrated using seven income groups, the trips made by each group being further stratified into three trip length categories. The estimated parameter values of MNL and EBH models were supported by corresponding tests of statistical significance. While the details of the results are given elsewhere (Sinha, 1981) typical results of income group Rs.500/- to Rs.800/- for the MNL and EBH models are shown in Tables 5 and 6. It is evident from these tables that the generalized cost does not have a significant effect on the mode choice. On the other hand, the mode specific constant derived from calibration could replicate the observed market share of the modes.

TABLE 5

MNL CALIBRATION FOR INCOME GROUP RS. 600-800

		Maximum Likelihood Estimate of		
Trip Length (km)	Mode	General Cost Coefficient	Model Constant	Likelihood Ratio
1-6	Cycle Scooter Minibus	-0.688 0.016 0.025	36.0 20.9 18.4	52.64
6-12	Scooter Minibus Train	0.004 0.006 -0.035	- 6.73 - 5.28 - 2.76	1.61

TABLE 6

EMB CALIBRATION FOR INCOME GROUP RS. 600-800

		Maximum Likelihood Estimate of		
Trip Length (km)	Mode	General Cost Coefficient	Model Constant	Likelihood Ratio
1-6	Cycle and Scooter versus Minibus	0.001	2.42	20.81
	Cycle versus Scooter	-1.57	-21.47	42.94
6-12	Minibus and Scooter versus Train	-0.018	0.445	13.20
	Minibus versus Train	-0.092	- 4.60	9.55

CONCLUSIONS

Any typical medium size city in India has a large variation in the socio-economic characteristics of the urban dweller which results in the use of a large variety of transport modes. In spite of the increased number of modes the different income groups were found to use only a subset of the total range available. Thus with appropriate stratification, the mode choice process can be modelled either as a multinomial logit choice process or even more simply as an equivalent binary choice phenomenon.

The focus on the city of Patna shows that there is a characteristic lead distance for each mode and the expansion of the city will necessitate commuter's readjustment in mode choice. Continuous increase in energy cost may also divert high income groups from private motorized modes to other alternative modes. Further, due to constraints on the total housing and travel budget, transport demands will have serious implications on future development of land use patterns.

ACKNOWLEDGMENTS

The assistance received from Dr. P. K. Sikdar, Reader in Civil Engineering, University of Roorkee, Roorkee, India, in going through the manuscript and making important suggestions is gratefully acknowledged by the authors.

REFERENCES

Domencich, T.A. and McFadden, D., 1975, Urban Travel Demand: A Behavioural Analysis, North Holland, Amsterdam.

Hensher, D.A., 1976, The Value of Commuter Travel Time Savings: Empirical Estimation Using an Alternative Valuation Model, Journal of Transport Economic and Policy, X, 167-176.

McFadden, D., 1973, Conditional Logit Analysis of Qualitative Choice Behaviour, in Zarembka, P. (Ed.) Frontiers of Econometrics, Academic Press, New York.

Sinha, H.K., 1981, Choice of Urban Transportation Modes for Work Trips, PhD thesis, Department of Civil Engineering, University of Roorkee, Roorkee, India.

Stopher, P.R., 1979, Urban Transport Planning in Developing Countries - Can the Technology be Transferred?, Proceedings, Second Symposium in Engineering, San Salavster.

Zahavi, Y., 1977, The UMOT Model, Paper of Urban Project Department, World Bank, Washington, DC.

GEOGRAPHIC TRANSFER OF TRAVEL CHOICE MODELS: EVALUATION AND PROCEDURES

Frank S. Koppelman and Geoffrey Rose
Department of Civil Engineering and
The Transportation Center
Northwestern University
Evanston, IL 60201
United States of America

Abstract. This paper reviews research results which evaluate model transferability and methods of updating in transfer application. Early expectations that disaggregate choice models would be generally transferable across a wide range of application contexts are not supported by research studies. Indeed, the reported level of transferability varies across model types and specification and differences in transfer contexts. These studies also indicate that methods of transfer model adjustment are very effective in both increasing the average level of transfer effectiveness and decreasing the variability of transfer effectiveness across specifications and contexts. This review establishes the need for additional research to identify the effect on transfer effectiveness of differences in model type and specification and differences in characteristics of transfer contexts. It also establishes the importance of adopting updating procedures when employing model transfer.

INTRODUCTION

Disaggregate modelling has been extensively used during the last fifteen years to describe, explain, and forecast travel and travel related behaviour (Lisco, 1967; Stopher, 1969; Lave, 1969; PMM, 1972; Ben-Akiva and Lerman, 1974; Lerman, 1975; Adler, 1975; Koppelman and Hauser, 1979). The models are formulated by application of utility maximization theory to the choice an individual makes among a set of alternatives (McFadden, 1973, 1976). The argument for adoption of disaggregate models is based on four main advantages of these models relative to aggregate models of travel. First, disaggregate models are expected to represent the true behavioural process better than aggregate models because they are formulated and estimated at the level of the decision makers. Second, disaggregate models are more efficient than aggregate models in their use of data. Third, disaggregate models are highly flexible in that they can be applied at any level of aggregate prediction. Fourth, because disaggregate models describe individual behaviour they are expected to be transferable to contexts other than those in which they are estimated.

Model transferability has important practical usefulness. The urban transportation planning process has become very expensive, particularly in terms of the time and cost associated with data collection and analysis. The possibility of transferring (or borrowing) a model developed in one region for use in a transportation study in another region offers the potential for considerable time and cost savings.

The expected transferability of disaggregate models combined with the practical advantages of model transfer has created increasing interest in this topic in recent years. This interest has led to research studies (Watson and Westin, 1975; Atherton and Ben-Akiva, 1976; Talvitie and Kirshner, 1978; Galbraith and Hensher, 1982; Koppelman and Wilmot, 1982b) and general discussion of the issues associated with model transfer (Lerman, 1981; Ben-Akiva, 1981; Louvierre, 1981). Further, there have been a number of practical applications of model transfer (Barton-Aschman Associates, 1979, 1981, 1982; Barton-Aschman Associates and Texas Transportation Institute, 1979; Schultz, 1983).

This paper provides an overview of the state-of-the-art in model transfer and the analysis of model transferability. We address not only the theoretical and empirical research into transferability but also the practical issues of how models can be effectively transferred. The structure of the paper is as follows. First, we discuss some of the important issues and concepts relating to model transfer as well as the conditions for effective transfer. Next, we discuss research which has been directed at evaluating model transferability. Then, we examine and evaluate techniques known as model updating which can be used to enhance transferability. Finally, we summarize the important issues raised in this paper and use these as a basis to draw conclusions about the state-of-the-art in this field.

ISSUES AND CONCEPTS IN MODEL TRANSFERABILITY

Although the issue of model transfer has been discussed widely in the literature, there appears to be some confusion between the transfer of a model and the appropriateness of that transfer. In this section, we define and distinguish between model transfer and model transferability, formulate some conditions for effective model transfer, and discuss selected issues relevant to the evaluation of model transferability and the practical use of model transfer.

Relevant Definitions

We define model transfer as the application of a model formulated in one context to another context. According to this definition, model transfer does not necessarily imply that the application is appropriate or useful. We define model transferability or effective model transfer as a measure of the usefulness of the information about behaviour in the application context which is provided by the transferred model.

It is useful to think of transferability as a property which may exist to greater or lesser degree depending on the formulation of the model and the characteristics of the estimation and application contexts (Lerman, 1981; Ben-Akiva, 1981). It is not satisfactory to describe transferability as a dichotomous property; rather, it is appropriate to consider the degree of transferability of a model, theory or information from one context to another (Lerman, 1981).

It is useful to further define the contexts of model estimation and model application. We argue that characteristics of the environment in a specific time and place determine the appropriateness of the application of a model estimated in a different time and place. We identify context differences in terms of time and space. Temporal transfer is the application of a model estimated at one point in time for prediction of behaviour in the same spatial environment at another point in time. Temporal transfer is employed and temporal transferability is implicitly invoked whenever models estimated on historic data are used to predict the future. Spatial transfer is the application of a model estimated in one location for prediction of behaviour in a different spatial environment. Spatial transferability is explicitly invoked when models developed in one geographic region are used to make predictions in another. Obviously, cases of spatial-temporal transfer may occur. More generally, transfers are potentially describable in terms of the characteristics of the contexts of model estimation and application. In the case of pure temporal transfer, we expect that most contextual characteristics are relatively unchanged and thus we expect a high level of temporal transferability and this expectation has been verified empirically (Train, 1978; Talvitie and Kirshner, 1978; McCarthy, 1981).

Conditions for Effective Model Transfer

There are general conditions, both theoretical and practical, which we believe need to be satisfied in order for a transferred model to be effective.

The theoretical condition for transferability is that the underlying behaviour process under study in the application context is the same as in the context in which the model was formulated and estimated. If this condition does not hold (if, for example, people in one context are utility maximizers and people in another context are satisficers, or if people in one context place great weight on one aspect of travel alternatives and people in another context place great weight on a different aspect of travel alternatives) models estimated in one context will describe a behavioural process different from that in the other context and will not be transferable between these contexts.

Even if the condition of behavioural equality holds, there are further practical conditions for transferability. First, the model to be transferred must be well specified so that it effectively describes the underlying behavioural process. Second, variable definitions and measurement procedures should be equivalent between the estimation and application contexts or satisfactory procedures should be adopted to make appropriate adjustments in the models. Third, the estimation data set should be large enough to assure reasonably precise parameter estimates (Koppelman and Chu, 1983) and of sufficient range to encompass the conditions in the application context. A well specified model, estimated with high quality data, should be transferable to contexts with expected similar behaviour and consistent variable definition and measurement.

Transferability of Aggregate versus Disaggregate Models

The argument in support of the transferability of disaggregate travel models is based in part on the presumed ability of these models to represent the choice process of the traveller. It is also based on an advantage in transferability relative to aggregate travel demand models. Theil (1955) and Green (1964) illustrate the bias which occurs in the estimation of linear regression models estimated with non-homogeneous aggregate population groups. Koppelman and Ben-Akiva (1977) and McFadden and Reid (1975) illustrate the application of these results in the case of choice models. The biases obtained are related to the distribution of variables within the aggregate population groups. Unless these distributions are identical between estimation and application contexts the disaggregate to aggregate level biases will be different. Thus, the aggregate models may be non-transferable even in cases where the underlying behaviour is identical and the disaggregate model is transferable. Thus, disaggregate models can be expected to have a transferability advantage over the corresponding aggregate models.

Prior versus Posterior Analysis of Model Transferability

We distinguish between prior and posterior analysis of transferability. Posterior analysis of transferability is the evaluation of the effectiveness of a transferred model in an application context after analogous models have been formulated and estimated in that context using locally collected data. There is no intent to apply the transferred model in this case as the locally estimated model against which the transferred model is compared will be preferred to the transferred model. The usefullness of posterior analyses of transferability is that they provide a basis from which to infer the transferability of comparable models in other contexts. These studies will provide a basis to undertake prior analysis of model transferability. The potential for prior analysis or prediction of model transferability implies some relationship between the level of transferability, the characteristics of the model considered for transfer, and the characteristics of the estimation and application contexts. Unfortunately, the inferences about the transferability which have been made to date are not sensitive enough for this purpose. Most studies conclude only that models are or are not transferable although Koppelman and Wilmot (1982b) have examined the effect of specification improvement on the level of model transferability and Koppelman and Pas (1983) have identified different levels of transferability among models for different choices. Studies to date have found a wide range of transferability for different contexts but the context characteristics which are responsible for this variability in transfer effectiveness are not identified.

Partial Model Transfer and Updating

Different portions of a model, theory or data may be more or less transferable than other portions. Thus it is appropriate to consider the notion of differential transferability of various model components. Westin and Manski (1979) and McFadden (1978) argue that the alternative specific constants, which represent the average effect of excluded variables, are least likely to be transferable and that parameter scale, which represents the variance of the stochastic component of the utility function, is next least likely to be transferable. These differences in transferability of model components have been empirically verified by Atherton and Ben-Akiva (1976), Koppelman and Wilmot (1982a) and Koppelman, Wilmot and Kuah (1983).

It is possible to transfer the most transferable portion of a model and update the non-transferred portion using data which describes the application context. Updating procedures can be used with a small amount of disaggregate or aggregate local data to adjust alternative specific constants of choice models (intercept constants of regression models) or constants and parameter scale to best fit conditions in the application context. These procedures are discussed in a later section of this paper.

EVALUATION OF MODEL TRANSFERABILITY

A number of study efforts have been undertaken to evaluate model transferability. In this section, we review a set of representative studies of transferability in various contexts and make some general inferences about transferability, methods to evaluate transferability, and research issues. The studies reviewed are inherently posterior in design. Each study employs multiple data bases to evaluate transferability between pairs of contexts. The general approach is to formulate and estimate models on one or more data bases and then apply these models to one or more other data bases. The results obtained from the transferred model are compared to both observed behaviour and a comparable estimated model in the application area. Various measures are formulated and interpreted to evaluate transferability for each directional transfer.

Inter-Regional Transferability

The general objective of spatial transfer is to apply models in regions different from those in which they are estimated. Studies of inter-regional transferability directly evaluate the effectiveness of such transfer applications. We review two studies: one undertaken by Ben-Akiva, Atherton and others at MIT and Cambridge Systematics (Atherton and Ben-Akiva, 1976; Cambridge Systematics, 1977) and the second by Talvitie and others at SUNY-Buffalo (Talvitie and Kirshner, 1978; Talvitie, et al 1981; Dehghani, et al 1981).

Ben-Akiva and colleagues examined the transfer application of a model estimated in Washington, DC, to New Bedford, Massachusetts, and Los Angeles. They evaluated transferability by use of statistical tests of parameter equality and disaggregate predictive accuracy and concluded that the models are transferable. Other general model comparisons, undertaken in a more judgmental fashion, are found to support model transferability.

Talvitie and colleagues examined transferabililty between Washington, Minneapolis-St. Paul and San Francisco. They reject transferability based on comparison between all city pairs except Minneapolis-St. Paul and San Francisco. However, they also concluded that only about 20 percent of aggregate prediction error is attributable to model transfer. The balance is attributable, almost equally, to model and aggregation errors.

It is difficult to make a general conclusion about the effectiveness of inter-regional transfer based on these results. The studies examined transfer of similar models and obtain substantially different conclusions. Apparently, the differences in contexts, data used, specifications employed, transfer tests, and judgment are more critical to the results obtained than any fundamental property of specific model types.

Intra-Regional Transferability

Intra-regional transferability is important to the study of transferability as within region analyses generally avoid the problem of differences in variable definition and measurement which may undermine the effectiveness of inter-regional model transfer. We review four studies of intra-regional transfer.

Watson and Westin (1975) examined transferability of intercity mode choice models between different regions in each of two cities. Based on tests of model equality and transfer prediction error, they conclude that there is a high level of transferability between some context pairs (those for which one end of the trip is in the CBD of either of the cities) but not between others. Talvitie and Kirshner (1978) rejected transferability across residential or work location boundaries in Washington and Minneapolis-St. Paul using tests of equality between transfer and local model parameters. Galbraith and Hensher (1982) rejected transferability between suburban portions of the Sydney, Australia region using test of model parameter equality as well as more general goodness-of-fit comparisons. Koppelman (1977) rejected transferabililty across sectors and rings of residential location in Washington using tests of model parameter equality but obtained acceptable cross-prediction performance measures for some transfers.

Thus each of these studies provides some evidence against the general adoption of model transferability. The relevance of these results is that it would seem unlikely for model transferability to exist across metropolitan regions if it does not exist within these regions. These results suggest that general acceptance of the transferability property of available disaggregate choice models may not be appropriate.

Temporal Transferability

While this paper is primarily directed towards spatial transfer, we examine studies of temporal transfer with three objectives. First, these studies may offer some insights into the potential for effective spatial model transfer. Second, these studies may suggest a limit to how well we can do in spatial transfer which includes temporal transfer. Further, these results are relevant to an understanding of the general usefullness of travel models in local prediction.

Train (1978), Talvitie and Kirshner (1978) and McCarthy (1981) investigated temporal transferability using pre-BART/post-BART data collected in the San Francisco Bay Area. Train examined the validity of forecasts made with a disaggregate mode choice model developed before the implementation of the Bay Area Rapid Transit (BART) for prediction of travel behaviour after the opening of BART. Train identified substantial prediction errors and diagnoses on sources of this error but asserts that the level of service parameters of the models estimated in the pre- and post-BART data sets are fairly similar. Talvitie and Kirshner examined models developed using pre- and post-BART samples and reports that equality of pre- and post-BART coefficients were rejected at the .05 level. McCarthy defined three time periods; pre-BART, early-BART and post-BART and rejected transferability across some of these periods at the .05 level with a reduced data set. However he argued that prediction with a model estimated on a combination of pre-BART and early-BART data for the post-BART period is not significantly inferior to that of a post-BART model.

The results of these studies are reasonably consistent, partially reflecting the use of a common data base. Equality of the models over time is generally rejected at the 0.05 level even though the data set used is relatively small. However, there is some disagreement about the level of error produced in prediction.

Empirical Studies of Predictive Validity

An alternative approach for evaluating the transferability of disaggregate choice models is to apply them to forecasting problems and compare the predicted aggregate travel choice shares obtained to those observed. Studies by Parody (1977), Benham and Tardiff (1981), Ben-Akiva and Atherton (1977) and Cambridge Systematics (1977) were interpreted by their authors to support the transfer validity of disaggregate choice models for the prediction of aggregate shares of individuals choosing a transportation mode to work. Despite the encouraging conclusions drawn by these researchers, three important issues should be considered before these results are generalized.

First, the test applied in each case is the prediction of aggregate mode shares in a corridor or region. This is not a strong test of the predictive validity of the models. Accurate prediction of total mode shares may obscure serious errors in the prediction of mode shares at a more detailed level of analysis.

Second, in each case except the Parody study, the initial predictions obtained from the disaggregate models were seriously in error. Subsequent adjustments made to the model input data significantly reduced the prediction error. While the adjustments in each case are reasonable, a number of alternative reasonable adjustments could have been adopted which would have produced substantially different prediction results. It is impossible to evaluate the validity of the predictions obtained in the face of these post-facto adjustments.

Third, only a small number of cases have been identified in which the predictive validity of disaggregate models has been tested. The errors reported in these cases vary considerably even after adjustments which improve the predictions. It is not clear which, if any of these results can be considered typical of general application of disaggregate models.

Interpretation of Empirical Studies

The most obvious conclusion which can be made from this review of transferability studies is the lack of consistency of the results obtained by different researchers and, in some cases, by the same researchers in different studies. The lack of consistency in findings can be attributed to a variety of differences among these studies. Most important among these may be differences in the contexts over which transferability is evaluated. The identification of the relationship between context characteristics and transferability is essential to any generalization of transferability results. Other of these differences are attributable to methodological differences among studies including differences in model specification, use of different updating procedures, use of different measures to describe the level of transferability and the judgment of the researchers in interpreting the results obtained. Establishment of a consistent approach to the evaluation of transferability is essential to developing generalizable results. If methodological consistency is established differences in results may be associated with context characteristics and thus may clarify the impact of these characteristics on model transferability.

Nevertheless, some very limited general conclusions may be tentatively drawn from these results. First, the effectiveness of pure temporal transfer appears to be greater than of spatial transfer. Second, differences in model specification and context characteristics may have substantial impact on model transferability. Third, updating alternative specific constants can substantially enhance transferability in most cases.

CURRENT RESEARCH ON MODEL TRANSFERABILITY

Researchers at The Transportation Center of Northwestern University are engaged in an extensive, ongoing investigation of model transferablility with the support of the US Department of Transportation, Office of University Research (Koppelman and Wilmot, 1982b). The results discussed in this section are based on that research. First, we describe an integrated set of transferability measures incorporating and relating measures used in earlier studies to provide a general framework for analyzing model transferability. Then, we analyze and interpret empirical study results of transfer effectiveness for both inter- and intra-regional transfer of selected disaggregate travel demand models.

Measures of Model Transferability

Measures of model transferability are organized into two different classification systems. The first classification groups measures by the level of analysis at which they evaluate transfer effectiveness. One set of measures evaluates model transfer at the disaggregate level and the other at a level of aggregation typical of practical applications. The second classification is by type of measure. There are three measure types in this classification. First are absolute measures of ability of the transferred model to replicate observed behaviour in an application context. Second are measures of this replication ability relative to the replication ability of a similarly specified model estimated on the observed data in the application environment. Third are statistical measures which test hypotheses about the appropriateness of the transferred model to describe behaviour in the application environment. These classes can be crossed so that we identify measures of each type at each level of analysis. There are clear analytical relations among the measures at each level of analysis; however, use of the full range of measures provides more insight into model transferability than any single measure. The relationships between aggregate and disaggregate measures are less easily defined. However, these measures generally give consistent results although they are not strictly monotonic.

The measure set is initially formulated in a general fashion so that they may be applied to different classes of models. Specifically, we define distinct measures which are appropriate for use with probabilistic choice models or which are appropriate for use with regression models. Thus, we obtain analogous measure sets for these two different model types.

We review six general measures, one for each of the joint classes defined earlier. First, we review the disaggregate measures starting with an absolute goodness-of-fit measure, followed by a relative goodness-of-fit measure, and finally by a statistical test of model applicability. Next, we review aggregate measures in the same order.

Disaggregate Measures of Model Transferability. These measures evaluate the effectiveness of the transferred model based on the ability to replicate observed behaviour at the disaggregate level. The first of these measures is the transfer goodness-of-fit measure. It is formulated in Table 1 for discrete choice models and for regression models. These measures are analogous to the likelihood ratio index or rho-square measure (McFadden, 1973) for discrete choice models and the common R-square measure for regression models. The differences between these transfer measures and the corresponding goodness-of-fit measures is the use of transferred model log likelihood or sum of squared errors in place of the corresponding values for the local models. Thus, we call these specific measures the transfer likelihood ratio index or transfer rho-square for choice models and the transfer R-square for regression models.

The second measure is the transferability index. This measure describes the disaggregate transfer prediction accuracy or goodness-of-fit relative to the corresponding goodness-of-fit of a similarly specified model estimated in the application context. The transferability index has an upper bound of one which it attains when the transferred model is identical to the locally estimated model. Although this index has no lower bound we expect it to generally be positive.

TABLE 1
MEASURE OF TRANSFERABILITY

Transferability Measure	Regression Models	Discrete Choice Models
(A) **Disaggregate Measures**		
1) Transfer Goodness-of-fit	$R^2_{ij} = 1 - \frac{ESS_i(\beta)_j}{TSS_i}$	$\rho^2_{ij} = 1 - \frac{LL_i(\beta_j)}{LL_i(BASE)}$
2) Transferability Index	$TI_{ij} = \frac{TSS_i - ESS_i(\beta_j)}{TSS_i - ESS_i(\beta_i)}$ $= R^2_{ij}/R^2_{ii}$	$TI_{ij} = \frac{LL_i(\beta_j) - LL_i(BASE)}{LL_i(\beta_i) - LL_i(BASE)}$ $= \rho^2_{ij}/\rho^2_{ii}$
3) Transferability Test Statistic	$\frac{[ESS_i(\beta_j) - ESS_i(\beta_i)]/NPAR}{ESS_i(\beta_i)/[N_i - NPAR]}$ (Distributed $F_{NPAR,\ N_i-NPAR}$)	$-2\ [LL_i(\beta_j) - LL_i(\beta_i)]$ (Distributed X^2_{NPAR})
(B) **Aggregate Measures**		
1) Root-Mean-Square-Error (RMSE)	$\left\{\frac{\sum_z N_z^P\ REM_z^2}{\sum_z N_z^P}\right\}^{1/2}$	$\left\{\frac{\sum_m \sum_z N_{mz}^P\ REM_{mz}^2}{\sum_m \sum_z N_{mz}^P}\right\}^{1/2}$
2) Relative Root-Mean-Square-Error	$REL.RMSE = \frac{RMSE_{ij}}{RMSE_{ii}}$	$REL.RMSE = \frac{RMSE_{ij}}{RMSE_{ii}}$
3) Aggregate Prediction Statistic	$\sum_z \frac{(N_z^P - N_z^O)^2}{N_z^P}$ (Distributed X^2_{Z-a})	$\sum_{m,z} \frac{(N_{m,z}^P - N_{m,z}^O)^2}{N_{m,z}^P}$ (Distributed $X^2_{(Z-a)(M-1)}$)

Key to Table 1

(A) Disaggregate Measures

1) Regression Models

R^2_{ij} = Transfer R^2 (Local R^2 if i=j).

$ESS_i(\beta_j)$ = Error Sum of Squares for a model with parameters estimated in context $j(\beta_j)$ and applied in context i.

TSS_i = Total Sum of Squares in Context i.

N_i = Number of observations in context i.

2) Discrete Choice Models

ρ^2_{ij} = Transfer ρ^2 (local ρ^2 if i=j).

$LL_i(\beta_j)$ = Log likelihood for a model with parameters estimated in context j and applied in context i.

$LL_i(BASE)$ = Log likelihood for a base model in context i.

3) Generic

T_{ij} = Transfer index for transfer from j to i.

NPAR = Number of Parameters in the Model.

(B) Aggregate Measures

1) Primary Variables

N^p_{sub}, N^o_{sub} = Number of individuals predicted/observed in the subscripted group (see below).

REM_{sub} = Relative error measure for subscripted group $\dfrac{N^p_{sub} - N^o_{sub}}{N^p_{sub}}$.

AE, AE_m = Average Error in prediction, Average Error in prediction for alternative m.

2) Subscripts

m = alternative index

z = zone index

M = total number of alternatives

Z = total number of zones

$$a = \begin{cases} 0 & \text{for full transfer} \\ 1 & \text{for partial transfer or local prediction} \end{cases}$$

The third disaggregate measure is used to test the hypothesis that the transferred model describes the behaviour in the application context and, thus, is transferable to it. The transferability test statistic formulated in Table 1 for both choice models and regression models tests the hypothesis that the parameters in the transferred model are equal to the population behaviour parameters in the application context. Effectively, this test compares the fit in the application environment of a locally estimated model to an identically specified model with parameters restricted to equal the estimated values in the transferred model. This test is based on the likelihood ratio statistic for discrete choice models, and the F-test for regression models. The transferability test statistic is distinctly different from the commonly used test for behavioural equality between two distinct populations. The transferability test statistic is inherently directional and it is possible and, we argue, reasonable to accept transferability in one direction but not in another.

All the tests described above evaluate transferability for an entire model estimated in one environment and applied to another. Each of these measures can be reformulated to test the transferability or portions of the model by modifying the transferred model so that selected portions are re-estimated to best fit the application context. These partial transfer measures (Koppelman and Wilmot, 1982b; Koppelman and Rose, 1983) measure the transferabililty of the balance, the non-updated portion, of the model. The tests are formulated and interpreted identically to the full transfer tests except that the statistical tests must be adjusted for differences in the degrees of freedom to represent the number of restrictions in the transferred model.

Aggregate Measures of Model Transferability. These measures evaluate the effectiveness of the transferred model based on the ability to replicate observed aggregate behaviour for aggregate population groups generally defined by spatial proximity. Each of the aggregate measures is based on the error in prediction in each aggregate group. We define this error in relative terms. The relative error measure for each aggregate prediction of travel activity is given by

$$REM = \frac{N^p - N^o}{N^p} \tag{1}$$

where REM = relative error measure for a single aggregate prediction; N^p = travel activity predicted; and N^o = travel activity observed.

This measure describes the error in prediciton as a portion of the actual prediction.

The Root-Mean-Square-Error in Table 1 summarizes the prediction error for all aggregate predictions. This measure is an index of the average relative error in prediction weighted by the size of the prediction element and structured to place emphasis on large relative errors. This measure has the useful property that it can be disaggregated into its average and standard deviation components as shown in Table 1, with the property that

$$RMSE^2 = AE^2 + SDE^2 \qquad (2)$$

where RMSE = root-mean-square-error; AE = average error; and SDE = standard deviation error.

In the case of disaggregate choice models it is also possible to develop corresponding error measure for each alternative (Koppelman and Wilmot, 1982b; Koppelman and Pas, 1983).

The root-mean-square-error can be used to measure the absolute error in aggregate prediction by either transferred or local models. We defined the relative aggregate transfer error as the ratio of these measures shown in Table 1. This measure indicates the degree to which aggregate prediction errors produced by the transferred model exceed those produced by a corresponding local model.

Finally, we formulate a statistical measure which can be used to test the hypothesis that the transferred model applied at the aggregate level generated the observed aggregate data. The aggregate prediction statistic, defined in Table 1, is equivalent to the chi-square one sample test (Spiegel, 1956) with degrees of freedom determined by the type of prediction employed as shown in Table 1.

Composite Transferability Measures. It is useful to have composite measures which can be used to describe the transfer effectiveness results for a number of transfers. In Table 2, we formulate composite measures of the transfer goodness-of-fit, transfer index, transfer root-mean-square error, and relative aggregate transfer error. In each case, these measures are weighted functions of the corresponding measures for each of the transfers included in the composition.

Empirical Analysis of Model Transferability

The empirical research conducted as part of this study investigates intra-regional and inter-regional transferability of models describing mode choice, automobile ownership, joint choice of mode and automobile ownership, and trip frequency. In this section we briefly discuss the results of some of these empirical analyses.

Data sets for three distinct urban regions are used in this analysis. These regions are Baltimore, 1977; Minneapolis-St. Paul, 1970; and Washington, D.C., 1968. Each data set contains the detailed socio-economic and level of service data necessary for estimation of disaggregate models. We examine intra-regional transferability for selected models in each region. The intra-regional transfers are between two sectors in each area. We also examine intra-regional transferability for mode choice models between each pair of urban regions.

TABLE 2

COMPOSITE TRANSFERABILITY MEASURES

Composite Measure	Regression Measure	Discrete Choice Model
1. Composite Local Goodness-of-Fit	$\tilde{R}^2_L = 1 \frac{\sum_{i \in I} ESS_i(\beta_i)}{\sum_{i \in I} TSS_i}$	$\tilde{\rho}^2_L = 1 - \frac{\sum_{i \in I} LL_i(\beta_i)}{\sum_{i \in I} LL_i(BASE)}$
2. Composite Transfer Goodness-of-Fit	$\tilde{R}^2_T = 1 - \frac{\sum_{i \in I} \sum_{j \in J_i} ESS_i(\beta_j)}{\sum_{i \in I} \sum_{j \in J_i} TSS_i}$	$\tilde{\rho}^2_T = 1 - \frac{\sum_{i \in I} \sum_{j \in J_i} LL_i(\beta_j)}{\sum_{i \in I} \sum_{j \in J_i} LL_i(BASE)}$
3. Composite Transfer Index	$\widetilde{TI} = \tilde{R}^2_T / \tilde{R}^2_L$	$\widetilde{TI} = \tilde{\rho}^2_T / \tilde{\rho}^2_L$
4. Composite Local Root-Mean-Square-Error	$\widetilde{RMSE}_L = \left\{ \frac{\sum_{i \in I} {}_iN^P \, RMSE^2_{ii}}{\sum_{i \in I} {}_iN^P} \right\}^{1/2}$	
5. Composite Transfer Root-Mean-Square-Error	$\widetilde{RMSE}_T = \left\{ \frac{\sum_{i \in I} \sum_{j \in J_i} {}_iN^P \, RMSE^2_{ij}}{\sum_{i \in I} \sum_{j \in J_i} {}_iN^P} \right\}^{1/2}$	
6. Composite Relative Root-Mean-Square-Error	$\widetilde{REL.RMSE} = \widetilde{RMSE}_T / \widetilde{RMSE}_L$	

Key to Table 2

$\tilde{R}^2$, $\tilde{R}^2_T$ = composite local and transfer R^2. $\tilde{\rho}^2_L$, $\tilde{\rho}^2_T$ = composite local and transfer ρ^2. $\widetilde{TI}$ = composite transfer index. I = set of application contexts. J_i = set of estimation contests from which models are applied in context i. $\widetilde{RMSE}_{ii}$, $\widetilde{RMSE}_{ij}$ = composite local and transfer RMSE. ${}_iN^P$ = aggregate predicted sample size in application context i.

Intra-Regional Transferability. We report the intra-regional transferability of trip generation and mode choice models in the Baltimore region in detail. We then report composite results for all intra-regional transfers within each area. More detailed results of these transfer analyses are available in Koppelman and Wilmot (1982a and b); Wilmot (1983); Koppelman and Pas (1983); and Koppelman and Rose (1983).

The trip generation analysis is formulated in terms of number of stops and number of tours which sum to the number of linked trips (Horowitz, 1976). We use least square regression models rather than the Poisson regression (Ruijgrok and van Essen, 1980) or the negative binomial regression (Litinas, et al 1981) as the consistency property of these models will tend to produce approximately equal estimations (Timmermans, 1982). Further, we adopt a linear functional form as the non-linearities tested were not significant and the linear form is more familar. We report here only the results for the stops generation model. The corresponding analysis for the tours models are reported in Koppelman and Rose (1983). The transferability results for the tours models are similar to those for the stops models.

The estimation results for the stops model for each Baltimore sector and the region are reported in Table 3. The coefficients of all the explanatory variables are significant and have the expected signs. There are large differences in parameter estimates, especially vehicles available and number of workers, between the two sectors. The impact of these differences on model transferability will be examined later.

The estimation results for the multinomial logit work mode choice model for each Baltimore sector and the region are reported in Table 4. These models describe the alternatives of drive alone, shared ride, and transit. Most of the estimated parameters have the expected sign and are significant. The only parameter with a counter-intuitive sign is that for out-of-pocket cost divided by income in the North sector model and this estimate is not significant.

We examine the transferability of these stop generation and mode choice models between the North and South sectors of Baltimore. We report the values of the local and transfer goodness-of-fit measures and the transfer indices for full and partial model transfer for stop generation and mode choice models in Tables 5 and 6, respectively. The goodness-of-fit measures, local and transferred, provide an indication of the degree to which variability of behaviour is explained by the local or transferred model. These measures are in a satisfactory range for the stops generation model but are low for the mode choice model. The transfer index measures the goodness-of-fit performance of the transferred model relative to the local model. These values are good for transfer of the stops generation model especially with partial transfer, but poor for the mode choice model. This is consistent with results of other transfer analyses that transferability measured by the transfer index is generally better for transfers into regions in which the behaviour under study is better described by the models used. The transfer index results also demonstrate the importance in performance of partial versus full transfer and indicate the transfer from the North to South sector is superior to transfer from South to North. Evaluation of the hypothesis of transferability using the transfer test statistic results in rejection of the hypothesis for both full and partial transfer at or near the .01 level in every case.

TABLE 3

BALTIMORE STOP GENERATION LINEAR REGRESSION MODELS PARAMETER ESTIMATES (Standard Errors)

VARIABLE	NORTH SECTOR	SOUTH SECTOR	WHOLE REGION
Constant	0.83 (0.51)	0.20 (0.48)	0.49 (0.35)
Persons per House-hold	0.90 (0.13)	0.78 (0.12)	0.83 (0.09)
Vehilces Available Available	0.42 (0.22)	1.19 (0.22)	0.78 (0.15)
Number of workers	1.08 (0.23)	0.58 (0.26)	0.91 (0.17)
Error Sum of Squares	6938	6120	13230
Total Sum of Square	9420	8877	18340
R^2	0.26	0.31	0.28

TABLE 4

BALTIMORE MODE CHOICE MODELS PARAMETER ESTIMATES (t-statistics)

VARIABLE	NORTH SECTOR	SOUTH SECTOR	WHOLE REGION
TTT	-0.0396 (2.8)	-0.0832 (4.5)	-0.0571 (5.2)
OVTTD	-0.1905 (2.6)	-0.3935 (3.3)	-0.2724 (4.0)
OPTCINC	0.0456 (0.8)	-0.1268 (2.7)	-0.0509 (1.7)
TAATDUM	-1.189 (1.5)	-4.057 (3.0)	-2.241 (3.2)
CPDDA	3.014 (5.3)	2.183 (3.1)	2.545 (6.0)
CPDSR	2.113 (4.4)	2.588 (4.2)	2.260 (6.2)
SRD	-0.1764 (0.4)	-2.029 (4.7)	-1.048 (3.7)
TRD	2.413 (3.7)	2.757 (3.4)	2.444 (4.9)
No. of cases	374	290	664
No. of observations	1069	824	1893
Log Likelihood			
at zero	-389.4	-299.9	-689.3
at market shares	-310.0	-228.8	-539.4
at convergence	-280.1	-185.1	-475.4
ρ^2 equal shares	0.281	0.383	0.310
market shares	0.096	0.191	0.119

TABLE 5

TRANSFERABILITY OF STOPS GENERATION MODELS WITHIN BALTIMORE: TRANSFER GOODNESS-OF-FIT (Transfer Index)

		PREDICTING ON SECTOR	
		North	South
Estimated on Sector	North	0.26 (1.00)	0.27 (0.88) 0.29 (0.93)
	South	0.22 (0.85) 0.24 (0.92)	0.31 1.00

TABLE 6

TRANSFERABILITY OF MODE CHOICE MODEL WITHIN BALTIMORE: TRANSFER GOODNESS-OF-FIT (Transfer Index)

		PREDICTING ON SECTOR	
		North	South
Estimated on Sector	North	0.096 (1.00)	.101 (0.53) .103 (0.54)
	South	0.024 (0.25) 0.029 (0.30)	.191 (1.00)

Key:

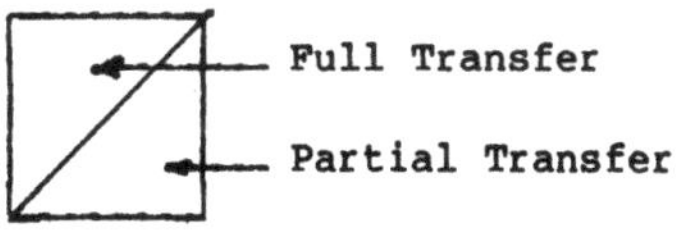

Next, we examine aggregate prediction measures of transferability for intra-region transfer. The absolute and relative values of root-mean-square error for the stops generation and mode choice models are reported in Tables 7 and 8, respectively. First, we observe that the root-mean-square errors for stops prediction are much smaller than those for mode choice prediciton. This difference in results is largely attributable to the poor performance of the modal choice models in the Baltimore sectors. Second, the relative transfer errors are highly directional for both model types and the better transfer direction is different for each model type. Finally, the use of partial versus full transfer generally produces substantial reduction in errors. The aggregate prediction statistics for these transfers are reported in Tables 9 and 10. These results indicate rejection of both the local and transferred stops generation models at the .01 level in every case and rejection of the South to North transfer of the mode choice models at the .01 level.

TABLE 7

TRANSFERABILITY OF STOPS GENERATION MODEL WITHIN BALTIMORE: ABSOLUTE AND (RELATIVE) ROOT MEAN SQUARE ERROR

Estimated on Sector	Predicting on Sector: North	Predicting on Sector: South
North	0.15 (1.0)	0.17 (1.55) / 0.16 (1.45)
South	0.17 (1.13) / 0.13 (0.87)	0.11 (1.0)

TABLE 8

TRANSFERABILITY OF MODE CHOICE MODEL WITHIN BALTIMORE: ABSOLUTE AND (RELATIVE) ROOT MEAN SQUARE ERROR

Estimated on Sector	Predicting on Sector: North	Predicting on Sector: South
North	0.33 (1.0)	0.37 (1.09) / 0.37 (1.09)
South	0.54 (1.64) / 0.50 (1.52)	0.34 (1.0)

Key:

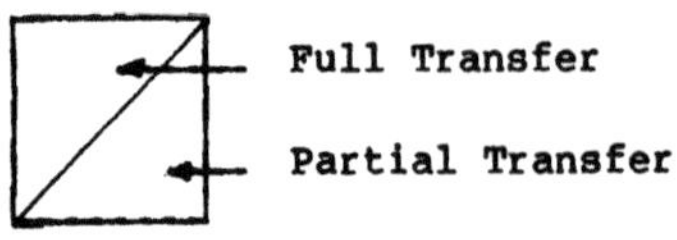

TABLE 9

TRANSFERABILITY OF STOPS GENERATION MODEL WITHIN BALTIMORE: AGGREGATE PREDICTION STATISTIC

		PREDICTING ON SECTOR	
		North	South
Estimated on Sector	North	56.6**	64.5** / 42.0**
	South	64.3** / 39.8**	26.8**

TABLE 10

TRANSFERABILITY OF MODE CHOICE MODEL WITHIN BALTIMORE: AGGREGATE PREDICTION STATISTIC

		PREDICTIONG ON SECTOR	
		North	South
Estimated on Sector	North	41.6	39.1 / 40.3
	South	107.3** / 93.7**	33.5

Key: 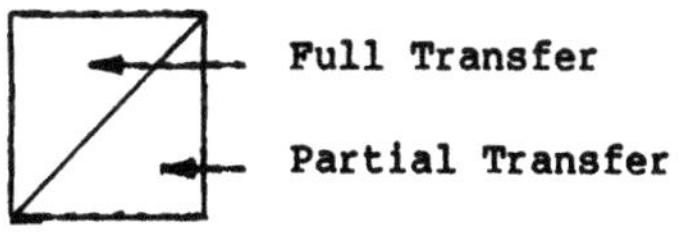

* Significant at .05 level
** Significant at .01 level

These results highlight the variability in transferability results. The level of transferability varies across the two model types examined, across the direction of transfer, and across the measure used to evaluate transferability. It will almost certainly be misleading to make an overall generalization about model transferability based on these or other limited studies. A broader range of analyses must be undertaken before it will be possible to identify the sources of variability and develop generalizations about transferability. One of the more obvious inconsistencies in these analyses has to do with the rejection of transferability by the statistical tests employed when the transfer goodness-of-fit or the prediction error is close to the corresponding values obtained by local models (eg., transfer index for the stops generation model). These results suggest that statistical tests may not be good indicators of the usefullness of model transfer.

We can broaden our perspective on intra-regional transferability by examining composite transfer measures for transfer within Baltimore, Washington and Minneapolis-St. Paul for mode choice, automobile ownership and stops generation models. Composite disaggregate measures for partial intra-regional transfer are reported in Table 11 and the corresponding composite aggregate measures are reported in Table 12. We observe that the mode choice model transfers within Baltimore have substantially lower transfer effectiveness than the corresponding models transferred within Washington and within Minneapolis-St. Paul. While the composite disaggregate goodness-of-fit measure is twice as large for Washington auto ownership models than for Washington mode choice models, the composite transfer index and absolute and relative root-mean-square errors are similar. This suggests that differences in performance between these two model types are not attributable to model transfer per se but differences in ability to describe the disaggregate behaviour with the models used. Overall, the results for intra-regional transfer within Washington and Minneapolis are close to those obtained using the corresponding local models while intra-regional transfer within Baltimore appears to be less effective. However, the test statistics, not reported here, reject the hypothesis of intra-regional transfer for almost all the transfers within each region.

<u>Inter-Regional Transferability.</u> We examine inter-regional transferability using work choice models developed for Baltimore, Minneapolis-St. Paul and Washington, DC (Wilmot, 1983). The estimation results for the regional models are reported in Table 13 and all coefficients are significant and have the expected signs. Full and partial model transfers were studied between each pair of regions. Partial transfer involved the transfer of all model parameters except the alternative specific constants which were updated using the disaggregate data in the application context.

TABLE 11

INTRA-REGIONAL PARTIAL MODEL TRANSFERABILITY: COMPOSITE GOODNESS OF FIT
(Composite Transfer Index)

Model Type		CITY		
		Baltimore	Washington	Minneapolis
Model Type	Mode Choice	0.006 (0.43)	0.124 (0.95)	0.107 (0.87)
	Automobile Ownership	NA	0.216 (0.94)	NA
	Stop Generation	0.265 (0.91)	NA	NA

TABLE 12

INTRA-REGIONAL TRANSFERABILITY - PARTIAL TRANSFER COMPOSITE ROOT-MEAN-SQUARE
ERROR, ABSOLUTE AND (Relative)

Model Type		REGION		
		Baltimore	Washington	Minneapolis
Model Type	Mode Choice	0.449 (1.34)	0.222 (1.06)	0.221 (1.02)
	Automobile Ownership	NA	0.238 (1.05)	NA
	Stop Generation	0.145 (1.32)	NA	NA

Key: NA = results not available

TABLE 13

URBAN REGION MODE CHOICE MODELS PARAMETER ESTIMATES (t-statistics)

Variable	Baltimore	Minneapolis	Washington
TTT	-0.0571 (5.2)	-0.0349 (5.2)	-0.0506 (7.4)
OVTTD	-0.2724 (4.0)	-0.3014 (4.8)	-0.1551 (1.9)
OPTCINC	-0.0509 (1.7)	-0.0697 (3.1)	-0.0342 (2.0)
TAATDUM	-2.241 (3.2)	-0.8856 (3.6)	-1.384 (4.5)
CPDDA	2.545 (6.0)	3.229 (9.5)	3.494 (14.5)
CPDSR	2.260 (6.2)	1.542 (5.2)	1.703 (10.2)
SRD	-1.048 (3.7)	-0.0782 (0.5)	1.114 (5.4)
TRD	2.444 (4.9)	1.864 (6.4)	2.769 (11.5)
No. of cases	664	1806	2000
No. of observations	1893	5267	5568
Log likelihood			
At zero	-689.3	-1923	-2020
At market shares	-539.4	-1252	-1957
At convergence	-475.4	-1091	-1731
ρ^2 equal shares	0.310	0.433	0.144
market shares	0.119	0.129	0.116

The transfer index measures reported in Table 14 demonstrate the importance of using partial rather than full model transfer in inter-regional transfer application. Two of the full model transfer indices are negative, indicating that the transferred model does not perform as well as a local market shares model, and the rest provide less than 60 percent of the information provided by the corresponding local model. The partial transfer results are much better than the full transfer results with values ranging from 69 percent to 97 percent. The hypothesis of inter-regional transferability is rejected for both full and partial model transferability at the .01 level in every case except Minneapolis-St. Paul to Washington where it is rejected at the .05 level.

The root-mean-square errors, reported in Table 15, also indicate the importance of using partial rather than full transfer in intercity transfer applicatons. While relative root-mean-square error for full model transfer varies from 1.12 to 2.24, the range for partial transfer is 1.03 to 1.12.

The aggregate prediction statistics for full and partial model transfer are reported in Table 16. The local model in Washington is rejected as suitably describing aggregate behaviour in that region. The transfer hypothesis is rejected for three of six full model transfers but only one of six partial model transfers.

These results provide a somewhat more optimistic indication of model transferablility. The transfer index indicates that transferred models provide a large portion of the goodness-of-fit which would be obtained by the corresponding local models (the composite transfer index across the six inter-regional transfers is 0.84). The relative root-mean-square error measure produces a similar interpretation (the composite relative root-mean-square error for the six inter-regional transfers is 1.03). Finally, while the transfer test statistic rejects the transferability hypothesis in all cases, the aggregate prediction statistic does so for only one case (the same application in which the local model is rejected).

TABLE 14

INTER-REGIONAL TRANSFERABILITY OF MODE CHOICE MODELS: TRANSFER INDEX

Estimated on	Predicted on: Minneapolis	Predicted on: Baltimore	Predicted on: Washington
Minneapolis	1.00	0.51 / 0.74	0.55 / 0.97
Baltimore	0.59 / 0.69	1.00	-0.10 / 0.85
Washington	-0.06 / 0.93	0.13 / 0.77	1.00

Key:

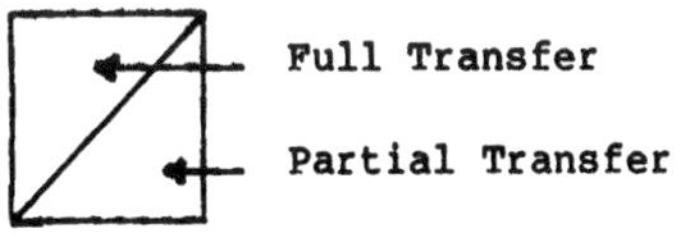

TABLE 15

INTER-REGIONAL TRANSFERABILITY OF MODE CHOICE MODELS: ABSOLUTE AND (RELATIVE) ROOT MEAN SQUARE ERROR

Estimated on	Predicted on: Minneapolis	Predicted on: Baltimore	Predicted on: Washington
Minneapolis	0.26 (1.00)	0.44 (1.29) / 0.35 (1.03)	0.42 (1.68) / 0.26 (1.04)
Baltimore	0.29 (1.12) / 0.29 (1.12)	0.34 (1.00)	0.56 (2.24) / 0.25 (1.00)
Washington	0.45 (1.73) / 0.27 (1.04)	0.47 (1.38) / 0.34 (1.00)	0.25 (1.00)

Key:

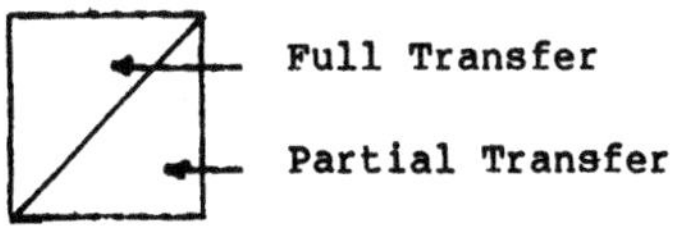

TABLE 16

INTER-REGIONAL TRANSFERABILITY OF MODE CHOICE MODESL: PARTIAL TRANSFER AGGREGATE PREDICTION STATISTIC

		PREDICTED ON		
		Minneapolis	Baltimore	Washington
Estimated on	Minneapolis	124.4	129.5 / 79.4	345.8** / 134.3**
	Baltimore	147.6 / 150.8	77.5	624.7** / 121.7
	Washington	366.7** / 130.2	148.2 / 76.4	126.8*

Key: 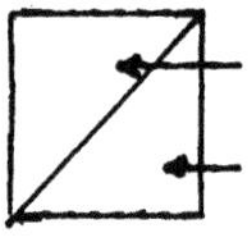
Full Transfer
Partial Transfer

* Significant at .05 level
** Significant at .01 level

Interpretation of Empirical Results. These analyses reinforce our interpretation of the results of earlier studies in terms of the variability of transfer effectiveness. This variability is observed between inter- and intra-region transfers, among either inter- and intra-region transfers for different regions, and across transfer measures. Two important issues arise from these analyses. First, there is a need to identify the characteristics of contexts which are associated with high or low levels of transfer effectiveness. Second, the use of partial transfer with adjustment of alternative specific constants substantially improves transfer effectiveness in most cases, especially when full model transfer is poor. The first issue requires continuing research. Studies designed to address this issue are in progress in Northwestern University. The second issue indicates the importance of partial model transfer and updating to improve transfer effectiveness. In the next section, we discuss methods for updating alternative specific constants and other model components.

IMPROVING MODEL TRANSFERABILITY

The possibility of applying existing models rather than estimating models in each new study area is very appealing. This use of transferred models can substantially reduce the resources needed and the time required for model development. However, the variability in transferability results suggest that such use of transferred models must be done carefully. It is generally recognized that models are not perfectly transferable between contexts. Further, different components of models are likely to be more or less transferable. For disaggregate choice models, the alternative specific constants which reflect the average effect of excluded variables are the least transferable components, the scale of other parameters which implicitly reflects the unexplained choice variability is next least transferable, and the relative parameter values are most transferable (McFadden, 1978; Westin and Manski, 1979). Whenever it is possible, the alternative specific constants and the scale of disaggregate choice models should also be adjusted. Similarly, the intercept constant of regression models should also be adjusted, when possible. In this section we discuss the updating of disaggregate choice models. Analogous procedures can be employed to update regression models.

Updating procedures use available application area data to modify or replace portions of the transferred model. We distinguish between updating with a small set of disaggregate data and updating with aggregate data since the nature of the available local data is an important consideration in choosing an updating method.

Updating with Disaggregate Data

To apply these techniques a small sample of observations of individual travel behaviour in the application context is required. One approach suggested by Atherton and Ben-Akiva (1976) is to use the small sample of local data to re-estimate all the coefficients in the original (transfer) specification, on the assumption that if that specification worked in one region it should work in another. Of course the small data set is likely to lead to high variance estimators which may be very far from the true values. Alternatively the local disaggregate data can be used to update the alternative specific constants (ASC) and scale of the transferred model or the parameters from the local and transfer models can be combined using Bayesian updating. Those procedures are discussed separately below.

Updating the Alternative Specific Constants. It is possible to use a small sample of local observations to update the alternative specific constants (ASC) of the transfer model. Usually parameter estimates for a choice model are obtained by maximizing a log likelihood expression of the form

$$L = \sum_{t}\sum_{i}\delta_{it} \ln P_{it}(X_t,\theta) \qquad (3)$$

where L = log likelihood; t = index of individuals; i = index of alternatives; δ_{it} = 1 if individual t chooses alternative i, or = 0 otherwise; $P_{it}(X_t,\theta)$ = probability that individual t chooses alternative i; X_t = vector of socio-economic characteristics and attributes of alternatives applicable to individual t; and θ = vector of parameters to be estimated.

Embedded in the probability function in eqn. (3) are expressions for the deterministic component of utility for each alternative. These expressions are usually formulated as linear in parameters

$$V_i = \alpha_i + X'_{it}\beta \tag{4}$$

where V_i = deterministic component of utility for alternative i; α_i = alternative specific constant for alternative i; X_{it} = vector of attributes of alternative i for individual t; and β = vector of slope parameters.

The alternative specific constants account for the average effect of factors not explicitly included in the model. While there may be theoretical justification for arguing that the effect of time, cost, and other variables are stable across estimation and application contexts, there is no such basis for transferring these constant terms. In general, we expect there to be average differences in the excluded factors between contexts. Therefore we are interested in transferring the parameters in expression (4) to the application context while obtaining a local estimate of the ASC. In this case we denote the parameters transferred to the application context with a T subscript, β_T. We now define

$$Z^A_{it} = X^{A\prime}_{it}\beta_T \tag{5}$$

where X^A_{it} = vector of attributes of alternative i for individual t in the application context.

To obtain the updated ASC we modify the utility function expression in eqn. (4) for the application context, using the following specification

$$V^A_i = \alpha^A_i + Z^A_{it} \tag{6}$$

where V_i^A = deterministic component of utility for alternative i in the application context; and α^A_i = updated ASC for alternative i in the application context.

The estimate of the updated ASC (α^A_i) is that which maximizes the log likelihood function

$$L = \sum_t\sum_i \delta_{it} \ln P_{it}(Z_t, \alpha^A) \tag{7}$$

where Z_t = vector of variables for individual t across all alternatives; and α^A = the vector of alternative specific constants for all alternatives.

The final utility function employed for transfer prediction becomes

$$V^A_i = \alpha^A_i + Z^{A\prime}_{it}\beta_T \tag{8}$$

That is, the resultant model includes all the transferred slope parameters, β_T, with the locally estimated alternative specific constants, α^A_i.

Updating the Alternative Specific Constants and Scale. We can extend the methodology outlined above to adjust the scale of the transferred parameters as well as the alternative specific constants. The coefficient of Z_{it} in eqn. (6) is restricted to equal one. When updating parameter scale we no longer impose that restriction. Instead we estimate a coefficient for Z^A_{it}. The deterministic component of utility becomes

$$V^A_i = \alpha^A_i + \lambda^A Z^A_{it} \tag{9}$$

where λ^A = scaling parameter for the application context.

Therefore updating the ASC and scale amounts to selecting values of α^A_i and λ^A which maximize the log likelihood function

$$L = \sum_t \sum_i \delta_{it} \ln P_{it}(Z^A_t, \alpha^A, \lambda^A) \tag{10}$$

The scaling parameter (λ^A) adjusts the scale of the explanatory variables but does not affect their relative impact on each alternatives utility.

Bayesian Updating. Another approach to adjusting transferred model parameters is to modify them by the correspondong parameter estimates obtained using local data. Bayesian statistics provide a framework for this type of updating. Bayesian statistics combine information about values of parameter estimates obtained from different sources. The underlying assumption of this method when applied to model transfer is that both the transferred and local models describe the same behaviour (Daganzo, 1979). That is, the transferred model is applicable to the local context. Thus, the benefit of Bayesian updating is to obtain more precise parameter estimates. If the transferred model represents different behaviour than that in the local environment, the Bayesian updated model will be inferior to a model based exclusively on local data.

Bayesian procedures compute updated coefficients as the weighted average of the coefficients from the local and transferred models with the weights being the inverse of the parameter variance. The relationships for updating a vector of coefficients and the corresponding covariance matrix are

$$\beta_{UPD} = [\Sigma_T^{-1} + \Sigma_L^{-1}]^{-1} \; [\Sigma_T^{-1}\beta_T + \Sigma_L^{-1}\beta_L] \tag{11a}$$

$$\Sigma_{UPD} = [\Sigma_T^{-1} + \Sigma_L^{-1}]^{-1} \tag{11b}$$

where β_{UPD} = Bayesian updated parameters; Σ_{UPD} = Bayesian updated convariance matrix; β_T ,β_L = transferred and locally estimated parameter vectors; and Σ_T, Σ_L = transferred and locally estimated covariance matrices.

Since the local area data set generally is small the local variance matrix will be large relative to the transferred covariance matrix and the updated parameters will be closer to the estimates from the transferred model than those from local estimation. However, as noted by Atherton and Ben-Akiva (1976) this procedure offers the opportunity to introduce subjective judgments by adjusting the weights to correspond with our feelings about the relevance of the transferred parameters. For example, if we have some doubt about the applicability of the transferred model, the transferred model covariance matrix can be artifically inflated to reduce its influence on the final parameter estimates.

Daganzo (1979) derives extensions of eqn. (11) for the case where a vector of parameters and the corresponding covariance matrix are to be updated using multiple sources of information. He also shows that the Bayesian approach obtains updated parameters which approximate the maximum likelihood estimates which would have been obtained if the samples had been combined and used in a single estimation.

Combining Alternative Specific Constants and Scale Adjustment with Bayesian Updating. The techniques outlined in the previous two sections can be combined into a two step updating procedure. First, the small sample of local data can be used to estimate a local model and the model coefficients updated using the Bayesian approach. These updated parameters could replace the pure transfer parameters in eqn. (5) and the second step would involve using the local sample to estimate the alternative specific constants and the scale of these parameters as described earlier. This combination of updating procedures has not been investigated in the literature.

Updating With Aggregate Data

When a disaggregate local data base is not available, local aggregate data can be used to update the parameters of the transferred disaggregate choice model. Aggregate mode shares and aggregate socioeconomic and level of service data are sufficient to perform the updating of alternative specific constants. Somewhat greater data is required to update scale as well. In this section we outline procedures for updating the alternative specific constant or both the alternative specific constant and parameter scale.

Updating Alternative Specific Constants With Aggregate Data. Using aggregate modal shares and zonal socioeconomic and interzonal level of service variables the alternative specific constants of the transfer model can be readily updated. The deterministic component for alternative i for members of aggregate group g can be written as

$$V_{ig} = \alpha_i^A + \overline{X}'_{ig}\,\beta_T \tag{12a}$$

$$= \alpha_i^A + \overline{Z}_{ig} \tag{12b}$$

where $\overline{X}_{iq}$ = the average values of socioeconomic and LOS variables for alternatives i for aggregate gorup g; α_i^A = alternative specific constant for alternatives i in the application context; and β_T = transfer parameters.

The updated alternative specific constants, α_i^A, are obtained by maximizing the log likelihood function

$$L = \sum_{g} \sum_{t \epsilon g} \sum_{i} \delta_{it} \ln P_{iq}(\overline{Z}_q, \alpha^A)$$

$$= \sum_{q} \sum_{i} f_{iq} \ln P_{ig}(\overline{Z}_q, \alpha^A) \qquad (13)$$

where P_{iq} = the probability of choosing alternative i for individuals in group g; $\overline{Z}_g$ = the average variable values for group g for all alternatives; and f_{iq} = the frequency of members of group g choosing alternative i.

The procedure is identical to that for updating alternative specific constants with disaggregate data except for the use of average rather than individual variable values. Estimates of $\alpha^A{}_i$ can be obtained even if the data are available for only the overall population representing a single group.

Talvitie (1981) discusses a hand calculation method which can be used to update the ASC when the aggregate modal shares, a (work) trip table and zonal socioeconomic and interzonal LOS variables are available in the application context. This is an iterative method where at each iteration j, a new value of the ASC is calculated as follows

$$\alpha_i^j = \alpha_i^{j-1} - \frac{P_i^{j-1} - S_i}{S_i(1 - S_i)} \qquad (14)$$

where a_i^j = alternative specific constant for alternative i at iteration j; P_i^{j-1} = predicted share for alternative i at iteration j-1; and S_i = observed share choosing alternative i.

This iterative process is repeated until $P_i^j \approx S_i$ which Talvitie indicates takes five to six iterations. This procedure is effectively identical to maximization of the log likelihood defined in eqn. (13) when data are available for the aggregate population as a single group.

An alternative approach to adjustment of the alternative specific constants when the multinomial logit model is used is to adopt the incremental form of that model (Koppelman, 1983; Atherton and Ben-Akiva, 1976). The incremental logit model has the form

$$S_i' = \frac{S_i \exp(V_i' - V_i)}{\sum_k S_k \exp(V_k' - V_k)} \tag{15}$$

where S_i , S_i' = present and future shares choosing alternative i, respectively; and V_i , V_i' = present and future values for the deterministic component of the utility function, respectively.

When the deterministic component of utility is a linear additive function as in eqn. (4), the alternative specific constants drop out of the computation of the differences, $V_k' - V_k$. Effectively, the present share values take account of the adjustment to the alternative specific constants which would otherwise be required.

Updating Alternative Specific Constants and Parameters Scale With Aggregate Data. We modify eqn. (12b) in the same manner as we modified eqn. (6) earlier to update alternative specific constants and scale to obtain

$$V_{ig} = \alpha_i^A + \lambda^A \overline{Z}_{iq} \tag{16}$$

and maximize the log likelihood

$$L = \sum_q \sum_i f_{ig} \ln P_{gt}(\overline{Z}_g, \alpha^A, \lambda^A) \tag{17}$$

with respect to α^A and λ^A. This estimation can be carried out providing we have aggregate information for at least two distinct aggregate groups in the application context.

Empirical Studies of Model Updating

Empirical studies have investigated the effect of model updating procedures on the transferability of disaggregate choice models (Atherton and Ben-Akiva, 1976; Galbraith and Hensher, 1982; Koppelman and Wilmot, 1982b; Koppelman, et al 1983) and regression models (Koppelman and Rose, 1983). In the case of choice models, studies have investigated updating the alternative specific constants and scale with both aggregate and disaggregate data and Bayesian updating of the full set of parameters.

Updating Choice Models With Disaggregate Data. Atherton and Ben-Akiva (1976) investigate updating when transferring mode choice to work models from Washington, DC, to the New Bedford, Massachusetts area. They apply two separate updating procedures, Bayesian updating and adjusting the alternative specific constants of the Washington model using sub-samples of the disaggregate New Bedford data. Unfortunately this study is unable to provide much useful information about the relative effectiveness of these updating schemes because the Washington model, even without updating, provides predictions in the New Bedford area which are almost as good as those obtained from the locally developed model. While the authors differentiate between the results obtained from the two updating procedures and conclude that the "Bayesian updating gives consistently better results", the difference in predictive ability between the pure Washington model and the updated model is so small that general conclusions cannot be based on these results.

Galbraith and Hensher (1982) investigate the transferability of disaggregate work mode choice models between two suburban areas (northwestern and southwestern) in the Sydney, Australia, region. To enhance the transferability of these models between these areas they apply two separate updating procedures: Bayesian updating and adjustment of the alternative specific constants and scale. The disaggregate data from the southwestern suburb is used to update the northwestern models for application in the southwestern suburb. They report that the model with updated alternative specific constants and scale is poorer than the non-adjusted transfer model. These results must be incorrect since the process of parameter adjustment can only improve the model transfer. Therefore we do not examine these results further. The Bayesian updating procedure resulted in a model which predictably performed better than the no update model but not as well as the locally developed southwestern model. Although the Bayesian updating improved the transfer models' performance, their statistical tests, using a .05 level of significance, rejected the hypothesis that the Bayesian updated and local models were identical.

Studies by Koppelman and Wilmot (1982b) and Koppelman, et al (1983) investigate the effect of updating methods for the intra-urban transfer of work mode choice models using the Washington, DC, data base and Wilmot (1983) extends this work to inter-regional transfer among Baltimore, Washington and Minneapolis-St. Paul. These results obtain a consistent improvement of transfer effectiveness from the full transfer model, to transfer with adjustment of alternative specific constants, to transfer with adjustment of alternative specific constants and scale.

Although there is variation in the impact of updating depending upon the specific contexts, several general conclusions can be drawn from this work. When the alternative specific constants are adjusted, the greatest improvements occur where the full transfer model performed poorly relative to the locally developed model. The transferred models with adjusted alternative specific constants generally provided in excess of 80 percent of the information which would be provided by a locally developed model.

The marginal improvement in model performance obtained by adjusting the scale in addition to updating the alternative specific constants is generally smaller than the improvement provided by adjusting the alternative specific constants alone. When the alternative specific constants and the scale are adjusted, the transferred model generally provides in excess of 90 percent of the information which would be provided by a locally developed model.

The work by Koppelman, et al (1983) also suggests that local adjustment of the alternative specific constants and scale mav partially compensate for relatively poor transfer model specifications.

Updating Choice Models With Aggregate Data. The studies by Atherton and Ben-Akiva (1976) and Koppelman, et al (1983) also investigate the effect of updating with aggregate local data. As mentioned earlier, the Atherton and Ben-Akiva study is unable to provide much information about different updating methods because the transfer model, even without updating, provides predictions in the application context which are almost as good as those obtained from the locally developed model. Koppelman, et al (1983) examine updating with aggregate local data when transferring models of four different specifications between three geographic sectors of Washington, DC. They obtain consistent results which indicate that aggregate updating of both the alternative specific constant and scale obtains a large proportion of the improvement in transferability which is obtainable through disaggregate updating.

Updating Regression Models. Koppelman and Rose (1983) investigate the transferability of linear regression trip generation models between two geographic sectors of the Baltimore region. Both full and partial transfer of the models were undertaken, where partial transfer involved the transfer of all parameters except the constant term which was re-estimated in the application context. Local adjustment of the constant consistently improved the performance of the transferred model. In excess of 90 percent of the information provided by the local model was obtained from the transfer model with an adjusted constant term.

Interpretation

The results reviewed here indicate the importance of updating in obtaining a model which can usefully describe travel behaviour in an application context. Updating of both choice models and linear regression models is extremely important. In both cases, the improvement is greatest where transfer without adjustment is relatively poor, regardless of whether the cause of this initially poor transfer is because of the nature of the application context or because of poor specification of the transfer model. Aggregate updating has been found to provide a large portion of the improvement in transferability which is obtainable with disaggregate updating.

SUMMARY AND CONCLUSIONS

This paper reviews research results designed to evaluate model transferability and methods of updating in transfer application. Interest in model transferability developed in parallel with the increasing use of disaggregate techniques in the estimation of travel demand models. These disaggregate models are expected to be transferable as they are formulated to represent the underlying individual behavioural process and are free of aggregation error. Initial studies of the transferability of disaggregate travel choice models obtained very promising results. As more studies have been undertaken, the expectation of the general transferability of disaggregate choice models has been placed in doubt.

This review highlights the wide range of transferability effectiveness and relates this variability of results to differences in model types, differences in specification and differences in transfer contexts as well as differences in transferability measures used, and differences in judgment. The paper further demonstrates this variability of results through a structured set of experiments in which subsets of these differences vary while others are fixed. It is apparent that while transferability appears to be good in a number of cases and composite measures of transferability across a range of contexts are generally good, the variability in transferability is large enough to caution against any general adoption of model transferability. However, these same results indicate that methods of transfer model adjustment are very effective in both increasing the average level of transfer effectiveness and decreasing the variability in transfer effectiveness results.

This review provides the basis to suggest a line of research which is necessary to improve the ability to understand the conditions under which model transfer is likely to be highly effective. Specifically, research should be directed at developing relationships which describe the effect of model type and specification and the effect of differences in regional contexts on the level of transfer effectiveness. Such relationshps can provide a basis for a priori prediction of the expected level of effectivences of specific model transfers and thus a basis for selecting models to be used in specific application contexts.

This review also provides a strong basis for the continued development and application of updating procedures which can be used to improve model transfer effectiveness. This review clearly establishes the need to at least update alternative specific constants for travel choice models and intercept constants for regression models. Further adjustment of parameter scale and individual parameters may also be appropriate in some cases.

The transfer of disaggregate travel models is becoming relatively common. Research results generally support the use of transferred models. However, until more is known about the conditions which determine transfer effectiveness, model transfer should be employed with care to assure that the transferred model is useful in the application context.

ACKNOWLEDGEMENTS

This paper is based in part on work undertaken at the Transportation Center of Northwestern University under contract with the US Department of Transportation, Office of University Research. James Ryan of the Urban Mass Transportation Administration, who is contract monitor, has provided important advice, encouragement, and support to the research team. Important contributions have been made to this work by Chester G. Wilmot, Geok-Koon Kuah, and Albert Lunde of the Transportation Center and Eric Pas of Duke University.

REFERENCES

Adler, T.J., 1975, A Joint Disaggregate Model of Non-Work Urban Passenger Travel Demand, MSc thesis, Department of Civil Engineering, MIT, Cambridge, MA.

Atherton, T.J. and Ben-Akiva, M.E., 1976, Transferability and Updating of Disaggregate Travel Demand Models, Transportation Research Record, 610, 12-18.

Barton-Aschman Associates, Inc., 1979, Development and Calibration of the Seattle Mode Choice Models, prepared for the Municipality of Metropolitan Seattle under subcontract with Parsons, Brinckerhoff, Quade and Douglas, Seattle, WN.

Barton-Aschman Associates, Inc., 1981, Development and Calibration of the New Orleans Mode Choice Models, prepared for the Regional Planning Commission, New Orleans, LA.

Barton-Aschman Associates, Inc., 1982, Calibration of the St. Louis Mode Choice Models, prepared for the East-West Gateway Coordinating Council and the Bi-State Development Agency, St. Louis.

Barton-Aschman Associates, Inc., and Texas Transportation Institute, 1979, Development and Calibration of the Travel Demand Models for the Houston-Galveston Area, prepared for the Metropolitan Transit Authority, Houston, TX.

Ben-Akiva, M.E., 1981, Issues in Transferring and Updating Travel Behavior Models, in Stopher, P.R., Meyburg, A.J. and Brog, W. (Eds.), New Horizons in Travel Behavior Research, D.C. Heath and Company, Lexington, MA.

Ben-Akiva, M.E. and Atherton, T.J., 1977, Methodology for Short-Range Travel Demand Predictions, Journal of Transport Economics and Policy, 224-261.

Ben-Akiva, M.E. and Lerman, S.R., 1974, Some Estimation Results of a Simultaneous Model of Auto Ownership and Mode Choice to Work, Transportation, 3, 4, 357-375.

Benham, J.L. and Tardiff, T.J., 1981, Evaluation of Methods to Predict Work Trip Mode Choice, 60th Annual Meeting, Transportation Research Board, Washington, DC.

Cambridge Systematics, Inc., 1977, Tests of Transferability and Validation of Disaggregate Behavioral Demand Models for Evaluating the Energy Conservation Potential of Alternative Transportation Policies in Nine US Cities, report prepared for the Federal Energy Administration, Office of Energy Conservation Policy.

Daganzo, C., 1979, Multinominal Probit: The Theory and Its Application to Demand Forecasting, Academic Press, New York.

Dehghani, Y., Koushesh, B., Sievert, R. and McKearney, T., 1981, Transferability and an Analysis of Prediction Errors in Mode Choice Models for Work Trips, 60th Annual Meeting, Transportation Research Board, Washington, DC.

Galbraith, R.A. and Hensher, D.A., 1982, Intra-Metropolitan Transferability of Mode Choice Models, Journal of Transport Economics and Policy, 16, 7-29.

Green, H.A.J., 1964, Aggregation in Economic Analysis: An Introductory Survey, Princeton University, New Jersey.

Horowitz, J., 1976, Effects of Travel Time and Cost on the Frequency and Structure of Automobile Travel, Transportation Research Record, 592, 1-5.

Koppelman, F.S., 1977, Intra-Urban Transferability of Disaggregate Choice Models, Transportation Center Working Paper, Northwestern University, Evanston, IL.

Koppelman, F.S., 1983, Predicting Transit Ridership in Response to Transit Service Changes, Journal of Transportation Engineering, ASCE, 107, TE 4, 548-564.

Koppelman, F.S. and Ben-Akiva, M.E., 1977, Aggregate Forecasting With Disaggregate Travel Demand Models Using Normally Available Data, Transportation Decisions in an Age of Uncertainty, Martinus-Nijhoff, Rotterdam.

Koppelman, F.S. and Chu, C., 1983, Sample Size Effect on Disaggregate Choice Model Estimation and Prediction, 62nd Annual Meeting, Transportation Research Board, Washington, DC.

Koppelman, F.S. and Hauser, J.R., 1979, Destination Choice Behavior for Non-Grocery Shopping Trips, Transportation Research Record, 673.

Koppelman, F.S., Wilmot, C.G. and Kuah, G.K., 1983, The Impact of Scale Adjustment on the Intra-City Transferability, Transportation Center Report, Northwestern University, Evanston, IL.

Koppelman, F.S. and Pas, E.I., 1983, Multidimensional Choice Model Transferability, Transportation Center Report, Northwestern University, Evanston, IL.

Koppelman, F.S. and Rose, G., 1983, Transferability of Disaggregate Linear Regression Trip Generation Models, Transportation Center Report, Northwestern University, Evanston, IL.

Koppelman, F.S. and Wilmot, C.G., 1982a, Transferability Analysis of Disaggregate Choice Models, Transportation Research Record, 895.

Koppelman, F.S. and Wilmot, C.G., 1982b, Identification of Conditions for Effective Transferability of Disaggregate Choice Models, Report UMTA-429-1, Prepared for US Department of Transportation, Office of University Research.

Lave, C., 1969, A Behavioral Approach to the Mode Split Forecasting, Transportation Research, 3, 4.

Lerman, S.R., 1975, A Disaggregate Behavioral Model of Urban Mobility Decisions, PhD dissertation, Department of Civil Engineering, MIT, Cambridge, MA.

Lerman, S.R., 1981, Interspatial, Intraspatial and Temporal Transferability, in Stopher, P.R., Meyburg, A.J. and Brog, W. (Eds.), New Horizons in Travel Behavior Research, D.C. Heath and Company, Lexington, MA.

Lisco, T.E., 1967, The Value of Commuters Travel Time: A Study in Urban Transportation, PhD dissertation, Department of Economics, University of Chicago, Chicago, IL.

Litinas, N., Gonzales, S.L., Lerman, S.R. and Solomon, I., 1981, A Theory of Travel Demand Processes with Integer Outcomes, Center for Transportation Studies, MIT, Cambridge, MA.

Louviere, J.J., 1981, Some Comments on Premature Expectations Regarding Spatial, Temporal and Cultural Transferability of Travel Choice Models, in Stopher, P.R., Meyburg, A.J. and Brog, W. (Eds.), New Horizons in Travel Behavior Research, D.C. Heath and Company, Lexington, MA.

McCarthy, P.S., 1981, Further Evidence on the Temporal Stability of Dissaggregate Travel Demand Models, Department of Economics, Purdue University.

McFadden, D., 1973, Conditional Logit Analysis in Qualitative Choice Behavior, in Zarembka, Z. (Ed.), Frontiers in Econometrics, Academic Press, New York.

McFadden, D., 1976, Properties of the Multinominal Model, Working Paper 7617, Urban Travel Demand Forecasting Project, Institute of Transportation Studies, University of California, Berkeley, CA.

McFadden, D., 1978, The Theory and Practice of Disaggregate Demand Forecasting for Various Models in Urban Transportation, Emerging Transportation Planning Method, Brown, W.F. (Ed.), US Department of Transportation, Office of University Research.

McFadden, D. and Reid, F., 1975, Aggregate Travel Demand Forecasting from Disaggregate Behavioral Models, Transportation Research Record, 534.

Parody, T.E., 1977, An Analysis of Disaggregate Mode Choice Models in Prediction, 56th Annual Meeting, Transportation Research Board, Washington, DC.

Peat, Marwick, Mitchell and Co., 1972, Implementation of the N-Dimensional Logit Model, Final Report to Comprehensive Planning Organization, San Diego, CA.

Ruijgrok, C.J. and van Essen, P.G., 1980, The Development and Application of Disaggregate Poisson Model for Trip Generation, 59th Annual Meeting, Transportation Research Board, Washington, DC.

Schultz, G.W., 1983, Development of a Travel Demand Model Set for the New Orleans Region, 62nd Annual Meeting of the Transportation Research Board.

Spiegel, S., 1956, Non-Parametric Statistics, McGraw-Hill, New York.

Stopher, P.R., 1969, A Probability Model of Travel Mode Choice for the Work Journey, Highway Research Record, 283, 57-65.

Talvitie, A., 1981, Refinement and Application of Individual Choice Models in Travel Demand Forecasting, Vol. 2, State University of New York at Buffalo, DOT Contract DOT-FH-11.

Talvitie, A., Dehghani, Y., Supernak, J., Morris, M., Anderson, M., Dejohn, A., Kousheski, B. and Feverstein, S., 1981, Refinement and Application of Individual Choice Models in Travel Demand Forecasting, Vol. 1, State University of New York at Buffalo, DOT contract DOT-FH-11.

Talvitie, A.P. and Kirshner, D., 1978, Specification, Transferability and the Effect of Data Outliers in Modelling the Choice of Mode in Urban Travel, Transportation, 7, 311-331.

Theil, H., 1955, Linear Aggregation of Economic Relationships, North Holland/ American Elsevier.

Timmermans, G.V.F., 1982, A Comparative Analysis of Disaggregate Trip Generation Models, MS thesis, Department of Civil Engineering, Northwestern University, Evanston, IL.

Train, K.E., 1978, The Sensitivity of Parameter Estimates to Data Specification in Mode Choice Models, Transportation, 7, 3, 301-309.

Watson, P.L. and Westin, R.B., 1976, Transferability of Disaggregate Mode Choice Models, Regional Science and Urban Economics, 5, 1-23.

Westin, R. and Manski, C.F., 1979, Theoretical and Conceptual Development in Demand Modelling, in Hensher, D.A. and Stopher, P.R. (Eds.), Behavioral Travel Modelling, Croom-Helm, London.

Wilmot, C.G., 1983, The Impact of Market Segmentation on the Transferability of Discrete Choice Models, PhD dissertation, Department of Civil Engineering, Northwestern University, Evanston, IL.

Discrete Analysis

HOUSING AFFORDABILITY: A REGIONAL PERSPECTIVE

William Goldner
Department of Urban and Regional Planning
San Jose State University
San Jose, CA 95192
United States of America

Abstract. A computer program, AFORD, is developed to deal with the complexity of house purchase transactions at the city, county, and regional levels. The transactional framework behind the program focuses on the measurement of affordability, aggregating households in selected income classes with houses in specified price groups. This matching includes selection of geographical locations, target year, tenure choice, consideration of federal and state income and local property taxes, and mortgage terms. These parameters are chosen by the user in an interactive mode using a time-share system that is user-friendly. Illustrative comparisons of computer output demonstrate affordability response to changes in interest rates and down payments.

INTRODUCTION

Housing economics has had to cope with recently renewed interest in a relatively old economic concept. In the past decade, a pervasive reference in the housing industry has been to affordability. In conventional market terms, affordability refers to the condition in which house prices asked by sellers are too high to clear the housing market. Consequently, an excess supply develops, but the unique characteristics of housing market transactions slow down the market adjustment substantially. The conceptual framework offers little guidance to identify the adjustment mechanism: will it be price reduction, or an expansion of market demand, or a decrease in supply? It appears that the concept needs some elaboration before it can fit into the more rigorous analytical framework that will satisfy housing economists.

Unfortunately, affordability and the socially more significant concept, non-affordability, reflect several layers of qualifications as pragmatic house purchase transactions are placed in a quasi-theoretical market structure. The following paragraphs itemize some of these.

Affordability is a quality that characterizes an individual confronting a transaction. When it is discussed and analyzed in the aggregate, the very process of aggregation introduces some very misleading relationships into the analysis. One obvious influence is the often unrecognized skewness in the distribution of incomes and also in house prices. The aggregation of diffuse segments from these consistently non-normal distributions does not lend itself to straightforward interpretation of the averaged results.

Another major aggregation bias involves differing geographical markets, or locations, which when blended together combine incomes from several markets with house prices and financing terms from these same markets, and implicitly assumes that averaging represents the larger geographical unit. State and national aggregates are especially subject to spurious matching to test for affordability.

In addition to biases of geographical aggregation, representations of affordability incorporate aggregates of households and persons, many of whom are not participants in the housing markets. To combine household incomes from complete (husband-wife present) families, households with a single head, and unrelated individuals incorporates a false representativeness to the typical transaction. Similar problems arise from the house-price side of the affordability comparison with regard to structure types, densities of development, and the many different size and quality characteristics of the structure. The use of hedonic functions to synthesize these distinctive features may ameliorate these problems.

It is necessary to distinguish the static equilibrium quality of a completed transaction in a housing market from the uncompletable transaction implied by non-affordability. In this sense, the important distinction is between realized demand and potential demand in a housing market, a distinction which differentiates ex post and ex ante conditions and static and dynamic market concepts.

The markets for real estate transactions encompass such a wide variety of determinants and a large spectrum of participants that the market framework needs both special elaboration and awkward simplification in order to be used for analysis. The conventional market structure of economic theory with price, quantity, supply, and demand is more representative of the production process than is applicable to the transaction mode. In spite of the many conventional market models that have been applied to land, housing, and construction markets, the tradition represented by transaction cost economics (Williamson, 1981) seems more relevant to the conceptual framework represented here.

One characteristic of affordability that is sometimes mentioned but rarely measured is the substantial financial advantage of tax benefits from the house purchase transaction (Villani, 1981). One possible cause of this oversight is the unique financial status of each buyer, which necessitates a detailed consideration of the buyer's wealth, assets, tax status, the tax rates to which he is subject, and other financial information. Nevertheless, some generalized assumptions reflecting fairly well-known attributes of house purchasers allow composite profiles to be used in estimating these tax advantages. These tax benefits have become more advantageous in recent years as house prices, associated financing terms, and property taxes have reached substantially higher levels and encountered higher marginal tax rates. The quantification of these concepts into the calculus of affordability represents an important addendum to the conventional view of the house purchase and to the process of qualifying buyers.

This paper presents a computer program that attempts to systematize some of the complexity referred to above. In this sense, it reflects an early stage of research into the multi-dimensional aspects of housing markets at the local level, with special attention being given to the spectrum of variables and the gallery of participants involved in the house-purchase transaction.

The program AFORD has been designed to cope with this complexity. It operates on a time-share system with a substantial portion of the program in interactive mode. The technical details of the program are supplied in a Technical Appendix available upon request from the author. However, the scope of the program and an overview of its operation is suggested by reference to the user-supplied parameters, the required data, the fixed but adjustable coefficients, and the program output.

CHARACTERISTICS OF THE MARKETS MODELLED

The program AFORD consists of a blend of data, user-supplied estimates of parameter values, and some fixed parameters. Out of this mixture, the program computes a set of income-house price comparisons, conditioned by relationships that guide the results to an index of affordability. Comparisons between these indices, given prescribed differences in the input parameters, provide the sensitivity analyses that are illustrated in this paper.

User-Supplied Variables and Parameters

The precautionary comments in the introduction to this paper are reflected in the selections of variables that elicit responses from users. The concepts which follow explain their place in the program.

Disaggregation. A universal characteristic encountered in confronting theory with evaluation and implementation is the necessity to accommodate to the strictures of available data. This unfortunate necessity has influenced the framework of analysis here in several ways. First, the differentiation by geographic units has been carried out, incorporating spatial disaggregation from the region to the county and city level of detail with regard to household incomes and house prices.

Second, home purchasers have been separated from renters mostly for the purpose of excluding renters from the complex treatment that purchasers are subjected to in the model. Admittedly, the data framework for tenure choice is not available to allow parallel treatment of the rental market, but the latter is the first element on this writer's agenda for further work on local housing markets.

Third, the family structure and size sharply condition the participants in the home purchase market as well as the rental market. From the innumerable sociological combinations possible among family size, marital status, number of working members, sex of household head, and number of children, the availability of household income data constrained the selection to (i) complete households with both husband and wife present along with a specified number of dependents; (ii) unmarried heads of households along with a specified number of dependents; and (iii) single individuals. Undifferentiated averaging across the three categories is frequently observed in evaluations involving affordability with the consequence that the lower income levels of (ii) and (iii) above significantly bias the outcomes.

Projections into Future Years. The model developed here does not include an internal mechanism to update household incomes and house prices to specified target years. This is due to the volatile fluctuations that have reflected the inflationary environment of the years since 1979 and the inability to model these meaningfully at the regional and local levels. Instead, these updating and projection processes have been left to exogenous determination by the user, reflecting either assumptions or estimates from a separate modelling effort. As a consequence, the model requires a target year to be specified (1980-1990 limits), and year-by-year inputs of percentage changes to income levels along with separately determined percentage changes in house prices. This flexibility allows the relationships between incomes and house prices in the base year (1980) to be carried out in current dollars reflecting inflation, or in real dollars with inflation factored out. Correspondingly, house prices can be incorporated as (i) current transaction prices in inflated terms; (ii) adjusted house values with the seller-financing incentives characteristic of real estate transactions in recent years discounted to true economic value; or (iii) adjusted to constant dollar values with inflation of house prices and the implied discounting of financial incentives taken into consideration.

Federal, State, and Local Taxes. US Federal and California State tax policies are substantially weighted in favour of homeowners in middle and upper income brackets (Kane, 1979). This has important consequences for the evaluation of affordability and the calculus of the rent-or-purchase decision of home seekers. The federal and state income tax provisions allow property taxes and interest expenses on home mortgages to be deducted from taxable income. Because the income tax schedules incorporate increasing marginal tax rates as income increases, the higher the income, the greater the benefit from the same amount of deductions. An interesting consequence of these relationships is that general decreases in tax rates reduce the amounts of tax benefits of higher incomes more than the benefit reductions to lower income households.

With regard to the contrast in treatment between renters and homeowners, property owners who rent to tenants must include their net profits as taxable income, whereas owner-occupants do not have to include the implicit value of their own occupancy as income. This comparison must be qualified by other provisions of the tax laws, including the contrasting expectations of property appreciation, the treatment of capital gains, the deferment of appreciation when purchasing another home, special provisions for depreciation write-offs, and other tax regulations affecting homeownership.

Given these complexities from the revenue-raising side of the public sector, and the on-going awareness that much of the taxing framework was subject to change during the period since 1980, a substantial effort was devoted to allow implementation of major tax changes as they occurred. This section of the program was modelled during the early part of 1980, a period during which legislative discussions in Washington and in Sacramento were directed toward alternative expectations regarding inflation, and also focused on different options regarding tax reduction. In May 1983, as this is being written, some of this controversy is still unresolved.

Three options, applicable separately to existing 1980 federal and state income tax schedules, were formulated. These were (i) the most likely (political) decisions regarding reductions in income tax rates: at the federal level, these were 10 percent reductions in each of the three years 1981, 1982, and 1983; at the state level, tax bracket adjustments equal to the rate of inflation in 1981 and 1982 and the rate of inflation minus 3 percent each year thereafter; (ii) to allow for changes in other possible formats, an option to adjust the tax brackets by an externally supplied percentage was provided; and (iii) the option which allowed specified across-the-board annual changes in the tax liability to be activated in the tax structure.

In retrospect, the most likely option at the federal level did not materialize exactly as anticipated, and the provision for alternative methods of adjusting income tax rates year-by-year has proved to be increasingly usable as fiscal policies are resolved.

Property Tax Rates. In order to calculate the tax benefits associated with affordability, it is necessary to estimate the property taxes accruing from the property. In California, Proposition 13, an initiative approved by the electorate in 1978, provides that property taxes are limited to one percent of full market value. Allowance is made for exceeding this limit for then-existing local bond issues and subsequent bonds issued with the approval of two-thirds majorities in appropriate jurisdictions. It is estimated that these allowances average about 0.25 percentage points on the property tax base. In specific jurisdictions, the amounts may be greater than this. Provision is made in the program to apply an appropriate property tax rate to the tax benefit calculations.

Mortgage Terms. The terms of home financing are relevant to the affordability analysis in two ways: first, these terms establish the payment schedule which is matched against the economic resources of the household. Second, the tax benefits associated with the tax write-off of interest paid is a partial and, in many cases, substantial offset to the level of house mortgage payments.

In AFORD, provision is made to install actual terms of existing mortgage markets into the model. These include the interest rate, the term of the mortgage, and the down payment associated with the house purchase transaction.

During the years 1980 to 1983, a variety of financing forms have been developed to augment the conventional fixed rate mortgage, including variable rate mortgages, wrap-around mortgages, graduated payment mortgages, reverse annuity mortgages, and other variants. Although each of these types affects the payment schedule in differing ways, many can be tanslated to interest rate and term equivalents. These, in turn, can be used as approximate inputs without major bias, especially when the model is used to analyze affordability in the near term of three to five years.

Program-Supplied Fixed Relationships

Income Expenditures for Housing. Among the most important parameters in the evaluations of affordability are the proportions of income spent on housing. These proportions are based on the Consumer Expenditure Surveys made by the US Bureau of Labor Statistics (BLS). These reports provide proportions expended on housing for lower, moderate, and high income families, as follows (i) .32 for high income family (greater than $30,091 in 1980); (ii) .29 for moderate income family ($20,085-30,091 in 1980); and (iii) .26 for lower income family (less than $20,085 in 1980).

In the BLS surveys, these proportions are applied to disposable income, ie., after taxes and savings are deducted. In addition, the surveys reflect wide variations in individual observations so that the averaging reflected in these parameters is subject to a great deal of variability for geographically disaggregated segments. Furthermore, this variability is augmented by the effect of inflation on more recent home purchasers as compared with pre-inflation owners whose mortgage payment schedules were established at much lower levels. Because of these qualifications, the proportions listed above have been used as preliminary indicators, to be adjusted to reflect more current practices of mortgage lenders as they become codified.

The bounds that separate these three income types have also been adjusted for ongoing inflation since 1980. The inflation projections for income have been used to implement these adjustments.

Treatment of Tax Benefit. A second assumption programmed into the model responds to the treatment of tax benefits. It is assumed that all of tax benefits associated with a specific income-house price comparison are fully offset against the housing expenditure level. This assumption was implemented to reflect the strong desire of house purchasers to qualify for financing in an inflationary environment. It might be argued that the marginal propensity to consume housing is less than one, and closer to the average propensities reflected in the Consumer Expenditure Surveys. The assumption in the program was judgmentally rationalized because the housing expenditure proportions reflected a sole dependence on income and did not include the potential effect of wealth accumulation on the propensity to consume housing.

Technical Aspects of the Program AFORD

Although every attempt has been made to establish the program in a user-friendly mode, there are several aspects of the program that are accommodations to the operation of the computer system, per se.

Default Values. First, to facilitate the user's learning in the interactive process, a set of default values has been used. These supply reasonable values of the input variables so that the user can observe the program's operation before using it for detailed analysis. The program has been used in university classes where this feature has proved to be of great pedagogic value.

Number and Layout of Output Tables. Second, the output format has been made flexible to accommodate simple to complex output tables. The user can supply an unlimited number of geographic comparisons of income with house prices in either of two forms. The user can input percentile steps or actual values, in either or both of income levels and house prices. Where percentile steps are input, the program supplies the corresponding actual value; where actual values are input, the program supplies the corresponding percentile step.

Explicit Listing of Assumptions. Third, attached to each set of output tables is a summary of the assumptions that have been used with that analysis. For each computer run, these document the significant variables and assumptions that have been mentioned above.

Data and Adjustable Parameters

The assembly of data for AFORD was a formidable job. In matching data from several sources, problems of non-congruences were serious requiring careful adjustments in order to establish a geographic-and time-consistent data set. The data collection process was carried out in 1980 before any of the 1980 Census publications were available. Adaptation of appropriate data from the 1980 Census of Population and Housing is underway as this is written and will provide validation for some of the estimates presently used in the model.

Income Data. The several sources of income data illustrate the problems that must be confronted in order to establish a congruent data base. Adjusted gross income data were available by counties from the State of California Franchise Tax Board for the 1979 tax year. Detailed distributions were available with fine-grain class intervals enabling a variety of statistical measurements to be calculated. Although questions of non-filing appeared to be reconcilable, the non-reporting of segments of the household's income by legitimate exclusion or by oversight made reconciliation with other sources a difficult process. However, these data did provide consistency on the shapes of the income distributions, and this source was heavily mined for these parameters.

A second source of income data was supplied by the US Department of Commerce, Bureau of Economic Analysis (BEA). These data, for counties, provided Family Income per Capita for 1977, including transfer payments and imputed rental value of owner-occupied housing in the definition of family income. Although this source purports to be measured at place of residence, a major source of information on wage and salary income was taken from payroll data at place of work. Adjustments to reallocate this income to place of residence are included in the BEA estimation process but appeared to greatly underestimate the geographical transfers involved in the San Francisco Bay Region. In addition, the transformation of per capita income to household income involved bold assumptions with regard to size of household and number of household workers.

House Price Data. Detailed data on house values are difficult to obtain and are subject to a host of conceptual and reporting biases. In the San Francisco Bay Area, a continuing program of value estimation has been carried out for at least two decades by the Northern California Real Estate Research Council (NCRERC). This organization has a corps of professional house appraisers who re-evaluate a selected sample of single-family houses and condominiums each quarter. Although there have been some replacements and additions as new construction and demolitions occur, the appraised values of each structure in a representative sample of 200 from the time the structure was included in the sample to the present is published regularly. Because the sample is small, it is remarkable that comparisons with house values reported in the 1970 Census of Housing are not significantly different for each of the nine counties in the region. On this basis, for 1980, the NCRERC data for house prices were used as the house price data base for counties. The thinness of the samples precluded determination on the shapes of the price distributions in each county. Consequently, the region wide aggregate of the sample of 200 was used, pegged to the median level of each county.

A second source of house price data was the file of completed mortgage transactions reported to the California Savings and Loan Department by each savings and loan association in the state. This file, updated each quarter on computer tape, records a long list of variables for each completed financial transaction. Among the items coded are the census tract location of the property, house price, mortgage amount, interest rate and terms, borrower's income, and other significant variables. These transactions were aggregated for cities and counties in the San Francisco Bay Area and the geographical structure of medians was used to estimate the price levels of cities within each county.

Relevelling Adjustments. In order to carry out the full range of affordability comparisons, it is necessary to provide a complete distribution of prices and of incomes for each geographical comparison that is selected by the user. This has been implemented by supplying a median level and a set of relative deviations from the median for each geographical unit in the study area; ie., the region, the nine counties, and 90 cities. The amalgam of data sources to construct this intricate mosaic is presented in Table 1.

TABLE 1

SOURCES OF DATA AND DATA ADJUSTMENTS

Statistical Concept	Region and Counties	Cities
Median Income Level	FTB Annual Report 1980; median return	BEA mean per capita income 1977; DOF population per household 1977; median/mean adjustment based on DOF county distributions; updated to 1980 by CPI for SFO
Income Distributions	FTB Annual Report 1980	City distributions assumed to correspond to FTB county distributions 1979; updated to 1980 by CPI for SFO
Median House Price Level	NCRERC sample of single-family house appraisals: 1980	California DSL median house price deviation from county median used as adjustment to county median from NCRERC
House Price Distribution	NCRERC sample: regional aggregation assumed to apply to each county	Same as Region and Counties

FTB = California Tax Board
DOF = California Department of Finance Population Research Unit
BEA = U.S. Department of Commerce Bureau of Economic Analysis
CPI = Consumer Price Index
SFO = San Francisco-Oakland Metropolitan Area
NCRERC = Northern California Real Estate Research Council
DSL = California Department of Savings and Loan

In addition to establishing a consistent data base for the year 1980 by the process described above, projections of these data are made by the price changes and income changes provided exogenously by the user. These changes are applied to the medians of the 1980 data base to project them forward to the selected target year. The assumption is made that the relative shape of the projected distribution remains unchanged.

Affordability Indices. Summary indications of the affordability status of specified income and house price comparisons are provided by AFORD. Starting with a specified set of income percentile or income level, the program estimates the normal state and federal income tax liability and deducts this from gross income to generate spendable income. The proportion of spendable income spent for housing is applied using the BLS housing expenditure ratios creating potential housing. These are converted from annual to monthly data for later use.

Parallel to this, the user specifies a set of house prices or house price percentiles. From user-supplied data, the program estimates the tax benefits associated with the house prices. These benefits converted from an annual to a monthly basis are added to monthly potential housing expenditures to create the potential expenditures available for housing. From the financial package and property tax estimates, the amount of monthly payments required are estimated.

The affordability index is the amount available divided by the amount required, expressed as a percentage. Affordable transactions are reported as percentages 100 and above. Non-affordability is measured by percentages below 100. The layout of illustrative comparisons is presented in Table 2.

ILLUSTRATIVE SENSITIVITY TESTS

Limitations on the size of this paper preclude the preparation of a large catalog of comparative tables. Instead, attention has been focused on two significant questions involving changes in financial terms and their effect on affordability, they are

1. What would be the effect of substantial reductions in interest rates?
2. How would the new home buyer with a small down payment be disadvantaged compared with an existing homeowner who would use his substantial existing equity in the purchase of a new house?

Illustrative Output Table

A typical format for the output of AFORD is displayed in Table 2 to illustrate the details of the affordability analysis. Table 2 compares two percentiles of the projected income distribution in Solano County, a low income area, with four levels of projected house prices. As can be observed, none of the household income levels is able to afford the house prices under the conditions assumed by the user in this run; ie., each of the affordabilty indices is less than 100.

There are several relationships observable in Table 2 that are of interest

1. The built-in progression of the income tax schedules is confirmed by the data in the ST FED/TAXES column.

2. Although the BLS data on monthly housing expenses have increasing proportion as spendable income increases, this proportion out of gross income is virtua ly constant at each income level.
3. For a house purchaser at middle and higher income levels, greater proportion tax benefits accrue as the house price is higher.
4. Low income households with consequent relatively small income tax liabilitie can only obtain tax benefits up to the maximum of their tax bills, if they were able to purchase a house.

With this introduction to the type of analysis provided by AFORD, let us tur to some illustrative sensitivity tests.

TABLE 2

REPRESENTATIVE EXAMPLE OF OUTPUT OF AFORD PROGRAM

Homeowners Affordability Analysis, 1985

Income Distribution: Solano Housing Price Distribution: Solano

INC PCTL	HH INC	ST FED TAXES	SPNDBL INC	MOHSG EXP	HOPR PCTL	HOUSE PRICE	TAX BENE	AVAIL-ABLE	REQU-IRED	AFFED INDEX
50	35731	6433	29299	708						
					50	98485	2437	911	1153	79
					35	89795	2068	880	1051	84
					20	81105	1698	850	949	89
					10	75312	1452	882	829	94
10	11455	404	11051	239	30	98485	404	273	1153	24
					35	89795	404	273	1051	26
					20	81105	404	273	949	29
					10	75312	404	273	882	31

The above calculations are based on the following assumptions

1. A representation household of two parents and two dependents.
2. Bureau of Labor Statistics figures for proportions of disposable income spent for housing;

   .32 for a high income family, 43230 or more annually;

   .29 for a moderate income family; between 28855 and 43230 annually;

   .26 for a lower income family; 28855 or less annually.
3. Federal tax deductions, exemptions and credits based on present or assumed 1985 tax schedules.
4. Family income based on data from the 1979 annual report of the Franchise Tax Board State of California, and updated to target year based on selected increases in the CPI.
5. Mortgage payments based on 10.0 percent down payment, 14.0 percent interest, and a 30 year term.

6. 1980 house price based on data from the Real Estate Research Council of Northern California. Target year prices assume selected increases in the trend of house prices.

The Framework of the Illustrative Sensitivity Tests

The process of sensitivity testing used here has been to select a high income county, a low income county, and the regional aggregate of the nine counties in the San Francisco Bay Area. Computer runs of AFORD have been made to simulate relationships among the programmed variables for the year 1981. Then, tables summarizing the affordability indices have been presented for evaluation. The summary tables have not included the detail that is shown in Table 2 so that the overwhelming volume of output would be compressed. Nevertheless, each comparison table involves three locations and two sensitivity levels, so that for our two examples, twelve tables have been used as the source of data.

In each case, incomes in a geographical area have been compared with house prices in the same area. This implies that houses in that area are being sought for purchase by existing residents. In the case of the region, the implication is that houses anywhere in the region are being sought by households from all locations in the region. The program also has the capability to compare houses in one geographical area with households and incomes from another area with the implication of inter-locational search taking place.

The representative household used for the tests illustrated here consists of a husband, wife, and two dependents who have made the tenure choice to purchase a house. They are assumed to file joint tax returns for federal and state income tax returns using the applicable income tax schedules for the 1981 tax year.

The proportion of household income normally devoted to housing varies with income level as follows (i) .32 for a high income level: more than $34,605 annually; (ii) .29 for a moderate income level: $23,098 to $34,605 annually; and (iii) .26 for a low income family: less than $23,098 annually.

Income and house price percentiles and their associated absolute values are shown in Table 3. Because of the interest in non-affordability, the percentiles at the lower ends of the income and house price distributions have been emphasized in the comparisons.

It should be reiterated that the tests presented here are illustrative and do not reflect actual conditions in the geographical areas specified. For such comparisons, a very careful recalibration would be required.

Interest Rate Reduction. In 1980 and 1981, interest rates on home mortgages moved to extremely high levels, reaching 20 percent in some cases. The sale of houses dropped to low levels because of the almost universal dependence on

TABLE 3

AFFORDABILITY INDICES FOR 1981 INCOME/HOUSE PRICE COMPARISONS IN SELECTED LOCATIONS

	SAN MATEO					SOLANO					REGION				
		Interest Rates		*Down Payment			Interest Rates		*Down Payment			Interest Rates		*Down Payment	
Percentile	Income and House Price	19%	11 %	10%	35%	Income and House Price	19%	11 %	10%	35%	Income and House price	19%	11 %	10%	35%
Income 50	$ 34.5					$ 28.6					$ 32.2				
House Price 50	$146.2	54	71	65	78	$ 82.9	67	88	80	98	$136.1	54	71	64	77
35	134.6	58	75	68	83	75.6	71	94	85	104	117.0	59	78	70	86
20	122.8	61	80	73	88	68.2	76	102	91	112	95.1	68	90	81	99
10	111.2	65	86	77	94	63.4	80	107	96	119	76.5	78	104	94	115
Income 25	23.0					17.6					20.8				
House Price 50	same	31	46	41	51	same	39	53	48	58	same	30	44	39	48
35	as	34	49	44	53	as	43	56	51	62	as	34	49	44	53
20	above	37	52	47	57	above	46	60	54	66	above	42	56	51	61
10		41	55	50	61		48	64	57	70		49	65	58	71
Income 10	13.1					9.2					11.1				
House Price 50	same	15	23	20	26	same	16	25	21	29	same	13	20	17	23
35	as	16	25	21	29	as	18	27	23	31	as	15	23	20	26
20	above	18	27	23	31	above	20	30	26	35	above	18	28	24	32
10		20	30	26	35		21	33	28	37		23	35	30	40

Calculated for a purchase transaction with 10 percent down payment, 30-year mortgage term and specified interest rates.
*Specified down payments, 30-year mortgage term and 14 percent interest rate.

mortgage financing in connection with house purchases. In May 1983, mortgages were being offered in the range of 11.5 to 13.0 percent. The question to be evaluated is what enlargement of the market would have been attributable to such a lower level of interest rates in 1981, ceteris paribus.

The relevant comparisons are shown in Table 3. For households at the median income level in each location, the non-affordability of houses under a regime of high interest rates is confirmed for all house price levels shown in the analysis. As is known, ex post, the housing market had virtually dried up because of the conditions of financing, and pervasive uncertainties.

In contrast, the lower interest rate option would have made houses in some locations affordable but only for those houses at lower levels on the price distribution. Even in San Mateo County, a high income area, the median income household was completely out of the affordable range. As for households with incomes below the median, their participation in the housing markets at even the lowest house price levels was precluded by the apparent non-affordability.

Down Payment Variations. Another concern of the real estate and housing industries was the inability of first-time house buyers to participate in the market. Those owner-occupants who chose to sell their existing houses to move to another usually had a significant down payment generated by the appreciation on their property. First-time house buyers had to obtain their front money from other sources. To evaluate the handicap of the first-time house purchase, the program was run to compare 10 percent down (first-time buyer) with 35 percent down (an existing owner-occupant). The results of these runs are presented in Table 3.

As was apparent for interest rates, the enlargement of the market took place exclusively among those households at the median income level. For median households with 35 percent down payments in Solano County, the higher down payment signaled a significant penetration of the market. This was also reflected to a lesser extent in the regional aggregate which included the Solano County relationships.

Another relationship displayed by Table 3 is the contrasting gain in affordability associated with the different income levels. At the median income, households gained from 13 to 23 points on the affordability index. For households at the 25th income percentile, the gain was in the 11 to 13 point range. At the 10th percentile income level, 6 to 10 points bracketed the gain. These relationships reflect the higher value of tax benefits generated against the progressively higher marginal income tax rates.

Measuring Market Enlargement. Although the affordability indices measure the deviation from affordability for a particular income/house price comparison, the percentiles in AFORD measure the degree by which the particular market would be enlarged as the adjustable variable generates a response.

Referring again to Table 3, it is observed that in Solano County, the lower interest rate alternative moved the affordability indices to above 100 for the 10th and 20th house price percentiles. In fact, it appears that a more detailed partitioning of these percentiles would show affordable indices up to the 25th percentile. This points to the measurement of market penetration that can be gleaned from the AFORD analysis. Measured at the regional level, the penetration can be observed at above the 10th and up to the 13th percentile. More exact measurements can easily be made by asking the program for more percentile steps near the affordability threshold.

Table 3 also provides an example of the market enlargement in response to the simulated change in down payment requirements. Again, in Solano County, the affordability indices for the 35 percent down option show that house prices close to the median level are affordable to the median income household under the changed down payment requirements. For the region, almost 20 percent of the market is attainable to median income households.

CONCLUDING REMARKS

The program AFORD has been designed for use by planning agencies for housing policy evaluation at the local level. It also has potential use for market measurement under simulated what if conditions. These conditions encompass an extensive range of geographic options, a time horizon from the present to the mid-range future, a meaningful breakdown of family types, alternative property and income tax levels, and a comprehensive selection of household incomes and house price levels based on the distributions of these variables.

The limited presentation of sensitivity tests in this paper suggests the potential for a significant expansion of these tests. Simulations involving changes through time in the level and distribution of incomes, and of house prices have immediate and direct interest to financial institutions, real estate practitioners, community developers, and local governments. Simulations involving simultaneous changes in several of the adjustable variables are also on this potential agenda.

The transferabilty of this mechanism to other regions depends on the availability of data from the 1980 Census of Population and Housing and other government statistical sources that are universally available in the USA. In addition, the accessibility to compatible computer systems is a fundamental requirement (See the Technical Appendix for greater details).

There are several developments that are high on the priority list for further research. First, there is the critical gap with regard to rental markets and their relationships to tenure choice decisions among those who seek housing.

Second, the tendency to treat the house purchase transaction as both the acquisition of shelter and the undertaking of an investment needs to be integrated into the generalized transaction framework illustrated by the AFORD program.

Third, the variety of financial instruments that are significant elements in the house purchase transaction needs to be codified and synthesized to standardized dimensions.

FOOTNOTES AND REFERENCES

The program for the model AFORD was originally created by Fred Vogler, working collaboratively with the author. Subsequent modifications were made by Dr. Chin Ming Yang. Most of this work was supported by the Association of Bay Area Governments, Berkeley, California.

Buckley, R.M. and Van Order, R.A., 1983, Housing and the Economy: Popular Myths, Journal of the American Real Estate and Urban Economics Association, 10, 421-441.

Kane, E.J., 1979, Micro and Macro Financial Policies and Housing Finance, Occasional Papers in Housing and Community Affairs, 5, US Department of Housing and Urban Development, 21-31.

Maisel, S.J., 1979, Housing and the Fight against Inflation, Occasional Papers in Housing and Community Affairs, 5, US Department of Housing and Urban Develoment, 14-20.

Villani, K., 1981, The Tax Subsidy to Housing in an Inflationary Environment: Implications for After-Tax Housing Costs, Occasional Papers in Housing and Community Affairs, 9, US Department of Housing and Urban Development, 1-66.

Williamson, O.E., 1981, The Modern Corporation: Origins, Evolution, Attributes, Journal of Economic Literature, XIX, 1537-68.

FORECASTING THE LONG TERM EFFECTS OF INCREASES IN THE COST OF TRAVEL

Roger Mackett
Institute for Transport Studies
University of Leeds
Leeds LS2 9JT
United Kingdom

Abstract. The paper describes the development of a methodology for forecasting the impact of an increase in the cost of travel, taking into account the effects of changes in life-cycle characteristics and the opportunity to migrate. Monte Carlo simulation is used to represent progression through a series of processes such as household formation and residential search. The operation of the model is illustrated by an example, and the paper concludes by the identification of areas for further work.

INTRODUCTION

The increasing cost of fuel and concern about the cost of providing public transport have stimulated the need to be able to forecast the impact of changes in the cost of travel. Over the past 25 years a number of techniques have been developed, but these have tended to emphasize short-run responses, and have largely ignored the interaction between travel and locational decisions. This paper is written within the context of a project to investigate these issues, which are discussed further in the next section. This is followed by a description of the overall structure and the individual components of a new model. The operation of the model is illustrated by means of an example. In the concluding section the various issues for further research are identified.

THE EFFECTS OF TRANSPORT COST INCREASES

One approach to developing better methods of forecasting the amount of travel is to treat it as a derived demand, with decisions linked to the demand for other activities (Van der Hoorn, 1979). The aggregate models of the 1960s were found to be wanting because of their inability to represent the social organization within which individuals make their decisions (Hagerstrand, 1970). The more recent disaggregate models are based on the assumption that travel decisions are free choices defined by the characteristics of the alternatives available and of the individuals concerned. There are several problems with this approach including

1. Travel decisions may be the outcome of processes other than free choices, for example habit, avoidance of undesirable alternatives or constrained choice (Burnett and Hanson, 1982).

2. There may be supply side constraints, resulting from competition between individuals for opportunities.

3. Decisions made by one member of a household, for example to start using the car for the journey to work, may affect the travel patterns of other members of the household.

4. Travel decisions are often linked with choices of home and job (Mackett, 1983a).

Since activity patterns tend to change as the life-cycle progresses (Chapin, 1968), the requirement for travel also varies as the size and nature of the household changes (Zimmerman, 1982). This is particularly important when the long term effects of changes in transport costs are being examined. For example, if the cost of travel to work by one mode is increased the traveller may change mode in the short run. In the longer run, he or she may purchase a car, or link various trips together. Furthermore, the cost of travel may well influence the choice of home or job location.

These issues have been examined in the context of a project to investigate the impact of rail fare increases in London and South East England. The study area was chosen because not only have rail fares increased substantially in real terms, but they are expected to continue to do so. The objective of the work was to identify the extent to which the cost of travel influences locational decisions as well as modal choice, since changes of location tend to be expensive in time and money and so cannot be easily reversed. The project has had two components: survey and modelling. In the surveys, the emphasis has been on obtaining information about the decisions made, and the characteristics of those making them. Initially information was collected by means of self-completion questionnaires distributed to current and former rail commuters at home, at workplaces in Central London. This revealed a variety of information about residential and workpace locational decisions and the characteristics of those making them, but it was recognized that two further types of information were required and these are (i) the reasons for the decisions made; and (ii) the characteristics of the individual and his or her household at the time of the decision.

Consequently, it was decided to carry out a number of household interviews of an exploratory nature to overcome these deficiencies. (The interviews were limited to 150 in number for budgetary reasons.) For each household, data on its history for the previous 10 years, or since its formation if more recent, were collected. These covered the following topics (i) members of the present household, by age and sex, and the date of joining the household; (ii) anybody who had left the household during the relevant period; (iii) residential locations of the household, the tenure and dwelling type, dates of change, and the reasons for both leaving the previous dwelling and choosing the new one; (iv) employment history of all household members who have had jobs during the relevant period, including the address of work, the date of starting work there, the reason for the change, and the mode of travel to work; and (v) car ownership history.

From this information it is possible to identify who was in the household, where they lived and worked and how they travelled in between, at any point in time, plus the changes of location made and the reasons for the decisions. From this information it is possible to identify the relationship between travel and other decisions. The following are examples of the sorts of behaviour that can be distinguished

1. A female aged 25 working in Central London living with her mother 30 kilometres from London, who is considering finding a flat nearer to work because of the high cost of travel.

2. The couple who moved from place A to place B in December 1980. The husband, a supermarket manager, had been transferred from A to B in April 1977, but commuted between the two towns until the cost of travel became so high that a residential move was felt justified.

3. Two females in their early twenties who moved jobs from Central London to nearer to their homes because of the cost of travel.

These cases illustrate the complexity of possible response to a change in the cost of travel. The original rationale of the project had been to apply an existing aggregate land use-transport model (Mackett, 1983b) to the area, but it was recognised that, while such a model could be very useful for forecasting overall trends, it could not handle the full complexity of behavioural responses. The initial approach to this was to develop a gaming approach on a microcomputer (Mackett and Ong, 1981) in which the player at the keyboard can respond to travel and locational choices, to achieve a predefined objective, given limited information about the future. This stimulated the development of a model that represents individuals, with the decisions at the keyboard replaced by stochastic functions within the model. It is the development of this model that is described in the next section.

THE MODEL

The approach being used is known as microanalytical simulation (or microsimulation). It works on the simple principle of classifying the population by a number of relevant characteristics (age, sex, stage in life cycle and so on) and simulating their progress through a set of processes (for example choice of mode or forming a household). The probability of each possible outcome must be defined, and may be a function of the individual's characteristics and the alternatives. Since individuals are being considered the outcome must be deterministic so Monte Carlo simulation is used. This means that the probabilities of the various outcomes are cumulated from 0 to 1, and a random number in this range generated. The value of the random number determines which outcome of the process occurs. This does not imply that behaviour is random, but can be regarded as recognition that there is a limit to the extent to which individual behaviour can be forecast. As the sample size increases the proportion of people choosing each outcome will tend towards the probability of that outcome occurring. With different random number sequences, individuals will follow different paths through the decision sequence, so the technique should not be seen as a method of forecasting individual behaviour, but as a technique for predicting impacts at an aggregate level, taking into account the responses of individuals. While the basic technique is very simple, the complexity comes from a number of factors (i) the characteristics of an individual may change as a result of a process, for example, car ownership; (ii) the sequencing of events may vary between individuals; (iii) some decisions are made at a household level, for example, residential migration; (iv) some decisions may change the household structure itself, for example, leaving home because of the high cost of travel; and (v) different choice sets (for example homes) can be made available to apparently similar individuals.

The advantages of this technique are its basic simplicity, the way in which the results can be traced through, and the modular structure, which means that new processes can be added to the model. The disadvantages are the computational complexity and the need to calibrate the various probability functions. The functions can be calibrated in several ways: as choice functions, for example of the multinomial logit form, or from demographic data, for example to give the probability of dying. More generally, the calibrations may be based on data reflecting stated intentions or revealed preferences. Neither are completely satisfactory because the former tends to be based on hypothetical questions while the revealed preferences may have been made under constraints that cannot be identified subsequently. A further problem with the technique may be caused by the need for data on individuals. This is not a problem in the case of the project on South East England, but may be in other cases. If only aggregate data are available a technique such as that devised by Wilson and Pownall (1976) can be used.

The technique has been used for representing various processes, for example socio-economic systems (Orcutt, Greenberger, Korbel and Rivlin, 1961; Clarke, 1981; Williams, 1981), modal split and trip distribution (Kreibich, 1979), car sharing (Bonsall, 1982) and the housing market (Wegener, 1983). The model being described here is not complete, and is regarded as a framework within which to develop the household dynamics and the computational algorithms. Further processes can be added later. The present state of the model is described below.

The Overall Structure of the Model

The model is a set of linked sub-models as shown in Fig. 1. The first process is represented by the death sub-model. Anybody not dying survives, and may undergo a change of marital status. Changes in marital status may cause the formation (or cessation) of households. The number of people being born is forecast next, then any changes in economic status, that is entering or leaving the job market. The final two sub-models represent the residential search and migration processes and the journey-to-work. There is a feedback loop from the journey-to-work sub-model, so that a change in the cost of travel can affect the pattern of residential location. At this stage both car availability and employment locations are being kept fixed, but these can be added later. Further feedback loops could also be added, for example, from the journey to work sub-model to the economic status sub-model, so that the cost of travel could influence an entry to or exit from the employment market.

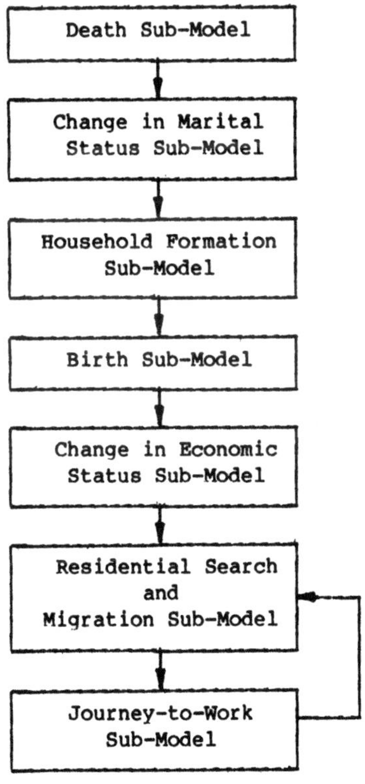

Figure 1 - The Overall Structure of the Model

The Death Sub-Model

The death sub-model is shown in Fig. 2. Death is taken to be a function of age and sex, so that when the random number is generated within the computer it is compared with the appropriate death probability. If the random number is less than or equal to this probability, death is assumed to have occurred, otherwise the person survives.

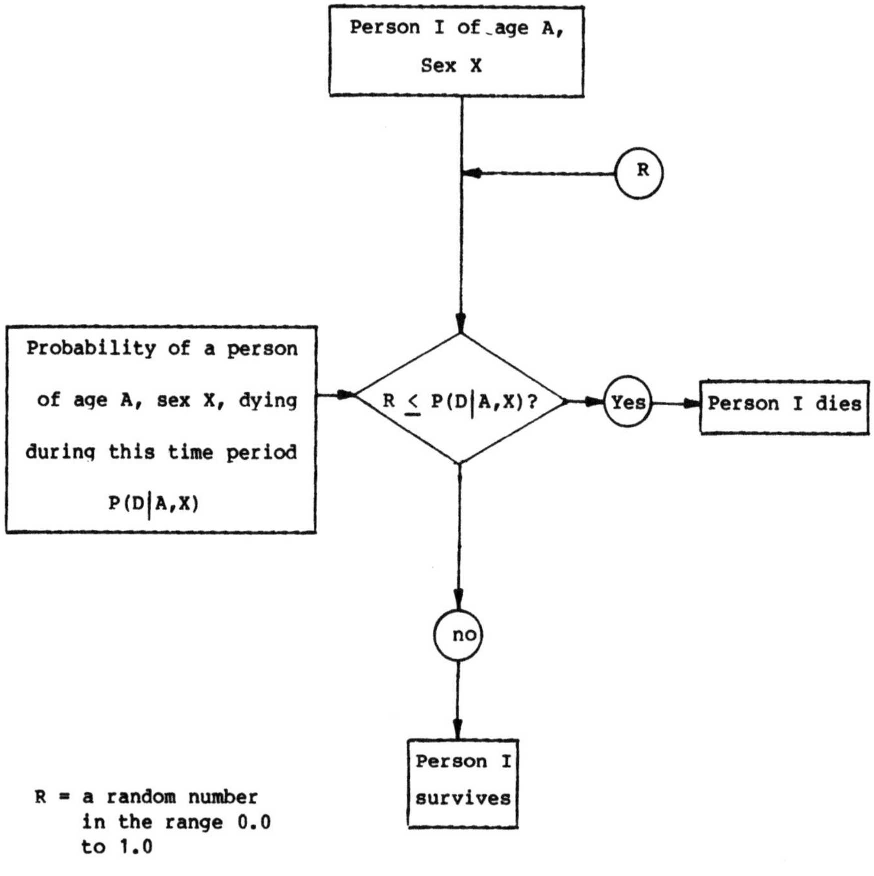

Figure 2 - The Death Sub-Model

The Change in Marital Status Sub-Model

Four states of marital status are considered within the model: single (never married), married, divorced and widowed. Not all the transitions are treated stochastically, nor are all transitions permitted. The process is shown in Fig. 3. Changes of state are a function of age, sex and present marital status. The possible transitions are shown in Table 1. Only one transition is permitted during a time period. If a person's spouse has died during this time period the person becomes widowed. The probability of divorce is applied to married persons using the Monte Carlo simulation method. However, if one person in a couple is divorced, then obviously that person's spouse also becomes divorced.

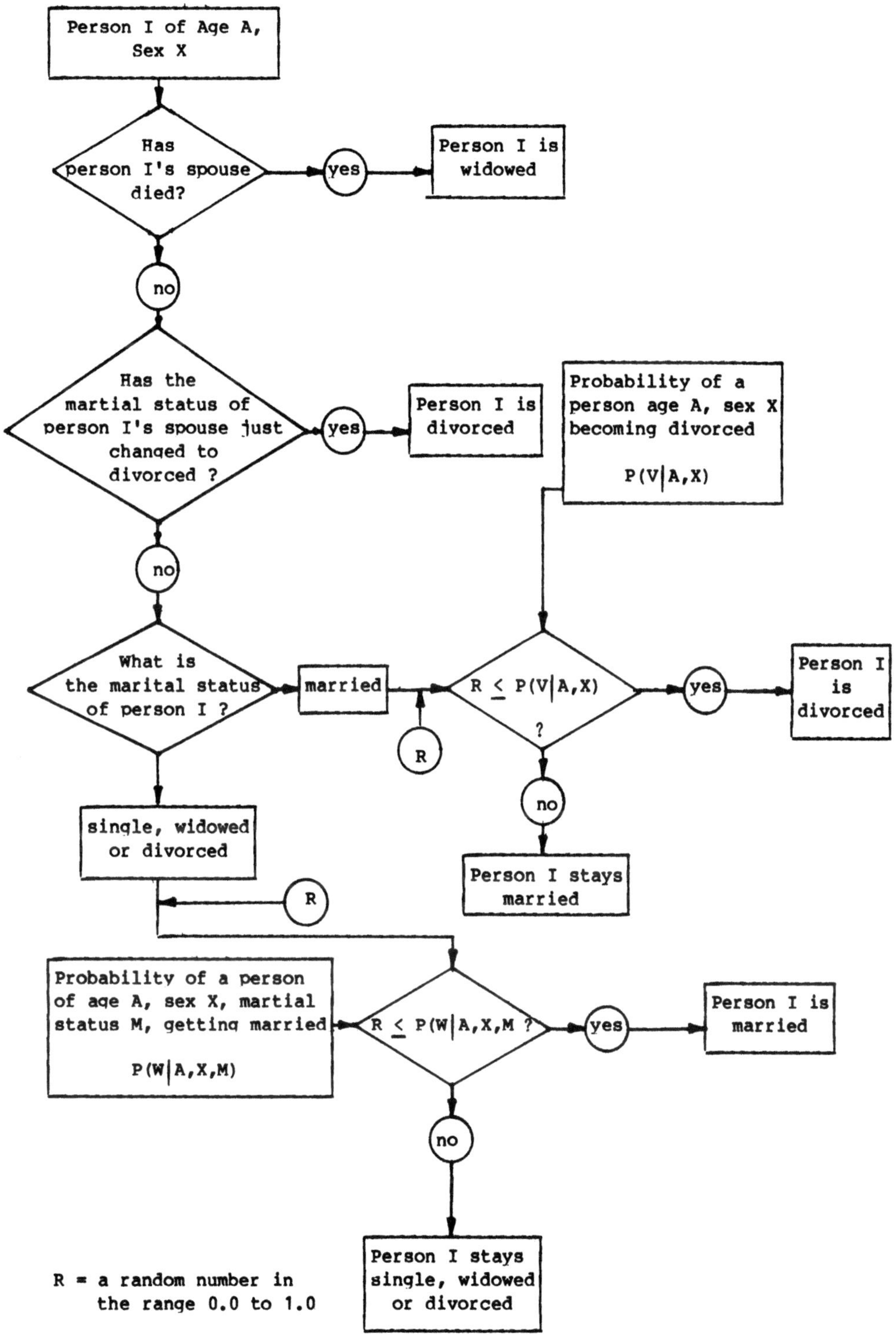

Figure 3 - The Change in Marital Status Sub-Model

TABLE 1

MECHANISMS FOR TRANSITIONS BETWEEN MARTIAL STATES

		Year t + 1			
		Single	Married	Divorced	Widowed
Year t	Single	s	s	n	n
	Married	n	s	s/d	d
	Divorced	n	s	s	n
	Widowed	n	s	n	s

s = stochastic (determined by Monte Carlo simulation)

d = deterministic (determined by events occurring to other people)

s/d = stochastic or deterministic

n = not possible in a single time period

Any couples that do not divorce stay married. Monte Carlo simulation is used to determine whether anyone who is not married becomes so during this time period. If the person does not marry, the present marital status is retained. Since a relatively small population is being considered it is not assumed that the spouse comes from within the simulated population. The spouse is added onto the list of people and given an age within 5 years of the person he or she is marrying.

The Household Formation Sub-Model

A change in marital status may cause the formation or cessation of a household so this process is considered next. The dynamics of these processes can be very complex, so a number of rules have to be applied. The various cases are as follows (i) a person living alone dies: that household ceases to exist; (ii) a person living with others dies: that household continues; (iii) a person living alone marries: a new household is formed and his or her old one ceases; (iv) a single person living with parents or friends marries and a new household may be formed: Monte Carlo simulation is used to determine whether the newly married couple stay living in the same household (a low probability) or leave and form a new household (a high probability); (v) a single person who lives with friends and does not marry may move out to be alone and so form a new household (low probability) or stay in the same household (high probability); (vi) a married couple living with others may leave to form a separate household (a low probability) or continue to share a dwelling (a high probability); and (vii) a married couple who divorce from two new households and their old one ceases and the children stay with their mother.

These procedures raise some interesting issues about the definition of households. The convention that has been followed here is that a new household is deemed to have been formed if the process that has occurred is likely to have a substantial effect on the household's behaviour, particularly in terms of migration decisions. It should be noted that it is not assumed that all households are conventional nuclear families. It was clear from the surveys carried out that other household formations do exist and should be considered. This may be particularly important in studies such as this where it appears that a significant proportion of the population is in these conventional households who often tend to be very mobile (in migration terms) and so cannot be regarded as locationally captive to a specific transport market.

The Birth Sub-Model

The birth sub-model is similar to the one for the death process, but, of course, is only applied to women, and the outcome of the Montre Carlo simulation is the number of childred (0, 1, 2 or 3) born to a woman of a particular age and martial status category during the time period. The sex of the newly born baby is determined at random.

The Change in Economic Status Sub-model

Whether or not a person is economically active is a function of his or her sex, age and, in the case of women, marital status. If a woman has just given birth she does not have a job, but may become eocnomically active the next year. The process is similar to that in the death sub-model.

The Residential Search and Migration Sub-model

In the model, space is represented by a zoning system. The supply of housing in each zone that is available for purchase by potential migrants is determined by the computer. The number of houses available in a zone (between 1 and 9) is generated at random, then the prices allocated to be within 10% of the mean value for the zone. At present a different set is defined for each household, so that they are not, strictly speaking, competing, but this can be revised later. Monte Carlo simulation is used to determine whether a household is considering migrating and if so, where it is considering relocating. At present, the migration probabilities are based on a matrix of such flows for a previous time period. The residential search process is shown in Fig. 4. A household is assumed to purchase the most expensive house that is available, subject to two constraints: firstly, that the capital cost of the dwelling does not exceed 2.5 times the head of household's income, reflecting the rule applied by Building Societies when providing a mortgage. The second constraint is that the annual cost of repayment of the mortgage plus the cost of travel to work by all workers in the household does not exceed a fixed proportion of the household's income. In order to check this, the mode of transport that would be used from the new residential location is calculated in the journey to work sub-model as described below. If no houses in a zone can be afforded another zone is selected for consideration. This process is repeated, if necessary, up to 6 times. If no suitable dwelling can be found the household does not migrate.

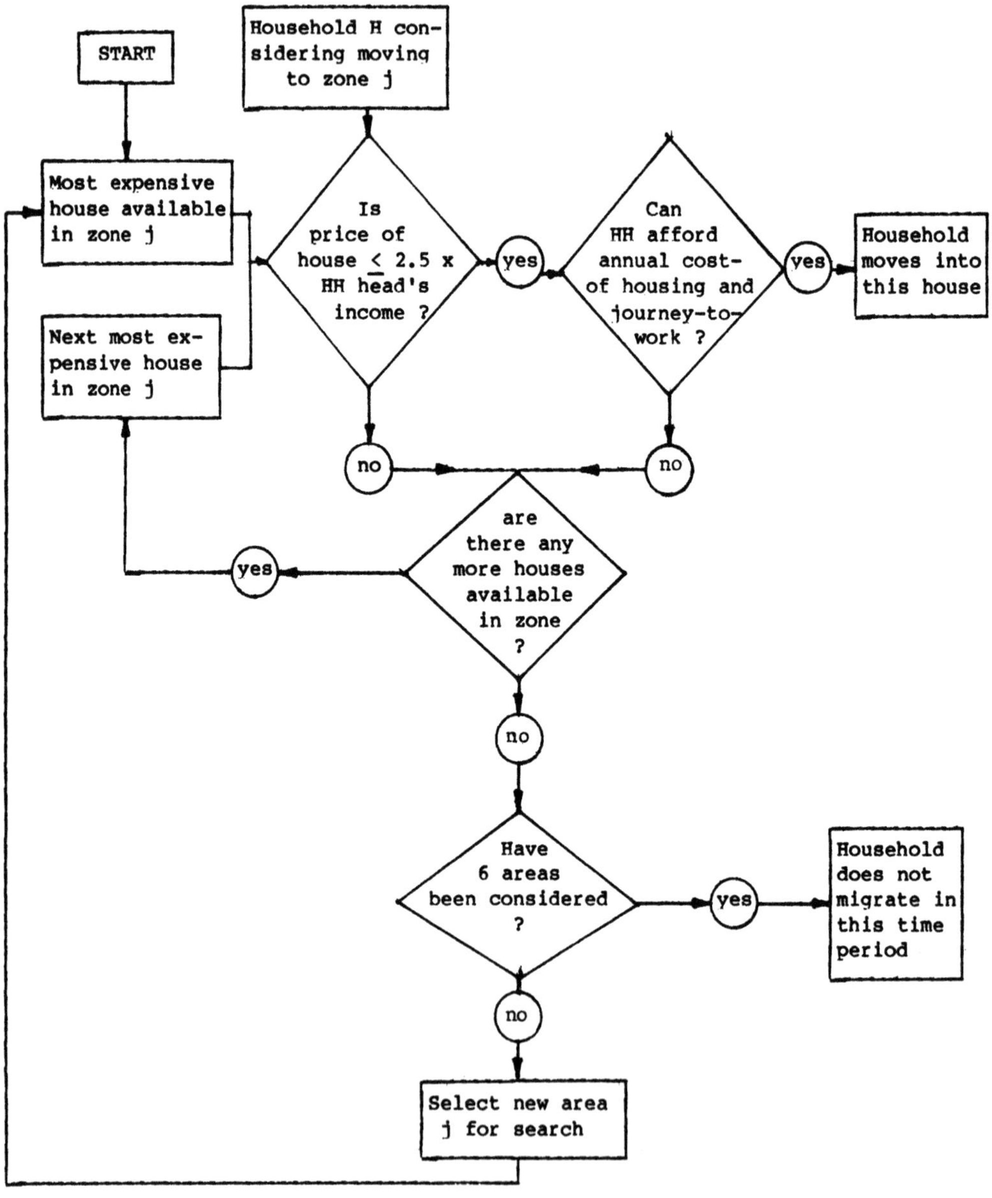

Figure 4. The Residential Search Process

The Journey to Work Sub-model

The residential location (or potential location) is defined as described in the previous section, or is the same as previously. As indicated previously, the employment location and car ownership level are taken as fixed, so only the mode needs to be determined. The probability of travelling by a particular mode between a pair of zones given the car availability level and occupational-income group (which determines the value of time) is defined by a spatial choice function based on the relative generalized cost of travel by each mode. The actual mode used is determined by Monte Carlo simulation.

Using the Model

The model is run for each household in turn. After all the households in the system have been processed the numbers in each category are aggregated to find not only the numbers of people in each category, such as, living in each zone, but also the numbers transferring between categories, for example migrating or switching modes.

OPERATION OF THE MODEL

The way the model operates at a microlevel can next be illustrated by example, as shown in Table 2. This shows household 68 which consisted of 4 people in year 1. The person identified as a rail commuter to Central London (zone 29) was person 186, a male aged 20, who is single and is in a technical or clerical profession. He lives in zone 10 with his parents aged 61 and 59 respectively, and his 89 year old grandmother. Both his parents have jobs, with his father travelling by rail to outer London (zone 30) and his mother by car to zone 3.

During the following year the married couple and son decide to move out and migrate to zone 9 from where the son still travels to work by rail, but his father switches to bus. The mother has ceased to be in employment. The grandmother has been left as a single person household, and so becomes the head of that household. The generation numbers are updated to reflect the change.

During the next year the grandmother died, so her household has ceased to exist. Meanwhile, the father in the other household has ceased to be economically active, and so the son becomes the head of the household as its chief economic supporter. This means that the relationships to the head of household all change.

It must be stressed that the model has not been designed to make forecasts for individual households, but this does illustrate the link between the location of residence and the mode of travel, and how progression over time affects

TABLE 2

THE PREDICTION BY MODEL OF THE CHANGES IN HOUSEHOLD 68

	Person Number	Rel. to HH Head	Age	Sex	Marital Status	Economic Status	Generation Number	Parent Number	Spouse Number	Occu-pation Group	Mode	Zone of Resi-dence	Zone of Work
Year 1	186	11	20	1	1	2	3	188	0	2	3	10	29
	187	1	61	1	2	2	2	189	188	1	3	10	30
	188	2	59	2	2	2	2	189	187	1	1	10	3
	189	31	89	2	4	1	1	0	0	0	0	10	0
Year 2	186	11	21	1	1	2	2	188	0	2	3	9	29
	187	1	62	1	2	2	1	189	188	1	2	9	30
	188	2	60	2	2	1	1	189	187	1	0	9	0
	189	1	90	2	4	1	1	0	0	0	0	10	0
Year 3	186	1	22	1	1	2	2	188	0	2	3	9	29
	187	31	63	1	2	1	1	189	188	1	0	9	0
	188	31	61	2	2	1	1	189	187	1	0	9	0

Relationship to Household Head	Sex	Marital Status	Economic Status	Generation Number	Occupation Group	Transport Mode to Work
1 = head 2 = spouse 11 = child 31 = parent	1 = male 2 = female	1 = single 2 = married 3 = divorced 4 = widowed	1 = economically inactive 2 = economically active	1 = oldest generation 2 = second oldest generation etc.	1 = managerial and professional 2 = technical and clerical 3 = manual	1 = car 2 = bus 3 = train

In all cases a value of 0 implies no known value.

the demand for travel. When the actions of many households are aggregated the impact of such processes can be determined. The effect of a change in the cost of travel by one mode will be reflected directly by the shift to alternative modes, and indirectly by the effect on the ability of households to purchase dwellings in different locations. The model would be run separately with and without the change in the cost of travel, and the differences would then be interpreted as resulting from the change in the cost of travel.

OPERATIONAL DETAILS

Some of the practical details of the implementation of the model will be considered in this section. The Monte Carlo simulation is carried out using a multiplicative congruence generator that produces a uniformly distributed random number in the range 0.0 to 1.0. The computer programs are written in FORTRAN 77 and implemented on the University of Leeds Amdahl V7A computer.

As discussed above the data for the initial descriptions of individuals and households are taken from 150 households surveyed as part of the Location and Commuting Project at the Institute for Transport Studies. The two major conversion operations carried out on the data were to convert the intra-household links from the relationship to the initial respondent (who was the person who commuted to Central London) to the equivalent for the head of the household, if that was a different person, and to convert the spatial references of home and workplace to the zoning system being used.

The probabilities of birth, dying and changing marital status were taken from tabulations of the Office of Population Censuses and Surveys. The data for the migration and economic activity probabilities were taken from reports produced by Hertfordshire County Council, and the modal choice probabilities based on parameters estimated using a journey-to-work trip matrix also supplied by Hertfordshire County Council, and interzonal generalized costs based on public transport timetables and networks taken from maps. The only other data that needs to be specified to run the model are the number of time periods being considered and an integer in the range 1 to 524287 to start the pseudo-random number generator.

FURTHER DEVELOPMENTS

As mentioned previously, this research is at a preliminary stage, and in the work to date emphasis has been placed on the development of suitable algorithms for the operation of the model and gaining experience of the techniques. The model is being extended to take into account other processes such as job choice, car purchase and other travel decisions. These will include the representation of search behaviour, the acquisition and use of information, learning processes, and, as far as possible, future expectations. These will raise a number of important issues about the sequencing of decisions, for example, whether to search for a new home first or find a new job, and then consider where to live. Similarly, the purchase of a car before moving home may increase the area of dwellings that are considered suitable, but for some people the choice might be between moving home and buying a car. Clearly it is important not to impose a fixed order but to make the sequence itself a function of the characteristics of the decision-maker and the supply-side constraints. Experiments will be carried out on different decision structures, with sensitivity analysis used to examine the significance of the ordering, and the robustness of the model.

The complexity of the interactions between the various processes implies the use of a large data set. In fact emphasis will be placed on the development of an internally consistent model structure rather than statistical estimation of all the parameters. The model will be calibrated against a number of existing data sets, including that collected within the context of the project on South East England and tests made on the validity of the model. There are a number of interesting methodological issues involved in the estimation of spatial choice models that will be considered in defining the probability functions (Lerman, this volume).

In this work the emphasis will be on the role of transport in long-term decision processes. Other work in the field will be drawn upon, for example, on the interaction of labour and housing markets at a regional scale (Clarke, Keys and Williams, 1980) and on the impact of fiscal policies (Orcutt, Glazer, Harris and Wertheimer, 1980), as well as work on the individual components of the decision processes such as residential choice (Young, this volume).

At present the supply side constraints are fairly weak. This is partly because of the small sample being considered: it is hardly realistic to regard 150 households as a self-contained society, from which all marriage partners have to be selected. When a larger population is being represented then there will be pools from which marriage partners, houses and jobs are selected, so that once one has been selected it is not available to others. The pools will be increased by the addition of people no longer married, vacant houses and jobs and so on.

The role of money will be made more explicit, with stronger links between income, housing expenditure, the cost of travel, car purchase, savings and expenditure on other goods. Then feedbacks between the ability to pay for houses and their prices could be introduced, so that if there was an increase in the demand for houses near to the city centre their price would tend to rise and houses further out would become relatively cheaper. Similarly there could be changes in wage levels if insufficient workers of a particular category, for example secretaries, could not be attracted.

It is important that the validity of such a model is assessed. As discussed previously, data on the history of 150 households are available, and so these can be used for comparison with the forecasts from the model. If it is found that there are systematic deviations between the model and the results, perhaps due to the fact that the population of rail commuters has some particular characteristics, some form of tracking mechanism could be introduced; that is, data would be used to adjust the forecasts to be closer to the aggregate patterns of change (Nakamura and Nakamura, 1978).

This model is being developed to examine the impact of increases in the cost of travel. A substantial amount of work on this topic has already been carried out using the Leeds Integrated Land Use-Transport (LILT) model (Mackett, 1983b) and so it will be possible to compare the results from the two approaches, which will lead to some interesting insights into the relationships at different aggregation levels. In the longer run the two models may be integrated, with LILT providing aggregate level constraints on the micro-model.

CONCLUSIONS

This paper has described the development of a micro level model that can be used to represent the effects of increases in transport costs, taking into account the responses of individuals and households. The work is not complete, but in its present state of development it offers scope for experimentation with different behavioural assumptions, and for the introduction of other processes quite easily. The availability of an aggregate model of the equivalent processes offers exciting opportunities for developing a better understanding of the relationships between the impacts of transport cost changes at different aggregation levels.

ACKNOWLEDGEMENTS

This work was sponsored by the Social Science Research Council, UK. The author would like to thank Chew Lan Ong for the computing that she has carried out as part of this work and Martin Clarke for some useful comments.

REFERENCES

Bonsall, P.W., 1982, Microsimulation: Its Application to Car Sharing, Transportation Research A, 16, 421-429.

Burnett, P. and Hanson, S., 1982, The Analysis of Travel as an Example of Complex Human Behaviour in Spatially-Constrained Situations: Definition and Measurement Issues, Transportation Research A, 16, 87-102.

Chapin, F.S., 1968, Activity Systems and Urban Structure: A Working Scheme, Journal of the American Institute of Planners, 34, 11-18.

Clarke, M., 1981, A First Principles Approach to Modelling Socio-Economic Interdependence Using Micro-Simulation, Computers, Environment and Urban Systems, 6, 211-227.

Clarke, M., Keys, P. and Williams, H.C.W.L., 1980, Microsimulation in Socio-Economic and Public Policy Analysis, in Voogd, H. (Ed.) Strategic Planning in a Dynamic Society, Delftsche Uitgevers Maatschappij, B.F., Delft, The Netherlands, 115-125.

Hagerstrand, T., 1970, What about People in Regional Science?, Papers and Proceedings of the Regional Science Association, 24, 7-21.

Kreibich, V., 1979, Modelling Car Availability, Modal Split and Trip Distribution by Monte Carlo Simulation: A Short Way to Integrated Models, Transportation, 8, 153-166.

Lerman, S.R., 1984, Random Utility Models of Spatial Choice, this volume.

Mackett, R.L., 1983a, The Inter-Relationships between Travel and Locational Decisions, in Carpenter, S.M. and Jones, P.M., (Eds.), Recent Advances in Travel Demand Analysis, Gower, London, 79-92.

Mackett, R.L., 1983b, The Leeds Integrated Land Use-Transport Model (LILT), Supplementary Report 805, Transport and Road Research Laboratory, Crowthorne, UK.

Mackett, R.L. and Ong, C.L., 1981, A Computer Simulation Game of the Locational Decision Process, Computers, Environment and Urban Systems, 6, 183-192.

Nakamura, A. and Nakamura, M., 1978, On Microanalytic Simulation and its Applications in Population Projection, Journal of the Operational Research Society, 29, 349-360.

Orcutt, G.H., Glazer, A., Harris, R. and Wertheimer, R., 1980, Microanalytic Modelling and the Analysis of Public Transfer Policies, in Haveman, R.H. and Hollenback, K., (Eds.), Microeconomic Simulation Models for Public Policy Analysis, Acadamic Press, New York, 81-106.

Orcutt, G.H., Greenberger, M., Korbel, J. and Rivlin, A.M., 1961, Microanalysis of Socioeconomic Systems: A Simulation Study, Harper and Row, New York.

Van der Hoorn, T., 1979, Travel Behaviour and the Total Activity Pattern, Transportration, 8, 309-328.

Wegener, M., 1983, The Dortmund Housing Market Model: A Monte Carlo Simulation of a Regional Housing Market, Arbeitspapier No. 7, Institut für Raumplanung, Universität Dortmund, Dortmund, West Germany.

Williams, H.C.W.L., 1981, Microsimulation in Location, Travel and Activity Analysis, a paper presented at the conference on Travel Demand Analysis: Activity-Based and Other New Approaches, University of Oxford, Oxford, UK.

Wilson, A.G. and Pownall, C.E., 1976, A New Representation of the Urban System for Modelling and for the Study of Micro-Level Interdependence, Area, 8, 246-254.

Young, W., 1984, The Application of an Elimination-by-Aspects Model to Urban Location Decisions, this volume.

Zimmerman, C.A., 1982, The Life Cycle Concept as a Tool for Travel Research, Transportation, 11, 51-69.

CONTINGENCY TABLE ANALYSIS AND URBAN TRAVEL ACCOUNTS

Bruce Hutchinson
Department of Civil Engineering
University of Waterloo
Waterloo, Ontario, N2L 3G1
Canada

Abstract. The use of log-linear models of multi-dimensional contingency tables in identifying the fundamental structures of observed travel accounts is described. It is pointed out that existing transport models such as the gravitational and logit families may be considered as special cases of the more general log-linear framework. The approach is illustrated through analyses of the Statistics Canada travel to work survey conducted in the Toronto Census Metropolitan Area in 1978. The approach advocated in the paper will help to bridge the gap between travel models and travel accounts.

TRAVEL ACCOUNTS AND TRAVEL MODELS

The development of transport and other urban models has followed closely the traditional approach used in the physical sciences. Model forms have been generated from various theoretical perspectives and the parameters have been estimated using information extracted from observed travel accounts. With urban systems it is impossible to produce observed travel accounts from which the effects of those factors not included in the model have been excluded through appropriate experimental design. Characteristics of urban residents such as income, household size and composition, car ownerhsip, residential location, transport system service properties and transport mode usage are spatially correlated. Any aggregation of elementary survey records has the potential for introducing spurious variations in an aggregated travel account.

Urban travel models are usually imposed a priori on observed travel accounts and in many cases the structure of the models have not been consistent with the structure of the data in an account. The creation of fallacious or paradoxical effects through the aggregation of data accounts is well known and has been discussed by Robinson (1950), Simpson (1951), Alker (1969), Bishop (1971), Whittemore (1978) and Kotzke (1982).

LOG-LINEAR MODELS

Consider a three dimensional account of trips to work which is cross-classified by origin of trip, destination of trip and mode of travel. The symbols O, D and M are used to identify the classificatory variables and the subscripts i, j and k are used to identify respectively the categories of each of these variables. Log-linear models represent expected cell frequencies as a linear combination of effects, where a saturated log-linear model of the data in the account

$$\ell n\, m_{ijk} = u + u_i^{O} + u_j^{D} + u_k^{M} + u_{ij}^{OD} + u_{ik}^{OM} + u_{jk}^{DM} + u_{ijk}^{ODM} \qquad (1)$$

where m_{ijk} = the expected number of trips in cell (i,j,k) estimated from a model of the travel accounts and the other terms are described in the following paragraphs.

The terms of eqn. (1) reflect the variations around some overall mean value that are induced by the various effects contained in the equation and these may be interpreted in the following way

1. the overall mean effect u which reflects the overall intensity of trip making with respect to the zone system used;
2. the main effects u_i^O, u_j^D and u_k^M which reflect the differences in cell magnitudes induced respectively by differences in origin zone size, differences in destination zone size and the aggregate differences in mode usage;
3. the two-way effects u_{ij}^{OD}, u_{ik}^{OM} and u_{jk}^{DM} which reflect the differences in cell magnitudes that are induced by deviations from the main effects, where for example, the first term represents differences in the average unit rate of spatial interaction between zones and the second term differences in transport mode choice due to the characteristics of the origin zones; and
4. the three-way effect u_{ijk}^{ODM} which reflects the impacts on trip flows of specific mode choice effects between pairs of origin and destination zones.

Eqn. (1) is known as a saturated model since it has a number of independent parameters equal to the number of cells in the account and allows, therefore, the cell entries in an account to be estimated exactly. Reduced forms of the log-linear model are usually of more interest since simpler model structures with some compromise in explanatory power are more preferable for forecasting. The following section outlines the strategy for exploring alternative model forms.

Table 1 illustrates the way in which the magnitude of each of these parameters may be estimated along with the constraints imposed on these parameters. Clearly, log-linear models provide a representation of a data account in a manner analagous to the analysis of variance paradigm. Unlike analysis of variance one is not exploring the relationship between a dependent variable and a variety of independent variables, but rather the inter-relationship between the attributes used to cross-classify the members of a population, which in this case are trips.

TABLE 1

ESTIMATION PROCEDURES FOR PARAMETERS OF SATURATED MODELS

$$u = \frac{1}{IJK} \sum_{i,j,k} \ell n\ m_{ijk} \qquad i = 1,\ldots, I;\ j = 1,\ldots, J;\ k - 1,\ldots, K \qquad (3)$$

$$u_i^O = \frac{1}{JK} \sum_{j,k} \ell n\ m_{ij} - u \qquad (4)$$

where u_j^D and u_k^C derived similarly

$$u_{ij}^{OD} = \frac{1}{K} \sum_{k} \ell n\ m_{ijk} - (u + u_i^A + u_j^B + u_k^C) \qquad (5)$$

with u_{ik}^{OM} and u_{jk}^{DM} derived similarly

$$u_{ijk}^{ODM} = n\ m_{ijk} - (u + u_i^O u_j^D + u_k^M + u_{ij}^{OD} + u_{ik}^{OM} + u_{jk}^{DM} \qquad (6)$$

with the following constraints

$$\sum_i u_i^O = \sum_j u_j^D = \sum_k u_k^M \qquad (7)$$

$$\sum_i u_{ij}^{OD} = \sum_j u_{ij}^{OD} = \sum_i u_{ik}^{OM} = \sum_k u_{ik}^{OM} = \sum_j u_{jk}^{DM} = \sum_k u_{jk}^{DM} = 0 \qquad (8)$$

$$\sum_i u_{ijk}^{ODM} = \sum_j i_{ijk}^{ODM} = \sum_k u_{ijk}^{ODM} = 0 \qquad (9)$$

This paper discusses only hierarchial models which means that for higher order terms to exist, all of the lower order terms that are subsets of this term must also exist. For example, the two- and three-way interaction terms involving the mode variable M could not exist if the main effect term involving M did not exist. With hierarchical models the model structure may be represented by a simplified notation. For example, the saturated model of eqn. (1) may be represented by [ODM] which implies that all two-way and main effects involving the three variables also exist. A notation [O,DM] would mean that the three main effects exist along with only one of the two-way effects. The relation between log-linear models of contingency tables and other techniques for establishing structural models of discrete data is described by Manski (1981).

Estimation of Cell Entries

Bishop, Fienberg and Holland (1975) show that maximum likelihood estimates of the elementary cell counts may be determined from sufficient statistics which are various marginal sums of an account. They also point out that direct estimates of the cell counts may be obtained whenever there are only two marginals, and in a limited number of cases when there are more than two. Maximum likelihood estimates of the cell counts can always be obtained from iterative proportional fitting to the sufficient statistics using the Deming-

Stephan algorithm. The sufficient marginal statistics required to represent the structure of observed travel accounts may be identified by a sequential step-wise evaluation of alternative model structures. The approach is described later in this paper.

Inadequacy of Fit Statistic

A most appropriate inadequacy of fit measure is the likelihood ratio chi-square, which for the two-dimensional case is given by

$$G^2 = 2 \sum_{ij}\sum x_{ij} \; \ell n(x_{ij}/m_{ij}) \tag{2}$$

where x_{ij} = the observed number of trips in cell (i,j).

One of the useful properties of this measure is that it is additive under partitioning for hierarchial models. Consider the models [O,D,M] and [O,DM] where the difference in G^2 between the two models is a test of the additional effects captured by [O,DM] conditional on the effects in [O,D,M]. Smith and Hutchinson (1981) have discussed the behaviour of this statistic for gravitational distribution models. Both the likelihood statistic G and the difference in G^2 are asymptotically distributed as chi-square.

TRAVEL SURVEY DATA SET

The data set used in this paper was collected during the Statistics Canada Travel to Work Survey which is conducted each November as a supplement to the Labour Force Survey. The travel survey was administered to five-sixths of the labour force survey sample of approximately 56,000 households throughout Canada. Respondents were Canadian residents 15 years or older who were employed during the week prior to the survey, which in this case was in November 1978. A detailed description of the survey methodology may be found in Statistics Canada (1979).

The data set collected for the Toronto CMA was used for the analyses described in this paper. Complete records for 1971 individuals were available after screening the initial 2800 records to eliminate those with missing data. Preliminary analyses of the data set yielded the six-way classification of trips counts shown in Table 2 where the dimensions are mode of transport (M), sex of trip maker (S), availability of other modes of transport (O), the dwelling unit type of the tripmaker (T), the parking charge (P) for those using the automobile mode, and the distance travelled to work (D). While the data are not coded spatially, the data set is adequate for illustrating the mechanics of the approach.

TABLE 2

SIX-WAY CLASSIFICATION OF TORONTO TRAVEL TO WORK DATA

0 = Yes								
M	S	T	P	D(km)				Total
				1	2	3	4	
		Single	< $2	0	2	13	4	19
			> $2	0	2	3	5	10
			Free	40	71	87	40	238
			NA	0	0	0	0	0
		Total		40	75	103	49	267
	Male	Double	< $2	0	1	2	0	3
			> $2	0	0	1	0	1
			Free	11	21	37	14	83
			Na	0	0	0	0	0
		Total		11	22	40	14	87
		Other	< $2	3	1	6	3	13
			> $2	0	1	0	0	1
			Free	31	50	61	45	187
			NA	0	0	0	0	0
Auto		Total		34	52	67	48	201
		Single	< $2	0	4	3	10	17
			> $2	0	1	1	1	3
			Free	32	46	41	10	129
			NA	1	0	0	0	1
		Total		33	51	45	21	150
	Female	Double	< $2	1	1	2	0	4
			> $2	0	0	0	0	0
			Free	5	14	15	5	39
			NA	0	0	0	0	0
		Total		6	15	17	5	43
		Other	< $2	1	8	4	5	18
			> $2	0	2	1	0	3
			Free	16	27	31	10	84
			NA	0	0	0	0	0
		Total		17	37	36	15	105
		Single	< $2	0	3	3	6	12
			> $2	0	2	7	9	18
			Free	1	2	2	6	11
			NA	0	0	2	0	2
		Total		1	7	14	21	43
	Male	Double	< $2	0	0	0	0	0
			> $2	1	0	0	2	3
			Free	1	1	2	3	7
			NA	0	0	1	0	1
		Total		2	1	3	5	11

TABLE 2
(continued)

M	S	T	P	D(km) 1	2	3	4	Total
0 = Yes								
		Other	< $2	2	1	5	0	8
			> $2	0	5	2	3	10
			Free	0	5	4	0	9
			NA	0	0	0	0	0
Transit		Total		2	11	11	3	27
		Single	< $2	0	1	1	1	3
			> $2	0	1	2	1	4
			Free	1	1	1	3	6
			NA	2	0	0	0	2
		Total		3	3	4	5	15
	Female	Double	< $2	0	1	0	0	1
			> $2	0	3	1	2	6
			Free	0	2	2	1	5
			NA	0	0	0	0	0
		Total		0	6	3	3	12
		Other	< $2	0	2	2	1	5
			> $2	4	5	3	3	15
			Free	2	1	6	4	13
			NA	0	0	0	0	0
		Total		6	8	11	8	33
0 = No								
		Single	< $2	0	0	1	0	1
			> $2	0	0	1	0	1
			Free	17	25	39	80	161
			NA	0	0	0	0	0
		Total		17	25	41	80	163
	Male	Double	< $2	0	0	0	0	0
			> $2	0	0	0	0	0
			Free	7	8	9	19	43
			NA	0	0	0	0	0
		Total		7	8	9	19	43
		Other	< $2	0	0	2	3	5
			> $2	0	1	0	0	1
			Free	10	7	25	34	76
			NA	0	0	0	0	0
Auto		Total		10	8	27	37	82
		Single	< $2	0	1	0	1	2
			> $2	0	0	0	0	0
			Free	23	14	15	17	69
			NA	0	0	0	0	0
		Total		23	15	15	18	71

TABLE 2
(continued)

0 = No

M	S	T	P	D(km) 1	2	3	4	Total
	Female	Double	< $2	0	0	0	0	0
			> $2	0	0	0	0	0
			Free	5	5	2	4	16
			NA	0	0	0	0	0
		Total		5	5	2	4	16
		Other	< $2	1	0	1	0	2
			> $2	0	0	0	0	0
			Free	12	4	9	13	38
			NA	0	0	0	0	0
		Total		13	4	10	13	40
		Single	< $2	2	0	8	6	16
			> $2	1	2	3	1	7
			Free	2	8	6	4	20
			NA	0	0	0	0	0
		Total		5	10	17	11	43
	Male	Double	< $2	1	1	5	0	7
			> $2	0	5	5	2	12
			Free	2	5	4	0	11
			NA	0	0	0	0	0
		Total		3	11	14	2	30
		Other	< $2	2	7	5	0	14
			> $2	7	7	14	6	34
			Free	11	15	10	7	43
			NA	0	1	0	0	1
		Total		20	30	29	13	92
Transit								
		Single	< $2	4	2	12	0	18
			> $2	4	14	20	6	44
			Free	11	12	21	9	53
			Na	0	2	1	1	4
		Total		19	30	54	16	119
	Female	Double	< $2	1	5	1	3	10
			> $2	3	18	10	6	37
			Free	4	13	6	3	26
			NA	0	0	2	0	2
		Total		8	36	19	12	75
		Other	< $2	7	8	14	8	37
			> $2	12	24	28	14	78
			Free	11	29	31	16	87
			NA	0	1	0	0	1
		Total		30	62	73	38	203

EXPLORING ALTERNATIVE MODEL FORMS

A number of standard computer programs exist for estimating and evaluating alternative log-linear models of data accounts and the program on which the analyses described in this paper are based is BMDP 4F (Brown 1981). This program allows alternative log-linear models to be built and evaluated in a step-wise manner. The strategy used for model building is that suggested by Brown (1976) and Benedetti and Brown (1978) which uses tests of partial association and of marginal association.

The test of partial association examines the difference in fit of a model of a given order and the same model excluding a given term of the model. For example, the significance of the term OD may be tested by examing the change in fit between [OD,OM,DM] and [OM,DM]. Relevant model terms are identified through differences in the likelihood ratio statistics that are significant.

The test of marginal association examines whether a particular interaction is zero in a table formed by the factors contained in the interaction. For example, the interaction OD may be tested by examining the difference in fit between the models [OD] and [O,D] on the original frequency table. Benedetti and Brown (1978) point out that the marginal association test is really an unconditional test of interaction since it ignores the effect of the other variables. When the inadequacy of fit statistic is non-significant the model provides an adequate fit to the observed table.

Brown (1976) suggests that both statistics should be used to develop model structures. If both statistics are large then the particular interaction is required in the model.

The step-wise development of alternative hierarchical log-linear models allows the trade-off between model goodness of fit and model parsimony to be considered explicitly. Model parsimony is an important criterion if model structures developed from the analysis of existing travel accounts are to be used to forecast future accounts. It should be recalled that forecasting involves the specification of the sufficient marginal distributions and the use of multi-proportional adjustment techniques to establish cell magnitudes.

ANALYSIS OF TRAVEL TO WORK DATA

The six-way classification of the travel account analyzed in this paper has been illustrated in Table 2. Since the travel account is derived from a sample of trip makers throughout the Toronto CMA it is important to develop a broad appreciation of the characteristics reflected in the account. There are 1268 auto trips in the sample versus 703 trips by transit; 994 of the trip makers indicated that they had a choice of modes, while 977 perceived that they were captives of one of the modes; 1089 of the trip makers were male and

882 were female; 871 lived in single family dwellings, 317 lived in double units while 783 lived in higher density forms of housing. Finally, about 74% of the trip makers had free parking available, about 11% paid less than $2 per day and about 15% paid more than $2 per day.

With a six-way table there are thousands of hierarchical log-linear models that could be developed. The first step is to reduce the number of options by identifying potentially relevant terms using the tests of partial and marginal association. The second step is to select an appropriate starting model and to test the change in the inadequacy of fit statistic as terms are added to the starting model. An alternative approach is to begin with a saturated model and to delete terms from this model. With the forward stepping approach all possible hierarchial models that are included in a current model and differ from it by one term only are tested and the most significant effect is added to the model.

This step-wise approach was used in the analysis of the account in Table 2. A large number of alternative equations were tested and the early stages of the analysis suggested that separate model forms should be developed for each of the two other mode available (yes/no) strata.

Table 3 shows the relevant model forms estimated and evaluated for the other mode available stratum where the base model form shown is that for the first two-way interaction term. The second step in the model sequence is for the addition of S (sex) to the base model which reduces the inadequacy of fit statistic to 511.41 - 71.69 = 439.72. The right-hand column of Table 3 demonstrates that the probability that this difference could have arisen from chance causes is close to zero which is also the case for the model [MP,S]. The effects of the systematic addition of higher order terms is illustrated in Table 3. The last step illustrated in Table 3 indicates that while the addition MT is significant, the model [MP,PS,MT] is not significant since the probability of 0.0699 is greater than the conventional magnitude of 0.05. The evidence presented in Table 3 suggests that the most appropriate model form is [MP,PS,T] although [MP,S,T] represents the best trade-off between model parsimony and inadequacy of fit.

Table 4 summarizes the sequence of models developed for the alternative mode unavailable stratum. The information presented in this table indicates that a much more complex model form is required to represent the structure of the data in the mode unavailable account. The last equation in the table indicates that four two-way interaction terms are required to represent the account.

An inspection of the travel account in Table 2 indicates that the number of trip records with parking not available is very small. In addition, a detailed analysis of the coded records suggested that there were some coding difficulties with this question since there are virtually no employment locations within the Toronto CMA where parking is unavailable. These records were deleted from the two strata and the analysis repeated.

TABLE 3

STEPWISE MODEL ASSESSMENT FOR OTHER MODE AVAILABLE STRATUM

Model	G^2	DF	Probability
[MP]	511.41	184	0.0
[MP,S]	439.72	183	0.0
adding S	71.69	1	0.0
[MP,S,T]	279.06	181	0.0
adding T	160.66	2	0.0
[MP,PS,T]	267.20	178	0.008
adding PS	11.84	3	0.0
[MP,PS,MT]	261.88	176	0.0699
adding MT	5.32	2	0.0

TABLE 4

STEPWISE MODEL ASSESSMENT FOR OTHER MODE UNAVAILABLE STRATUM

Model	G^2	DF	Probability
[MP]	627.83	124	0.0
[MP,D]	581.94	181	0.0
adding D	45.94	3	0.0
[MP,D,S]	577.22	180	0.0
adding S	4.72	1	0.0
[MP,D,MS]	434.27	179	0.0
adding MS	142.95	1	0.0
[MP,D,MS,T]	312.16	177	0.0
adding T	122.11	2	0.0
[MP,D,MS,MT]	240.88	175	0.0
adding MT	71.28	2	0.0007
[MP,DS,MS,MT]	208.00	172	0.0
adding DS	32.88	3	0.0

Table 5 summarizes the sequence of equations developed for the other mode available stratum. The most appropriate model suggested by this analysis is [MP,S,T,D]. The distance to work variable has been added to the basic model form identified for the analyses summarized in Table 3.

TABLE 5

STEPWISE MODEL ASSESSMENT FOR OTHER MODE AVAILABLE STRATUM WITH PARKING NOT AVAILABLE DELETED

Model	G^2	DF	Probability
[MP]	502.65	138	0.0
[MP,S]	428.86	137	0.0
adding S	73.77	1	0.0
[MP,S,T]	266.07	135	0.0
adding T	162.79	2	0.0
[Mp,S,T,D]	174.54	132	0.0008
adding D	91.53	3	0.0078
[MP,MS,T,D]	169.94	131	0.0125
adding MS	4.39	3	0.0317
[MP,MS,MT,D]	164.24	129	0.0196
adding MT	5.71	2	0.0576
[MP,MS,MT,DS]	153.86	126	0.0463
adding DS	10.38	3	0.0156

Table 6 illustrates the sequence of equations developed for the other mode unavailable stratum. This table indicates that a five or six two-way interaction model is required to represent the structure of the data in the account Once again the distance variable assumes a much more important role; in this case, in the form of three two-way interaction terms involving distance.

TABLE 6

STEPWISE MODEL ASSESSMENT FOR OTHER MODE AVAILABLE STRATUM WITH PARKING NOT AVAILABLE DELETED

Model	G^2	DF	Probability
[MP]	619.09	138	0.0
[MP,S]	615.03	137	0.0
adding S	4.06	1	0.0
[MP,MS]	471.50	136	0.0
adding MS	143.51	1	0.0
[MP,MS,T]	346.10	134	0.0
adding T	125.40	2	0.0
[MP,MS,T,D]	300.43	141	0.0
adding D	45.67	3	0.0
[MP,MS,MT,D]	226.17	129	0.0
adding MT	74.26	2	0.0
[MP,MS,MT,DS]	192.55	126	0.0
adding DS	33.62	3	0.00001
[MP,MS,MT,DS,DP]	164.68	120	0.0043
adding DP	14.98	6	0.0001
[MP,MS,MT,DS,DP,DT]	149.71	114	0.0140
adding DT	40.13	3	0.0

Interpretation of Model Structures

The mode available analyses suggested model forms of [MP,S,T] or [MP,S,T,D]. These models indicate that the sufficient statistics consist of a bivariate marginal relating mode choice to parking charges for all trip makers along with two (or three) univariate marginals. The univariate marginals indicate that mode choice mechanism is independent of sex, dwelling unit type and distance to work. They simply scale the choice structures to the appropriate magnitude for the region.

The mode unavailable stratum analyses suggested model forms of [MP,DS,MS, MT] and [MP,DS,MS,MT,DT]. These model forms indicate that mode choice is influenced not only by parking charges but also by sex and dwelling unit type and that there are interactions between these variables and distance.

In interpreting the above model forms it is useful to distinguish between individual characteristics (sex), transport system characteristics (parking charges and distance to work) and urban structural characteristics (dwelling unit type and distance). While parking charges are normally thought of as a transport system variable, they represent, in the case of the Toronto CMA, a measure of urban structure since significant parking charges are levied only in the central business district area. The dominant theme suggested by the above analyses is the over-riding importance of urban structure on modal choice.

Relation to Existing Travel Models

The essence of the log-linear approach is the derivation of elementary cell entries from the adjustment of a starting matrix to the sufficient marginal distributions. The starting matrix normally consists of ones, except in any cells that are structural zeros. Existing distribution models use a similar approach where an initial matrix is adjusted by bi-proportional balancing techniques to specified origin and destination trip ends using a technique developed by Bacharach (1970) for input-output tables.

The Fratar growth factor method adjusts an observed base year trip matrix to the estimated horizon year trip ends using the bi-proportional algorithm. Evans and Kirby (1974) have noted the connection between the doubly constrained maximum entropy gravity model and Bacharach's bi-proportional adjustment procedure. A starting matrix of inter-zonal travel deterrence measures is adjusted bi-proportionally to the forecast trip ends. Evans and Kirby have also suggested an alternative form of the doubly constrained gravity model in which a trip matrix is estimated which is tri-proportional to trip origins, trip destinations and an area-wide trip cost distribution. Willekens (1981) has pointed out that existing trip distribution models may be viewed as part of the family of log-linear models.

It is well known that the logit model is a special case of a log-linear model in which one variable is dichotomous and is treated as the dependent variable, Bishop (1969), Manski (1981). Swafford (1980) points out that the coefficients of a logit model may be obtained from an appropriate log-linear model by doubling the coefficients of those terms in the log-linear model which involve the dependent variable and disregarding the others.

CONCLUDING REMARKS

Calibrated transport models forecast travel behaviour which reflects information obtained from travel surveys as well as information contributed by the logical structure of the model imposed on the data account. The difficulty with this approach is that the richness of the information contained in observed travel accounts is compromised when the few parameters of the models are estimated from an account.

The log-linear modelling framework offers a relatively neutral way of understanding the structure of observed travel accounts. Parsimonious model structures may be developed which are morphologically consistent with observed accounts. The log-linear approach attempts to integrate the individual behavioural perspective with the ecological perspective of aggregate models.

An important advantage of the log-linear approach to data analysis is that existing multinomial models, such as the gravitational and logit models, are special cases of the log-linear framework.

REFERENCES

Alker, H.R., 1969, A Typology of Ecological Fallacies. In M. Dogan and S. Rokkan (Eds.) Qualitative Ecological Analysis in the Social Sciences, The MIT Press, Cambridge, MA.

Bacharach, M., 1970, Biproportional Matrices and Input-Output Change, Cambridge University Press, London.

Benedetti, J.K. and Brown, M.B., 1978, Strategies for the Selection of Log-Linear Models, Biometrics, 34, 680-686

Bishop, Y.M.M., 1971, Effects of Collapsing Multidimensional Contingency Tables, Biometrics, 27, 545-562.

Bishop, Y.M.M., Fienberg, S.E. and Holland, P.W., 1975, Discrete Multivariate Analysis : Theory and Practice, MIT Press, Cambridge, MA.

Brown, M.B., 1976, Screening Effects in Multidimensional Contingency Tables, Applied Statistics, 25, 37-46.

Brown, M.B., 1981, BMDP 4F Two-Way and Multiway Frequency Tables - Measures of Assocation and the Log-Linear Model, in Dixon, W.J. (Ed.) BMDP Statistical Software 1981, University of California Press, 143-206.

Evans, S.P. and Kirby, H.R., 1974, A Three-Dimensional Furness Procedure for Calibrating Models, Transportation Research, 8, 105-122.

Kotze, T.J.V.W., 1982, The Log-Linear Model and Its Application to Multi-Way Contingency Tables, in Hawkins, D.M. (Ed.) Topics in Applied Multi-variate Analysis, Cambridge University Press, 142-182.

Manski, C.F., 1981, Structural Models for Discrete Data: The Analysis of Discrete Choice, in Leinhardt, S. (Ed.) Sociological Methodology, Jossery Bass, San Francisco, CA.

Robinson, W.S., 1950, Ecological Correlations and the Behavior of Individuals, American Sociological Review, 15, 351-357.

Simpson, E.H., 1951, The Interpretation of Interaction in Contingency Tables, Journal Royal Statistical Society, B, 13, 238-241.

Smith, D.P., and Hutchinson, B.G., 1981, Goodness of Fit Statistics for Trip Distribution Models, Transportation Research, 15A, 295-303.

Statistics Canada, 1979, Culture Statistics: Travel to Work 1973-1977, Ministry of Industry, Trade and Commerce, Ottawa, Canada.

Swafford, M., 1980, Three Parametric Techniques for Contingency Table Analysis: A Nontechnical Commentary, American Sociological Review, 45, 664-690.

Whittemore, A.S., 1978, Collapsibility of Multidimensional Contingency Tables, Journal Royal Statistical Society, B, 40, 328-340.

Willikens, F. (1981). Multi-Dimensional Population Analysis with Incomplete Data, WP 20, Netherlands Interuniversity Demographic Institute, Voorburg, The Netherlands.

TRANSPORT IMPACTS OF CHANGING HOUSEHOLD STRUCTURE

Neil Monkman
Regional Municipality of Ottawa-Carleton
Ottawa, Ontario K1P 5Z3
and
John Shortreed
Department of Civil Engineering
University of Waterloo
Waterloo, Ontario N2L 3G1
Canada

Abstract. Extensive time series transport and land use data for Montreal are available for 1970, 1974 and 1978. A log-linear model was used to model household structure over time in order to isolate the effects of household structure on transit ridership from other effects which included new subway lines. The data were also used to test the performance of the log-linear model in forecasting household structure for future time periods. The changes in transit ridership in Montreal from 1970 to 1978 were due both to changes in household structure and to changes in transit trip making because of improved levels of transit service. The log-linear formulation was very useful in decoupling these effects.

INTRODUCTION

The growing availability of extensive transport data and the development of new techniques for data analysis provide an opportunity to address critical issues in urban transportation. In this paper the log-linear model which has been used extensively to understand travel behaviour (Hutchinson, this volume) is extended to explore its use as a forecasting tool for the short-term policy analysis of urban transit systems. The urban transit policy issues are introduced first, then the log-linear model is estimated and used to forecast transit trips for the City of Montreal.

The dramatic shifts in household structure in the recent past and its impact on transit ridership have been identified by Shortreed (1980). Fig. 1 illustrates the changes in persons per dwelling unit in Canada during this period. It was estimated that in this period most of the rapid decline in transit productivity (ie., passenger-km/bus-km) was due to the decline in household size. Transit ridership also responds to car ownership as well as household size and this is illustrated in Fig. 2. Fig. 2 shows the relative transit trip rates per household with changing household size and car ownership. Plotted points are relative to an arbitrary value of 1.0 for 1 car, 2 person households. While the relative consistency between cities of the data in Fig. 2 is of interest it is the linearity of the relationships between transit ridership and persons per dwelling unit that is of most interest. Given the level of car ownership the transit ridership is almost proportional to household size. In Fig. 2 there is a slight non-linearity at the level of 4 and 5 person households which is probably due to families with younger children. Further disaggregation of households to include age of head of household should provide more information on this non-linearity.

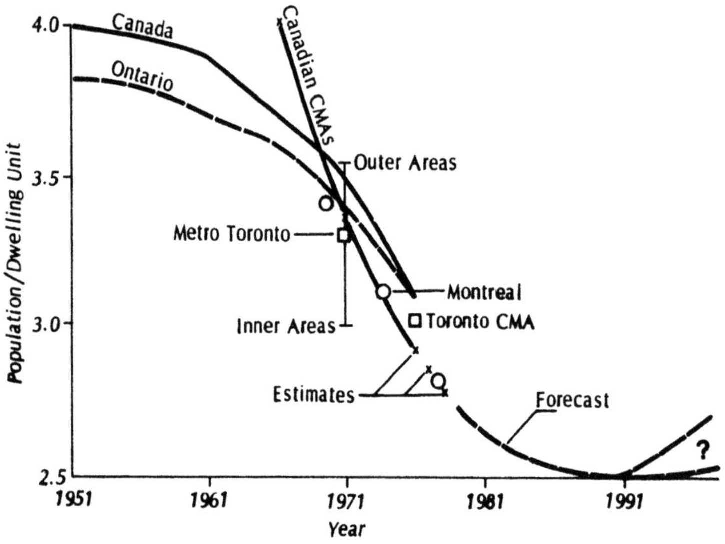

Source: Shortreed (1980)

Figure 1 - Changes in Persons per Dwelling Unit in Canada 1951

The impacts of changing household structure and the effect on transit ridership illustrated in Figs. 1 and 2 are clearly of considerable importance to transit authorities as they have a direct and significant impact on their revenues. The changes in household structure have been studied by the Toronto Transit Commission (1981), Miron (1979) and Hutchinson (1981) with a view to understanding these changes. Miron (1979) identified three main reasons for the changes observed in Toronto from 1951-1976 and these are (i) the maturing of the baby boom; (ii) the increasing tendency for families to maintain their own household; and (iii) the increasing tendency for non-married individuals to reside on their own. The report of the Toronto Transit Commission (1981) indicated that the trend to smaller households would continue until 2001, with the household size dropping from 3.1 persons per household to 2.7 persons per household.

The purpose of the study described in this paper was to explore methods of forecasting the changes in household structure and using these forecasts for predicting the impact on transit ridership. Moreover it was very desirable to predict changes in transit ridership on a geographical basis for the transit authority's planning activity.

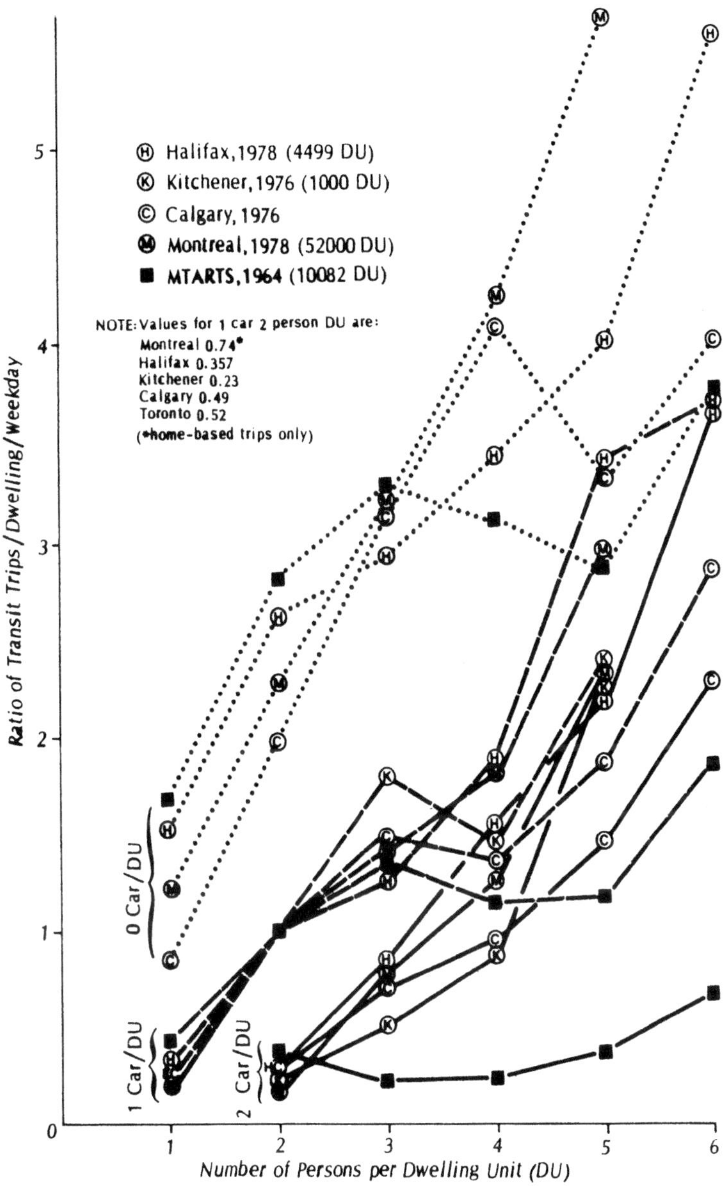

Source: Shortreed (1980)

Note: values for 1 car, 2 person DU are: Montreal .74 (home based trips only), Halifax 0.357, Kitchener 0.23, Calgary 0.49 and Toronto 0.52

Figure 2 - Relative Transit Ridership per Dwelling Unit

Travel behaviour forecasting models have shown considerable improvement by disaggregating them by households into life-cycle groups as shown by Clarke (1981), Kostyniuk and Kitamura (1981) and Solomon and Ben-Akiva (1982). These authors all reported an improvement in model performance with a consideration of household structure but they did not include any spatial disaggregaton.

On the other hand, the traditional gravity and Lowry models incorporate spatial effects but do not generally include household characteristics. Typically households are stratified by income, car ownership, occupation of head, etc. Andreassen (1973) predicted the spatial distribution of households by income, size and age of head of household for Ottawa using contingency table analysis based on forecast total characteristics for Ottawa. However, he did not incorporate car ownership, or interaction terms.

Willekens (1981) used a log-linear model to model migration flows which identified some population characteristics on a spatial basis. He also demonstrated the use of prior data for forecasting purposes. Based on Willekens results and others (Manski, 1981; Fingleton, 1981) as well as a review of model requirements, the log-linear model was selected to explore if it could be used to predict future shifts in household structure on a spatial basis.

THE STUDY AREA

The Commission de Transport de la Communauté Urbaine de Montréal (CTCUM) as a part of its planning function undertakes a traditional transportation telephone home interview survey every four years. The survey data used was for 1970, 1974 and 1978 with data for 28,000, 43,000 and 52,000 dwellings, representing a 4.0%, 4.7% and 5.3% random sample of the population, respectively. The data were summarized for the 66 sectors shown in Fig. 3.

A dwelling was defined as .... 'a home, usually occupied by a family group with lodgers, etc., or .... group of unrelated persons, of two or more families, or of one person living alone'. For each dwelling the data contained (i) the number of persons; (ii) the number of autos; and (iii) the sex and age (<18, 18-65, >65) of each person. The daily travel data included for home-based trips only, origin sector, destination sector, purpose (work, shop, study, leisure, other) and mode (drive, auto passenger, CTCUM transit, other transit, taxi, train and walk).

The main transport variable of interest in this study was the transit trips for all purposes per dwelling per weekday. Fig. 2 shows the relative trip rates for the whole of the study area for 1978. In Fig. 2 there were 0.78 home based transit trips per day for a 1 car, 2 person dwelling; the corresponding values for 1970 and 1974 are 0.61 and 0.68, thus there is a continued increase in the transit trips per household over the period. The data indicated about an 11 percent increase from 1970 to 1974 and about a 20 percent increase from 1970 to 1978, for similar types of households.

The dwellings, hereafter called households were classified in three dimensions corresponding to the three dimensions of the log-linear model and these are (i) life cycle expressed as the age of oldest household member (3 levels); (ii) household structure expressed as persons per household (5 levels) and cars per household (4 levels) for a total of 20 levels; and (iii) sector, the 66 geographical zones of Montreal.

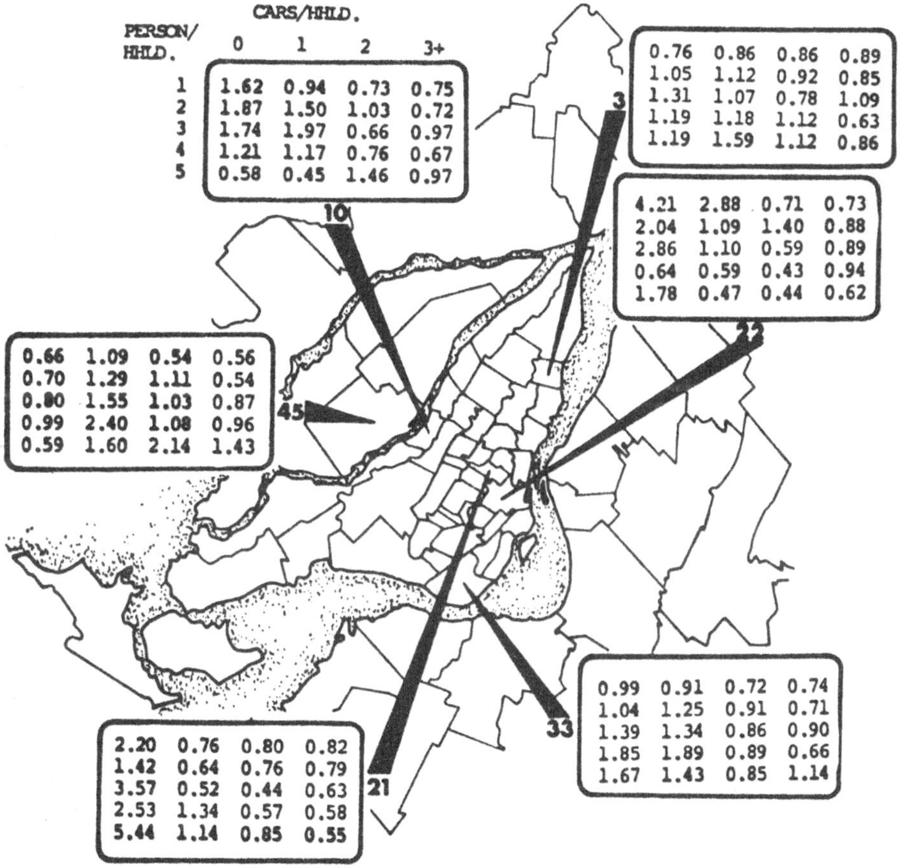

Figure 3 - Selected Log-Linear Household Structure Parameters for Montreal 1970

Over the 1970 to 1978 period average household size fell from 3.40 to 2.86 persons per household. Non-car-owning households fell from 28.4 percent to 25.7 percent and two car households increased from 10.7 percent to 16.6 percent of all households. Total trips per household by all modes, in the study area increased by 3 to 4 percent in the 8 year period.

THE MODEL STRUCTURE

The log-linear model was used in the product form (Birch, 1963). Payne (1977) developed procedures for testing the significance of particular model terms by testing the significant difference between two models, one with and one without the term (Nijkamp, 1983).

Goodness of Fit

Payne (1977) identified the G^2 statistic to test the goodness of fit of a log-linear model. G^2 is interpreted as the unexplained variation in the log of the frequencies (Hutchinson, this volume).

The Model Hierarchical Principle

In searching for a partial model which contains all the significant terms Bishop (1975) recommends that the hierarchical principle be followed to reduce the search for a model to manageable proportions. Using the hierarchial principle the search for possible models is reduced to the following

Model 1 - the overall mean U only,

Model 2 - MUTUAL INDEPENDENCE where there is no interaction between the variables and the model is U, U1, U2, U3,

MODEL 3 - MULTIPLE INDEPENDENCE where two of the three variables interact but they are independent of the third; the model is U, U1, U2, U3 and one of M1, M2, or M3,

MODEL 4 - CONDITIONAL INDEPENDENCE where two of the three possible first order interactive effects are present but the third is absent and thus the second order interaction term is also absent; the model is U, U1, U2, U3 and two of M1, M2, and M3,

MODEL 5 - PAIRWISE ASSOCIATION where all terms but the UU(ijk) are present, and

MODEL 6 - SATURATED where all terms are present.

Model Calibration

Table 1 gives the summary results for all possible heirarchical models for the Montreal households in 1970, 1974 and 1978. Because of the different sample size G^2 varies and it cannot be interpreted directly. The best MODEL 3 for all three years is 3c which includes only M3, the interaction between household structure and sector. For the Conditional Independence model, the best model,

4b, adds the interaction, M1, between age of head and structure. The change in G^2 (eg., for 1970 is 5,440 - 1,280 = 4,160 with 400 degrees of freedom) is significant at the 5 percent level. The partial correlation of model 4b compared to model 36 is .88 for 1970, that is the addition of M1 in model 4b explains 88 percent of the variance unexplained in model 3c.

Model 5 in Table 1 versus model 4b has a partial correlation of .24, .26 and .29 for the three years. This is significant at the 5 percent level using a conditional G^2 test. Model 6 is both less parsimonious than 5 and does not represent a significant improvement over Model 5. Therefore the pairwise association model which includes all the first order interactions was selected as the model which best describes the household allocation for prediction purposes.

TABLE 1

LOG-LINEAR MODEL RESULTS FOR MONTREAL HOUSEHOLDS IN 1970, 1974, 1978

All Entries x 10^{-3}		1970		1974		1978	
Model	Terms Present	G^2	df	G^2	df	G^2	df
1	U	87.84	3.42	125.4	3.96	148.98	3.96
2	U,U1,U2,U3	12.25	3.34	18.92	3.87	23.87	3.87
3a	U,U1,U2,U3,M1	8.10	3.30	11.85	3.84	15.03	3.84
3b	U,U1,U2,U3, M2	11.52	2.28	17.59	3.74	22.23	3.74
3c	U,U1,U2,U3, M3	5.44	2.28	8.89	2.64	10.95	2.64
4a	U,U1,U2,U3,M1,M2	7.36	3.19	10.52	3.71	13.39	3.71
4b	U,U1,U2,U3,M1, M3	1.28	2.24	1.83	2.60	2.11	2.60
4c	U,U1,U2,U3, M2,M3	4.71	2.17	7.57	2.51	9.30	2.51
5	U,U1,U2,U3,M1,M2,M3	0.92	2.13	1.35	2.47	1.51	2.47
6	All	0.0	0	0.0	0	0.0	0
Critical χ^2 for α = 5%		χ^2	df	χ^2	df	χ^2	df
		2.39	2.28	2.76	2.64	2.76	2.64
		2.35	2.24	2.72	2.60	2.72	2.60

TRENDS IN HOUSEHOLD ALLOCATIONS

Besides being used for prediction, the model coefficients can be examined to see how household structure is changing over time. Table 2 presents the main model effects for the three study years. The increase in the overall mean effect from 1.67 to 2.22 represents the absolute increase in the number of households in the study area. For other than the main effect, in the multiplicative formulation, a value of 1.0 has an average allocation while values greater than one reflect more than average number of households. In Table 2 the 18-64 age group not unexpectedly has the largest age effect parameter. However, from 1970 to 1978 the aging of the baby boom with the growth in the seniors group and the decline in the under 18 group is quite evident.

TABLE 2

LOG-LINEAR PARAMETERS FOR THE HOUSEHOLD STRUCTURE MAIN EFFECTS MONTREAL, 1970, 1974, 1978

Overall Mean Effect (U)	1970	1974	1978		
	1.668	1.923	2.223		
Age-of-Head of Household Effect (U1)	Under 18	18 to 64	Over 64		
	0.445	3.945	0.570		
	0.398	4.309	0.584		
	0.367	4.601	0.584		
Household Structure Effect (U2)					
Persons Per Household	Cars Per Household				
	1	2	3	4	5
0	1.886	2.637	1.390	1.103	1.139
	2.426	2.643	1.166	0.848	0.751
	2.732	2.731	1.178	0.688	0.566
1	0.934	3.253	2.573	2.682	3.076
	1.188	4.158	2.589	2.600	2.703
	1.631	4.591	2.873	2.387	1.884
2	0.308	0.692	0.894	0.925	1.196
	0.265	0.817	0.960	1.061	1.399
	0.244	1.002	1.258	1.193	1.193
3+	0.300	0.311	0.388	0.420	0.558
	0.262	0.282	0.385	0.437	0.620
	0.228	0.261	0.391	0.490	0.606

In Table 2 the trends in the household structure parameters over time are consistent with the overall trends in the study area with shifts to smaller households and also shifts to more cars per household. The sector parameters are not shown since they mainly reflect the relative size of the individual sectors. However, the relative growth in the sector parameter over the time period reflects its relative attractivity for households. This attractivity represents both accessibility and availability of land for development. As expected for core sectors such as 28, the sector parameter decreased from 1.06 in 1970 to .93 in 1978, while for suburban sector 7 it increased from 1.16 in 1970 to 1.53 in 1978.

The product of the model parameters gives the estimated number of households. Thus for sector 7 in 1978 the number of 2 person 1 car households with a head between 18 and 64 years is approximately 2.22 x 4.60 x 4.59 x 1.53 or 71.7 households. This is only approximate since the (age-sector), (structure-sector), and (age-structure) interactions must also be included. These values are not shown because of space limitations.

The spatial pattern of household structure is illustrated in Figs. 3 and 4. These are the household structure parameters by sector for a selected sample of sectors for 1970 and 1978. Sectors 21 and 22 are adjacent to the Montreal CBD and the higher propensity for smaller households with lower car ownership is evident. Sectors 3, 10, and 33 are at the terminals of the Montreal Metro rapid transit system. The Metro was just new at this time and comparing 1978 to 1970 the growth in transit oriented households (smaller, no car) is quite evident. Sectors 45 and 58 are suburban sectors off the island of Montreal. As expected they exhibit larger households with higher car ownership.

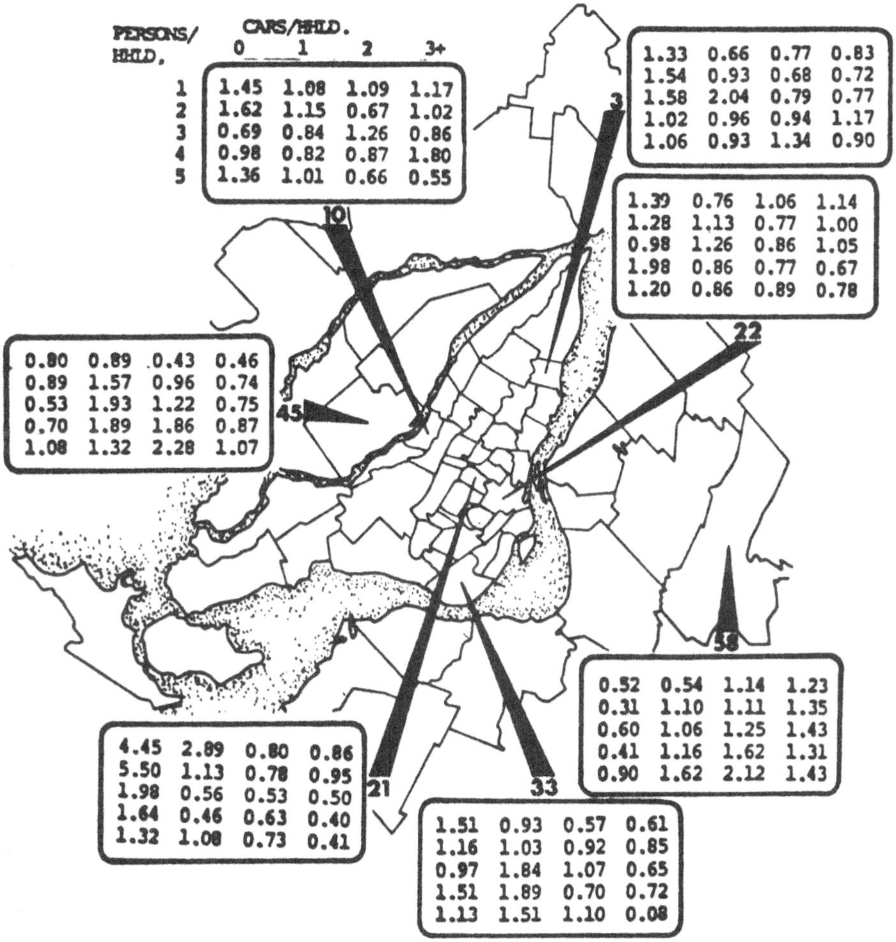

Figure 4 - Selected Log-Linear Household Structure Parameters for Montreal 1978

Figs. 3 and 4 illustrate the differences in household structure with the spatial location of the sector. Visual examination of the log-linear results for all the sectors suggested that they could be aggregated into three groups and these are (i) sectors served by the Metro (inner); (ii) other sectors on the island of Montreal (intermediate); and (iii) sectors off the island of Montreal (outer). It would be desirable to stratify the sectors by a clustering procedure and this will be done in the ongoing research.

Montreal has grown around some self-contained communities such as the City of Laval (sector 45 in Figs. 3 and 4) which exhibited a household structure different to other sectors in a similar spatial location. It appears that the log-linear parameters defining household structure could also be used in the study of community structure.

PREDICTION OF HOUSEHOLD STRUCTURE

Willekens (1981) demonstrated how the log-linear model could be used as a forecasting tool utilizing the ability to incorporate prior information by using previously found interaction parameters. The Montreal time series data were used to test this capability. Following Bishop (1975) the prior information was used to find the Maximum Likelihood Estimate (MLE) by successive balancing of the contingency table. For example, suppose the (household-sector) interaction face is the prior information in Model 3c with the overall mean the age, structure and sector marginals taken as given for the forecast period. Then the MLE for the household allocation is

$$M^{o}_{ijk} = \left(\frac{X_{i..}}{\Sigma X_{i..}}\right)\left(\frac{X_{.j.}}{\Sigma X_{.j.}}\right)\left(\frac{X_{..k}}{\Sigma X_{..k}}\right) M3(j,k) \qquad (1)$$

where M_{ijk} = initial estimate of households in cell i,j,k; and $X_{i..}$ = marginal total for a level of dimension i with summation over j and k dimensions. The initial estimate is balanced to the known marginal totals in a step by step procedure, eg.

$$M^{1}_{ijk} = M^{o}_{ijk} \left(\frac{X_{.jk}}{\sum_i M_{ijk}}\right) \qquad (2)$$

which is continued successively over i,j,k until there is no change in the estimate of Mijk. Willekens (1981) and Bishop (1975) give estimation algorithims for all the heirarchical models for the three dimensional case.

Fig. 5 summarizes the results of the household forecasting analysis. Models 2, 3b, 5 and 6 were estimated for 1978 using prior data from 1974 and 1970. For example, in Fig. 5 the top curve shows the reduction in G^2 as the known 1978 model structure is added; ie., initially Model 2 had the known age, structure and sector main effects; then the (structure-sector) face was added in model 3b then the (age-structure) and (age-sector) faces were added for Model 5; and finally the 2nd order interaction terms were added. This curve is the same as the results illustrated in Table 1. The other curves represent the use of the same 1978 parameters but with the addition of all the interactions from prior data. Thus reading Fig. 5 vertically the improvement in G^2 due to the use of the prior interaction information can be seen. The use of 1974 prior data performs better than the use of 1970 prior data. Also the use of prior interaction terms does make a significant improvement in the amount of variance unexplained by Model 2 in Fig. 5. It is reduced by 59 percent with the use of 1970 prior information and by 76 percent with 1974 prior information.

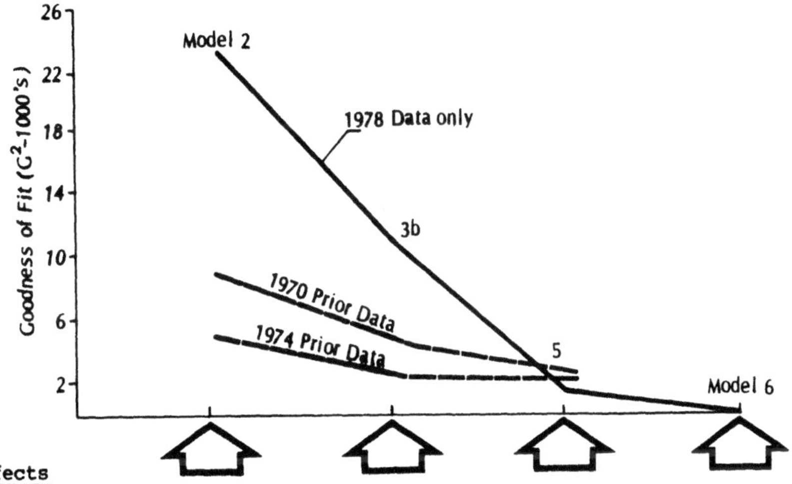

Main Effects				
Age	78	[78]*	78	78
Structure	78	[78]	78	78
Sector	78	[78]	78	78
1st Order Interactions				
Age-Structure	-	-	78	78
	70	70	78	78
	74	74	78	78
Age-Sector	-	-	78	78
	70	70	78	78
	74	74	78	78
Structure-Sector	-	78	78	78
	70	78	78	78
	74	78	78	78
2nd Order Interactions				
	-	-	-	78
	70	70	70	78
	74	74	74	78

*Source of Model Structure (Year) for 3 curves shown

Figure 5 - Unexplained Variance in 1978 Household Allocation versus Use of Prior Data in the Model Structure

Fig. 5 also illustrates the importance of the model significance level. For the Montreal data the pairwise association Model 5 was significant but Model 6 was not. When the prior second order interaction effects were added to the 1978 model, as shown in Fig. 5, they actually reduced the goodness of fit of the model, since they have no explanatory power and act as random variables.

TRANSIT RIDERSHIP PREDICTION

Table 3 presents the transit ridership rates in terms of daily home based transit trips per household for 1970, 1974 and 1978. The data is disaggregated by (i) inner Metro served sectors; (ii) intermediate sectors; and (iii) outer

TABLE 3

HOME BASED TRANSIT TRIPS PER HOUSEHOLD PER WEEKDAY FOR MONTREAL, 1970, 1974, 1978

Persons/ Household	Cars per Household								
	0			1			2		
	Inner Sectors								
	1970	1974	1978	1970	1974	1978	1970	1974	1978
1	0.77	0.84	1.00	0.30	0.41	0.45	0.00	0.00	0.00
2	1.49	1.63	1.84	0.73	0.88	1.00	0.30	0.43	0.46
3	2.19	2.45	2.48	1.12	1.29	1.49	0.70	0.75	1.04
4	2.58	3.04	3.26	1.44	1.73	2.09	1.42	1.57	1.82
5	3.51	3.96	4.31	2.19	2.77	3.22	2.43	2.54	3.04
	Intermediate Sectors								
	1970	1974	1978	1970	1974	1978	1970	1974	1978
1	0.80	0.93	1.04	0.20	0.26	0.28	0.00	0.00	0.17
2	1.55	1.83	1.86	0.69	0.82	0.95	0.18	0.23	0.29
3	2.50	2.90	2.75	1.14	1.27	1.51	0.72	0.77	0.88
4	3.08	3.38	3.80	1.36	1.75	2.12	1.11	1.58	1.77
5	3.86	4.25	5.00	2.36	2.95	3.49	2.06	2.88	3.28
	Other Sectors								
	1970	1974	1978	1970	1974	1978	1970	1974	1978
1	0.37	0.36	0.35	0.09	0.08	0.06	0.00	0.00	0.00
2	0.72	0.92	0.80	0.29	0.29	0.31	0.09	0.11	0.10
3	1.14	1.25	1.27	0.34	0.46	0.45	0.27	0.23	0.26
4	1.57	1.75	1.56	0.38	0.54	0.60	0.42	0.45	0.39
5	1.79	2.14	2.63	0.68	0.89	0.90	0.66	0.91	0.85
	Total Area								
	1970	1974	1978	1970	1974	1978	1970	1974	1978
1	0.74	0.81	0.93	0.23	0.29	0.29	0.00	0.00	0.21
2	1.43	1.59	1.69	0.61	0.68	0.74	0.18	0.22	0.21
3	2.20	2.47	2.40	0.91	0.99	1.07	0.53	0.49	0.58
4	2.64	2.96	3.20	1.06	1.23	1.36	0.88	0.98	0.91
5	3.44	3.80	4.28	1.65	1.98	2.18	1.51	1.69	1.75

sectors, since these areas were found to have common characteristics. The data for the total area is provided for comparison purposes. In the inner and intermediate areas there has been a significant increase in transit trip rates, partly due to extensions of the subway system. It is thought that this effect could be modelled by a logit modal split model as a separate exercise from the forecasts of household allocation.

To evaluate the need to disaggregate the transit trip rates the household allocations were forecast using model 5, then the transit trip rates were applied to the forecast households for each of the four levels shown in Table 4. The resulting total sector transit trips were compared to the observed using the G^2 statistic as shown in Table 4. For practical purposes the disaggregation of trip rates to household structure and two geographic areas of sector location appear to be satisfactory, given the household allocation. Research is continuing into the appropriate combined level of disaggregation for the transit trip rates and the household allocation, given the observed changes in the transit trip rates over time.

TABLE 4

GOODNESS OF FIT FOR PREDICTED versus ACTUAL SECTOR TRANSIT TRIPS BY DISAGGREGATION OF TRANSIT TRIP RATES GIVEN THE ALLOCATION OF HOUSEHOLDS

Level of Disaggregation of Transit Trip Rates	Goodness of Fit G^2 (1000s)		
	1970	1974	1978
1. Household structure . whole study area	13.47	22.70	35.57
2. Household structure . inner and intermediate sectors . outer sectors	5.82	9.13	12.57
3. Household Structure . inner sectors . intermediate sectors . outer sector	5.73	9.00	12.42
4. Household structure . age of head . inner sectors . intermediate sectors . outer sectors	4.50	7.31	9.83

CONCLUSIONS

The distribution of households in Montreal can be modelled by a pairwise association log-linear model with the three main effects of age of head, persons per household and cars per household, and sector, and three interaction faces;

age-structure, age-sector and structure-sector. The interaction between age and sector was significant but had a low partial correlation coefficient and could be omitted. The second order interaction age-structure-sector was not significant.

The use of prior interaction data in the log-linear model with forecast marginals leads to improved prediction of household distribution. Over a four year period the use of prior interactions lead to a 75 percent reduction in the residual variance of the household allocation and over an eight year period a 60 percent reduction. The structure of households in the Montreal area demonstrated considerable change over the eight year period. These changes varied by spatial location of the sector. The log-linear formulation provided a useful vehicle for measuring these changes and the parameters of the model could form a data base for further analysis of changes in the urban structure. Given the forecast of the allocation of households, transit trip rates need only be disaggregated to the level of household structure and two spatial levels, on-island and off-island sectors. After accounting for the changes in household structure, transit usage in Montreal exhibited a growth of about 20 percent overthe 8 year period. Further research using a logit model is recommended to see if this increase can be accounted for by the improved level of service provided by the Metro Subway System. The Montreal data sets provide a very rich source of data on urban structure. The study reported in this paper has really only scratched the surface.

ACKNOWLEDGEMENT

This research was funded by a grant from the Natural Sciences and Engineering Research Council of Canada.

REFERENCES

Andreassen, A., 1973, Estimating Regional Population Distribution by Selected Socio-Economic Characteristics, unpublished MASc thesis, Department of Civil Engineering, University of Waterloo, Waterloo, Ontario.

Birch, M.W., 1963, Maximum Likelihood in Three-way Contingency Tables, Journal Royal Statistical Society (B), 25, 220-233.

Bishop, Y.M., Fienburg, S.E., Holland, P.W., 1975, Discrete Multivariate Analysis, MIT Press, Cambridge, MA.

Clarke, M.I., 1981, Some Recent Developments in Activity-Travel Analysis and Modelling, Transportation Research Record, 794.

CTCUM, 1970, (also 1974 and 1978), Mobilité de Montréalais, Enquête Origine Destination 1970, Montréal, Québec.

Fingleton, B., 1981, Log Linear Modelling of Geographical Contingency Tables, Environment and Planning, 2, 1539-1551.

Goodman, L.A., 1972, A Modified Multiple Regression Approach to the Analysis of Dichotomous Variables, American Sociological Review, 37, 28-46.

Hutchinson, B.G. 1981, Urban Transport Policy and Review, Transport Reviews, 1, 169-188.

Hutchinson, B.G., 1984, Contingency Table Analysis and Urban Travel Accounts (this volume).

Kostyniuk, L. and Kitamura, R., 1982, Cycle and Household Time-Space Paths: Empirical Investigation, Transportation Research Record, 879.

Manski, C.F., 1981, Structural Models for Discrete Data: The Analysis of Discrete Choice, in Leinhart, S., 1981, (Ed.), Sociological Methodology 1981, Jossery-Bass, Washington.

Miron, Juma, 1979, Changing Patterns of Household Formation in the Toronto CMA: 1951 to 1976, Research Paper 106, Centre for Urban and Community Studies, University of Toronto Press, Toronto.

Nijkamp, P., 1983, Quantitative Methods For Urban and Regional Impact Analysis a paper presented at the International Symposium on New Directions in Urban Systems Models, University of Waterloo, Waterloo, Ontario.

Payne, C., 1977, The Log Linear Model of Contingency Tables, in O'Muinchen Muircheartaigh, C.A., Payne, C., (Eds.), The Analysis of Survey Data Vol. 2: Model Fitting, Wiley, New York.

Salomon, I., Ben-Akiva M., 1982, Use of Life Style Concept in Travel Demand Models, Transportation Research Record, 879.

Shortreed, J.H. and Bessette, H., 1980, Changing Socio-Economic Characteristics and Urban Transit, Proceedings, RTAC, Ottawa, Ontario.

Toronto Transit Commission, 1981, Report on Spatial Patterns of Urban Activity, Toronto, Ontario.

Willekens, F., 1981, Multidimensional Population Analyses with Incomplete Data: A Generalized Approach, WP 19, Netherlands Interuniversity Demographic Institute, Voorburg, The Netherlands.

Vol. 157: Optimization and Operations Research. Proceedings 1977. Edited by R. Henn, B. Korte, and W. Oettli. VI, 270 pages. 1978.

Vol. 158: L. J. Cherene, Set Valued Dynamical Systems and Economic Flow. VIII, 83 pages. 1978.

Vol. 159: Some Aspects of the Foundations of General Equilibrium Theory: The Posthumous Papers of Peter J. Kalman. Edited by J. Green. VI, 167 pages. 1978.

Vol. 160: Integer Programming and Related Areas. A Classified Bibliography. Edited by D. Hausmann. XIV, 314 pages. 1978.

Vol. 161: M. J. Beckmann, Rank in Organizations. VIII, 164 pages. 1978.

Vol. 162: Recent Developments in Variable Structure Systems, Economics and Biology. Proceedings 1977. Edited by R. R. Mohler and A. Ruberti. VI, 326 pages. 1978.

Vol. 163: G. Fandel, Optimale Entscheidungen in Organisationen. VI, 143 Seiten. 1979.

Vol. 164: C. L. Hwang and A. S. M. Masud, Multiple Objective Decision Making – Methods and Applications. A State-of-the-Art Survey. XII, 351 pages. 1979.

Vol. 165: A. Maravall, Identification in Dynamic Shock-Error Models. VIII, 158 pages. 1979.

Vol. 166: R. Cuninghame-Green, Minimax Algebra. XI, 258 pages. 1979.

Vol. 167: M. Faber, Introduction to Modern Austrian Capital Theory. X, 196 pages. 1979.

Vol. 168: Convex Analysis and Mathematical Economics. Proceedings 1978. Edited by J. Kriens. V, 136 pages. 1979.

Vol. 169: A. Rapoport et al., Coalition Formation by Sophisticated Players. VII, 170 pages. 1979.

Vol. 170: A. E. Roth, Axiomatic Models of Bargaining. V, 121 pages. 1979.

Vol. 171: G. F. Newell, Approximate Behavior of Tandem Queues. XI, 410 pages. 1979.

Vol. 172: K. Neumann and U. Steinhardt, GERT Networks and the Time-Oriented Evaluation of Projects. 268 pages. 1979.

Vol. 173: S. Erlander, Optimal Spatial Interaction and the Gravity Model. VII, 107 pages. 1980.

Vol. 174: Extremal Methods and Systems Analysis. Edited by A. V. Fiacco and K. O. Kortanek. XI, 545 pages. 1980.

Vol. 175: S. K. Srinivasan and R. Subramanian, Probabilistic Analysis of Redundant Systems. VII, 356 pages. 1980.

Vol. 176: R. Färe, Laws of Diminishing Returns. VIII, 97 pages. 1980.

Vol. 177: Multiple Criteria Decision Making-Theory and Application. Proceedings, 1979. Edited by G. Fandel and T. Gal. XVI, 570 pages. 1980.

Vol. 178: M. N. Bhattacharyya, Comparison of Box-Jenkins and Bonn Monetary Model Prediction Performance. VII, 146 pages. 1980.

Vol. 179: Recent Results in Stochastic Programming. Proceedings, 1979. Edited by P. Kall and A. Prékopa. IX, 237 pages. 1980.

Vol. 180: J. F. Brotchie, J. W. Dickey and R. Sharpe, TOPAZ – General Planning Technique and its Applications at the Regional, Urban, and Facility Planning Levels. VII, 356 pages. 1980.

Vol. 181: H. D. Sherali and C. M. Shetty, Optimization with Disjunctive Constraints. VIII, 156 pages. 1980.

Vol. 182: J. Wolters, Stochastic Dynamic Properties of Linear Econometric Models. VIII, 154 pages. 1980.

Vol. 183: K. Schittkowski, Nonlinear Programming Codes. VIII, 242 pages. 1980.

Vol. 184: R. E. Burkard and U. Derigs, Assignment and Matching Problems: Solution Methods with FORTRAN-Programs. VIII, 148 pages. 1980.

Vol. 185: C. C. von Weizsäcker, Barriers to Entry. VI, 220 pages. 1980.

Vol. 186: Ch.-L. Hwang and K. Yoon, Multiple Attribute Decision Making – Methods and Applications. A State-of-the-Art-Survey. XI, 259 pages. 1981.

Vol. 187: W. Hock, K. Schittkowski, Test Examples for Nonlinear Programming Codes. V. 178 pages. 1981.

Vol. 188: D. Bös, Economic Theory of Public Enterprise. VII, 142 pages. 1981.

Vol. 189: A. P. Lüthi, Messung wirtschaftlicher Ungleichheit. IX, 287 pages. 1981.

Vol. 190: J. N. Morse, Organizations: Multiple Agents with Multiple Criteria. Proceedings, 1980. VI, 509 pages. 1981.

Vol. 191: H. R. Sneessens, Theory and Estimation of Macroeconomic Rationing Models. VII, 138 pages. 1981.

Vol. 192: H. J. Bierens: Robust Methods and Asymptotic Theory in Nonlinear Econometrics. IX, 198 pages. 1981.

Vol. 193: J. K. Sengupta, Optimal Decisions under Uncertainty. VII, 156 pages. 1981.

Vol. 194: R. W. Shephard, Cost and Production Functions. XI, 104 pages. 1981.

Vol. 195: H. W. Ursprung, Die elementare Katastrophentheorie. Eine Darstellung aus der Sicht der Ökonomie. VII, 332 pages. 1982.

Vol. 196: M. Nermuth, Information Structures in Economics. VIII, 236 pages. 1982.

Vol. 197: Integer Programming and Related Areas. A Classified Bibliography. 1978 – 1981. Edited by R. von Randow. XIV, 338 pages. 1982.

Vol. 198: P. Zweifel, Ein ökonomisches Modell des Arztverhaltens. XIX, 392 Seiten. 1982.

Vol. 199: Evaluating Mathematical Programming Techniques. Proceedings, 1981. Edited by J.M. Mulvey. XI, 379 pages. 1982.

Vol. 200: The Resource Sector in an Open Economy. Edited by H. Siebert. IX, 161 pages. 1984.

Vol. 201: P. M. C. de Boer, Price Effects in Input-Output-Relations: A Theoretical and Empirical Study for the Netherlands 1949–1967. X, 140 pages. 1982.

Vol. 202: U. Witt, J. Perske, SMS – A Program Package for Simulation and Gaming of Stochastic Market Processes and Learning Behavior. VII, 266 pages. 1982.

Vol. 203: Compilation of Input-Output Tables. Proceedings, 1981. Edited by J. V. Skolka. VII, 307 pages. 1982.

Vol. 204: K.C. Mosler, Entscheidungsregeln bei Risiko: Multivariate stochastische Dominanz. VII, 172 Seiten. 1982.

Vol. 205: R. Ramanathan, Introduction to the Theory of Economic Growth. IX, 347 pages. 1982.

Vol. 206: M.H. Karwan, V. Lotfi, J. Telgen, and S. Zionts, Redundancy in Mathematical Programming. VII, 286 pages. 1983.

Vol. 207: Y. Fujimori, Modern Analysis of Value Theory. X, 165 pages. 1982.

Vol. 208: Econometric Decision Models. Proceedings, 1981. Edited by J. Gruber. VI, 364 pages. 1983.

Vol. 209: Essays and Surveys on Multiple Criteria Decision Making. Proceedings, 1982. Edited by P. Hansen. VII, 441 pages. 1983.

Vol. 210: Technology, Organization and Economic Structure. Edited by R. Sato and M. J. Beckmann. VIII, 195 pages. 1983.

Vol. 211: P. van den Heuvel, The Stability of a Macroeconomic System with Quantity Constraints. VII, 169 pages. 1983.

Vol. 212: R. Sato and T. Nôno, Invariance Principles and the Structure of Technology. V, 94 pages. 1983.

Vol. 213: Aspiration Levels in Bargaining and Economic Decision Making. Proceedings, 1982. Edited by R. Tietz. VIII, 406 pages. 1983.

Vol. 214: M. Faber, H. Niemes und G. Stephan, Entropie, Umweltschutz und Rohstoffverbrauch. IX, 181 Seiten. 1983.

Vol. 215: Semi-Infinite Programming and Applications. Proceedings, 1981. Edited by A. V. Fiacco and K. O. Kortanek. XI, 322 pages. 1983.

Vol. 216: H. H. Müller, Fiscal Policies in a General Equilibrium Model with Persistent Unemployment. VI, 92 pages. 1983.

Vol. 217: Ch. Grootaert, The Relation Between Final Demand and Income Distribution. XIV, 105 pages. 1983.

Vol. 218: P. van Loon, A Dynamic Theory of the Firm: Production, Finance and Investment. VII, 191 pages. 1983.

Vol. 219: E. van Damme, Refinements of the Nash Equilibrium Concept. VI, 151 pages. 1983.

Vol. 220: M. Aoki, Notes on Economic Time Series Analysis: System Theoretic Perspectives. IX, 249 pages. 1983.

Vol. 221: S. Nakamura, An Inter-Industry Translog Model of Prices and Technical Change for the West German Economy. XIV, 290 pages. 1984.

Vol. 222: P. Meier, Energy Systems Analysis for Developing Countries. VI, 344 pages. 1984.

Vol. 223: W. Trockel, Market Demand. VIII, 205 pages. 1984.

Vol. 224: M. Kiy, Ein disaggregiertes Prognosesystem für die Bundesrepublik Deutschland. XVIII, 276 Seiten. 1984.

Vol. 225: T. R. von Ungern-Sternberg, Zur Analyse von Märkten mit unvollständiger Nachfragerinformation. IX, 125 Seiten. 1984

Vol. 226: Selected Topics in Operations Research and Mathematical Economics. Proceedings, 1983. Edited by G. Hammer and D. Pallaschke. IX, 478 pages. 1984.

Vol. 227: Risk and Capital. Proceedings, 1983. Edited by G. Bamberg and K. Spremann. VII, 306 pages. 1984.

Vol. 228: Nonlinear Models of Fluctuating Growth. Proceedings, 1983. Edited by R. M. Goodwin, M. Krüger and A. Vercelli. XVII, 277 pages. 1984.

Vol. 229: Interactive Decision Analysis. Proceedings, 1983. Edited by M. Grauer and A. P. Wierzbicki. VIII, 269 pages. 1984.

Vol. 230: Macro-Economic Planning with Conflicting Goals. Proceedings, 1982. Edited by M. Despontin, P. Nijkamp and J. Spronk. VI, 297 pages. 1984.

Vol. 231: G. F. Newell, The $M/M/\infty$ Service System with Ranked Servers in Heavy Traffic. XI, 126 pages. 1984.

Vol. 232: L. Bauwens, Bayesian Full Information Analysis of Simultaneous Equation Models Using Integration by Monte Carlo. VI, 114 pages. 1984.

Vol. 233: G. Wagenhals, The World Copper Market. XI, 190 pages. 1984.

Vol. 234: B. C. Eaves, A Course in Triangulations for Solving Equations with Deformations. III, 302 pages. 1984.

Vol. 235: Stochastic Models in Reliability Theory. Proceedings, 1984. Edited by S. Osaki and Y. Hatoyama. VII, 212 pages. 1984.

Vol. 236: G. Gandolfo, P. C. Padoan, A Disequilibrium Model of Real and Financial Accumulation in an Open Economy. VI, 172 pages. 1984.

Vol. 237: Misspecification Analysis. Proceedings, 1983. Edited by T. K. Dijkstra. V, 129 pages. 1984.

Vol. 238: W. Domschke, A. Drexl, Location and Layout Planning. IV, 134 pages. 1985.

Vol. 239: Microeconomic Models of Housing Markets. Edited by K. Stahl. VII, 197 pages. 1985.

Vol. 240: Contributions to Operations Research. Proceedings, 1984. Edited by K. Neumann and D. Pallaschke. V, 190 pages. 1985.

Vol. 241: U. Wittmann, Das Konzept rationaler Preiserwartungen. XI, 310 Seiten. 1985.

Vol. 242: Decision Making with Multiple Objectives. Proceedings, 1984. Edited by Y. Y. Haimes and V. Chankong. XI, 571 pages. 1985.

Vol. 243: Integer Programming and Related Areas. A Classified Bibliography 1981–1984. Edited by R. von Randow. XX, 386 pages. 1985.

Vol. 244: Advances in Equilibrium Theory. Proceedings, 1984. Edited by C. D. Aliprantis, O. Burkinshaw and N. J. Rothman. II, 235 pages. 1985.

Vol. 245: J. E. M. Wilhelm, Arbitrage Theory. VII, 114 pages. 1985.

Vol. 246: P. W. Otter, Dynamic Feature Space Modelling, Filtering and Self-Tuning Control of Stochastic Systems. XIV, 177 pages. 1985.

Vol. 247: Optimization and Discrete Choice in Urban Systems. Proceedings, 1983. Edited by B. G. Hutchinson, P. Nijkamp and M. Batty. VI, 371 pages. 1985.

GPSR Compliance

The European Union's (EU) General Product Safety Regulation (GPSR) is a set of rules that requires consumer products to be safe and our obligations to ensure this.

If you have any concerns about our products, you can contact us on ProductSafety@springernature.com

In case Publisher is established outside the EU, the EU authorized representative is:

Springer Nature Customer Service Center GmbH
Europaplatz 3
69115 Heidelberg, Germany

Batch number: 10838062

Printed by Printforce, the Netherlands